Data Science Handbook

Scrivener Publishing
100 Cummings Center, Suite 541J
Beverly, MA 01915-6106

Next-Generation Computing and Communication Engineering

Series Editors: Dr. G. R. Kanagachidambaresan and Dr. Kolla Bhanu Prakash

Developments in articial intelligence are made more challenging because the involvement of multi-domain technology creates new problems for researchers. erefore, in order to help meet the challenge, this book series concentrates on next generation computing and communication methodologies involving smart and ambient environment design. It is an eective publishing platform for monographs, handbooks, and edited volumes on Industry 4.0, agriculture, smart city development, new computing and communication paradigms. Although the series mainly focuses on design, it also addresses analytics and investigation of industry-related real-time problems.

Publishers at Scrivener
Martin Scrivener (martin@scrivenerpublishing.com)
Phillip Carmical (pcarmical@scrivenerpublishing.com)

Data Science Handbook

A Practical Approach

Kolla Bhanu Prakash

K. L. University, Vaddeswaram, Andhra Pradesh, India

Scrivener
Publishing

Preface

Data Science is one of the leading research-driven areas in the modern era. It is having a critical role in healthcare, engineering, education, mechatronics and medical robotics. Building models and working with data is not value neutral. We choose the problems with which we work on, we make assumptions in these models and we decide metrics and algorithms for the problems. The data scientist identifies the problem which can be solved with data and expert tools of modelling and coding. The main aim of writing this book is to give a hands-on experience on different algorithms and popular techniques used in real time in data science to all the researchers working in various domains.

The book starts with introductory concepts in data science like data munging, data preparation, transforming data. Chapter 2 discusses data visualization, drawing various plots and histograms. Chapter 3 covers mathematics and statistics for data science. Chapter 4 mainly focuses on machine learning algorithms in data science. Chapter 5 comprises of outlier analysis and DBSCAN algorithm. Chapter 6 focuses on clustering. Chapter 7 discusses network analysis. Chapter 8 mainly focuses on regression and naive-bayes classifier. Chapter 9 covers web-based data visualizations with Plotly. Chapter 10 discusses web scraping. Various projects in data science are then discussed.

Kolla Bhanu Prakash
June 2022

Data Munging Basics

1 Introduction

Data gains value by transforming itself in to useful information. Every firm is more significant about the data generated from its all assets. The firm's data helps the different personnel in the organization to improve their business tasks, save time and expenditure amount on maintenance of it. The top level management fails in taking appropriate decision if they don't consider the data as important factor in understanding the business process. Many poor decisions related to the advertisement of company products leads to wastage of resources and affect the fame of the organization at every level. Companies may avoid squandering money by tracking the success of numerous marketing channels and concentrating on the ones that provide the best return on investment. As a result, a business can get more leads for less money spent on advertising [1].

Data Science provides study of discovering different data patterns from inter-disciplinary domains like business, education, research etc... Much of the information extracted is of the form unstructured like text and images and structured like in tabular format. The basic functional feature of data science involves the statistical techniques, inference rules, analytics for prediction, fundamental algorithms in machine learning, and novel methods for gleaning insights from huge data.

Business use cases which uses data science for serving the customers in different domains.

- Banking organization provides a mobile app to send recommendation on various loan offers to their applicants.
- One of the car manufacturing firms uses data science to build a 3-D printing screen for guiding driver less cars by enabling the object detection mechanism with more accuracy.

Kolla Bhanu Prakash. *Data Science Handbook: A Practical Approach*, (1–22) © 2022 Scrivener Publishing LLC

- An automation solution provider using cognitive approach develops an incident response system for failure detection in functionalities offered to their clients.
- General viewer behaviour is analysed by different channel subscribers based on the study of audience analytical platform and provide solution of grouping favourable TV channels.
- Cyber police department uses statistical tools to analyse the crime incidents occurring in particular locality with the capturing images from different CCTV footages and caution citizens to be-aware about those criminals.
- To safeguard the old age patients with memory loss or suffering with paralysis using body sensor information to analyse their health condition for their close relatives or care givers as part of building smart health care system.

Data science adopts four popular strategies [8] while exploring data they are (i) Understanding the problem in real time world (Probing Reality) (ii) Usage patterns of data (Discovery Patterns) (iii) Building Predictive data model for future perspective (predicting future events) (iv) Being empathetic business world (Understanding the people and the world)

(i) Understanding the problem in real time world:- Active and passive methods are used in collecting data for a particular problem in business process to take action. All the responses collected during the business process are more important to perform analysis in taking appropriate decision and leads success in further subsequent decisions.

(ii) Usage Patterns of Data (Discovery Patterns):- Divide and Conquer mechanism can be used to analyze the complex problems but it may not always the perfect solution without understanding the purpose of data. Much of the data is analyzed by clustering the data usage patterns this mechanism of clustering study helps to deal with real time digital marketing data.

(iii) Building Predictive models (Predicting future events): Right from the study of statistics it is clear that many of the techniques in mathematics are evolved to analyze the current data and predict the future. The predictive analysis will really help in decision making in dealing with the current scenarios of data collection. The prediction of future endeavors will help us to add valuable knowledge for the current data.

(iv) Emphatic in business world (Understanding the People and the world):- The toughest task by any organization in building the teams to understand the people in the real time world who are interacting with your organization for multiple reasons. Optimal decision making is possible only by understanding the real time scenarios of data generated during interaction and provides supported evidence for framing strategy in decision making solution for organization. High end domain knowledge like deep learning are used to understand the visual object recognition for study of the real time world.

Purpose of Data Science

Simple business intelligence tools are analyzed for unstructured data which is very small. Most of the data collected in traditional system were of the form of unstructured. The data was generated from different sources like financial reports, textual files, multimedia information, sensors and instrumental data. The business intelligence solutions cannot deal with huge volume of data with different complex formats. To process the complex formatted data we need high processing ability with improved analytical tools and algorithms for getting better insights that is done as part of data science.

Past and Future of Data Science

In 1962, John Tukey published a paper on the convergence of statistics and computers, showing how they may provide measurable results in hours. In 1974, Peter Naur written a book on Concise Survey of Computer Methods in which he coined the term data science many times to refer processing of data through specific mathematical methods. In 1977, an international association was established for statistical processing of data with the purpose of translating data into knowledge by combining modern computer technology, traditional statistical techniques, and domain knowledge. Tukey released Exploratory Data Analysis in the same year, emphasizing the importance of data.

Businesses began collecting enormous volumes of personal data in anticipation of new advertising efforts as early as 1994. Jacob Zahavi emphasized the need for new technology to manage the large volume of data generated by different organizations. William S. Cleveland published an article outlining on specialized learning methods and scope for Data Scientists which was used as case studies for businesses and education institute.

In 2002, a journal for Data Science was launched by international council for science. It focused on Data Science topics such as data systems modeling and its application. In 2013, IBM claimed that much of digital data collected all over the world is generated in the last two years, from then all organizations planned to build good amount of data for their benefits in decision making and started gaining good insights for improvement in the organization growth.

According to IDC, global data will exceed 175 zettabytes by 2025. Data Science allows businesses to swiftly interpret large amounts of data from a number of sources and turn that data into actionable insights for better data-driven decisions which is widely used in marketing, healthcare, finance, banking, policy work, and other fields. The market for Data Science platforms is expected to reach 178 billion dollars by 2025. Data science provides a platform for data scientists to explore many options for business organizations to track the latest developments in relevant to data gathering and maintenance for appropriate decision making.

BI (Business Intelligence) Vs DS (Data Science)

Business Intelligence is a process involved in decision making by getting insights in to the current data available as part of their organization transactions with respective all stake holders. It gathers data from all sources which can be from external or internal of the organization. The set of BI tools provide support for running queries, displaying results of data with good visualization mechanisms by performing analysis on revenue earned in that quarterly by facing business challenges. BI enables to provide suggestions based on market study, revealing revenue opportunities and business processes improvement. It is purely meant for building business strategies to earn profits in long run for the organization. Tools Like OLAP, warehouse ETL are used for storing and visualizing data in BI.

Data Science is a multi-disciplinary domain which performs study on data by extracting meaningful insights. It also uses tools relevant to data processing from machine learning and artificial intelligence to develop predictive models. It is further used for forecasting the future perspective growth in business organization carried functionalities. Python, R programming used to build the predictive data models by implementing efficient machine learning algorithms and the results are tracked based on high end visual communication techniques.

Data Munging Basics

Data Science is multi-disciplinary field which derives its features from artificial intelligence, machine learning and deep learning to uncover the more insights of data which is in different forms like structured (Tabular format of data) and unstructured (text, images). It performs study on specific problem domain areas and find or define solutions with available input data usage patterns and reveals good insights [1, 2].

Data Science deals with data to provide appropriate solutions to the relevant questions made by the study of those real time scenarios in the process of business. It is different from the business intelligence mechanism which only works on framing good business strategies for improving the future trends of the organization based on the collection of insights from the existing data rather than instance decisions on the current available data [3, 4].

In practical data scientists explore large amount of data for understanding the patterns and to frame the solutions by performing the correlation among the appropriate data sets which were not considered in the previous approaches. Data science builds the data sets which forms the basis for the machine learning algorithms for further analysis in the process of information. High end tools of different domains like statistical, analytical, and intelligent software are needed for processing big data [11].

Data Science broadens the scope of using data for different levels of processing like macro or micro depending on the need of problem solution [12]. It majorly supports in narrow down the solution approaches for sending the data as a unique formats for large queries as part of analytical tools. It processes the data either dividing the data into usable chunks or cluster the data into different groups for providing easy insights [5].

Popular uses cases of using data science in our daily routine are like the Google search which uses the ranking of the web pages of relevant searches made by users while surfing on the internet is made possible using data science [13]. The inbuilt recommended systems for choosing friends on Facebook or sharing videos on You Tube are implemented using data science approaches [14]. The dynamic automatic decision making of Alexa or Siri devices uses techniques of data science for processing the image and voice recognition data instantly. Online gaming websites uses data science to track the experience of users and promote those popular with latest version releases. Online pricing of products will be compared among the popular online shopping websites by extracting the data from relevant websites using inbuilt packages of data science [15].

Advantages of Data Science

1. The demand for data scientists is more as the complexity of dealing data is critical.
2. Highly paid jobs are data scientists and more people are recruited to work on specific domains to analyze all aspects of data generated by the organizations.
3. It provides wide variety platforms to make better understanding of data for building effective business solutions.
4. Many of the data science projects are working on improving the products features, saving lives of people and provide better insights for the organizations to make their business reach to common man.

Disadvantages of Data Science

1. The term relates to much confusion while analyzing the data without any specific objective.
2. Data Scientists need to update the new technology features of data science if not they will set back in providing effective solutions to business.
3. Without prefect domain knowledge data science becomes useless landing into bad insights which will bring great loss to the business.
4. Privacy of data becomes a big question without which data science cannot proceed for next level of analysis. Arbitrary data results in unexpected outcome of organization which causes great defame.

1.1   Filtering and Selecting Data

Segment 1 - Filtering and selecting data

```
import numpy as np
import pandas as pd

from pandas import Series, DataFrame
```

Selecting and retrieving data

```
In [8]: series_obj = Series(np.arange(8), index=['row 1', 'row 2','row 3','row 4','row 5', 'row 6', 'row 7', 'row 8'])
        series_obj

Out[8]: row 1    0
        row 2    1
        row 3    2
        row 4    3
        row 5    4
        row 6    5
        row 7    6
        row 8    7
        dtype: int32
```

```
In [9]: # ['label-index']
        # -@-@-@-( WHAT THIS DOES ) -@-@-@
        # When you write square brackets with a label-index inside them, this tells Python to select and
        # retrieve all records with that label-index.
        series_obj['row 7']

Out[9]: 6
```

```
In [10]: # [integer index]
         # -@-@-@-( WHAT THIS DOES )-@-@-@
         # When you write square brackets with an integer index inside them, this tells Python to select and
         # retrieve all records with the specified integer index.
         series_obj[[0,7]]

Out[10]: row 1    0
         row 8    7
         dtype: int32
```

```
In [22]: np.random.seed(25)
         DF_obj = DataFrame(np.random.rand(36).reshape((6,6)),
                            index=['row 1', 'row 2', 'row 3', 'row 4', 'row 5', 'row 6'],
                            columns=['column 1', 'column 2', 'column 3', 'column 4', 'column 5', 'column 6'])
         DF_obj
```

Out[22]:

	column 1	column 2	column 3	column 4	column 5	column 6
row 1	0.870124	0.582277	0.278839	0.185911	0.411100	0.117376
row 2	0.684969	0.437611	0.556229	0.367080	0.402366	0.113041
row 3	0.447031	0.585445	0.161985	0.520719	0.326051	0.699186
row 4	0.366395	0.836375	0.481343	0.516502	0.383048	0.997541
row 5	0.514244	0.559053	0.034450	0.719930	0.421004	0.436935
row 6	0.281701	0.900274	0.669612	0.456069	0.289804	0.525819

```
In [13]: # object_name.ix[[row indexes], [column indexes]]
         # -@-@-@-( WHAT THIS DOES )-@-@-@
         # When you call the .ix[] special indexer, and pass in a set of row and column indexes, this tells
         # Python to select and retrieve only those specific rows and columns.
         DF_obj.ix[['row 2', 'row 5'], ['column 5', 'column 2']]
```

Out[13]:

	column 5	column 2
row 2	0.402366	0.437611
row 5	0.421004	0.559053

Data slicing

```
In [14]: # ['starting label-index':'ending label-index']
         # -@-@-@-( WHAT THIS DOES )-@-@-@
         # Data slicing allows you to select and retrieve all records from the starting label-index, to the
         # ending label-index, and every record in between.
         series_obj['row 3':'row 7']

Out[14]: row 3    2
         row 4    3
         row 5    4
         row 6    5
         row 7    6
         dtype: int32
```

Comparing with scalars

```
In [25]: # object_name < scalar value
         # -@-@-@-( WHAT THIS DOES )-@-@-@
         # You can use comparison operators (like greater than or less than) to return True / False values for
         # all records, to indicate how each element compares to a scalar value.
         DF_obj < .2
```

Out[25]:

	column 1	column 2	column 3	column 4	column 5	column 6
row 1	False	False	False	True	False	True
row 2	False	False	False	False	False	True
row 3	False	False	True	False	False	False
row 4	False	False	False	False	False	False
row 5	False	False	True	False	False	False
row 6	False	False	False	False	False	False

Filtering with scalars

```
In [26]: # object_name[object_name > scalar value]
         # -@-@-@-( WHAT THIS DOES )-@-@-@
         # You can also use comparison operators and scalar values for indexing, to return only the records
         # that satisfy the comparison expression you write.
         series_obj[series_obj > 6]

Out[26]: row 8    7
         dtype: int32
```

Setting values with scalars

```
In [27]: # ['label-index', 'label-index', 'label-index'] = scalar value
         # -@-@-@-( WHAT THIS DOES )-@-@-@
         # Setting is where you select all records associated with the specified label-indexes and set those
         # values equal to a scalar.
         series_obj['row 1', 'row 5', 'row 8'] = 8

In [28]: series_obj
Out[28]: row 1    8
         row 2    1
         row 3    2
         row 4    3
         row 5    8
         row 6    5
         row 7    6
         row 8    8
         dtype: int32
```

Data Preparation

The process of data preparation starts with understanding the context of problem domain from which data is collected. After collection of data it needs to be cleaned and normalized by transforming it into equivalent understandable type of data. The main motivation for data preparation is to enrich data with more interesting facts by reframing the types of values it holds and corrections of the values according to the relevancy of domain [6, 7].

Data preparation is considered as lengthy procedure which to be critically dealt by data scientists. It is primary job of data science professional to understand the data in the context of problem domain to get better insights from it [8]. Always data science professional should ensure that poor data quality will lead to great confusion and poor decision making which is great loss to the business. Thus data preparation process usually include following standard format while collecting raw data, ensure the source data is enriched with meaningful context and finally eliminate the unwanted data as part of outliers analysis [9].

Data Preparation Steps

Data preparation process is similar for all organizations, industry and individuals. It follows the common framework steps as mentioned in fig 1.1.

The first stage is Gather which provides the source for collection of data from all available problem domain areas. Some problem domain areas may

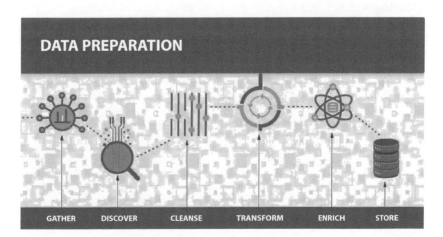

Fig 1.1 Stages of data preparation process.

provide data catalogue to refer and some provide at run time depending on the problem occurrence in real time world as on ad-hoc basis.

Second stage of data preparation is Discover, Whose primary task is to understand the data to determine its usefulness in the current context of problem domain. It's a very critical task for which Talend's provided a data preparation platform to determine the usefulness of data with good visual effects based on the users profile and acts as a tool for browsing the data [10].

Third stage of data preparation is cleaning the data which is a crucial part of processing the data where more effective techniques are used to remove the unwanted data by performing outliers mechanism, Need to fill the missed values in the data, ensure the data following standard patterns, and mask the critical or sensitive data by categorizing it while entry of data. In this stage the validation of data is also done to check the errors by putting check points while processing. If validation of data is not done at initial stage for finding errors further they lead to great disaster of not having clarity on the context of problem domain from where data is collected.

The fourth and fifth stages of data preparation are transform and enriching data. In this stage the data is transformed in to standard format of value entries which leads to perfect determined outcome and make easy understandable of data for all the users who are interacting with the data. Enriching provides the flavor of improving the data with more facts and makes the connectivity among those relevant data strongly bounded to provide good and better insights.

The final stage of data preparation where the data is loaded in to specific storage areas where it can be channelized to different analytical tools for processing and helping the organization to gain good insights for further decision making.

The major advantages of data preparation are identifying the errors at initial stages of processing the data. If the errors were not caught at the third stage of data preparation i.e cleaning it will be difficult in the next stages where it is converted to another format and tracing of error at this stage is highly unachievable. The data preparation process assures us providing good quality of data after completion of cleaning phase and transformation phase and further analytical tools task is made easy for getting better insights. The job of decision making was made easy possible by all phases of data preparation. The data which is made available at the storage stage is highly qualified data which could be analyzed at any instant for effective decision making in business.

1.2 Treating Missing Values

Segment 2 - Treating missing values

```
In [10]: import numpy as np
         import pandas as pd

         from pandas import Series, DataFrame
```

Figuring out what data is missing

```
In [11]: missing = np.nan

         series_obj = Series(['row 1', 'row 2', missing, 'row 4','row 5', 'row 6', missing, 'row 8'])
         series_obj
```

```
Out[11]: 0    row 1
         1    row 2
         2      NaN
         3    row 4
         4    row 5
         5    row 6
         6      NaN
         7    row 8
         dtype: object
```

```
In [12]: # object_name.isnull()
         # 👉-👉-( WHAT THIS DOES )-👉-👉
         # The .isnull() method returns a Boolean value that describes (True or False) whether an element in a
         # Pandas object is a null value.
         series_obj.isnull()
```

```
Out[12]: 0    False
         1    False
         2     True
         3    False
         4    False
         5    False
         6     True
         7    False
         dtype: bool
```

Filling in for missing values

```
In [13]:  np.random.seed(25)
          DF_obj = DataFrame(np.random.randn(36).reshape(6,6))
          DF_obj
```

Out[13]:

	0	1	2	3	4	5
0	0.228273	1.026890	-0.839585	-0.591182	-0.956888	-0.222326
1	-0.619915	1.837905	-2.053231	0.868583	-0.920734	-0.232312
2	2.152957	-1.334661	0.076380	-1.246089	1.202272	-1.049942
3	1.056610	-0.419678	2.294842	-2.594487	2.822756	0.680889
4	-1.577693	-1.976254	0.533340	-0.290870	-0.513520	1.982626
5	0.226001	-1.839905	1.607671	0.388292	0.399732	0.405477

```
In [14]:  DF_obj.ix[3:5, 0] = missing
          DF_obj.ix[1:4, 5] = missing
          DF_obj
```

Out[14]:

	0	1	2	3	4	5
0	0.228273	1.026890	-0.839585	-0.591182	-0.956888	-0.222326
1	-0.619915	1.837905	-2.053231	0.868583	-0.920734	NaN
2	2.152957	-1.334661	0.076380	-1.246089	1.202272	NaN
3	NaN	-0.419678	2.294842	-2.594487	2.822756	NaN
4	NaN	-1.976254	0.533340	-0.290870	-0.513520	NaN
5	NaN	-1.839905	1.607671	0.388292	0.399732	0.405477

```
In [15]:  # object_name.fillna(numeric value)
          # 🌼-🌼-🌼-( WHAT THIS DOES )-🌼-🌼-🌼
          # The .fillna method() finds each missing value from within a Pandas object and fills it with the
          # numeric value that you've passed in.
          filled_DF = DF_obj.fillna(0)
          filled_DF
```

Out[15]:

	0	1	2	3	4	5
0	0.228273	1.026890	-0.839585	-0.591182	-0.956888	-0.222326
1	-0.619915	1.837905	-2.053231	0.868583	-0.920734	0.000000
2	2.152957	-1.334661	0.076380	-1.246089	1.202272	0.000000
3	0.000000	-0.419678	2.294842	-2.594487	2.822756	0.000000
4	0.000000	-1.976254	0.533340	-0.290870	-0.513520	0.000000
5	0.000000	-1.839905	1.607671	0.388292	0.399732	0.405477

```
In [17]:  # object_name.fillna(dict)
          # 🌼-🌼-🌼-( WHAT THIS DOES )-🌼-🌼-🌼
          # You can pass a dictionary into the .fillna() method. The method will then fill in missing values
          # from each column Series (as designated by the dictionary key) with its own unique value
          # (as specified in the corresponding dictionary value).
          filled_DF = DF_obj.fillna({0: 0.1, 5: 1.25})
          filled_DF
```

Out[17]:

	0	1	2	3	4	5
0	0.228273	1.026890	-0.839585	-0.591182	-0.956888	-0.222326
1	-0.619915	1.837905	-2.053231	0.868583	-0.920734	1.250000
2	2.152957	-1.334661	0.076380	-1.246089	1.202272	1.250000
3	0.100000	-0.419678	2.294842	-2.594487	2.822756	1.250000
4	0.100000	-1.976254	0.533340	-0.290870	-0.513520	1.250000
5	0.100000	-1.839905	1.607671	0.388292	0.399732	0.405477

```
In [18]: # -*-*-( WHAT THIS DOES )-*-*-*
         # You can also pass in the method='ffill' argument, and the .fillna() method will fill-forward any
         # missing values with values from the last non-null element in the column Series.
         fill_DF = DF_obj.fillna(method='ffill')
         fill_DF
```

Out[18]:

	0	1	2	3	4	5
0	0.228273	1.026890	-0.839585	-0.591182	-0.956888	-0.222326
1	-0.619915	1.837905	-2.053231	0.868583	-0.920734	-0.222326
2	2.152957	-1.334661	0.076380	-1.246089	1.202272	-0.222326
3	2.152957	-0.419678	2.294842	-2.594487	2.822756	-0.222326
4	2.152957	-1.976254	0.533340	-0.290870	-0.513520	-0.222326
5	2.152957	-1.839905	1.607671	0.388292	0.399732	0.405477

Counting missing values

```
In [21]: np.random.seed(25)
         DF_obj = DataFrame(np.random.randn(36).reshape(6,6))
         DF_obj.ix[3:5, 0] = missing
         DF_obj.ix[1:4, 5] = missing
         DF_obj
```

Out[21]:

	0	1	2	3	4	5
0	0.228273	1.026890	-0.839585	-0.591182	-0.956888	-0.222326
1	-0.619915	1.837905	-2.053231	0.868583	-0.920734	NaN
2	2.152957	-1.334661	0.076380	-1.246089	1.202272	NaN
3	NaN	-0.419678	2.294842	-2.594487	2.822756	NaN
4	NaN	-1.976254	0.533340	-0.290870	-0.513520	NaN
5	NaN	-1.839905	1.607671	0.388292	0.399732	0.405477

```
In [22]: # object_name.isnull().sum()
         # -*-*-( WHAT THIS DOES )-*-*-*
         # To generate a count of how many missing values a DataFrame has per column, just call the .isnull()
         # method off of the object, and then call the .sum() method off of the matrix of Boolean values it
         # returns.
         DF_obj.isnull().sum()
```

```
Out[22]: 0    3
         1    0
         2    0
         3    0
         4    0
         5    4
         dtype: int64
```

Filtering out missing values

```
In [30]: # object_name.dropna()
         # ☆-☆-☆-( WHAT THIS DOES )-☆-☆-☆
         # To identify and drop all rows from a DataFrame that contain ANY missing values, simply call the
         # .dropna() method off of the DataFrame object. NOTE: If you wanted to drop columns that contain
         # any missing values, you'd just pass in the axis=1 argument to select and search the DataFrame
         # by columns, instead of by row.
         DF_no_NaN = DF_obj.dropna(axis=1)
         DF_no_NaN
```

Out[30]:

	1	2	3	4
0	1.026890	-0.839585	-0.591182	-0.956888
1	1.837905	-2.053231	0.868583	-0.920734
2	-1.334661	0.076380	-1.246089	1.202272
3	-0.419678	2.294842	-2.594487	2.822756
4	-1.976254	0.533340	-0.290870	-0.513520
5	-1.839905	1.607671	0.388292	0.399732

```
In [31]: # object_name.dropna(how='all')
         # ☆-☆-☆-( WHAT THIS DOES )-☆-☆-☆
         # To identify and drop only the rows from a DataFrame that contain ALL missing values, simply
         # call the .dropna() method off of the DataFrame object, and pass in the how='all' argument.
         DF_obj.dropna(how='all')
```

Out[31]:

	0	1	2	3	4	5
0	0.228273	1.026890	-0.839585	-0.591182	-0.956888	-0.222326
1	-0.619915	1.837905	-2.053231	0.868583	-0.920734	NaN
2	2.152957	-1.334661	0.076380	-1.246089	1.202272	NaN
3	NaN	-0.419678	2.294842	-2.594487	2.822756	NaN
4	NaN	-1.976254	0.533340	-0.290870	-0.513520	NaN
5	NaN	-1.839905	1.607671	0.388292	0.399732	0.405477

1.3   Removing Duplicates

Segment 3 - Removing duplicates

```
In [1]: import numpy as np
        import pandas as pd

        from pandas import Series, DataFrame
```

Removing duplicates

```
In [6]: DF_obj = DataFrame({'column 1': [1, 1, 2, 2, 3, 3, 3],
                            'column 2': ['a', 'a', 'b', 'b', 'c', 'c', 'c'],
                            'column 3': ['A', 'A', 'B', 'B', 'C', 'C', 'C']})
        DF_obj
```

Out[6]:

	column 1	column 2	column 3
0	1	a	A
1	1	a	A
2	2	b	B
3	2	b	B
4	3	c	C
5	3	c	C
6	3	c	C

In [7]:
```
# object_name.duplicated()
# ☆-☆-☆-( WHAT THIS DOES )-☆-☆-☆
# The .duplicated() method searches each row in the DataFrame, and returns a True or False value to
#indicate whether it is a duplicate of another row found earlier in the DataFrame.
DF_obj.duplicated()
```

Out[7]:
```
0    False
1    True
2    False
3    True
4    False
5    True
6    True
dtype: bool
```

In [8]:
```
# object_name.drop_duplicates()
# ☆-☆-☆-( WHAT THIS DOES )-☆-☆-☆
# To drop all duplicate rows, just call the drop_duplicates() method off of the DataFrame.
DF_obj.drop_duplicates()
```

Out[8]:

	column 1	column 2	column 3
0	1	a	A
2	2	b	B
4	3	c	C

In [10]:
```
DF_obj = DataFrame({'column 1': [1, 1, 2, 2, 3, 3, 3],
                    'column 2': ['a', 'a', 'b', 'b', 'c', 'c', 'c'],
                    'column 3': ['A', 'A', 'B', 'B', 'C', 'D', 'C']})
DF_obj
```

Out[10]:

	column 1	column 2	column 3
0	1	a	A
1	1	a	A
2	2	b	B
3	2	b	B
4	3	c	C
5	3	c	D
6	3	c	C

```
In [11]: # object_name.drop_duplicates(['column_name'])
         # 卷-卷-卷-( WHAT THIS DOES )-卷-卷-卷
         # To drop the rows that have duplicates in only one column Series, just call the drop_duplicates()
         # method off of the DataFrame, and pass in the label-index of the column you want the de-duplication
         # to be based on. This method will drops all rows that have duplicates in the column you specify.
         DF_obj.drop_duplicates(['column 3'])
```

Out[11]:

	column 1	column 2	column 3
0	1	a	A
2	2	b	B
4	3	c	C
5	3	c	D

1.4   Concatenating and Transforming Data

Segment 4 - Concatenating and transforming data

```
In [6]: import numpy as np
        import pandas as pd

        from pandas import Series, DataFrame
```

```
In [7]: DF_obj = pd.DataFrame(np.arange(36).reshape(6,6))
        DF_obj
```

Out[7]:

	0	1	2	3	4	5
0	0	1	2	3	4	5
1	6	7	8	9	10	11
2	12	13	14	15	16	17
3	18	19	20	21	22	23
4	24	25	26	27	28	29
5	30	31	32	33	34	35

```
In [8]: DF_obj_2 = pd.DataFrame(np.arange(15).reshape(5,3))
        DF_obj_2
```

Out[8]:

	0	1	2
0	0	1	2
1	3	4	5
2	6	7	8
3	9	10	11
4	12	13	14

Concatenating data

```
In [10]: # pd.concat([left_object, right_object], axis=1)
         # 凸-凸-凸-( WHAT THIS DOES )-凸-凸-凸
         # The concat() method joins data from seperate sources into one combined data table. If you want to
         # join objects based on their row index values, just call the pd.concat() method on the objects you
         # want joined, and then pass in the axis=1 argument. The axis=1 argument tells Python to concatenate
         # the DataFrames by adding columns (in other words, joining on the row index values).
         pd.concat([DF_obj, DF_obj_2], axis =1)
```

Out[10]:

	0	1	2	3	4	5	0	1	2
0	0	1	2	3	4	5	0.0	1.0	2.0
1	6	7	8	9	10	11	3.0	4.0	5.0
2	12	13	14	15	16	17	6.0	7.0	8.0
3	18	19	20	21	22	23	9.0	10.0	11.0
4	24	25	26	27	28	29	12.0	13.0	14.0
5	30	31	32	33	34	35	NaN	NaN	NaN

```
In [11]: pd.concat([DF_obj, DF_obj_2])
```

Out[11]:

	0	1	2	3	4	5
0	0	1	2	3.0	4.0	5.0
1	6	7	8	9.0	10.0	11.0
2	12	13	14	15.0	16.0	17.0
3	18	19	20	21.0	22.0	23.0
4	24	25	26	27.0	28.0	29.0
5	30	31	32	33.0	34.0	35.0
0	0	1	2	NaN	NaN	NaN
1	3	4	5	NaN	NaN	NaN
2	6	7	8	NaN	NaN	NaN
3	9	10	11	NaN	NaN	NaN
4	12	13	14	NaN	NaN	NaN

Transforming data

Dropping data

```
In [12]: # object_name.drop([row indexes])
         # 凸-凸-凸-( WHAT THIS DOES )-凸-凸-凸
         # You can easily drop rows from a DataFrame by calling the .drop() method and passing in the index
         # values for the rows you want dropped.
         DF_obj.drop([0,2])
```

Out[12]:

	0	1	2	3	4	5
1	6	7	8	9	10	11
3	18	19	20	21	22	23
4	24	25	26	27	28	29
5	30	31	32	33	34	35

```
In [13]:  DF_obj.drop([0,2], axis=1)
```

Out[13]:

	1	3	4	5
0	1	3	4	5
1	7	9	10	11
2	13	15	16	17
3	19	21	22	23
4	25	27	28	29
5	31	33	34	35

Adding data

```
In [14]:  series_obj = Series(np.arange(6))
          series_obj.name = "added_variable"
          series_obj
```

```
Out[14]:  0    0
          1    1
          2    2
          3    3
          4    4
          5    5
          Name: added_variable, dtype: int32
```

```
In [15]:  # DataFrame.join(left_object, right_object)
          # ✿-✿-✿-( WHAT THIS DOES )-✿-✿-✿
          # You can use .join() method two join two data sources into one. The .join() method works by joining
          # the two sources on their row index values.
          variable_added = DataFrame.join(DF_obj, series_obj)
          variable_added
```

Out[15]:

	0	1	2	3	4	5	added_variable
0	0	1	2	3	4	5	0
1	6	7	8	9	10	11	1
2	12	13	14	15	16	17	2
3	18	19	20	21	22	23	3
4	24	25	26	27	28	29	4
5	30	31	32	33	34	35	5

```
In [19]:  added_datatable = variable_added.append(variable_added, ignore_index=False)
          added_datatable
```

Out[19]:

	0	1	2	3	4	5	added_variable
0	0	1	2	3	4	5	0
1	6	7	8	9	10	11	1
2	12	13	14	15	16	17	2
3	18	19	20	21	22	23	3
4	24	25	26	27	28	29	4
5	30	31	32	33	34	35	5
0	0	1	2	3	4	5	0
1	6	7	8	9	10	11	1
2	12	13	14	15	16	17	2
3	18	19	20	21	22	23	3
4	24	25	26	27	28	29	4
5	30	31	32	33	34	35	5

In [20]:
```
added_datatable = variable_added.append(variable_added, ignore_index=True)
added_datatable
```

Out[20]:

	0	1	2	3	4	5	added_variable
0	0	1	2	3	4	5	0
1	6	7	8	9	10	11	1
2	12	13	14	15	16	17	2
3	18	19	20	21	22	23	3
4	24	25	26	27	28	29	4
5	30	31	32	33	34	35	5
6	0	1	2	3	4	5	0
7	6	7	8	9	10	11	1
8	12	13	14	15	16	17	2
9	18	19	20	21	22	23	3
10	24	25	26	27	28	29	4
11	30	31	32	33	34	35	5

Sorting data

In [21]:
```
# object_name.sort_values(by=[index value], ascending=[False])
# -&-&-&-( WHAT THIS DOES )-&-&-&
# To sort rows in a DataFrame, either in ascending or descending order, call the .sort_values()
# method off of the DataFrame, and pass in the by argument to specify the column index upon which
# the DataFrame should be sorted.
DF_sorted = DF_obj.sort_values(by=[5], ascending=[False])
DF_sorted
```

Out[21]:

	0	1	2	3	4	5
5	30	31	32	33	34	35
4	24	25	26	27	28	29
3	18	19	20	21	22	23
2	12	13	14	15	16	17
1	6	7	8	9	10	11
0	0	1	2	3	4	5

1.5   Grouping and Data Aggregation

Segment 5 - Grouping and data aggregation

```
In [25]:  import numpy as np
          import pandas as pd
          from pandas import Series, DataFrame
```

Grouping data by column index

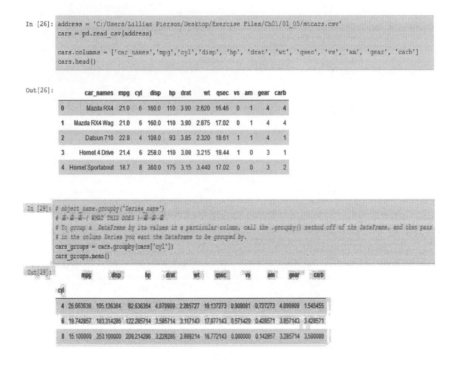

```
In [26]:  address = 'C:/Users/Lillian Pierson/Desktop/Exercise Files/Ch01/01_05/mtcars.csv'
          cars = pd.read_csv(address)

          cars.columns = ['car_names','mpg','cyl','disp', 'hp', 'drat', 'wt', 'qsec', 'vs', 'am', 'gear', 'carb']
          cars.head()
```

Out[26]:

	car_names	mpg	cyl	disp	hp	drat	wt	qsec	vs	am	gear	carb
0	Mazda RX4	21.0	6	160.0	110	3.90	2.620	16.46	0	1	4	4
1	Mazda RX4 Wag	21.0	6	160.0	110	3.90	2.875	17.02	0	1	4	4
2	Datsun 710	22.8	4	108.0	93	3.85	2.320	18.61	1	1	4	1
3	Hornet 4 Drive	21.4	6	258.0	110	3.08	3.215	19.44	1	0	3	1
4	Hornet Sportabout	18.7	8	360.0	175	3.15	3.440	17.02	0	0	3	2

```
In [29]:  # object_name.groupby('Series_name')
          # -B-B-B-( WHAT THIS DOES )-B-B-B-
          # To group a DataFrame by its values in a particular column, call the .groupby() method off of the DataFrame, and then pass
          # in the column Series you want the DataFrame to be grouped by.
          cars_groups = cars.groupby(cars['cyl'])
          cars_groups.mean()
```

Out[29]:

	mpg	disp	hp	drat	wt	qsec	vs	am	gear	carb
cyl										
4	26.663636	105.136364	82.636364	4.070909	2.285727	19.137273	0.909091	0.727273	4.090909	1.545455
6	19.742857	183.314286	122.285714	3.585714	3.117143	17.977143	0.571429	0.428571	3.857143	3.428571
8	15.100000	353.100000	209.214286	3.229286	3.999214	16.772143	0.000000	0.142857	3.285714	3.500000

References

1. Dhar, V. (2013). "Data science and prediction". Communications of the ACM. 56 (12): 64–73. doi:10.1145/2500499.
2. Jeff Leek (12 December 2013). "The key word in "Data Science" is not Data, it is Science". Simply Statistics.
3. Hayashi, Chikio (1 January 1998). "What is Data Science? Fundamental Concepts and a Heuristic Example". In Hayashi, Chikio; Yajima, Keiji; Bock,

Hans-Hermann; Ohsumi, Noboru; Tanaka, Yutaka; Baba, Yasumasa (eds.). Data Science, Classification, and Related Methods. Studies in Classification, Data Analysis, and Knowledge Organization. Springer Japan. pp. 40–51. doi:10.1007/978-4-431-65950-1_3. ISBN 9784431702085.

4. Tony Hey; Stewart Tansley; Kristin Michele Tolle (2009). The Fourth Paradigm: Data-intensive Scientific Discovery. Microsoft Research. ISBN 978-0-9825442-0-4. Archived from the original on 20 March 2017.

5. Bell, G.; Hey, T.; Szalay, A. (2009). "COMPUTER SCIENCE: Beyond the Data Deluge". Science. 323 (5919): 1297–1298. doi:10.1126/science.1170411. ISSN 0036-8075. PMID 19265007. S2CID 9743327.

6. Davenport, Thomas H.; Patil, D. J. (October 2012). "Data Scientist: The Sexiest Job of the 21st Century". Harvard Business Review. 90 (10): 70–6, 128. PMID 23074866. Retrieved 18 January 2016.

7. "About Data Science | Data Science Association". www.datascienceassn.org. Retrieved 3 April 2020.

8. "Introduction: What Is Data Science? - Doing Data Science [Book]". www.oreilly.com. Retrieved 3 April 2020.

9. "the three sexy skills of data geeks". m.e.driscoll: data utopian. 27 May 2009. Retrieved 3 April 2020.

10. Yau, Nathan (4 June 2009). "Rise of the Data Scientist". FlowingData. Retrieved 3 April 2020.

11. Develop algorithms to determine the status of car drivers using built-in accelerometer and GBDT, Nguyen, T.T., Doan, P.T., Le, A.-N., ...Tran, D.-N., Prakash K B, Tran, D.-T., International Journal of Electrical and Computer Engineering, 2022, 12(1), pp. 785–792.

12. Ganesan, V., Sobhana, M., Anuradha, G., Yellamma, P., Devi, O.R., Prakash, K.B. &Naren, J. 2021, "Quantum inspired meta-heuristic approach for optimization of genetic algorithm", Computers and Electrical Engineering, vol. 94.

13. Kavuri, M. & Prakash, K.B. 2019, "Performance comparison of detection, recognition and tracking rates of the different algorithms", International Journal of Advanced Computer Science and Applications, vol. 10, no. 6, pp. 153-158.

14. Kumar Vadla, P., Prakash Kolla, B. & Perumal, T. 2020, "FLA-SLA aware cloud collation formation using fuzzy preference relationship multi-decision approach for federated cloud", Pertanika Journal of Science and Technology, vol. 28, no. 1, pp. 117-140.

15. Kumar, V.P. & Prakash, K.B. 2021, "Optimize the Cost of Resources in Federated Cloud by Collaborated Resource Provisioning and Most Cost-effective Collated Providers Resource First Algorithm", International Journal of Advanced Computer Science and Applications, vol. 12, no. 1, pp. 58-65.

Data Visualization

Data visualization provides a mechanism to view the data in good graphical format with curves or bars to give insights of the analysis [1, 2]. The basic visual elements like curve graphs, bar graphs, charts and maps all are part of visualization mechanism to make available data for tend analysis, removing the unwanted data i.e. outlier's mechanism and understanding the patterns of data [11]. The data visualization tools provide analysis of large amount of data which are popularly known as Big Data in the form of graphs and charts and support data-driven decisions for the organizations [3, 4].

The popular areas where the visualization of data gains more importance are the study of complex events like predicting the death rate with new variant of covid-19 virus. Some of the other assets of data visualization are natural phenomenon of weather reporting, medical diagnosis for different type of cancers and mathematical interpretations for computing the astronomical measurements [5, 6].

The three different type of analysis done by data visualization are univariate, Bivariate and multivariate [7]. The univariate analysis provides analysis by prioritizing a single feature of data among all its available properties [8]. The bivariate analysis does the similar task of analyzing on at least two features of available properties of data. The multivariate doe's analysis more than two features for getting appropriate findings of the data [12].

The wide varieties of applications are making use of data visualization mechanisms [13]. The popular are healthcare care industry for visualizing the patient's data for identifying any common facts of occurrence of diseases with bacteria or virus [9]. Business Intelligence tools are popularly used by all types of industries to analyze the decisions made by them affecting their product sales. Military uses the data visualization to develop a high end defense tools to protect their nation. Food delivery apps use the data visualization for identifying the popular restaurant foods requested by the customers [10].

Kolla Bhanu Prakash. *Data Science Handbook: A Practical Approach*, (23–56) © 2022 Scrivener Publishing LLC

Advantages of Data Visualization

In business most of the situations are analyzed on comparison basis at-least two components are two features are targeted for better analysis and decision making. In normal method large amount of data need to examine with good knowledge experts with many business factors for taking the decision. Data visualization comparison analysis will save time and provide better agreement among the business management team to take appropriate decisions.

Data visualization provides a superior method of understanding data with good pictorial structures. This undoubtedly provides clear visual facts for supporting decision making or understanding patterns.

The visual tools provide improved perception of information and provide conclusions on usable patterns with more superior knowledge [14].

Instead of sharing huge cumbersome amount of data the visual tools provide the information in more abstract form with more observations.

Data visualizations helps the different organization teams to work with visualized facts and helps them to deeply investigate before coming to conclusions. Much of the situations or occasions can be correlated in business with visual facts for better decision making in improving their insights by comparisons.

The visual information can be adjusted to improve the perception of information and altered changes can be analyzed for further decision making. It opens doors for many top level management people in the organization to easily investigate on the visual facts and influence their decisions while discussion with expert teams. It also helps the geological perception of information for further investigation to study day to day effects on the visual data.

Disadvantages of Data Visualization

The data visualization sometimes foresees the actual fact values and provides perception on fault data. As the data changes for assessment it is difficult for data science team to draw conclusions with corrupted information. The results may be only changed graphs but that leads to misguidance in taking exact decisions.

Many of the conclusions drawn from the data used for visualization is done only one sided decision which means the information perception is absolutely failed if an individual will carry the data interpretation. Thus one-sided interpretation always makes the job of data science to draw conclusions from the significant information with one-sided results.

The data visualization tools provide perceptions which can't provide help with other alternative choices and consider those results as unexpected [15].

The information perception which is viewed as a correspondence need to be clarified with specific reasons and the plan will fail if any data provided at that point is not relevant to consider the results as inappropriate.

If the personnel involved in the data science team doesn't have clarity on the domain relevant data then they may fed wrong input for visualization tool which results in wrong interpretations.

2.1   Creating Standard Plots (Line, Bar, Pie)

Segment 1 - Creating standard plots (line, bar, pie)

```
In [1]: ! pip install Seaborn

        Requirement already satisfied (use --upgrade to upgrade): Seaborn in c:\program files\anaconda2\lib\site-packages

        You are using pip version 8.1.2, however version 9.0.1 is available.
        You should consider upgrading via the 'python -m pip install --upgrade pip' command.
```

```
In [2]: import numpy as np
        from numpy.random import randn
        import pandas as pd
        from pandas import Series, DataFrame

        import matplotlib.pyplot as plt
        from matplotlib import rcParams
        import seaborn as sb
```

```
In [3]: %matplotlib inline
        rcParams['figure.figsize'] = 5, 4
        sb.set_style('whitegrid')
```

Creating a line chart from a list object

Plotting a line chart in matplotlib

```
In [4]: x = range(1,10)
        y = [1,2,3,4,0,4,3,2,1]

        plt.plot(x, y)
```

```
Out[4]: [<matplotlib.lines.Line2D at 0xbf691d0>]
```

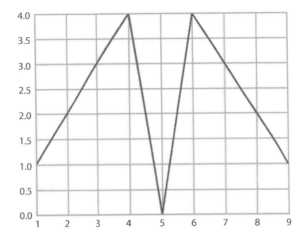

Plotting a line chart from a Pandas object

```
In [5]: address = 'C:/Users/Lillian Pierson/Desktop/Exercise Files/Ch02/02_01/mtcars.csv'
        cars = pd.read_csv(address)
        cars.columns = ['car_names','mpg','cyl','disp', 'hp', 'drat', 'wt', 'qsec', 'vs', 'am', 'gear', 'carb']
        mpg = cars['mpg']
```

```
In [6]: mpg.plot()
Out[6]: <matplotlib.axes._subplots.AxesSubplot at 0xc13cda0>
```

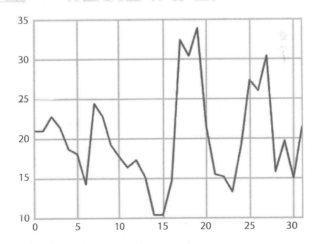

```
In [7]: df = cars[['cyl', 'wt', 'mpg']]
        df.plot()
Out[7]: <matplotlib.axes._subplots.AxesSubplot at 0xc008898>
```

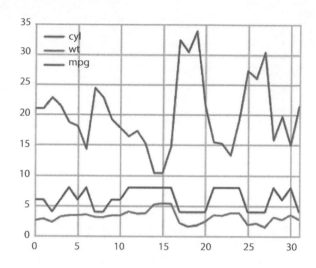

Creating bar charts

Creating a bar chart from a list

```
In [8]: plt.bar(x, y)
Out[8]: <Container object of 9 artists>
```

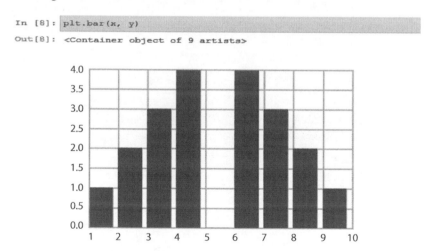

Creating bar charts from Pandas objects

```
In [9]: mpg.plot(kind='bar')
Out[9]: <matplotlib.axes._subplots.AxesSubplot at 0xc7f41d0>
```

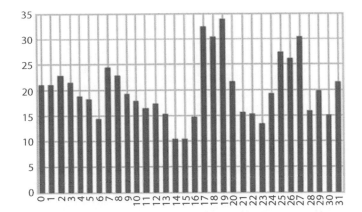

```
In [12]:  mpg.plot(kind='barh')

Out[12]:  <matplotlib.axes._subplots.AxesSubplot at 0xdec1358>
```

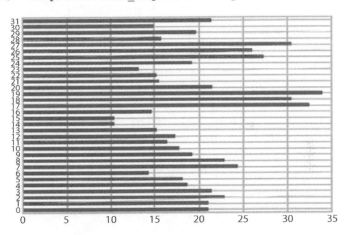

Creating a pie chart

```
In [13]:  x = [1,2,3,4,0.5]
          plt.pie(x)
          plt.show()
```

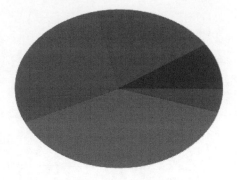

Saving a plot

```
In [14]: plt.savefig('pie_chart.jpeg')
         plt.show()
```

```
<matplotlib.figure.Figure at 0xcc44f98>
```

```
In [16]: %pwd
```

```
Out[16]: u'C:\\Users\\Lillian Pierson\\Documents\\Notebooks'
```

2.2   Defining Elements of a Plot

Segment 2 - Defining elements of a plot

```
In [1]: import numpy as np
        from numpy.random import randn
        import pandas as pd
        from pandas import Series, DataFrame

        import matplotlib.pyplot as plt
        from matplotlib import rcParams
```

```
In [2]: %matplotlib inline
        rcParams['figure.figsize'] = 5, 4
```

Defining axes, ticks, and grids

```
In [4]: x = range(1,10)
        y = [1,2,3,4,0,4,3,2,1]

        fig = plt.figure()

        ax = fig.add_axes([.1, .1, 1, 1])

        ax.plot(x,y)
Out[4]: [<matplotlib.lines.Line2D at 0x9f646d8>]
```

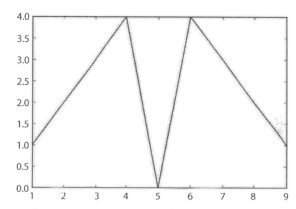

```
In [5]: fig = plt.figure()
        ax = fig.add_axes([.1, .1, 1, 1])

        ax.set_xlim([1,9])
        ax.set_ylim([0,5])

        ax.set_xticks([0,1,2,4,5,6,8,9,10])
        ax.set_yticks([0,1,2,3,4,5])

        ax.plot(x,y)
Out[5]: [<matplotlib.lines.Line2D at 0xa051da0>]
```

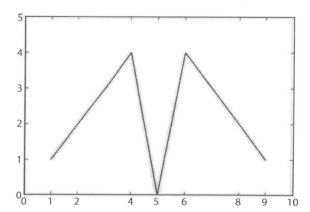

```
In [6]:   fig = plt.figure()
          ax = fig.add_axes([.1, .1, 1, 1])

          ax.set_xlim([1,9])
          ax.set_ylim([0,5])

          ax.grid()
          ax.plot(x, y)
```

```
Out[6]:   [<matplotlib.lines.Line2D at 0xa5c5048>]
```

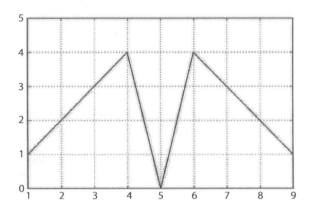

Generating multiple plots in one figure with subplots

```
In [7]:   fig = plt.figure()
          fig, (ax1, ax2) = plt.subplots(1,2)

          ax1.plot(x)
          ax2.plot(x,y)
```

```
Out[7]:   [<matplotlib.lines.Line2D at 0xa8db908>]

          <matplotlib.figure.Figure at 0xa5d3c18>
```

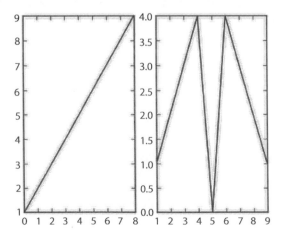

2.3   Plot Formatting

Segment 3 - Plot formatting

In [1]:
```python
import numpy as np
import pandas as pd
from pandas import Series, DataFrame

import matplotlib.pyplot as plt
from pylab import rcParams

import seaborn as sb
```

In [2]:
```python
%matplotlib inline
rcParams['figure.figsize'] = 5, 4
sb.set_style('whitegrid')
```

Defining plot color

In [3]:
```python
x = range(1, 10)
y = [1,2,3,4,0.5,4,3,2,1]

plt.bar(x, y)
```
Out[3]:   <Container object of 9 artists>

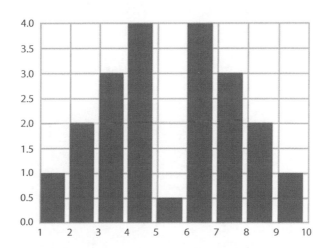

In [4]:
```
wide = [0.5, 0.5, 0.5, 0.9, 0.9, 0.9, 0.5, 0.5, 0.5]
color = ['salmon']
plt.bar(x, y, width=wide, color=color, align='center')
```

Out[4]:   <Container object of 9 artists>

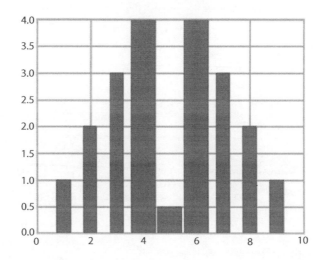

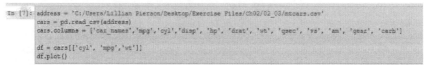

In [7]:
```
address = 'C:/Users/Lillian Pierson/Desktop/Exercise Files/Ch02/02_03/mtcars.csv'
cars = pd.read_csv(address)
cars.columns = ['car_names','mpg','cyl','disp', 'hp', 'drat', 'wt', 'qsec', 'vs', 'am', 'gear', 'carb']

df = cars[['cyl', 'mpg','wt']]
df.plot()
```

Out[7]:   <matplotlib.axes._subplots.AxesSubplot at 0xc259da0>

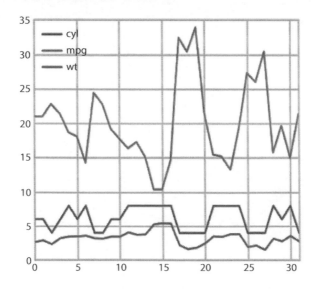

```
In [8]:  color_theme = ['darkgray', 'lightsalmon', 'powderblue']
         df.plot(color=color_theme)
```

```
Out[8]:  <matplotlib.axes._subplots.AxesSubplot at 0xc680860>
```

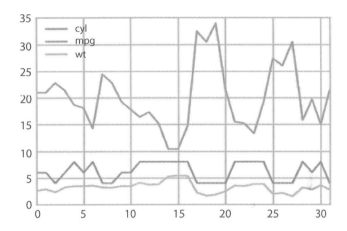

```
In [9]:  z = [1,2,3,4,0.5]
         plt.pie(z)
         plt.show()
```

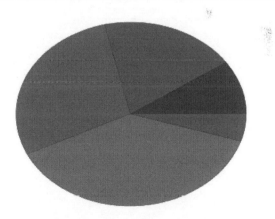

```
In [15]:  color_theme = ['#A9A9A9', '#FFA07A', '#B0E0E6', '#FFE4C4', '#BDB76B']
          plt.pie(z, colors = color_theme)
          plt.show()
```

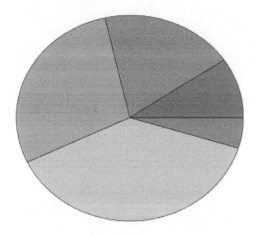

Customizing line styles

```
In [16]:  x1 = range(0,10)
          y1 = [10, 9, 8, 7, 6, 5, 4, 3, 2, 1]

          plt.plot(x, y)
          plt.plot(x1,y1)

Out[16]:  [<matplotlib.lines.Line2D at 0xdbfd7b8>]
```

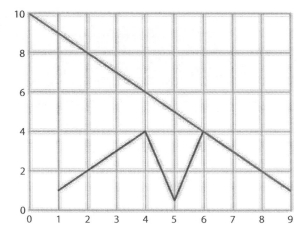

In [17]:
```
plt.plot(x, y, ls = 'steps', lw=5)
plt.plot(x1,y1, ls='--', lw=10)
```

Out[17]: [<matplotlib.lines.Line2D at 0xdff2048>]

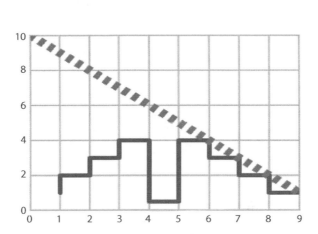

Setting plot markers

In [18]:
```
plt.plot(x, y, marker = '1', mew=20)
plt.plot(x1,y1, marker = '+', mew=15)
```

Out[18]: [<matplotlib.lines.Line2D at 0xe394198>]

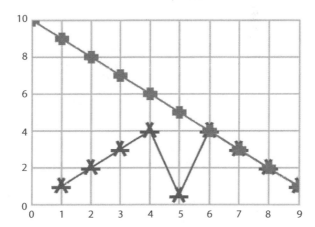

2.4   Creating Labels and Annotations

Segment 4 - Creating labels and annotations

```
In [1]:  import numpy as np
         import pandas as pd
         from pandas import Series, DataFrame

         import matplotlib.pyplot as plt
         from pylab import rcParams
         import seaborn as sb
```

```
In [2]:  %matplotlib inline
         rcParams['figure.figsize'] = 8,4
         sb.set_style('whitegrid')
```

Labeling plot features

The functional method

```
In [3]:  x = range(1,10)
         y = [1,2,3,4,0.5,4,3,2,1]
         plt.bar(x,y)

         plt.xlabel('your x-axis label')
         plt.ylabel('your y-axis label')
```
```
Out[3]:  <matplotlib.text.Text at 0xbecb748>
```

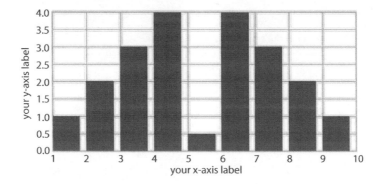

```
In [4]:  z = [1 , 2, 3, 4, 0.5]
         veh_type = ['bicycle', 'motorbike','car', 'van', 'stroller']
         plt.pie(z, labels= veh_type)
         plt.show()
```

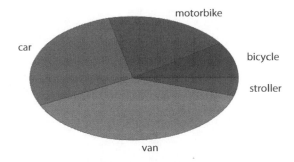

The object-oriented method

```
In [5]:  address = 'C:/Users/Lillian Pierson/Desktop/Exercise Files/Ch02/02_04/mtcars.csv'
         cars = pd.read_csv(address)
         cars.columns = ['car_names','mpg','cyl','disp', 'hp', 'drat', 'wt', 'qsec', 'vs', 'am', 'gear', 'carb']

         mpg = cars.mpg

         fig = plt.figure()
         ax = fig.add_axes([.1, .1, 1, 1])

         mpg.plot()

         ax.set_xticks(range(32))

         ax.set_xticklabels(cars.car_names, rotation=60, fontsize='medium')
         ax.set_title('Miles per Gallon of Cars in mtcars')

         ax.set_xlabel('car names')
         ax.set_ylabel('miles/gal')
```

```
Out[5]:  <matplotlib.text.Text at 0x02c4495>
```

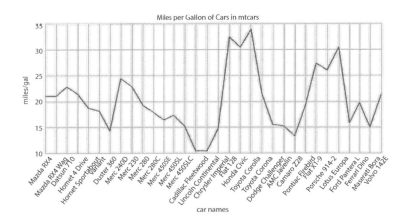

Adding a legend to your plot

The functional method

```
In [6]: plt.pie(z)
        plt.legend(veh_type, loc='best')
        plt.show()
```

The object-oriented method

```
In [7]: fig = plt.figure()
        ax = fig.add_axes([.1,.1,1,1])
        mpg.plot()

        ax.set_xticks(range(32))

        ax.set_xticklabels(cars.car_names, rotation=60, fontsize='medium')
        ax.set_title('Miles per Gallon of Cars in mtcars')

        ax.set_xlabel('car names')
        ax.set_ylabel('miles/gal')

        ax.legend(loc='best')
```

```
Out[7]: <matplotlib.legend.Legend at 0xc9cab00>
```

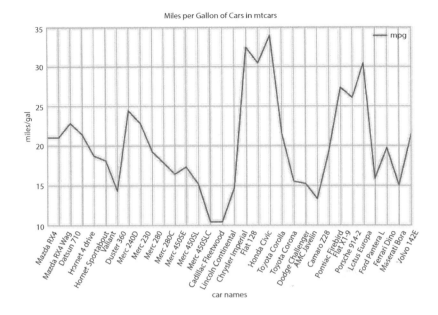

Annotating your plot

In [8]: `mpg.max()`

Out[8]: 33.899999999999999

```
In [9]: fig = plt.figure()
ax = fig.add_axes([.1,.1,1,1])
mpg.plot()
ax.set_title('Miles per Gallon of Cars in mtcars')
ax.set_ylabel('miles/gal')

ax.set_ylim([0,45])

ax.annotate('Toyota Corolla', xy=(19,33.9), xytext = (21,35),
            arrowprops=dict(facecolor='black', shrink=0.05))
```

Out[9]: <matplotlib.text.Annotation at 0xc1f8390>

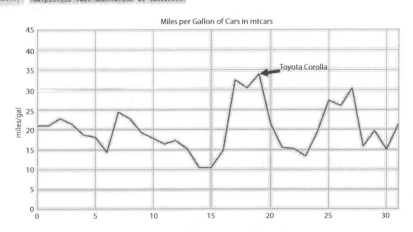

2.5   Creating Visualizations from Time Series Data

Segment 5 - Creating visualizations from time series data

```
In [1]:  import numpy as np
         from numpy.random import randn
         import pandas as pd
         from pandas import Series, DataFrame

         import matplotlib.pyplot as plt
         from pylab import rcParams
         import seaborn as sb
```

```
In [2]:  %matplotlib inline
         rcParams['figure.figsize'] = 5, 4
         sb.set_style('whitegrid')
```

The simplest time series plot

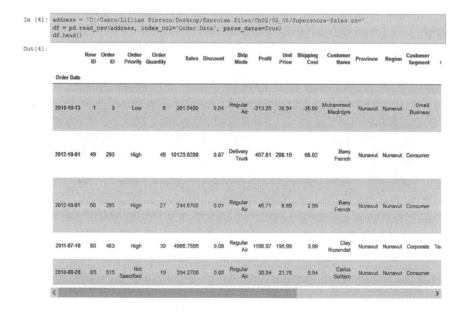

```
In [4]:  address = 'C:/Users/Lillian Pierson/Desktop/Exercise Files/Ch02/02_05/Superstore-Sales.csv'
         df = pd.read_csv(address, index_col='Order Date', parse_dates=True)
         df.head()
```

Order Date	Row ID	Order ID	Order Priority	Order Quantity	Sales	Discount	Ship Mode	Profit	Unit Price	Shipping Cost	Customer Name	Province	Region	Customer Segment	
2010-10-13	1	3	Low	6	261.5400	0.04	Regular Air	-213.25	38.94	35.00	Muhammed Macintyre	Nunavut	Nunavut	Small Business	
2012-10-01	49	293	High	49	10123.0200	0.07	Delivery Truck	457.81	208.16	68.02	Barry French	Nunavut	Nunavut	Consumer	
2012-10-01	50	293	High	27	244.5700	0.01	Regular Air	46.71	8.69	2.99	Barry French	Nunavut	Nunavut	Consumer	
2011-07-10	80	483	High	30	4965.7595	0.08	Regular Air	1198.97	195.99	3.99	Clay Rozendal	Nunavut	Nunavut	Corporate	Te
2010-08-28	85	515	Not Specified	19	394.2700	0.08	Regular Air	30.94	21.78	5.94	Carlos Soltero	Nunavut	Nunavut	Consumer	

The simplest time series plot

```
In [4]:  address = 'C:/Users/Lillian Pierson/Desktop/Exercise Files/Ch02/02_05/Superstore-Sales.csv'
         df = pd.read_csv(address, index_col='Order Date', parse_dates=True)
         df.head()
```

Out[4]:

Ship Mode	Profit	Unit Price	Shipping Cost	Customer Name	Province	Region	Customer Segment	Product Category	Product Sub-Category	Product Name	Product Container	Product Base Margin	Ship Date
Regular Air	-213.25	38.94	35.00	Muhammed Macintyre	Nunavut	Nunavut	Small Business	Office Supplies	Storage & Organization	Eldon Base for stackable storage shelf, platinum	Large Box	0.80	10/20/2010
Delivery Truck	457.81	208.16	68.02	Barry French	Nunavut	Nunavut	Consumer	Office Supplies	Appliances	1.7 Cubic Foot Compact "Cube" Office Refrigera...	Jumbo Drum	0.58	10/2/2012
Regular Air	46.71	8.69	2.99	Barry French	Nunavut	Nunavut	Consumer	Office Supplies	Binders and Binder Accessories	Cardinal Slant-D◆ Ring Binder, Heavy Gauge Vinyl	Small Box	0.39	10/3/2012
Regular Air	1198.97	195.99	3.99	Clay Rozendal	Nunavut	Nunavut	Corporate	Technology	Telephones and Communication	R380	Small Box	0.58	7/12/2011
Regular Air	30.94	21.78	5.94	Carlos Soltero	Nunavut	Nunavut	Consumer	Office Supplies	Appliances	Holmes HEPA Air Purifier	Medium Box	0.50	8/30/2010

```
In [5]: df['Order Quantity'].plot()
```

```
Out[5]: <matplotlib.axes._subplots.AxesSubplot at 0xc25e860>
```

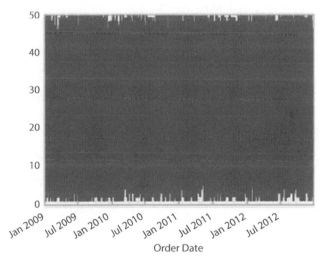

Order Date

```
In [6]: df2 = df.sample(n=100, random_state=25, axis=0)

        plt.xlabel('Order Date')
        plt.ylabel('Order Quantity')
        plt.title('Superstore Sales')

        df2['Order Quantity'].plot()
```

```
Out[6]: <matplotlib.axes._subplots.AxesSubplot at 0xc92bd30>
```

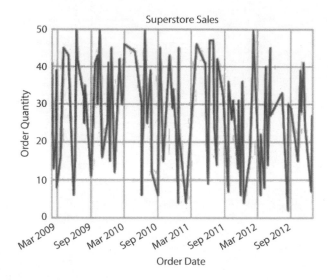

2.6   Constructing Histograms, Box Plots, and Scatter Plots

Histogram

The data visualization tool which works on continuous interval of data for a particular period of time. It combines features of vertical bar and line charts. The x-axis is broken into discrete intervals based on the continuous variable and the amount of data in that time interval relates to that height of the histogram bar. The general interpretations which happens from histogram are they provide data in that specific interval with more concentrated bars and capable of finding gaps or unusual values throughout the dataset.

The popular reason for using histogram are most of the datasets are compared over an interval of time with good distribution of data. The data set more than three featured variable values should not be considered for interpretation in histogram.

The best practices of using histogram for data visualization are as follows:

- o   Try to avoid distribution of data with too wide carrying more important details or too narrow which relates to large noisy data.

- o Always use equal round numbers for creating good bar size graphs.
- o Consistent colors need to be used with fine labeling throughout the graph so that it is easy to identify relationships.

Advantages and Disadvantages of Histogram

- Histograms are mostly used for continuous, discrete and unordered data and very useful to draw.
- They consume more ink and space to display small information
- Simultaneous comparisons are somewhat difficult using histograms.

Segment 6 - Constructing histograms, box plots, and scatter plots

```
In [9]:  import numpy as np
         import pandas as pd
         from pandas import Series, DataFrame

         from pandas.tools.plotting import scatter_matrix

         import matplotlib.pyplot as plt
         from pylab import rcParams
         import seaborn as sb
```

```
In [10]:  %matplotlib inline
          rcParams['figure.figsize'] = 5, 4
          sb.set_style('whitegrid')
```

Eyeballing dataset distributions with histograms

```
In [3]:  address = 'C:/Users/Lillian Pierson/Desktop/Exercise Files/Ch02/02_06/mtcars.csv'
         cars = pd.read_csv(address)
         cars.columns = ['car_names','mpg','cyl','disp', 'hp', 'drat', 'wt', 'qsec', 'vs', 'am', 'gear', 'carb']
         cars.index = cars.car_names
         mpg = cars['mpg']

         mpg.plot(kind='hist')
```

```
Out[3]:  <matplotlib.axes._subplots.AxesSubplot at 0xbec74e0>
```

Best practices for a scatter plot visualization

If you use a scatterplot, here are the key design best practices:

- Scatter plot will analyze data to identify the possible trends of data and ensure it to plot for only two possible trends to remove confusion.
- Always start at 0 for y-axis plot.

Advantages of Scatter plots

- Good trends of relationship are identified using this visualization technique.
- All possible outliers data are identified with in the range of minimum to maximum
- Correlations are highlighted
- Exact data values are retained for a particular sample size
- Both positive type correlation and negative type correlation are revealed in the plotting.

Disadvantages of Scatter Plots

- Flat plot of straight line gives confused results.
- Most of the data interpretations are done in subjective
- The correlation does not reveal perfect reasons for their cause
- It only deals with continuous data for plotting on both axes.
- Multivariate analysis cannot be done using scatter plots

Seeing scatterplots in action

```
In [6]: cars.plot(kind='scatter', x='hp', y='mpg', c=['darkgray'], s=150)
Out[6]: <matplotlib.axes._subplots.AxesSubplot at 0xc44c4a8>
```

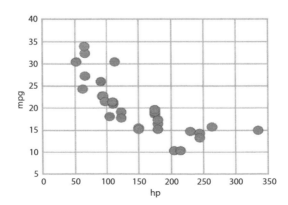

```
In [7]: sb.regplot(x='hp', y='mpg', data=cars, scatter=True)
Out[7]: <matplotlib.axes._subplots.AxesSubplot at 0xc5f68d0>
```

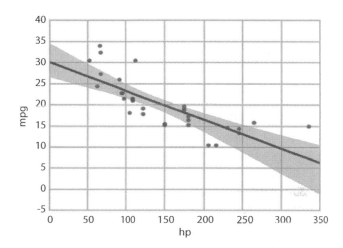

Generating a scatter plot matrix

```
In [8]: sb.pairplot(cars)
Out[8]: <seaborn.axisgrid.PairGrid at 0xc4c630>
```

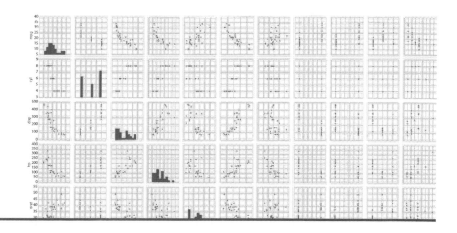

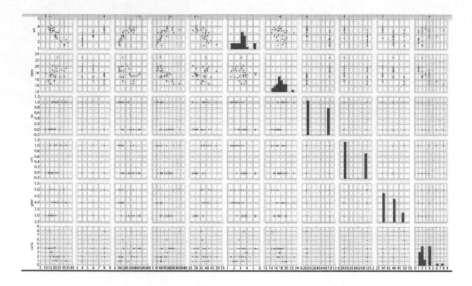

```
In [14]: cars_df = pd.DataFrame((cars.ix[:,(1,3,4,6)].values), columns = ['mpg', 'disp', 'hp', 'wt'])
         cars_target = cars.ix[:,9].values
         target_names = [0, 1]

         cars_df['group'] = pd.Series(cars_target, dtype="category")
         sb.pairplot(cars_df, hue='group', palette='hls')

Out[14]: <seaborn.axisgrid.PairGrid at 0x29587048>
```

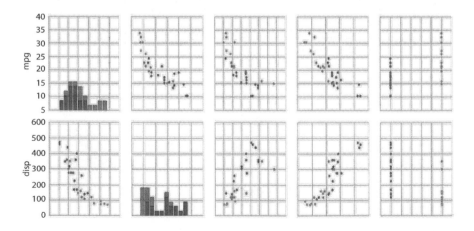

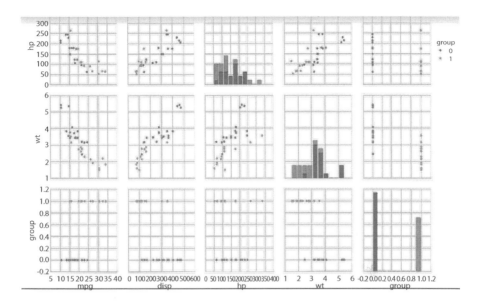

Building boxplots

Boxplots

Data visualization which deals with more amount of distribution of data across different ranges of maximum to minimum with many partition is possible using box plot or whisker diagram. It summarizes data in to five categories like minimum range, first quartile range, median range, third quartile range, and the maximum.

Much of the outlier's data is clearly interpreted in box plot with full length of data variation from minimum to maximum.

Reasons for utilization of box plot visualization.

- Distribution of data is interpreted with neat comparison.
- The interpretation of box plot all possible ranges of data from min to max and then to median.

Don't use a box plot for the following reason:

- Data set with no perfect conclusion forunivariate interpretation

Best practices for a box plot visualization

If you use a box plot, here are the key design best practices:

- The labels of the box plot need to be with good font size and legend need to be highlighted and the line thickness and width need to be highlighted for good and easy understanding of the interpretation.
- Different color, line borders and symbols need to be used to differentiate while plotting multiple data sets.
- Unwanted clutter need to remove while plotting the data with boxplot.

Advantages

- Most of the statistical data can be easily plotted for large amount of data in a single box plot.
- During display of box plot the range of data need to be clearly specified on a number line.
- Symmetry and skew-ness of data easily captured using box plots
- Most outliers are detected are shown using box plot

Disadvantages

- The originality of data misses in the box plot and other statistical parameters like mean and mode cannot be plotted.
- Numerical data is only suitable for box plot other variety of data samples cannot be interpreted.

Building boxplots

```
In [15]:  cars.boxplot(column='mpg', by='am')
          cars.boxplot(column='wt', by='am')

Out[15]:  <matplotlib.axes._subplots.AxesSubplot at 0x29ae7f60>
```

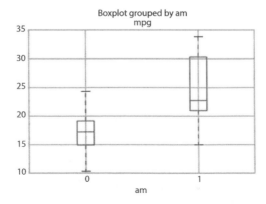

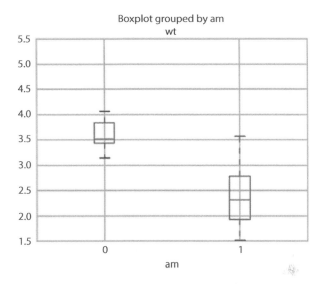

```
In [16]: sb.boxplot(x='am', y='mpg', data=cars, palette='hls')
```

Out[16]: <matplotlib.axes._subplots.AxesSubplot at 0x2d7f5f28>

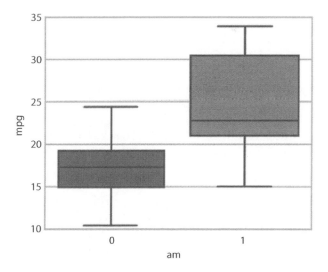

References

1. Shewan, Dan (5 October 2016). "Data is Beautiful: 7 Data Visualization Tools for Digital Marketers". Business2Community.com. Archived from the original on 12 November 2016.
2. Nussbaumer Knaflic, Cole (2 November 2015). Storytelling with Data: A Data Visualization Guide for Business Professionals. ISBN 978-1-119-00225-3.
3. "What is Data Visualization? - Whizlabs Blog".
4. Gershon, Nahum; Page, Ward (1 August 2001). "What storytelling can do for information visualization". Communications of the ACM. 44 (8): 31–37. doi:10.1145/381641.381653. S2CID 7666107.
5. Mason, Betsy (November 12, 2019). "Why scientists need to be better at data visualization". Knowable Magazine. doi:10.1146/knowable-110919-1.
6. O'Donoghue, Seán I.; Baldi, Benedetta Frida; Clark, Susan J.; Darling, Aaron E.; Hogan, James M.; Kaur, Sandeep; Maier-Hein, Lena; McCarthy, Davis J.; Moore, William J.; Stenau, Esther; Swedlow, Jason R.; Vuong, Jenny; Procter, James B. (2018-07-20). "Visualization of Biomedical Data". Annual Review of Biomedical Data Science. 1 (1): 275–304. doi:10.1146/annurev-biodatasci-080917-013424. hdl:10453/125943. S2CID 199591321. Retrieved 25 June 2021.
7. "Stephen Few-Perceptual Edge-Selecting the Right Graph for Your Message-2004" (PDF). Archived (PDF) from the original on 2014-10-05. Retrieved 2014-09-08.
8. "10 Examples of Interactive Map Data Visualizations".
9. Vitaly Friedman (2008) "Data Visualization and Infographics" Archived 2008-07-22 at the Wayback Machine in: Graphics, Monday Inspiration, January 14th, 2008.
10. Fernanda Viegas and Martin Wattenberg (April 19, 2011). "How To Make Data Look Sexy". CNN.com. Archived from the original on May 6, 2011. Retrieved May 7, 2017.
11. Pawan, Y.V.R.N. & Prakash, K.B. 2020, "Block chain for tertiary education", *Journal of Engineering Education Transformations*, vol. 33, no. Special Issue, pp. 608-612.
12. Pawan, Y.V.R.N. & Prakash, K.B. 2020, "Improved PSO Performance using LSTM based Inertia Weight Estimation", *International Journal of Advanced Computer Science and Applications*, vol. 11, no. 11, pp. 582-599.
13. Pradeep Kumar, V. & Prakash, K.B. 2019, "QoS aware resource provisioning in federated cloud and analyzing maximum resource utilization in agent based model", *International Journal of Innovative Technology and Exploring Engineering*, vol. 8, no. 8, pp. 2689-2697.

14. Prakash, K.B., Kumar, V.P. & Pawan, V.R.N. 2021, "Machine learning in blockchain" in *Blockchain and Machine Learning for e-Healthcare Systems*, pp. 137-160.
15. Prakash, K.B. & Rajaraman, A. 2016, "Mining of Bilingual Indian Web Documents", *Procedia Computer Science*, pp. 514.

Eigenvalue Decomposition

Eigen value decomposition perform reduction operation on matrices to boost the matrix to generate new vector data which are having similar features and further this vector data is decomposed in to eigenvalues and eigenvectors.

Principal Component Analysis

Higher reduction of dimensional data is possible using principal component analysis. It is popular dimensionality reduction technique among the variables without losing strong variables among the correlate data [14].

3.2 Calculus

Calculus plays very important role in Data Science [15]. It majorly involved in optimization techniques which are popular in machine learning. It is also used as mathematical modeling technique as part of neural networks to improve the performance and accuracy. Calculus is classified as Differential calculus and Integral calculus [5].

3.2.1 Differential Calculus

Derivatives are mostly used as part of differential calculus to find the max and min functions and rate at which the quantity changes. Derivatives are popular used in optimization techniques to find the minimal as to minimize the error function. Partial derivatives are generally used for back propagation chain rule concept of neural networks. Game theory also uses differential calculus for generative adversarial neural networks.

3.2.2 Integral Calculus

Integral calculus is popularly used for aggregating the quantities and find area under the given curve. Integral calculus is performed in two ways definite and indefinite integrals. Most of the probability density functions and variance computation for random variable is dealt by integral calculus.

Bayesian interference popular technique in machine learning uses only integral calculus.

Statistics for Data Science

Data science derives most of its features from statistics like gathering, analysis of raw data, data interpretation and data visualization [6]. Both are data–driven mechanisms which are popularly used for decision making [7]. It provides very popular tools to reveal features of large amount of data. Comprehensive results can be derived by data summarization and interference mechanism [8]. The two popular approaches of statistics are Descriptive statistics and inferential statistics [9].

Descriptive statistics is mostly used for describing the data. It performs the quantitative analysis of data for summarization. It does summarization using graphs. Following are some of the key concepts learned as per descriptive statistics [10].

Large no of data samples are plotted using normal distribution in to a bell shaped curve which is popularly known as Gaussian curve. The Gaussian curve is symmetric in nature means all the sample values are equally distributed in both directions of center axis.

Central tendency identifies the central point of data from which mean, mode and median are computed. The average of sample data gives the mean value, the middle value of the data which is arranged in ascending order signifies the median and mode is the most frequently occurring value in the sample data.

In the Gaussian curve if the sample data does not lead to equal distribution on both sides from the center then it leads to skewness. The left side accumulation of sample data leads to positive skew similarly right side accumulation of sample data leads negative skew.

If the sample data in Gaussian curve accumulates on the tail end of the graph then it is called kurtosis. If more data is present the tail of the graph then it called large kurtosis similarly small data at tail of graph represent small kurtosis.

The other measures which are computed on the sample data which are occurred in variable manner in Gaussian curve are range value, variance value, inter quartile and standard deviation of data.

3.3   Inferential Statistics

Inferential Statistics is the procedure of inferring or concluding from the data. Through inferential statistics, we make a conclusion about the larger population by running several tests and deductions from the smaller sample.

The concluding of data or inferring the results of sample data is a procedure followed in inferential statistics. The conclusions are made by running several tests on large population and finding results from the sample data. Example of election survey which is done by selecting some sample of population and choose some specific observation parameters to identify the views of the public.

Some of the popular techniques studied under inferential statistics are as follows.

3.3.1   Central Limit Theorem

Central limit theorem is estimation of the population mean where in the mean value same between small population and large population. The margin error is computed by the product of standard error of the mean with z-score of percentage of confidence level.

3.3.2   Hypothesis Testing

Hypothesis testing is performed by computing the attribute results from smaller sample for a much larger group. Two hypotheses are tested against each other i.e null and alternate hypothesis. Always alternate hypothesis is computed to prove that null hypothesis is wrong.

3.3.3   ANOVA

ANOVA is used for performing the hypothesis test for multiple groups. It improves the popular hypothesis of t-test. It tries to perform testing on minimal error rate. It is normally used for computing F-ratio. It is the ratio of mean square of internal group and mean square in between the groups.

3.3.4   Qualitative Data Analysis

The two important techniques of qualitative data analysis are correlation and regression. The process of finding relationship between random variables and bivariate data is called correlation. Regression is used to find relationship between variables. Different model of regression are chosen based on no of variables used for estimation it ranges from simple regression where only two variables are used and multi-variable regression where more than two variables are considered for estimating the relationship. Non-linear regression is performed of non-linear data.

3.4   Using NumPy to Perform Arithmetic Operations on Data

Arithmetic Operations on NumPy Arrays

Numpy performs element wise arithmetic operations on the array elements.

np.add( )- performs the addition operation on the array elements.
np.subtract( )- Performs the subtraction operation on the array elements.
np.mulitply( )- Performs the multiplication operation on the array elements.
np.divide( )- Performs the division operation on the array elements.
np.power( )- Performs the exponentiation operation on the array elements.
np.mod( )- Performs the modulus operation on the array elements.
np.negative( )- performs the negation operation on the array elements.
np.sqrt( )- computes the square root operation on the array elements.
np.abs( )- gives the absolute value of the array elements.
np.exp ( ) and np.exp2( )- computes **e^x and 2^x for each array element.**
np.log( ) and np.log10( )- computes natural logarithm and base-10 operation for the array elements.

Segment 1 - Using NumPy to perform arithmetic operations on data

```
In [1]: import numpy as np
        from numpy.random import randn
```

```
In [2]: np.set_printoptions(precision=2)
```

Creating arrays

Creating arrays using a list

```
In [3]: a = np.array([1,2,3,4,5,6])
         a

Out[3]: array([1, 2, 3, 4, 5, 6])
```

```
In [4]: b = np.array([[10,20,30], [40,50,60]])
         b

Out[4]: array([[10, 20, 30],
               [40, 50, 60]])
```

Creating arrays via assignment

```
In [5]: np.random.seed(25)
        c = 36*np.random.randn(6)
        c

Out[5]: array([  8.22,  36.97, -30.23, -21.28, -34.45,  -8.  ])
```

```
In [6]: d = np.arange(1,35)
        d

Out[6]: array([ 1,  2,  3,  4,  5,  6,  7,  8,  9, 10, 11, 12, 13, 14, 15, 16, 17,
               18, 19, 20, 21, 22, 23, 24, 25, 26, 27, 28, 29, 30, 31, 32, 33, 34])
```

Performing arthimetic on arrays

```
In [7]: a * 10

Out[7]: array([10, 20, 30, 40, 50, 60])
```

```
In [8]: c + a

Out[8]: array([  9.22,  38.97, -27.23, -17.28, -29.45,  -2.  ])
```

```
In [9]: c - a
```
Out[9]: array([7.22,   34.97, -33.23, -25.28, -39.45, -14.])

```
In [10]: c * a
```
Out[10]: array([8.22,   73.94,   -90.68,   -85.13, -172.24,   -48.02])

```
In [11]: c / a
```
Out[11]: array([8.22,   18.48, -10.08,   -5.32,   -6.89,   -1.33])

Multiplying matrices and basic linear algebra

```
In [12]: aa = np.array([[2.,4.,6.], [1.,3.,5.], [10.,20.,30.]])
         aa
```
Out[12]: array([[2.,   4.,   6.],
               [1.,   3.,   5.],
               [10.,   20.,   30.]])

```
In [13]: bb = np.array([[0.,1.,2.], [3.,4.,5.], [6.,7.,8.]])
         bb
```
Out[13]: array([[0.,   1.,   2.],
               [3.,   4.,   5.],
               [6.,   7.,   8.]])

```
In [14]: aa*bb
```
Out[14]: array([[0.,   4.,   12.],
               [3.,   12.,   25.],
               [60.,   140.,   240.]])

```
In [16]: np.dot(aa,bb)
```
Out[16]: array([[48.,   60.,   72.],
               [39.,   48.,   57.],
               [240.,   300.,   360.]])

3.5   Generating Summary Statistics Using Pandas and Scipy

Segment 2 - Generating summary statistics using pandas and scipy

```
In [17]: import numpy as np
         import pandas as pd
         from pandas import Series, DataFrame

         import scipy
         from scipy import stats
```

```
In [ ]: address = 'C:/Users/Lillian Pierson/Desktop/Exercise Files/Ch01/01_05/mtcars.csv'
        cars = pd.read_csv(address)
        cars.columns = ['car_names','mpg','cyl','disp', 'hp', 'drat', 'wt', 'qsec', 'vs', 'am', 'gear', 'carb']

        cars.head()
```

Looking at summary statistics that describe a variable's numeric values

```
In [20]: cars.sum()
```

```
Out[20]: car_names    Mazda RX4Mazda RX4 WagDatsun 710Hornet 4 Drive...
         mpg                                                     642.9
         cyl                                                       198
         disp                                                   7383.1
         hp                                                       4694
         drat                                                   115.09
         wt                                                    102.952
         qsec                                                   571.16
         vs                                                        14
         am                                                        13
         gear                                                      118
         carb                                                       90
         dtype: object
```

```
In [21]: cars.sum(axis=1)
```

```
Out[21]: 0      328.980
         1      329.795
         2      259.580
         3      426.135
         4      590.310
         5      385.540
         6      656.920
         7      270.980
         8      299.570
         9      350.460
         10     349.660
         11     510.740
         12     511.500
         13     509.850
         14     728.560
         15     726.644
         16     725.695
         17     213.850
         18     195.165
```

```
In [21]:  cars.sum(axis=1)
```

```
          14      728.560
          15      726.644
          16      725.695
          17      213.850
          18      195.165
          19      206.955
          20      273.775
          21      519.650
          22      506.085
          23      646.280
          24      631.175
          25      208.215
          26      272.570
          27      273.683
          28      670.690
          29      379.590
          30      694.710
          31      288.890
          dtype:  float64
```

```
In [22]:  cars.median()
```

```
Out[22]:  mpg       19.200
          cyl        6.000
          disp     196.300
          hp       123.000
          drat       3.695
          wt         3.325
          qsec      17.710
          vs         0.000
          am         0.000
          gear       4.000
          carb       2.000
          dtype:  float64
```

```
In [23]: cars.mean()
```

```
Out[23]: mpg      20.090625
         cyl       6.187500
         disp    230.721875
         hp      146.687500
         drat      3.596563
         wt        3.217250
         qsec     17.848750
         vs        0.437500
         am        0.406250
         gear      3.687500
         carb      2.812500
         dtype: float64
```

```
In [24]: cars.max()
```

```
Out[24]: car_names    Volvo 142E
         mpg                33.9
         cyl                   8
         disp                472
         hp                  335
         drat               4.93
         wt                5.424
         qsec               22.9
         vs                    1
         am                    1
         gear                  5
         carb                  8
         dtype: object
```

```
In [29]: mpg = cars.mpg
         mpg.idxmax()
```

```
Out[29]: 19
```

Looking at summary statistics that describe variable distribution

```
In [31]: cars.std()
```

```
Out[31]: mpg       6.026948
         cyl       1.785922
         disp    123.938694
         hp       68.562868
         drat      0.534679
         wt        0.978457
         qsec      1.786943
         vs        0.504016
         am        0.498991
         gear      0.737804
         carb      1.615200
         dtype: float64
```

```
In [32]: cars.var()
```

```
Out[32]: mpg          36.324103
         cyl           3.189516
         disp     15360.799829
         hp        4700.866935
         drat          0.285881
         wt            0.957379
         qsec          3.193166
         vs            0.254032
         am            0.248992
         gear          0.544355
         carb          2.608871
         dtype: float64
```

```
In [33]: gear = cars.gear
         gear.value_counts()
```

```
Out[33]: 3    15
         4    12
         5     5
         Name: gear, dtype: int64
```

```
In [34]: cars.describe()
```

Out[34]:

	mpg	cyl	disp	hp	drat	wt	qsec	vs	am	gear	carb
count	32.000000	32.000000	32.000000	32.000000	32.000000	32.000000	32.000000	32.000000	32.000000	32.000000	32.0000
mean	20.090625	6.187500	230.721875	146.687500	3.596563	3.217250	17.848750	0.437500	0.406250	3.687500	2.8125
std	6.026948	1.785922	123.938694	68.562868	0.534679	0.978457	1.786943	0.504016	0.498991	0.737804	1.6152
min	10.400000	4.000000	71.100000	52.000000	2.760000	1.513000	14.500000	0.000000	0.000000	3.000000	1.0000
25%	15.425000	4.000000	120.825000	96.500000	3.080000	2.581250	16.892500	0.000000	0.000000	3.000000	2.0000
50%	19.200000	6.000000	196.300000	123.000000	3.695000	3.325000	17.710000	0.000000	0.000000	4.000000	2.0000
75%	22.800000	8.000000	326.000000	180.000000	3.920000	3.610000	18.900000	1.000000	1.000000	4.000000	4.0000
max	33.900000	8.000000	472.000000	335.000000	4.930000	5.424000	22.900000	1.000000	1.000000	5.000000	8.0000

3.6   Summarizing Categorical Data Using Pandas

Data Ingestion

Data ingestion is a process where data transferring take place from different sources for performing analysis, storing and utilizing by the other applications. The general steps involved in the process are collecting data from its current location, converting into other normalized forms finally loaded in to storage for performing further research. Python bags up many tools for performing data ingestion the popular are Airflow, Bonobo, Sopu4, Beautiful Pandas etc. Now data ingestion is explored with pandas.

Initially data is shifted from different sources, into pandas data frame structure. The source can be any file formats such as comma separated value, JSON, HTML, Excel data.

Approach:

The basic approach, for transferring any such data, into a dataframe object, is as follows –

The general approach of transferring of any data, into a dataframe object is done as follows:-

Prepare source data- Data is collected from remote server using URL path or path of a file on a local machine.

Use Pandas 'read_x' method- The read_x method is used for loading and converting data into a dataframe object. Depending on the data format will use the respective read method.

Finally print the data from dataframe object to ensure the conversion is done perfectly or not.

Read data from CSV file

To load, data present in Comma-separated value file(CSV),

Prepare sample dataset. Here we collect the sample data of different cities data as part of teir1 and tier2 in CSV format.

Use Pandas method 'read_csv'

- o read_csv(file_path)
- o File_Path can be URL or file path of a local machine holding .csv or .txt files.

The file contents are as follows:

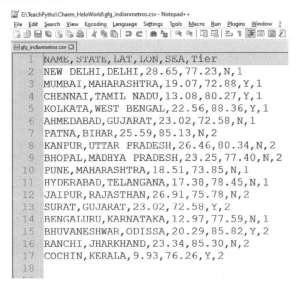

The contents of "gfg_indianmetros.csv" file

The code to get the data in a Pandas Data Frame is:

# Import the Pandas library
import pandas

# Load data from Comma separated file
# Use method - read_csv(filepath)
# Parameter - the path/URL of the CSV/TXT file
dfIndianMetros2 = pandas.rcad_csv("gfg_IndianMctros2.csv")

# print the dataframe object
print(dfIndianMetros2)

Output:

```
# print the dataframe object
print(dfIndianMetros)
```

```
           NAME          STATE   LAT   LON SEA  Tier
0      NEW DELHI         DELHI  28.65 77.23  N     1
1         MUMBAI   MAHARASHTRA  19.07 72.88  Y     1
2        CHENNAI    TAMIL NADU  13.08 80.27  Y     1
3        KOLKATA   WEST BENGAL  22.56 88.36  Y     1
4      AHMEDABAD       GUJARAT  23.02 72.58  N     1
5          PATNA         BIHAR  25.59 85.13  N     2
6         KANPUR UTTAR PRADESH  26.46 80.34  N     2
7         BHOPAL MADHYA PRADESH 23.25 77.40  N     2
8           PUNE   MAHARASHTRA  18.51 73.85  N     1
9      HYDERABAD     TELANGANA  17.38 78.45  N     1
10        JAIPUR     RAJASTHAN  26.91 75.78  N     2
11         SURAT       GUJARAT  23.02 72.58  Y     2
12     BENGALURU     KARNATAKA  12.97 77.59  N     1
13   BHUVANESHWAR       ODISSA  20.29 85.82  Y     2
14        RANCHI     JHARKHAND  23.34 85.30  N     2
15        COCHIN        KERALA   9.93 76.26  Y     2
```

The CSV data, in dataframe object

Read data from an Excel file

To load data present in an Excel file(.xlsx, .xls) we will follow steps as below-

- Prepare your sample dataset. Here Excel file, with Bakery information of different braches.
- Use Pandas method 'read_excel' .
  - Method used – read_excel(file_path)
  - File_Path can be URL or file path of a local machine holding .xlx, .xlsx files

The file contents are as follows:

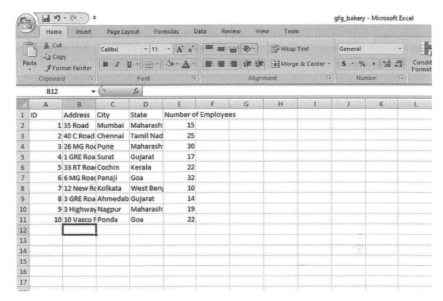

The contents of "gfg_bakery.xlsx" file

The code to get the data in a Pandas DataFrame is:

```
# Import the Pandas library
import pandas

# Load data from an Excel file
# Use method - read_excel(filepath)
# Method parameter - The file location(URL/path) and name
dfBakery2 = pandas.read_excel("gfg_Bakery.xlsx")

# print the dataframe object
print(dfBakery2)
```

Output:

```
# print the dataframe object
print(dfBakery)
```

```
   ID      Address       City        State  Number of Employees
0   1      35 Road     Mumbai  Maharashtra                   15
1   2     40 C Road    Chennai   Tamil Nadu                   25
2   3     26 MG Road      Pune  Maharashtra                   30
3   4     1 GRE Road     Surat     Gujarat                    17
4   5     33 RT Road    Cochin      Kerala                    22
5   6      6 MG Road    Panaji         Goa                    32
6   7    12 New Road   Kolkata  West Bengal                   10
7   8     3 GRE Road Ahmedabad     Gujarat                    14
8   9     3 Highway     Nagpur  Maharashtra                   19
9  10   10 Vasco Road    Ponda         Goa                    22
```

The Excel data, in dataframe object

Read data from a JSON file

To load data present in a JavaScript Object Notation file(.json) we will follow steps as below:

- Prepare your sample dataset. Here JSON file, with Countries and their dial code.
- Use Pandas method 'read_json'.
  o Method used – read_json(file_path)
  o File_Path can be URL or file path of a local machine holding .json files

The file contents are as follows:

The contents of "gfg_codecountry.json" file

The code to get the data in a Pandas DataFrame is:

# Import the Pandas library
import pandas

# Load data from a JSON file
# Use method - read_json(filepath)
# Method parameter - The file location(URL/path) and name
dfCodeCountry2 = pandas.read_json("gfg_Codecountry.json")

# print the dataframe object
print(dfCodeCountry2)

Output:

```
# print the dataframe object
print(dfCodeCountry)
```

	code	dial_code	name
0	IL	+972	Israel
1	AU	+61	Australia
2	AT	+43	Austria
3	BE	+32	Belgium
4	BW	+267	Botswana
5	BR	+55	Brazil
6	GR	+30	Greece
7	GL	+299	Greenland
8	GD	+1 473	Grenada
9	GP	+590	Guadeloupe
10	GU	+1 671	Guam
11	GY	+595	Guyana
12	HT	+509	Haiti

The JSON data, in dataframe objects

Read data from Clipboard

We can also transfer data present in Clipboard to a dataframe object. A clipboard is a part of Random Access Memory (RAM), where copied data is present. Whenever we copy any file, text, image, or any type of data, using the 'Copy' command, it gets stored in the Clipboard. To convert, data present here, follow the steps as mentioned below –

- Select all the contents of the file. The file should be a CSV file. It can be a '.txt' file as well, containing comma-separated values, as shown in the example. Please note, if the file contents are not in a favorable format, then, one can get a Parser Error at runtime.

- Right, Click and say Copy. Now, this data is transferred, to the computer Clipboard.
- Use Pandas method 'read_clipboard'.
  - o Method used – read_clipboard
  - o Parameter – The method, does not accept any parameter. It reads the latest copied data as present in the clipboard, and, converts it, into a valid two-dimensional dataframe object.

The file contents selected are as follows:

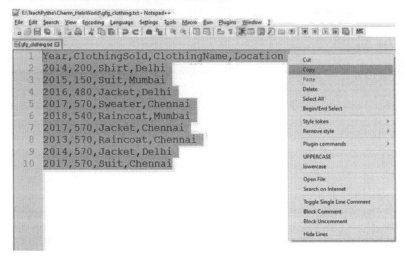

The contents of "gfg_clothing.txt" file

The code to get the data in a Pandas DataFrame is:

```
# Import the required library
import pandas

# Copy file contents which are in proper format
# Whatever data you have copied will
# get transferred to dataframe object
# Method does not accept any parameter
pdCopiedData = pd.read_clipboard()

# Print the data frame object
print(pdCopiedData)
```

Output:

```
#Print the dataframe object
print(pdCopiedData)
```

```
   Year,ClothingSold,ClothingName,Location
0              2014,200,Shirt,Delhi
1              2015,150,Suit,Mumbai
2              2016,480,Jacket,Delhi
3            2017,570,Sweater,Chennai
4           2018,540,Raincoat,Mumbai
5             2017,570,Jacket,Chennai
6           2013,570,Raincoat,Chennai
7              2014,570,Jacket,Delhi
8              2017,570,Suit,Chennai
```

The clipboard data, in dataframe object

Read data from HTML file

A webpage is usually made of HTML elements. There are different HTML tags such as <head>, <title>, <table>, <div> based on the purpose of data display, on browser. We can transfer, the content between <table> element, present in an HTML webpage, to a Pandas data frame object. Follow the steps as mentioned below –

- Select all the elements present in the <table>, between start and end tags. Assign it, to a Python variable.
- Use Pandas method 'read_html' .
  - Method used – read_html(string within <table> tag)
  - Parameter – The method, accepts string variable, containing the elements present between <table> tag. It reads the elements, traversing through the table, <tr> and <td> tags, and, converts it, into a list object. The first element of the list object is the desired dataframe object.

The HTML webpage used is as follows:

<!DOCTYPE html>
<html>
<head>

```
<title>Data Ingestion with Pandas Example</title>
</head>
<body>
<h2>Welcome To GFG</h2>
<table>
 <thead>
  <tr>
   <th>Date</th>
   <th>Empname</th>
   <th>Year</th>
   <th>Rating</th>
   <th>Region</th>
  </tr>
 </thead>
 <tbody>
  <tr>
   <td>2020-01-01</td>
   <td>Savio</td>
   <td>2004</td>
   <td>0.5</td>
   <td>South</td>
  </tr>
  <tr>
   <td>2020-01-02</td>
   <td>Rahul</td>
   <td>1998</td>
   <td>1.34</td>
   <td>East</td>
  </tr>
  <tr>
   <td>2020-01-03</td>
   <td>Tina</td>
   <td>1988</td>
   <td>1.00023</td>
   <td>West</td>
  </tr>
  <tr>
   <td>2021-01-03</td>
   <td>Sonia</td>
   <td>2001</td>
   <td>2.23</td>
```

```
    <td>North</td>
   </tr>
  </tbody>
</table>
</body>
</html>
```

Write the following code to convert the HTML table content in the Pandas Dataframe object:

```
# Import the Pandas library
import pandas
# Variable containing the elements
# between <table> tag from webpage
html_string = """
<table>
  <thead>
   <tr>
     <th>Date</th>
     <th>Empname</th>
     <th>Year</th>
     <th>Rating</th>
     <th>Region</th>
   </tr>
  </thead>
  <tbody>
   <tr>
     <td>2020-01-01</td>
     <td>Savio</td>
     <td>2004</td>
     <td>0.5</td>
     <td>South</td>
   </tr>
   <tr>
     <td>2020-01-02</td>
     <td>Rahul</td>
     <td>1998</td>
     <td>1.34</td>
     <td>East</td>
   </tr>
```

```
  <tr>
   <td>2020-01-03</td>
   <td>Tina</td>
   <td>1988</td>
   <td>1.00023</td>
   <td>West</td>
  </tr>
   <tr>
   <td>2021-01-03</td>
   <td>Sonia</td>
   <td>2001</td>
   <td>2.23</td>
   <td>North</td>
  </tr>
  <tr>
   <td>2008-01-03</td>
   <td>Milo</td>
   <td>2008</td>
   <td>3.23</td>
   <td>East</td>
  </tr>
  <tr>
   <td>2006-01-03</td>
   <td>Edward</td>
   <td>2005</td>
   <td>0.43</td>
   <td>West</td>
  </tr>
 </tbody>
</table>"""

# Pass the string containing html table element
df = pandas.read_html(html_string)

# Since read_html, returns a list object,
# extract first element of the list
dfHtml2 = df[0]

# Print the data frame object
print(dfHtml2)
```

Output:

```
#Print the data frame object
print(dfHtml)
```

```
        Date  Empname  Year    Rating Region
0  2020-01-01    Savio  2004   0.50000  South
1  2020-01-02    Rahul  1998   1.34000   East
2  2020-01-03     Tina  1988   1.00023   West
3  2021-01-03    Sonia  2001   2.23000  North
4  2008-01-03     Milo  2008   3.23000   East
5  2006-01-03   Edward  2005   0.43000   West
```

The HTML <table> data, in dataframe object,

Read data from SQL table

We can convert, data present in database tables, to valid dataframe objects as well. Python allows easy interface, with a variety of databases, such as SQLite, MySQL, MongoDB, etc. SQLite is a lightweight database, which can be embedded in any program. The SQLite database holds all the related SQL tables. We can load, SQLite table data, to a Pandas dataframe object. Follow the steps, as mentioned below –

- Prepare a sample SQLite table using 'DB Browser for SQLite tool' or any such tool. These tools allow the effortless creation, edition of database files compatible with SQLite. The database file, has a '.db' file extension. In this example, we have 'Novels. db' file, containing a table called "novels". This table has information about Novels, such as Novel Name, Price, Genre, etc.
- Here, to connect to the database, we will import the 'sqlite3' module, in our code. The sqlite3 module, is an interface, to connect to the SQLite databases. The sqlite3 library is included in Python, since Python version 2.5. Hence, no separate installation is required. To connect to the database, we will use the SQLite method 'connect', which returns a connection object. The connect method accepts the following parameters:
  - database_name – The name of the database in which the table is present. This is a .db extension file. If the file is present, an open connection object is returned. If the file is not present, it is created first and then a connection object is returned.

- Use Pandas method 'read_sql_query'.
  - ○ Method used – read_sql_query
  - ○ Parameter – This method accepts the following parameters
    - ▪ SQL query – Select query, to fetch the required rows from the table.
    - ▪ Connection object – The connection object returned by the 'connect' method. The read_sql_query method, converts, the resultant rows of the query, to a dataframe object.
- Print the dataframe object using the print method.

The **Novels.db** database file looks as follows –

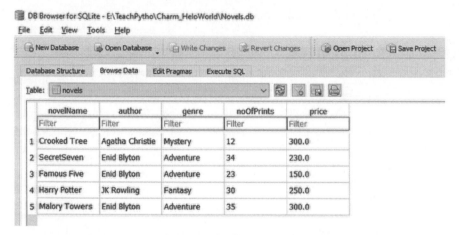

The novels table, as seen, using DB Browser for SQLite tool

Write the following code to convert the Novels table, in Pandas Data frame object:

```
# Import the required libraries
import sqlite3
import pandas

# Prepare a connection object
# Pass the Database name as a parameter
conn = sqlite3.connect("Novels.db")

# Use read_sql_query method
# Pass SELECT query and connection object as parameter
pdSql2 = pd.read_sql_query("SELECT * FROM novels", conn)
```

# Print the dataframe object
print(pdSql2)

# Close the connection object
conn.close()

Output:

```
#Print the dataframe object
print(pdSql)
```

	novelName	author	genre	noOfPrints	price
0	Crooked Tree	Agatha Christie	Mystery	12	300.0
1	SecretSeven	Enid Blyton	Adventure	34	230.0
2	Famous Five	Enid Blyton	Adventure	23	150.0
3	Harry Potter	JK Rowling	Fantasy	30	250.0
4	Malory Towers	Enid Blyton	Adventure	35	300.0

The Novels table data in dataframe object

Segment 3 - Summarizing categorical data using pandas

```
In [1]: import numpy as np
        import pandas as pd
```

The basics

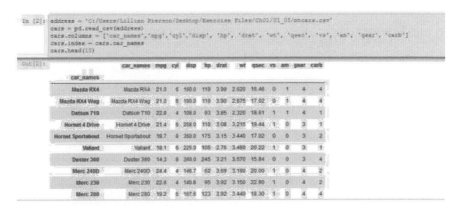

```
In [2]:  address = 'C:/Users/Lillian Pierson/Desktop/Exercise Files/Ch01/01_05/mtcars.csv'
         cars = pd.read_csv(address)
         cars.columns = ['car_names','mpg','cyl','disp', 'hp', 'drat', 'wt', 'qsec', 'vs', 'am', 'gear', 'carb']
         cars.index = cars.car_names
         cars.head(15)
```

Hornet 4 Drive	Hornet 4 Drive	21.4	6	258.0	110	3.08	3.215	19.44	1	0	3	1
Hornet Sportabout	Hornet Sportabout	18.7	8	360.0	175	3.15	3.440	17.02	0	0	3	2
Valiant	Valiant	18.1	6	225.0	105	2.76	3.460	20.22	1	0	3	1
Duster 360	Duster 360	14.3	8	360.0	245	3.21	3.570	15.84	0	0	3	4
Merc 240D	Merc 240D	24.4	4	146.7	62	3.69	3.190	20.00	1	0	4	2
Merc 230	Merc 230	22.8	4	140.8	95	3.92	3.150	22.90	1	0	4	2
Merc 280	Merc 280	19.2	6	167.6	123	3.92	3.440	18.30	1	0	4	4
Merc 280C	Merc 280C	17.8	6	167.6	123	3.92	3.440	18.90	1	0	4	4
Merc 450SE	Merc 450SE	16.4	8	275.8	180	3.07	4.070	17.40	0	0	3	3
Merc 450SL	Merc 450SL	17.3	8	275.8	180	3.07	3.730	17.60	0	0	3	3
Merc 450SLC	Merc 450SLC	15.2	8	275.8	180	3.07	3.780	18.00	0	0	3	3
Cadillac Fleetwood	Cadillac Fleetwood	10.4	8	472.0	205	2.93	5.250	17.98	0	0	3	4

```
In [7]:  # object_name.value_counts()
         # -#-#-#-( WHAT THIS DOES )-#-#-#-#
         # The .value_counts() method makes a count of all unique values in an array or Series object.
```

```
In [8]:  carb = cars.carb
         carb.value_counts()
```

```
Out[8]:  4    10
         2    10
         1     7
         3     3
         8     1
         6     1
         Name: carb, dtype: int64
```

```
In [9]:  # object_name.groupby('column_index')
         # -#-#-#-( WHAT THIS DOES )-#-#-#-#
         # To group a DataFrame by its values in a particular column, call the .groupby() method off of the DataFrame, and then pass
         # in the index value of the column Series you want the DataFrame to be grouped by.
         cars_cat = cars[['cyl','vs','am','gear','carb']]
         cars_cat.head()
```

Out[9]:

car_names	cyl	vs	am	gear	carb
Mazda RX4	6	0	1	4	4
Mazda RX4 Wag	6	0	1	4	4
Datsun 710	4	1	1	4	1
Hornet 4 Drive	6	1	0	3	1
Hornet Sportabout	8	0	0	3	2

```
In [10]:  gears_group = cars_cat.groupby('gear')
          gears_group.describe()
```

Out[10]:

gear		am	carb	cyl	vs
	count	15.000000	15.000000	15.000000	15.000000
	mean	0.000000	2.666667	7.466667	0.200000
	std	0.000000	1.175139	1.187234	0.414039
3	min	0.000000	1.000000	4.000000	0.000000
	25%	0.000000	2.000000	8.000000	0.000000
	50%	0.000000	3.000000	8.000000	0.000000
	75%	0.000000	4.000000	8.000000	0.000000
	max	0.000000	4.000000	8.000000	1.000000
	count	12.000000	12.000000	12.000000	12.000000
	mean	0.666667	2.333333	4.666667	0.833333
	std	0.492366	1.302678	0.984732	0.389249
4	min	0.000000	1.000000	4.000000	0.000000
	25%	0.000000	1.000000	4.000000	1.000000
	50%	1.000000	2.000000	4.000000	1.000000
	75%	1.000000	4.000000	6.000000	1.000000
	max	1.000000	4.000000	6.000000	1.000000
	count	5.000000	5.000000	5.000000	5.000000
	mean	1.000000	4.400000	6.000000	0.200000
	std	0.000000	2.607681	2.000000	0.447214
5	min	1.000000	2.000000	4.000000	0.000000
	25%	1.000000	2.000000	4.000000	0.000000
	50%	1.000000	4.000000	6.000000	0.000000
	75%	1.000000	6.000000	8.000000	0.000000
	max	1.000000	8.000000	8.000000	1.000000

Transforming variables to categorical data type

```
In [12]:  # pd.Series(a variable, dtype)
          # @-@-@-( WHAT THIS DOES )-@-@-@
          # To create a Series of categorical data type, call the pd.Series() function on the array or Series that holds the data you
          # want the new Series object to contain. When you pass in the dtype="category" argument, this tells Python to assign the new
          # Series a data type of "category". Here we create a new categorical Series from the gear variable, and then assign it to a
          # new column in the cars DataFrame, called 'group'.
          cars['group'] = pd.Series(cars.gear, dtype="category")
```

```
In [13]:  cars['group'].dtypes

Out[13]:  category
```

```
In [14]:  cars['group'].value_counts()

Out[14]:  3    15
          4    12
          5     5
          Name: group, dtype: int64
```

Describing categorical data with crosstabs

```
In [15]:  # pd.crosstab(y_variable, x_variable)
          # -#-#-#-( WHAT THIS DOES )-#-#-#-#
          # To create a cross-tab, just call the pd.crosstab() function on the variables you want included in
          # the output table.
          pd.crosstab(cars['am'], cars['gear'])

Out[15]:  gear   3  4  5
          am
          0     15  4  0
          1      0  8  5
```

3.7   Starting with Parametric Methods in Pandas and Scipy

Segment 4 - Starting with parametric methods in pandas and scipy

```
In [1]:  import pandas as pd
         import numpy as np

         import matplotlib.pyplot as plt
         import seaborn as sb
         from pylab import rcParams

         import scipy
         from scipy.stats.stats import pearsonr
```

```
In [2]:  %matplotlib inline
         rcParams['figure.figsize'] = 8, 4
         plt.style.use('seaborn-whitegrid')
```

The Pearson Correlation

```
In [3]: address = 'C:/Users/Lillian Pierson/Desktop/Exercise Files/Ch03/03_04/mtcars.csv'
        cars = pd.read_csv(address)
        cars.columns = ['car_names','mpg','cyl','disp', 'hp', 'drat', 'wt', 'qsec', 'vs', 'am', 'gear', 'carb']
```

```
In [4]: sb.pairplot(cars)
```

```
Out[4]: <seaborn.axisgrid.PairGrid at 0xbe87240>
```

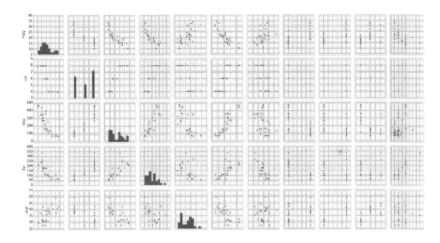

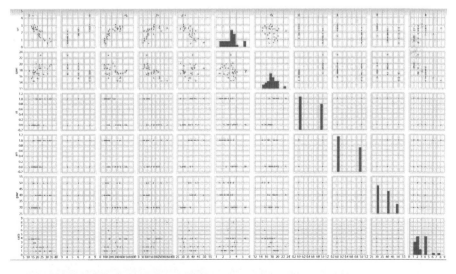

```
In [7]: X = cars[['mpg', 'hp', 'qsec','wt']]
        sb.pairplot(X)
```

```
Out[7]: <seaborn.axisgrid.PairGrid at 0x1bb6c978>
```

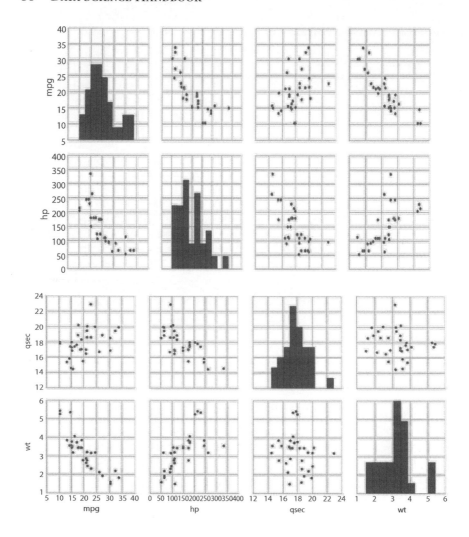

Using scipy to calculate the Pearson correlation coefficient

```
mpg = cars['mpg'] hp = cars['hp'] qsec = cars['qsec'] wt = cars['wt']

pearsonr_coefficient, p_value = pearsonr(mpg, hp) print 'PearsonR Correlation Coefficient %0.3f' % (pearsonr_coefficient)
```

```
In [12]:  pearsonr_coefficient, p_value = pearsonr(mpg, qsec)
          print 'PearsonR Correlation Coefficient %0.3f' % (pearsonr_coefficient)

          PearsonR Correlation Coefficient 0.419
```

```
In [13]: pearsonr_coefficient, p_value = pearsonr(mpg, wt)
         print 'PearsonR Correlation Coefficient %0.3f' % (pearsonr_coefficient)
```

PearsonR Correlation Coefficient -0.868

Using pandas to calculate the Pearson correlation coefficient

```
In [14]: corr = X.corr()
         corr
```

Out[14]:

	mpg	hp	qsec	wt
mpg	1.000000	-0.776168	0.418684	-0.867659
hp	-0.776168	1.000000	-0.708223	0.658748
qsec	0.418684	-0.708223	1.000000	-0.174716
wt	-0.867659	0.658748	-0.174716	1.000000

Using Seaborn to visualize the Pearson correlation coefficient

```
In [16]: sb.heatmap(corr, xticklabels=corr.columns.values, yticklabels=corr.columns.values)
```
Out[16]: <matplotlib.axes._subplots.AxesSubplot at 0x20afc160>

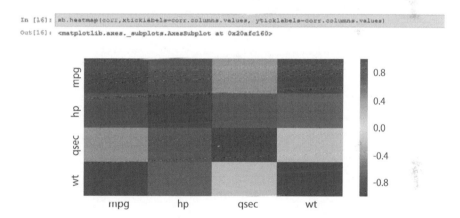

3.8   Delving Into Non-Parametric Methods Using Pandas and Scipy

Segment 5 - Delving into non-parametric methods using pandas and scipy

```
In [6]: import numpy as np
        import pandas as pd

        import matplotlib.pyplot as plt
        import seaborn as sb
        from pylab import rcParams

        import scipy
        from scipy.stats import spearmanr
```

In [2]:
```
%matplotlib inline
rcParams['figure.figsize'] = 14, 7
plt.style.use('seaborn-whitegrid')
```

The Spearman Rank Correlation

In [3]:
```
address = 'C:/Users/Lillian Pierson/Desktop/Exercise Files/Ch03/03_05/mtcars.csv'
cars = pd.read_csv(address)
cars.columns = ['car_names','mpg','cyl','disp', 'hp', 'drat', 'wt', 'qsec', 'vs', 'am', 'gear', 'carb']
cars.head()
```

Out[3]:

	car_names	mpg	cyl	disp	hp	drat	wt	qsec	vs	am	gear	carb
0	Mazda RX4	21.0	6	160.0	110	3.90	2.620	16.46	0	1	4	4
1	Mazda RX4 Wag	21.0	6	160.0	110	3.90	2.875	17.02	0	1	4	4
2	Datsun 710	22.8	4	108.0	93	3.85	2.320	18.61	1	1	4	1
3	Hornet 4 Drive	21.4	6	258.0	110	3.08	3.215	19.44	1	0	3	1
4	Hornet Sportabout	18.7	8	360.0	175	3.15	3.440	17.02	0	0	3	2

In [7]: sb.pairplot(cars)

Out[7]: <seaborn.axisgrid.PairGrid at 0x280d4978>

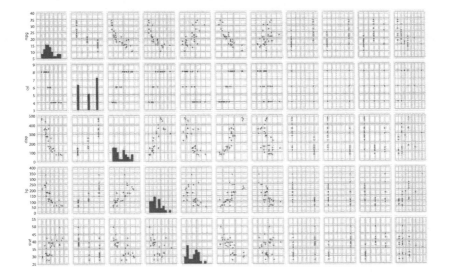

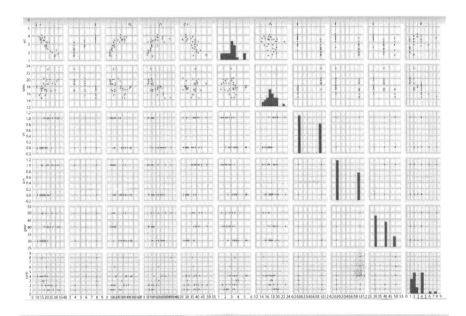

```
In [8]: X = cars[['cyl', 'vs', 'am', 'gear']]
        sb.pairplot(X)

Out[8]: <seaborn.axisgrid.PairGrid at 0x398e5898>
```

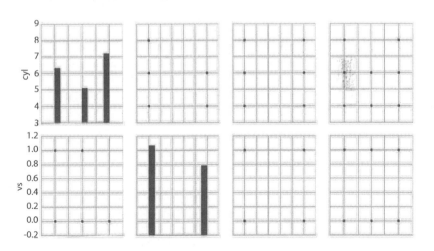

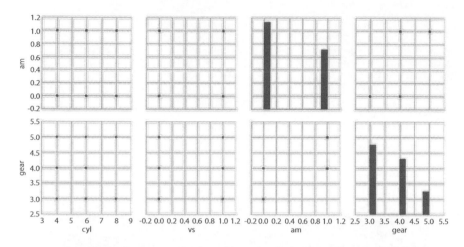

```
In [9]:  cyl = cars['cyl']
         vs = cars['vs']
         am = cars['am']
         gear = cars['gear']
         spearmanr_coefficient, p_value = spearmanr(cyl, vs)
         print 'Spearman Rank Correlation Coefficient %0.3f' % (spearmanr_coefficient)
```

Spearman Rank Correlation Coefficient -0.814

```
In [10]:  spearmanr_coefficient, p_value = spearmanr(cyl, am)
          print 'Spearman Rank Correlation Coefficient %0.3f' % (spearmanr_coefficient)
```

Spearman Rank Correlation Coefficient -0.522

```
In [11]:  spearmanr_coefficient, p_value = spearmanr(cyl, gear)
          print 'Spearman Rank Correlation Coefficient %0.3f' % (spearmanr_coefficient)
```

Spearman Rank Correlation Coefficient -0.564

Chi-square test for independence

```
In [14]:  table = pd.crosstab(cyl, am)

          from scipy.stats import chi2_contingency
          chi2, p, dof, expected = chi2_contingency(table.values)
          print 'Chi-square Statistic %0.3f p_value %0.3f' % (chi2, p)
```

Chi-square Statistic 8.741 p_value 0.013

```
In [15]:  table = pd.crosstab(cars['cyl'], cars['vs'])
          chi2, p, dof, expected = chi2_contingency(table.values)
          print 'Chi-square Statistic %0.3f p_value %0.3f' % (chi2, p)
```

Chi-square Statistic 21.340 p_value 0.000

```
In [16]:  table = pd.crosstab(cars['cyl'], cars['gear'])
          chi2, p, dof, expected = chi2_contingency(table.values)
          print 'Chi-square Statistic %0.3f p_value %0.3f' % (chi2, p)
```

```
Chi-square Statistic 18.036 p_value 0.001
```

3.9   Transforming Dataset Distributions

Segment 6 - Transforming dataset distributions

```
In [1]:  import numpy as np
         import pandas as pd
         import scipy

         import matplotlib.pyplot as plt
         from matplotlib import rcParams
         import seaborn as sb

         import sklearn
         from sklearn import preprocessing
         from sklearn.preprocessing import scale
```

```
In [2]:  %matplotlib inline
         rcParams['figure.figsize'] = 5, 4
         sb.set_style('whitegrid')
```

Normalizing and transforming features with MinMaxScalar() & fit_transform()

```
In [3]:  address = 'C:/Users/Lillian Pierson/Desktop/Exercise Files/Ch03/03_06/mtcars.csv'
         cars = pd.read_csv(address)
         cars.columns = ['car_names','mpg','cyl','disp', 'hp', 'drat', 'wt', 'qsec', 'vs', 'am', 'gear', 'carb']
```

```
In [4]:  mpg = cars.mpg
         plt.plot(mpg)
```
```
Out[4]:  [<matplotlib.lines.Line2D at 0xc184a58>]
```

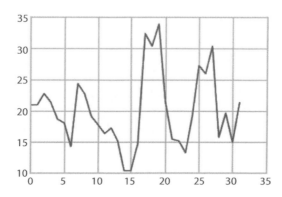

In [6]: `cars[['mpg']].describe()`

Out[6]:

	mpg
count	32.000000
mean	20.090625
std	6.026948
min	10.400000
25%	15.425000
50%	19.200000
75%	22.800000
max	33.900000

In [8]:
```
mpg_matrix = mpg.reshape(-1,1)
scaled = preprocessing.MinMaxScaler()
scaled_mpg = scaled.fit_transform(mpg_matrix)
plt.plot(scaled_mpg)
```

Out[8]: `[<matplotlib.lines.Line2D at 0xc951fd0>]`

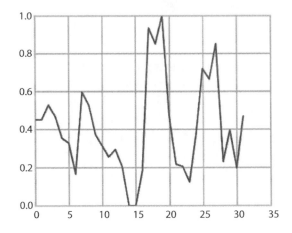

In [9]:
```
mpg_matrix = mpg.reshape(-1,1)
scaled = preprocessing.MinMaxScaler(feature_range=(0,10))
scaled_mpg = scaled.fit_transform(mpg_matrix)
plt.plot(scaled_mpg)
```

Out[9]: `[<matplotlib.lines.Line2D at 0xcc26748>]`

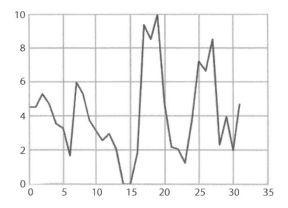

Using scale() to scale your features

```
In [11]: standardized_mpg = scale(mpg, axis=0, with_mean=False, with_std=False)
         plt.plot(standardized_mpg)

Out[11]: [<matplotlib.lines.Line2D at 0xcc9c208>]
```

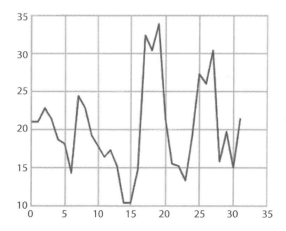

```
In [12]: standardized_mpg = scale(mpg)
         plt.plot(standardized_mpg)

Out[12]: [<matplotlib.lines.Line2D at 0xd9925f8>]
```

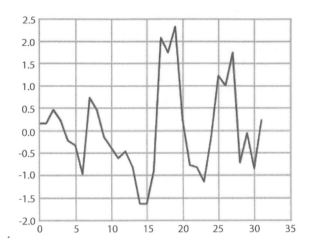

References

1. "Statistics". Oxford Reference. Oxford University Press. January 2008. ISBN 978-0-19-954145-4.
2. Romijn, Jan-Willem (2014). "Philosophy of statistics". Stanford Encyclopedia of Philosophy.
3. "Cambridge Dictionary".
4. Dodge, Y. (2006) The Oxford Dictionary of Statistical Terms, Oxford University Press. ISBN 0-19-920613-9
5. Lund Research Ltd. "Descriptive and Inferential Statistics". statistics.laerd. com. Retrieved 2014-03-23.
6. "What Is the Difference Between Type I and Type II Hypothesis Testing Errors?". About.com Education. Retrieved 2015-11-27.
7. Moses, Lincoln E. (1986) Think and Explain with Statistics, Addison-Wesley, ISBN 978-0-201-15619-5. pp. 1–3
8. Hays, William Lee, (1973) Statistics for the Social Sciences, Holt, Rinehart and Winston, p.xii, ISBN 978-0-03-077945-9
9. Moore, David (1992). "Teaching Statistics as a Respectable Subject". In F. Gordon; S. Gordon (eds.). Statistics for the Twenty-First Century. Washington, DC: The Mathematical Association of America. pp. 14–25. ISBN 978-0-88385-078-7.
10. Chance, Beth L.; Rossman, Allan J. (2005). "Preface" (PDF). Investigating Statistical Concepts, Applications, and Methods. Duxbury Press. ISBN 978-0-495-05064-3.
11. Prakash, K.B. & Rangaswamy, M.A.D. 2016, "Content extraction of biological datasets using soft computing techniques", Journal of Medical Imaging and Health Informatics, vol. 6, no. 4, pp. 932-936.

12. Prakash, K.B., Rangaswamy, M.A.D. & Raja Raman, A. 2012, *ANN for multi-lingual regional web communication.*

13. Prakash, K.B., Rangaswamy, M.A.D. & Raman, A.R. 2012, *Statistical interpretation for mining hybrid regional web documents.*

14. Ruwali, A., Sravan Kumar, A.J., Prakash, K.B., Sivavaraprasad, G. & Venkata Ratnam, D. 2020, "Implementation of hybrid deep learning model (LSTM-CNN) for ionospheric TEC forecasting using GPS data", *IEEE Geoscience and Remote Sensing Letters.*

15. Sivakumar, S., Rajalakshmi, R., Prakash, K.B., Kanna, B.R. & Karthikeyan, C. 2020, *Virtual Vision Architecture for VIP in Ubiquitous Computing.*

Introduction to Machine Learning

4.1 Introduction to Machine Learning

Now a day's most of the computer machines are fed with more amounts of relevant data generated from a particular problem domain [1]. Artificial Intelligence considered being major part of making the computer machines to understand the data [2]. Machine learning will be a subset of artificial intelligence which specifies set of algorithms to help the computer machines to learn that data automatically without any human being intervention [3].

The main theme behind using machine learning is to make machines fed with the data and specifying features to understand and enable it to adapt for new data without using explicit programming [4]. The computers observe the changes in the new data set identify the patterns to understand their behavior for making predictions [5].

Role of Machine Learning in Data Science

Much of concepts of data science like Analysis of data, extraction of data features, and decision making in business are automated and over performed by machine learning and artificial intelligence [6].

Large chunks of data were automatically analyzed by machine learning [7]. It basically does the data analysis and performs data prediction on real time data without any intervention of human beings [8]. Machine learning algorithms have become part of Data science life cycle as it does automatic building of data sets and any further changes in data are predicted automatically and train the machine for further processing [9].

Machine Learning process starts from feeding data which to be analyzed for specific features and build a data model [10]. The data model is further trained to generate new conclusions by using machine learning algorithm and further it performs predictions for the new dataset which are uploaded [11].

Kolla Bhanu Prakash. Data Science Handbook: A Practical Approach, (97–122) © 2022 Scrivener Publishing LLC

Steps of Machine Learning in the Data Science Lifecycle

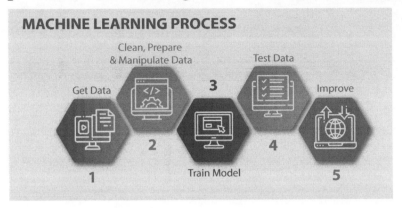

- **Collection of Data**
  The primary step of machine learning is collection of data from the real time domain area of problem occurrence. The data collection should be reliable and relevant so as to improve its quality [12].
- **Preparation of Data**
  In the preparation of data the first step is data cleaning which makes the data ready for data analysis. Most of the unwanted and error prone data points are removed from data set and convert all data in to standard format and further the data is partitioned into two parts one for training and other for performance evaluation [13].
- **Model Training**
  The dataset which is part of training will help in output value prediction. The output value would exhibit the much diversity with expected desired value for the first iteration [14]. The epoch or iterations are repeated by performing some adjustments with initial values and further the prediction accuracy of training data increases incrementally.
- **Evaluation Model**
  The rest of the data which is not used for training the model is used for performance evaluation [15]. The testing of the model against the left amount of data will really estimate the applicability of the data model in providing us with effective solution for all real time problems.

- **Prediction**
  After completion of training and evaluation of data model now it's time to deploy the model in real time environments and improve the accuracy by parameter tuning. As we deploy the model in real time it need to learn new data and predict the perfect output to answer new questions.

Machine Learning Techniques for Data Science

When you have a dataset, you can classify the problem into three types:

- Regression
- Classification
- Clustering

1) **Regression**
   Regression is used for the output variables which are in continuous space. The curve-fitting methodology in mathematics is followed in regression. It also tries to fits the data for a given equation of a curve and predicts the output value. The linear regression, Neural Network maintenance and perceptron management are popular implementation using regression mechanisms. Many of the financial institutions like stock markets try to predict the growth of the investments made by the shareholders. Rental brokers also try to use prediction of house prices in a given location to manage real estate business.

2) **Classification**
   Classification is a process of managing the output variables which are discrete and meant for identifying the categories of data. Most of the algorithms of classification type deal with processing data and divide them in to categories. It is like finding different categories of curves for fitting the data points. The example scenario of labeling the emails for spam in Gmail would be one type of classification problem where the different factors of email are checked for categorizing them to spam upon matching at least 80%-90% of anomalies match. Naïve Bayes, KNearest Neighbor, support vector machine, Neural Networks and Logistic Regression are some popular examples of classification algorithms.

3) Clustering

Grouping data of without labeling and having similar features leads to mechanism of clustering. Similarity functions are used to group the data points with similar characteristics. Dissimilar features of different clusters exist among the different grouped data points and unique patterns can be identified among the data sets which are not labeled in clustering. K-means and agglomerative are popular examples of clustering. Customer purchases can be categorized using clustering techniques.

Supervised Learning model- Regression and Classification
Unsupervised Learning model- Clustering.

Popular Real Time Use Case Scenarios of Machine Learning in Data Science

Machine Learning has its roots of implementation way back from previous years even without our knowledge of utilizing it in our daily life. Many popular industry sector starting finance to entertainments are applying machine learning techniques to manage their tasks effectively. Most popular mobile app's like Google Maps, Amazon online shopping uses machine learning at background to respond to the users with relevant information. Some of the popular real time scenarios where machine learning is used with data science are as follows:

- **Fraud Detection**
  Banking sectors implement machine learning algorithm to detect fraudulent transactions to ensure their customer safety. Popular machine learning algorithms are used to train the system to identify transactions with suspicious features and fault transaction patterns to get detected with in no time when the authorized customer performing his normal transactions. Thus the huge amount of daily transactional data is used to train the machine learning model to detect the frauds in time and provide customer safety while utilizing online banking services.
- **Speech Recognition**
  Popular chat bot implementations like Alexa, Siri, and normal Google Assistant work on many machine learning

mechanisms along with natural language processing are used for responding their users instantly by listening to their audio. Much amount of audio inputs is used to train the system with different ascent of users and prepare the response.

- **Online Recommendation Engines**

  Most of the recommendation systems are built using machine learning to automatically track the customer interests while doing shopping online, querying the search engine for relevant information and browsing websites for gaming. The behavioral characteristics of consumers are tracked by machine learning mechanisms and provide better suggestions for the business domain to improve their features to attract them. The popular applications like Amazon shopping tracks customer interests and pop only those specific products which he is interested, YouTube delivers the relevant search of videos on users interest and Facebook with better friend suggestions by using efficient trained machine learning models.

4.2   Types of Machine Learning Algorithms

Machine learning (ML) algorithms are of three types:

1. **Supervised Learning Algorithms:**

   It uses a mapped function f that works on mapping a trained label data for an input variable X to an output variable Y. In simple it solves following equation:

   $$Y = f(X)$$

   The above equation does generate accurate outputs for a given new inputs.

   Classification and Regression are two ML mechanisms which come under this supervised learning.

   Classification is a mechanism of ML which predicts for the sample data to the form of output variable in categories. For example from a patient's health record sample data of his symptoms the classification try to categorize by labeling his profile to either "sick" or "healthy".

Regression is a mechanism of ML which predicts for the sample data to the form of output variable in to real values. For example most of the regression models works on predicting the weather report on intensive rainfall for a particular year based on the available factors of sample data on different weather conditions.

The popular algorithms like linear and logistic regression, Naïve Bayes CART and KNN are of type supervised learning.

Ensembling is a new type of ML mechanism where two or more popular algorithms are used for training and try to use all the appropriate features of it to predict accurately on the sample data. Random Forest Bagging and XG Boost boosting are popular for ensemble techniques.

2. **Unsupervised Learning Algorithms:**
The learning models which does process the input variable X and doesn't relate it to any specific output variables is called unsupervised learning. Most of the unsupervised learning leads to unlabeled data without any specific structure defined for it.

There are three important techniques which come under unsupervised learning (i) Association (ii) Clustering (iii) Dimensionality reduction.

Association is a technique which correlates the occurrence of items in a specific collection. Market Basket Analysis is good examples which correlate the purchases made by the customers when they visit the grocery store for buying a bread will be 80% sure of making purchase of eggs.

Clustering is a technique of grouping similar featured input variables from a given sample data. It tries to find the specific criteria for grouping the sample data and differentiate them from each other clusters.

Dimensionality reduction is a technique of choosing specific criteria for reducing the input data sample for conveying the appropriate information relevant to the problem solution. The specific criteria for selection relate to the mechanism of feature selection similarly extracting the sample data fitting to the solution is known as feature extraction. Thus feature selection performs the selection of specific input variables satisfying the criteria for solution and feature extraction does simplify the data collection which suits to the solution space.

Popular algorithms like Apriori, K-means and PCA come under this unsupervised learning techniques.

3. **Reinforcement learning:**
The learning model in which an agent does the decision making to choose the best action based on its current learning behavior to improve the reward value. It does choice of providing optimal solution to the problem space in getting better gain by performing appropriate actions. Most of the automated solution uses this mechanism to improve in obtaining optimal solution. Example in a gaming application the reinforcement learning mechanism is applied on player objects initially to learn the game by moving randomly to gain points, but slowly it tries to find an optimal way of gaining points with appropriate moves so as to achieve maximum points with in an optimal time.

1. Linear Regression

Most of the algorithms in machine learning does quantifying the relationship between input variable (x) and output variable (y) with specific function. In Linear regression the equation $y = f(x) = a + bx$ is used for establishing relationship between x and y and a and b are the coefficients which need to be evaluated where 'a' represents the intercept and 'b' represent the slope of the straight line. The Fig 4.1 shows the plotted values of random points (x, y) of a particular data set. The major objective is to construct a

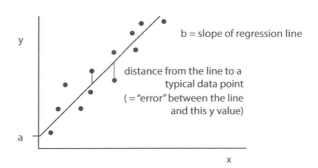

Fig 4.1 Plot of the points for equation y=a+bx.

straight line which is nearest to all the random points. The error value is computed for each point with its y value.

2. Logistic Regression

Most of the predictions made by the linear regression are on the data of type continuous like fall of rain in cm for a given location and predictions made by the logistic regression is on the type of data which is discrete like no of students who are passed/failed for a given exam by applying function of transformation.

Logistic regression is used for binary classification where data sets are denoted in two classes either 0 or 1 for y. Most of the event predictions will be only two possibilities i.e. either they occur denoted by 1 and not by 0. Like if patient health was predicted for sick using 1 and not by 0 in the given data set.

The transformation function which is used for logistic expression is $h(x) = 1/(1 + e^x)$ it normally represents s-shaped curve.

The output of the logistic expression represents in the form of probability and it value always ranges from 0 to 1. If the probability of patient health for sick is 0.98 that means the output is assigned to class 1. Thus the output value is generated using log transforming with x value with function $h(x) = 1/(1 + e^x)$. A binary classification is mostly realized using these functions by applying threshold.

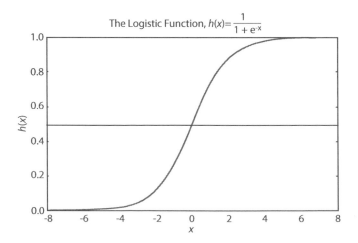

Fig 4.2 Plot of the transformation function h(x).

In fig 4.2 the binary classification of the tumor is malignant or not is computed using transformation function h(x). Most of the various x-values of instantaneous data of the tumor is ranged between 0 to 1. For any data which crosses the shown horizontal line is considered as threshold limit and to be classified as malignant tumor.

$P(x) = e \wedge (b0 + b1x) / (1 + e(b0 + b1x))$ logistic expression is transformed into $ln(p(x) / 1-p(x)) = b0 + b1x$. Thus resolving for bo and b1 coefficient with the help of training data set will try to predict the error between the actual outcome to estimated outcome. The technique called maximum likelihood estimation can be used to identify the coefficients.

3. CART

Classification and Regression Trees (CART) are one implementation of Decision Trees.

In Classification and Regression Trees contains non-terminal (internal) node and terminal (leaf) nodes. One of the internal node acts as a root node and all non-terminal nodes as decision making nodes for an input variable (x) and split the node in two branches and this branching of nodes will stop at leaf nodes which results in the output variable (y). Thus these trees acts as

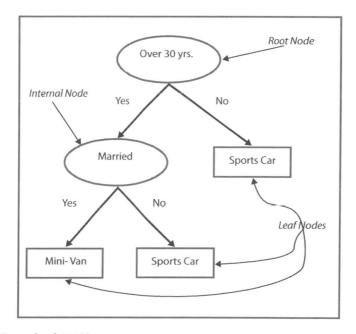

Fig 4.3 Example of CART.

a path of prediction to have walked through complete path of internal nodes and leading to the output result at the end of the terminal node.

The fig 4.3 is an example decision tree which uses CART features to find whether a person will purchase sport car or minivan by considering the factors of age and marital status. The decision factors considered at the internal node are first if the age is over 30 yrs and married will result in purchase of minivan. If age is not 30 yrs will result in sports car and age over 30 yrs and not married also result in sports car.

4. Naïve Bayes

Bayes theorem uses probability occurrence of an event when it occurs in real time. The probability for bayes theorem is computed by a given hypothesis (h) and by prior knowledge (d).

$$Pr(h|d)= (Pr(d|h)\ Pr(h))\ /\ Pr(d)$$

where:
- Pr(h|d) represents the posterior probability. Where hypothesis probability of h is true, for the given data d, where Pr(h|d)= Pr(d1| h) Pr(d2| h)....Pr(dn| h) Pr(d)

Table 4.1 Data set for Naïve bayes computation.

Weather	Play
Sunny	No
Overcast	Yes
Rainy	Yes
Sunny	Yes
Sunny	Yes
Overcast	Yes
Rainy	No
Rainy	No
Sunny	Yes
Rainy	Yes
Sunny	No
Overcast	Yes
Overcast	Yes
Rainy	No

- Pr(d|h) represents likelihood where the probability of the data d for given hypothesis h is true.
- Pr(h) represents the class prior probability where the probability of hypothesis h being true (irrespective of any data)
- Pr(d) represents the predictor prior probability where probability of the data (irrespective of the hypothesis)

This algorithm is called 'naive' because it assumes that all the variables are independent of each other, which is a naive assumption to make in real-world examples.

The algorithm is naïve because the treating of variables is independent of each other with different assumptions with real world sample examples.

Using the data in above Table 4.1, what is the outcome if weather = 'sunny'?

To determine the outcome play = 'yes' or 'no' given the value of variable weather = 'sunny', calculate Pr(yes|sunny) and Pr(no|sunny) and choose the outcome with higher probability.

->Pr(yes|sunny)= (Pr(sunny|yes) * Pr(yes)) / Pr(sunny) = (3/9 * 9/14) / (5/14) = 0.60

-> Pr(no|sunny)= (Pr(sunny|no) * Pr(no)) / Pr(sunny) = (2/5 * 5/14) / (5/14) = 0.40

Thus, if the weather = 'sunny', the outcome is play = 'yes'.

5. KNN

K-Nearest Neighbors algorithm mostly uses the data set which considers all the data to be training.

The KNN algorithm works through the entire data set for find the instances which are near to K-nearest or similar with record values then outputs the mean for solving the regression or the mode for a classification problem with k value specified. The similarity is computed by using the measures as a Euclidean distance and hamming distance.

Unsupervised learning algorithms

6. Apriori

Apriori algorithm usually generates association rules by mining frequent item sets from a transactional database. The market basket analysis is an

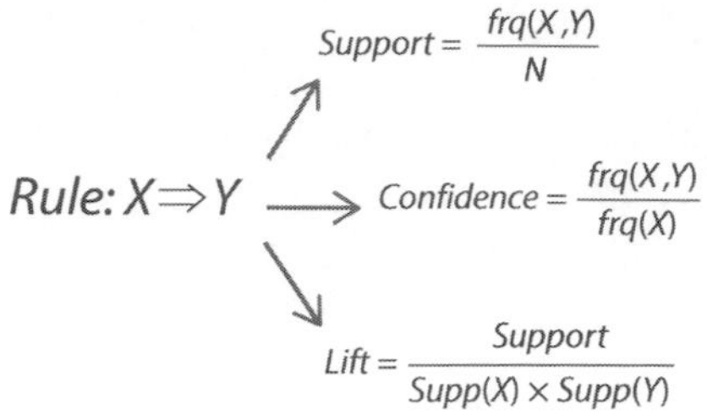

$$Support = \frac{frq(X,Y)}{N}$$

$$Rule: X \Rightarrow Y \longrightarrow Confidence = \frac{frq(X,Y)}{frq(X)}$$

$$Lift = \frac{Support}{Supp(X) \times Supp(Y)}$$

Fig 4.4 Rule defining for support, confidence and lift formulae.

good example for identifying the products which are purchased more frequently in combination from the available database of customer purchase. The association rule looks like f:X->Y where if a customer purchase X then only he purchase the item Y.

Example: The association rule defined for a customer purchase made for milk and sugar will surely buy the coffee powder can be given as {milk, sugar} -> coffee powder. These association rules are generated whenever the support and confidence will cross the threshold.

The fig 4.4 provides the support, confidence and lift formulae specified for X and Y. The support measure will help in pruning the number of candidate item sets for generating frequent item sets as specified by the Apriori principle. The Apriori principle states that for a frequent item sets, and then all of its subsets must all also be frequent.

7. K-means

K-means algorithm is mostly used for grouping the similar data into clusters through more iteration. It computes the centroids of the k cluster and assigns a new data point to the cluster based on the less distance between its centroid and data point.

Working of K-means algorithm:

Let us consider the value of k=3 from the fig 4.5 we see there are 3 clusters for which we need to assign randomly for each data point. The centroid is computed for each cluster. The red, blue and green are treated as the centroids for three clusters. Next will reassign each data point which is closest to the centroid. The top data points are assigned to blue centroid similarly the other nearest data points are grouped to red and green centroids. Now compute the centroid for new clusters old centroids are turned to gray color stars, the new centroids are made to red, green and blue stars.

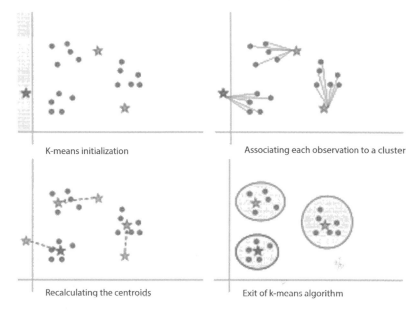

| K-means initialization | Associating each observation to a cluster |

| Recalculating the centroids | Exit of k-means algorithm |

Fig 4.5 Pictorial representation of working of k-means algorithm.

Finally, repeat the steps of identifying new data points for nearing to centroid and switch from one cluster to another to get new centroid until two consecutive steps the centroids are same and then exit the algorithm.

8. PCA

PCA is a Principal Component Analysis which explores and visualizes the data for less number of input variables. The reduction of capturing the new data input values is done based of the data for the new coordinate systems with axes called as "Principal Components".

Each component is the result of linear combination of the original variables which are orthogonal to one another. Orthogonality always leads to specifying that the correlation between components is zero as shown in Fig 4.6.

Initial principal component captures the data which are variable at maximum in one specific direction similarly second principal component is resulted with computation of variance on the new data other than used for first component. The other principal components are constructed while the remaining variance is computed with different correlated data from the previous component.

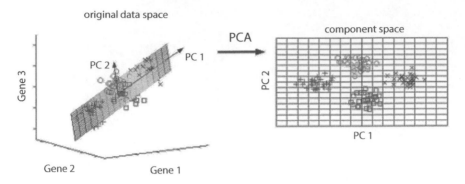

Fig 4.6 Construction of PCA.

Ensemble learning techniques:

The combination of two or more multiple learning techniques for improvement in the results with voting or averaging is called Ensembling. The voting is due done for classification and averaging is done based on regression. Ensemblers try to improve the results with combination of two or more learners. Bagging, Boosting and Stacking are three types of ensembling techniques.

9. Bagging with Random Forests

Bagging uses bootstrap sampling method to create multiple model data sets where each training data set comprises of random subsamples taken from original data set.

The training data sets are of same size of the original data set, but some data is repeated multiple times and some are missing in the records. Thus entire original data set is considered for testing. If original data set is of N size then generated training set is also N, with unique records would be about (2N/3) and the size of test data set is of N.

The second step in bagging is to provide multiple models for same algorithm for different generated training sets.

The Random forests are the results of bagging technique, it looks similar to the decision tree where each node is split to minimize the error but in random forest a set of random selected features are used for constructing the best split. The reason for randomness usage over decision tree is because of choosing multiple datasets for random split. The splitting over random subset features means less correlation among predictions leading to many sub trees.

The unique parameter which is used for splitting in random forest always provides with wide variety of features used for searching at each split point. Thus always bagging results in random forest tree construction with random sample of records where each split leads to more random samples of predictors.

10. Boosting with AdaBoost

Adaptive Boosting is popularly known as Adaboost. Bagging is an ensemble technique which is built parallel for each model of data set whereas boosting works on sequential ensemble techniques where each new data model is constructed based on the misclassification of the old model.

Bagging involves simple voting mechanism where each ensemble algorithm votes to obtain a final outcome. At first to determine the resultant model in bagging the earlier models are parallel treated with multiple models. In boosting the weighted voting mechanism is used where each classifier obtains the vote for final outcome based on the majority. The sequential models were built based on the previous assignment for attaining greater weights for different misclassified data models.

The fig 4.7 briefs the graphical illustration of AdaBoost algorithm where a weak learner known as decision stump with 1-level decision tree using a prediction based on the value of the one feature with a decision tree with root node directly connected to leaf nodes.

The construction of weak learners continues until a user-defined no of weak learners until no further improvement by training. Finally it results

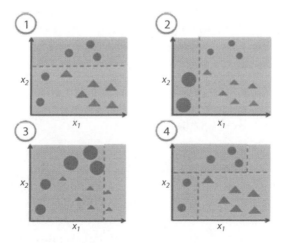

Fig 4.7 Steps of AdaBoost algorithm.

in step 4 with three decision stumps from the study of the previous models and applying three splitting rules.

First, start with one decision tree stump to make a decision on one input variable.

The size of the data points show that we have applied equal weights to classify them as a circle or triangle. The decision stump has generated a horizontal line in the top half to classify these points. We can see that there are two circles incorrectly predicted as triangles. Hence, we will assign higher weights to these two circles and apply another decision stump.

First splitting rule is done with one input variable to make a decision. Equal weights of data points were considered to classify them in to circle or triangle. The decision stump shows the separated horizontal line to categorize the points. In fig 4.7 step-1 clearly shows that two circles were wrongly predicted for triangles. Now we will assign more weightage to these circles and go for second decision stump.

In the second splitting rule for decision stump is done on another input variable. As we observe the misclassified circles were assigned with heavier weights in the second decision stump so they are categorized correctly and classified to vertical line on the left but three small circles which are not matching with that heavier weight are not considered in the current decision stump. Hence will assign another weights to these three circles which are at the top and go for another stump.

Third, train another decision tree stump to make a decision on another input variable.

The third splitting rule the decision tree stump try to make decision on another input variable. The three misclassified circles in second decision tree stump are raised to heavier weights thus a vertical line separates them from rest of the circles and triangles as shown in figure.

On fourth step will combine all decision stumps from the previous models and define a complex rule to classify the data points correctly from previous weak learners.

Dimensionality Reduction

In machine learning to resolve classification problems very often many factors are considered for the final classification. The factors which are considered for classification are known as variables or features. The more the numbers of features were considered it would be difficult to visualize the training set and to work on it. Most of the features are correlated hence possibility of occurrence of redundant is more. This technique of getting redundant features on the given training data set is done using dimensionality reduction algorithm. Dimensionality reduction is a mechanism where the no of random variables are reduced based on the availability principal variables on a given data set. The major steps involved in dimensionality reduction is extraction of features and selection of features.

Why is Dimensionality Reduction important in Machine Learning and Predictive Modeling?

The predominant example for understanding dimensionality reduction can be considered for classifying the simple e-mail messages which we receive in our inbox. The classification would be the e-mail message received is spam or not. More no of features can be considered for classifying the e-mail messages they are like subject title, content, usage of templates etc.., some of the features can overlap. Another example simple classification would be for predicting the humidity and rainfall for a given day. Most of the features which will be used are correlated to a high degree hence we need to reduce the features and try to classify. Most of the 3-D data classification leads too hard to visualize, 2-D data can be easily mapped to any two dimensional space and 1-D data can be made on to a straight line.

Components of Dimensionality Reduction

Dimensionality reduction is carried under two major steps:

- **Selection of Features:** A trial of subset of data is considered original data set with specified features of variables or features, to get minimal data set which can provide solution to the problem. It uses three popular techniques in choosing the minimal data set they are filtering technique, wrapper technique and embedded technique.
- **Extraction of Features:** In this mechanism the higher dimensional space are reduced to a lower dimension space and test set of data can be for lesser no of dimensions.

Methods of Dimensionality Reduction

The various methods used for dimensionality reduction include:

- Principal Component Analysis (PCA)
- Linear Discriminant Analysis (LDA)
- Generalized Discriminant Analysis (GDA)

Advantages of Dimensionality Reduction

- Low storage space and promotes high data compression
- Less computation time
- Eliminate more redundant features, if available.

Disadvantages of Dimensionality Reduction

- Data loss can occur after elimination of redundant data.
- Undesirable output can occur for data sets which have features more linearly correlated.
- It fails to define mean and covariance as sufficient data sets are not available for process.
- The no of principal components considered for implementation is uncertain but thumb rules are used to resolve the choice of selection.

4.3   Explanatory Factor Analysis

Segment 2 - Explanatory factor analysis

```
In [1]:  import pandas as pd
         import numpy as np

         import sklearn
         from sklearn.decomposition import FactorAnalysis

         from sklearn import datasets
```

Factor analysis on iris dataset

```
In [3]:  iris =  datasets.load_iris()

         X = iris.data

         variable_names = iris.feature_names

         X[0:10,]
```

```
Out[3]:  array([[ 5.1,  3.5,  1.4,  0.2],
                [ 4.9,  3. ,  1.4,  0.2],
                [ 4.7,  3.2,  1.3,  0.2],
                [ 4.6,  3.1,  1.5,  0.2],
                [ 5. ,  3.6,  1.4,  0.2],
                [ 5.4,  3.9,  1.7,  0.4],
                [ 4.6,  3.4,  1.4,  0.3],
                [ 5. ,  3.4,  1.5,  0.2],
                [ 4.4,  2.9,  1.4,  0.2],
                [ 4.9,  3.1,  1.5,  0.1]]])
```

```
In [4]:  factor = FactorAnalysis().fit(X)

         pd.DataFrame(factor.components_, columns=variable_names)
```

Out[4]:

	sepal length (cm)	sepal width (cm)	petal length (cm)	petal width (cm)
0	0.707227	-0.153147	1.653151	0.701569
1	0.114676	0.159763	-0.045604	-0.014052
2	-0.000000	0.000000	0.000000	0.000000
3	-0.000000	0.000000	0.000000	-0.000000

4.4   Principal Component Analysis (PCA)

The popular dimensionality reduction technique is the principal component analysis (PCA). It transforms the large set of dataset in to smaller dimension which still contains much of the information to represent that large dataset. As we reduce the selected features the accuracy will get reduced but the major feature of PCA algorithm it simplifies the data set with little change in accuracy. The PCA results in to smaller data sets which are easy to process and can be visualized and analyzed properly without loss of information or variables. Thus PCA preserve the actual important featured data from the available data set which gives more clarity on the solution space.

Step by Step Explanation of PCA

Step 1: Standardization

It is a procedure in which range of continuous initial variables which will contribute equally are analyzed. Most specifically the standardization is done prior to PCA because latter it would be challenging to compute the variances of initial data set variables. The variables with large differences between the range of initial variables will dominate over small differences over the small range which will provide us with biased result. So transforming the data on to comparable scales would be better choice to prevent this issue.

The below formulae can be used to standardize the data variables by subtracting the mean from the variable value and dividing it by its standard deviation.

$$z = \frac{value - mean}{standard\ deviation}$$

The standardization always results in unique scale form of arranging the data.

Step 2: Covariance Matrix computation

The variables correlation must be identified among the standardized data. This step is important because it identifies how input data will vary from the mean value of the other and results in to reduce that data which is leading more correlation. Thus covariance matrix helps in identifying the strong correlated data.

The below is the example covariance matrix for three dimensional data which will check for all variables possible correlation on x, y, and z.

$$
\begin{bmatrix}
Cov(x,x) & Cov(x,y) & Cov(x,z) \\
Cov(y,x) & Cov(y,y) & Cov(y,z) \\
Cov(z,x) & Cov(z,y) & Cov(z,z)
\end{bmatrix}
$$

Covariance Matrix for 3-Dimensional Data
Most of the diagonal will be same variable variance and the cumulative covariance will be same values hence in the above matrix the lower and upper triangular portions will have similar data. The positive value of covariance will build strong correlation and negative will result in inverse correlation.

Thus covariance matrix will help us in summarizing the correlated data between all possible pairs of variables.

Step 3: Compute the eigenvectors and eigenvalues of the covariance matrix to identify the principal components

Eigen vectors and Eigen values are linear algebra concepts that need to be computed on covariance matrix to determine the principal components of the data. Principal components are constructed with linear combinations or mixture of different variables. The new combinations are done such a way that uncorrelated data and most of the data within the initial variables will be compressed or squeezed to form the components. Thus depending on the dimension of data the principal components can be created. The principal components will always tries to maximize the possible information on to first component, then second components with next maximum remaining data.

The fig 4.8 provides with the possible data as grouped into principal components. This way of organizing the data without loss of information will provide the reduction in the unwanted or uncorrelated data. Thus the principal components with less data can be neglected and remaining are used for further process.

The pictorial representation of principal components will represent the directions of the data that gives the maximum computed variance data on the lines of capture for most of the information. The major relationship between variance and information are that the larger the variance carried by a line, larger the dispersion of data which provides more information. The difference between the data can be clearly observed from the principal component axes.

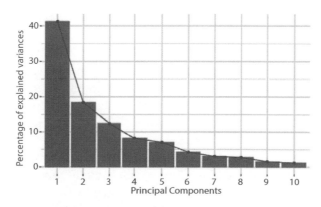

Fig 4.8 Percentage of Variance (Information) for each by PC.

Step 4: Feature Vector

The continuation previous step of construction of principal components from eigen vectors and order based on the Eigen values in descending order allows us to identify the significance of it. In this step will choose which components to be discarded (low eigenvalues) and the remaining will be resultant feature vector.

The feature vector is simply a matrix which has columns with eigen vectors of the components that will be used for further operations. This would be the first step to achieve dimensionality reduction, among p eigen vectors out of n, thus the final data set would be only p dimensions.

Last Step: Recast the Data Along the Principal Components Axes

From all above steps it is clear that after standardization you make changes to the data based on the principal component selection and result new feature vector, but the given input dat is always same.

In this step, which is the last one, the aim is to use the feature vector formed using the eigenvectors of the covariance matrix, to reorient the data from the original axes to the ones represented by the principal components (hence the name Principal Components Analysis). This can be done by multiplying the transpose of the original data set by the transpose of the feature vector.

In the final step will multiply the transposed feature vector with the transposed original datset.

$$FinalDataSet = FeatureVector^T * StandardizedOriginalDataSet^T$$

Advantages of Principal Component Analysis

1. **Separate the correlated featured data:**
   In real time scenarios there would be large amount of data set with variable no of features. It is difficult to run the algorithm for all features and visualize them graphically. So it is mandatory to reduce the number of features to understand the data set. The correlation among the features will help us in selecting the selected features which will result with close proximity of understanding which is quite impossible with manual intervention. Thus PCA provides the construction of principal components with featured vectors which will

help us finding the strong correlated features by removing from the original data.

2. **Improving the performance of algorithms:**
   Most of the algorithms performance depends on the valued data supplied for its input. If the data is not valid then it will degrade its performance and result in wrong results. If we provide the highly correlated data it will significantly improve the performance of algorithms. So if input data is more to process then PCA would be better choice to reduce the uncorrelated data.

3. **Overfitting reduction:**
   When more variable features are used in the dataset then overfitting is the common issue. So PCA reduces the no of features which will result less over fitting.

4. **Visualization is improved:**
   High dimensional data is difficult to visualize. PCA transforms the high dimensional to low dimensional to improve the visibility of data. Example IRIS data with four dimension can be transformed to two dimension by PCA which will improve the data visualization for processing.

Disadvantages of Principal Component Analysis

1. **Interpretation on independent variables is difficult:**
   PCA results in to the linear combination where original feature of data will be missing and these resulted principal components are less interpretable then with original features.

2. **PCA purely depends on data standardization:**
   The optimal principal components will not be possible if the input data is not standardized. Scaling factor is very important among the chosen available data. Any strong variation will result in biased results which will lead to wrong output. To get optimal performance form the machine learning algorithms we need to standardize the data to mean 0 and standard deviation 1.

3. **Loss of information:**
   Principal components will try to cover much of the highly correlated data with wide features but some information may be lost due to more convergence then with available original features.

Segment 3 - Principal component analysis (PCA)

```
In [2]:  import numpy as np
         import pandas as pd

         import matplotlib.pyplot as plt
         import pylab as plt
         import seaborn as sb
         from IPython.display import Image
         from IPython.core.display import HTML
         from pylab import rcParams

         import sklearn
         from sklearn import decomposition
         from sklearn.decomposition import PCA
         from sklearn import datasets
```

```
In [11]:  %matplotlib inline
          rcParams['figure.figsize'] = 5, 4
          sb.set_style('whitegrid')
```

PCA on the iris dataset

```
In [3]:  iris = datasets.load_iris()
         X = iris.data
         variable_names = iris.feature_names
         X[0:10,]
```

```
Out[3]:  array([[ 5.1,  3.5,  1.4,  0.2],
                [ 4.9,  3. ,  1.4,  0.2],
                [ 4.7,  3.2,  1.3,  0.2],
                [ 4.6,  3.1,  1.5,  0.2],
                [ 5. ,  3.6,  1.4,  0.2],
                [ 5.4,  3.9,  1.7,  0.4],
                [ 4.6,  3.4,  1.4,  0.3],
                [ 5. ,  3.4,  1.5,  0.2],
                [ 4.4,  2.9,  1.4,  0.2],
                [ 4.9,  3.1,  1.5,  0.1]])
```

```
In [4]:  pca = decomposition.PCA()
         iris_pca = pca.fit_transform(X)

         pca.explained_variance_ratio_
```

```
Out[4]:  array([ 0.92461621,  0.05301557,  0.01718514,  0.00518309])
```

```
In [5]:  pca.explained_variance_ratio_.sum()
```

```
Out[5]:  1.0
```

```
In [6]:  comps = pd.DataFrame(pca.components_, columns=variable_names)
         comps
```

Out[6]:

	sepal length (cm)	sepal width (cm)	petal length (cm)	petal width (cm)
0	0.361590	-0.082269	0.856572	0.358844
1	-0.656540	-0.729712	0.175767	0.074706
2	0.580997	-0.596418	-0.072524	-0.549061
3	0.317255	-0.324094	-0.479719	0.751121

```
In [12]:  sb.heatmap(comps)
```

Out[12]: <matplotlib.axes._subplots.AxesSubplot at 0xf03bb38>

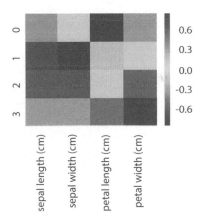

References

1. Mitchell, Tom (1997). Machine Learning. New York: McGraw Hill. ISBN 0-07-042807-7. OCLC 36417892.
2. Hu, J.; Niu, H.; Carrasco, J.; Lennox, B.; Arvin, F., "Voronoi-Based Multi-Robot Autonomous Exploration in Unknown Environments via Deep Reinforcement Learning" IEEE Transactions on Vehicular Technology, 2020.
3. Bishop, C. M. (2006), Pattern Recognition and Machine Learning, Springer, ISBN 978-0-387-31073-2

4. Machine learning and pattern recognition "can be viewed as two facets of the same field."[4]:vii

5. Friedman, Jerome H. (1998). "Data Mining and Statistics: What's the connection?". Computing Science and Statistics. 29 (1): 3–9.

6. "What is Machine Learning?". www.ibm.com. Retrieved 2021-08-15.

7. Zhou, Victor (2019-12-20). "Machine Learning for Beginners: An Introduction to Neural Networks". Medium. Retrieved 2021-08-15.

8. Domingos 2015, Chapter 6, Chapter 7.

9. Ethem Alpaydin (2020). Introduction to Machine Learning (Fourth ed.). MIT. pp. xix, 1–3, 13–18. ISBN 978-0262043793.

10. Samuel, Arthur (1959). "Some Studies in Machine Learning Using the Game of Checkers". IBM Journal of Research and Development. 3 (3): 210–229. CiteSeerX 10.1.1.368.2254. doi:10.1147/rd.33.0210.

11. Prakash K.B. Content extraction studies using total distance algorithm, 2017, Proceedings of the 2016 2nd International Conference on Applied and Theoretical Computing and Communication Technology, iCATccT 2016, 10.1109/ICATCCT.2016.7912085

12. Prakash K.B. Mining issues in traditional indian web documents,2015, Indian Journal of Science and Technology,8(32),10.17485/ijst/2015/v8i1/77056

13. Prakash K.B., Rajaraman A., Lakshmi M. Complexities in developing multilingual on-line courses in the Indian context, 2017, Proceedings of the 2017 International Conference On Big Data Analytics and Computational Intelligence, ICBDACI 2017, 8070860, 339-342, 10.1109/ICBDACI.2017.8070860

14. Prakash K.B., Kumar K.S., Rao S.U.M. Content extraction issues in online web education, 2017,Proceedings of the 2016 2nd International Conference on Applied and Theoretical Computing and Communication Technology, iCATccT 2016, 7912086,680-685,10.1109/ICATCCT.2016.7912086

15. Prakash K.B., Rajaraman A., Perumal T., Kolla P. Foundations to frontiers of big data analytics,2016,Proceedings of the 2016 2nd International Conference on Contemporary

5

Outlier Analysis

5.1   Extreme Value Analysis Using Univariate Methods

Segment 1 - Extreme value analysis using univariate methods

```
In [1]:  import numpy as np
         import pandas as pd

         import matplotlib.pyplot as plt
         from pylab import rcParams
```

```
In [3]:  %matplotlib inline
         rcParams['figure.figsize'] = 5,4
```

```
In [5]:  df = pd.read_csv(
             filepath_or_buffer='C:/Users/Lillian Pierson/Desktop/Exercise Files/Ch05/05_01/iris.data.csv',
             header=None,
             sep=',')
         df.columns=['Sepal Length','Sepal Width','Petal Length','Petal Width', 'Species']
         X = df.ix[:,0:4].values
         y = df.ix[:,4].values

         df[:5]
```

Out[5]:

	Sepal Length	Sepal Width	Petal Length	Petal Width	Species
0	5.1	3.5	1.4	0.2	setosa
1	4.9	3.0	1.4	0.2	setosa
2	4.7	3.2	1.3	0.2	setosa
3	4.6	3.1	1.5	0.2	setosa
4	5.0	3.6	1.4	0.2	setosa

Kolla Bhanu Prakash. Data Science Handbook: A Practical Approach, (123–134) © 2022 Scrivener Publishing LLC

Identifying outliers from Tukey boxplots

```
In [6]:  df.boxplot(return_type='dict')
         plt.plot()
```

Out[6]: []

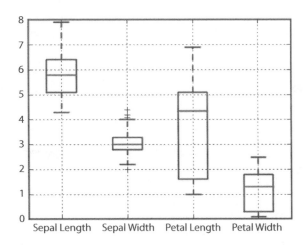

```
In [7]:  Sepal_Width = X[:,1]
         iris_outliers = (Sepal_Width > 4)
         df[iris_outliers]
```

Out[7]:

	Sepal Length	Sepal Width	Petal Length	Petal Width	Species
15	5.7	4.4	1.5	0.4	setosa
32	5.2	4.1	1.5	0.1	setosa
33	5.5	4.2	1.4	0.2	setosa

```
In [8]:  Sepal_Width = X[:,1]
         iris_outliers = (Sepal_Width < 2.05)
         df[iris_outliers]
```

Out[8]:

	Sepal Length	Sepal Width	Petal Length	Petal Width	Species
60	5.0	2.0	3.5	1.0	versicolor

Applying Tukey outlier labeling

```
In [9]:  pd.options.display.float_format = '{:.1f}'.format
         X_df = pd.DataFrame(X)
         print X_df.describe()
```

```
              0     1     2     3
count     150.0 150.0 150.0 150.0
mean        5.8   3.1   3.8   1.2
std         0.8   0.4   1.8   0.8
min         4.3   2.0   1.0   0.1
25%         5.1   2.8   1.6   0.3
50%         5.8   3.0   4.3   1.3
75%         6.4   3.3   5.1   1.8
max         7.9   4.4   6.9   2.5
```

5.2   Multivariate Analysis for Outlier Detection

Segment 2 - Multivariate analysis for outlier detection

```
In [1]:  import pandas as pd

         import matplotlib.pyplot as plt
         from pylab import rcParams
         import seaborn as sb
```

```
In [2]:  %matplotlib inline
         rcParams['figure.figsize'] = 5, 4
         sb.set_style('whitegrid')
```

Visually inspecting boxplots

```
In [3]:  df = pd.read_csv(
             filepath_or_buffer='C:/Users/Lillian Pierson/Desktop/Exercise Files/Ch05/05_02/iris.data.csv',
             header=None,
             sep=',')

         df.columns=['Sepal Length','Sepal Width','Petal Length','Petal Width', 'Species']
         data = df.ix[:,0:4].values
         target = df.ix[:,4].values
         df[:5]

         sb.boxplot(x='Species', y='Sepal Length', data=df, palette='hls')
```

```
Out[3]:  <matplotlib.axes._subplots.AxesSubplot at 0xbecf898>
```

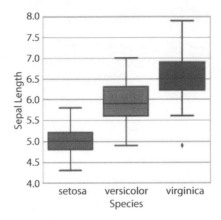

Looking at the scatterplot matrix

```
In [4]: sb.pairplot(df, hue='Species', palette='hls')
Out[4]: <seaborn.axisgrid.PairGrid at 0xbeb9470>
```

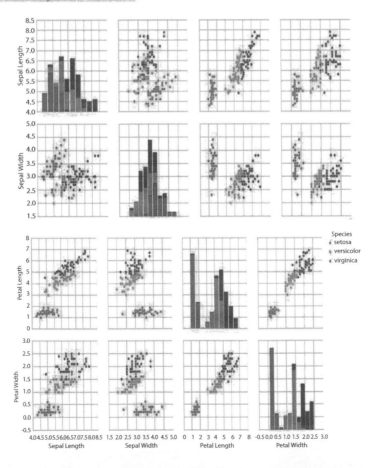

5.3   DBSCan Clustering to Identify Outliers

Outlier Detection Using DBSCAN (Density-Based Spatial Clustering Application with Noise)

Introduction

The unsupervised machine learning technique which uses density-based clustering algorithm to deal with outliers data of random shape and size to form cluster is a DBSCAN [1]. The knowledge of this algorithm is mandatory for Data scientist [2].

The main characteristic of the DBSCAN algorithm is used to detect the points which lie outside the dense regions are considered as outliers or noisy points [3]. It perfectly fits to outlier detection and from the cluster with different shape and size [4].

The epsi and Min_Pts are two parameters used for parametric approach.

- **epsi:** This represents the radius of the neighbourhood cluster around a point x.
- **Min_Pts:** The minimum points of neighborhood for defining a new cluster.

DBSCAN Algorithm step by step.

The major steps followed during the DBSCAN algorithm are as follows:

Step-1: Initialize the parameter values of **eps** and **Min_Pts.**
Step-2: For given data set repeat for each x:
- Euclidean distance is computed between data points and check if it is less than or equal to eps then consider as new neighbor of x.
- After identifying the new neighbor beside the data point x are counted and checked for greater than or equal to Min_Pts, and mark it as visited.
Step-3: For each core point, if it is not already assigned to a cluster then create a new cluster. Further, all the neighbouring points are recursively determined and are assigned the same cluster as that of the core point.

A new cluster is created for each core point if it is not assigned to a cluster. Further, recursively new neighboring points are determined and assigned a cluster for the each core point.

Step-4: The above steps are repeated until all new nodes are visited.

Input parameters given to the DBSCAN Algorithm.

The two-user defined input parameters considered for DBSCAN algorithm for clustering:

- **Epsilon (eps):** It is defined as radius around each neighboring points which is having the maximum distance [5].
- **Minimum Points (min_samples or min_pts):** It is defined as the minimum no of neighboring points which are around the core point with in that radius [6].

For example if Min_Pts is 6 means atleast the new point should be 5 or more neighboring points around the core point [7].

A cluster is considered when minimum no of points equals the epsilon distance of core point [8].

Terms related to DBSCAN Algorithm:

– Direct Density Reachable
– Density Reachable
– Density Connected

Direct density reachable:
If a point is near to the core point neighborhood then it is known as direct density reachable [9].

Density Reachable:
If a point is connected through a series of core points then it is known as density reachable.

Density Connected:
If two points are density reachable to core point then it is known as density connected.

We get three types of points upon applying a DBSCAN algorithm to a particular dataset – **Core point, Border point, and noise point.**

- **Core Point:**
  A core point is that data point which has a minimum no of neighboring points with in the epsilon distance of it.
- **Border Point:**
  Border point is that point with less no of minimum number of data points with atleast one point as core point in neighborhood.
- **Noise Point:**
  Noise point is that point which is neither core point nor border point. It also known as outlier data point.

Time complexity of the DBSCAN Clustering Algorithm

The different complexities of the algorithm are (**N= no of data points**) as follows:

Best Case:
KD-tree or R-tree are used for storing the data set using spatial indexing system to query the neighborhood points to get executed in logarithmic time i.e. $O(N \log N)$ time complexity.

Worst Case:
The worst case is $O(N^2)$ which will not use index on a degenerated data.

Average Case:
It is similar to best case or worst case with same implementation of algorithm.

How is the parameter "Min_Pts" estimated in the DBSCAN Algorithm?

Min_Pts ≥ Dim + 1 where Dim is the dimension of data set

Case-1:
The minimum value for Min_Pts is not equal to 1 because every point will be part of a cluster.

Case-2:
For Min_Pts<=2 then the points will be part of hierarchical clustering with single link and dendrogram cut to a height of epsilon.

So, Min_Pts value should be atleast 3.

Larger value of Min_Pts will be better for any dataset as they have more noisy points which will yield many clusters [10, 11].

At max the thumb rule could be Min_Pts ≥ 2* Dim + 1

To choose larger values, it may be necessary that the:

- Data values should be **large**
- The Data with more noisy, it leads to more **outliers**
- Data should have more **duplicates**

Advantages of the DBSCAN algorithm

1. No need of initial clusters to be defined [12].
2. Clusters can be any random shape or size even with non-spherical ones can be considered.
3. Outliers are easily identified which are considered as noisy data [13].
4. DBSCAN never provides initial no of cluster as input to algorithm which K Means does.
5. Any shape of cluster can be found [14].
6. Most of the cluster does not have any specific shape.
7. Many of the outliers is eliminated by forming new cluster and finally on more repetition none of the outliers will exist in our data set.

Disadvantages of the DBSCAN algorithm

1. It fails when there are more density drops among the clusters.
2. If there are more variations among the variable clusters it is difficult to detect the outliers or noisy points.
3. It is difficult to set the initial parameters as it is highly sensitive to the parameter settings.
4. The quality of DBSCAN algorithm lies with distance metric.
5. Effective clusters cannot be generated for the high dimensional data.
6. Multi processor system cannot be involved to partition the algorithm computation.

Segment 3 - DBSCan clustering to identify outliers

```
In [2]: import pandas as pd

        import matplotlib.pyplot as plt
        from pylab import rcParams
        import seaborn as sb

        import sklearn
        from sklearn.cluster import DBSCAN
        from collections import Counter
```

```
In [3]: %matplotlib inline
        rcParams['figure.figsize'] = 5, 4
        sb.set_style('whitegrid')
```

DBSCan clustering to identify outliers

Train your model and identify outliers

```
In [5]: df = pd.read_csv(
            filepath_or_buffer='C:/Users/Lillian Pierson/Desktop/Exercise Files/Ch05/05_03/iris.data.csv',
            header=None,
            sep=',')

        df.columns=['Sepal Length','Sepal Width','Petal Length','Petal Width', 'Species']
        data = df.ix[:,0:4].values
        target = df.ix[:,4].values
        df[:5]
```

Out[5]:

	Sepal Length	Sepal Width	Petal Length	Petal Width	Species
0	5.1	3.5	1.4	0.2	setosa
1	4.9	3.0	1.4	0.2	setosa
2	4.7	3.2	1.3	0.2	setosa
3	4.6	3.1	1.5	0.2	setosa
4	5.0	3.6	1.4	0.2	setosa

In [8]:
```
model = DBSCAN(eps=0.8, min_samples=19).fit(data)
print model

DBSCAN(algorithm='auto', eps=0.8, leaf_size=30, metric='euclidean',
    min_samples=19, p=None, random_state=None)
```

Visualize your results

In [9]:
```
outliers_df = pd.DataFrame(data)

print Counter(model.labels_)

print outliers_df[model.labels_ ==-1]

Counter({1: 94, 0: 50, -1: 6})
        0    1    2    3
98    5.1  2.5  3.0  1.1
105   7.6  3.0  6.6  2.1
117   7.7  3.8  6.7  2.2
118   7.7  2.6  6.9  2.3
122   7.7  2.8  6.7  2.0
131   7.9  3.8  6.4  2.0
```

In [10]:
```
fig = plt.figure()
ax = fig.add_axes([.1, .1, 1, 1])

colors = model.labels_

ax.scatter(data[:,2], data[:,1], c=colors, s=120)
ax.set_xlabel('Petal Length')
ax.set_ylabel('Sepal Width')
plt.title('DBScan for Outlier Detection')
```

Out[10]: <matplotlib.text.Text at 0xca6c320>

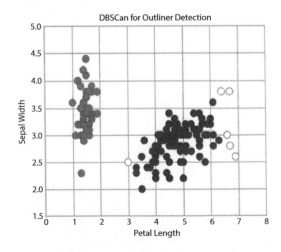

References

1. Liu, J.; Cosman, P. C.; Rao, B. D. (2018). "Robust Linear Regression via L0 Regularization". IEEE Transactions on Signal Processing. 66 (3): 698–713. doi:10.1109/TSP.2017.2771720.
2. Andersen, R. (2008). Modern Methods for Robust Regression. Sage University Paper Series on Quantitative Applications in the Social Sciences, 07-152.
3. Ben-Gal I., Outlier detection, In: Maimon O. and Rockach L. (Eds.) Data Mining and Knowledge Discovery Handbook: A Complete Guide for Practitioners and Researchers," Kluwer Academic Publishers, 2005, ISBN 0-387-24435-2.
4. Bobko, P., Roth, P. L., & Buster, M. A. (2007). "The usefulness of unit weights in creating composite scores: A literature review, application to content validity, and meta-analysis". Organizational Research Methods, volume 10, pages 689-709. doi:10.1177/1094428106294734
5. Daemi, Atefeh, Hariprasad Kodamana, and Biao Huang. "Gaussian process modelling with Gaussian mixture likelihood." Journal of Process Control 81 (2019): 209-220. doi:10.1016/j.jprocont.2019.06.007
6. Ester, Martin; Kriegel, Hans-Peter; Sander, Jörg; Xu, Xiaowei (1996). Simoudis, Evangelos; Han, Jiawei; Fayyad, Usama M. (eds.). A density-based algorithm for discovering clusters in large spatial databases with noise. Proceedings of the Second International Conference on Knowledge Discovery and Data Mining (KDD-96). AAAI Press. pp. 226–231.
7. Schubert, Erich; Sander, Jörg; Ester, Martin; Kriegel, Hans Peter; Xu, Xiaowei (July 2017). "DBSCAN Revisited, Revisited: Why and How You Should (Still) Use DBSCAN". ACM Trans. Database Syst. 42 (3): 19:1–19:21. doi:10.1145/3068335. ISSN 0362-5915. S2CID 5156876.
8. Sander, Jörg; Ester, Martin; Kriegel, Hans-Peter; Xu, Xiaowei (1998). "Density-Based Clustering in Spatial Databases: The Algorithm GDBSCAN and Its Applications". Data Mining and Knowledge Discovery. Berlin: Springer-Verlag. 2 (2): 169–194. doi:10.1023/A:1009745219419. S2CID 445002.
9. Sander, Jörg (1998). Generalized Density-Based Clustering for Spatial Data Mining. München: Herbert Utz Verlag. ISBN 3-89675-469-6.
10. Prakash K.B. Content extraction studies using total distance algorithm, 2017, Proceedings of the 2016 2nd International Conference on Applied and Theoretical Computing and Communication Technology, iCATccT 2016, 10.1109/ICATCCT.2016.7912085
11. Prakash K.B. Mining issues in traditional indian web documents,2015, Indian Journal of Science and Technology,8(32),10.17485/ijst/2015/v8i1/77056
12. Prakash K.B., Rajaraman A., Lakshmi M. Complexities in developing multilingual on-line courses in the Indian context, 2017, Proceedings of the 2017 International Conference On Big Data Analytics and

Computational Intelligence, ICBDACI 2017, 8070860, 339-342, 10.1109/ICBDACI.2017.8070860

13. Prakash K.B., Kumar K.S., Rao S.U.M. Content extraction issues in online web education, 2017,Proceedings of the 2016 2nd International Conference on Applied and Theoretical Computing and Communication Technology, iCATccT 2016, 7912086,680-685,10.1109/ICATCCT.2016.7912086

14. Prakash K.B., Rajaraman A., Perumal T., Kolla P. Foundations to frontiers of big data analytics,2016,Proceedings of the 2016 2nd International Conference on Contemporary Computing and Informatics, IC3I 2016, 7917968,242-247, 10.1109/IC3I.2016.7917968

Cluster Analysis

Clustering

Clustering is one of the most common exploratory data analysis technique used to get an intuition about the structure of the data [1]. It can be defined as the task of identifying subgroups in the data such that data points in the same subgroup (cluster) are very similar while data points in different clusters are very different [2]. In other words, we try to find homogeneous subgroups within the data such that data points in each cluster are as similar as possible according to a similarity measure such as euclidean-based distance or correlation-based distance [3]. The decision of which similarity measure to use is application specific [4].

Clustering analysis can be done on the basis of features where we try to find subgroups of samples based on features or on the basis of samples where we try to find subgroups of features based on samples [5]. We'll cover here clustering based on features. Clustering is used in market segmentation; where we try to find customers that are similar to each other whether in terms of behaviors or attributes, image segmentation/compression; where we try to group similar regions together, document clustering based on topics, etc. [6].

Unlike supervised learning, clustering is considered an unsupervised learning method since we don't have the ground truth to compare the output of the clustering algorithm to the true labels to evaluate its performance [7]. We only want to try to investigate the structure of the data by grouping the data points into distinct subgroups [8].

6.1 K-Means Algorithm

Kmeans algorithm is an iterative algorithm that tries to partition the dataset into K pre-defined distinct non-overlapping subgroups (clusters) where each data point belongs to only one group [9]. It tries to make

---

Kolla Bhanu Prakash. Data Science Handbook: A Practical Approach, (135–156) © 2022 Scrivener Publishing LLC

the intra-cluster data points as similar as possible while also keeping the clusters as different (far) as possible [10]. It assigns data points to a cluster such that the sum of the squared distance between the data points and the cluster's centroid (arithmetic mean of all the data points that belong to that cluster) is at the minimum [11]. The less variation we have within clusters, the more homogeneous (similar) the data points are within the same cluster [12].

The way kmeans algorithm works is as follows:

1. Specify number of clusters K.
2. Initialize centroids by first shuffling the dataset and then randomly selecting K data points for the centroids without replacement.
3. Keep iterating until there is no change to the centroids. i.e assignment of data points to clusters isn't changing.

- Compute the sum of the squared distance between data points and all centroids.
- Assign each data point to the closest cluster (centroid).
- Compute the centroids for the clusters by taking the average of the all data points that belong to each cluster.

The approach kmeans follows to solve the problem is called **Expectation-Maximization**. The E-step is assigning the data points to the closest cluster. The M-step is computing the centroid of each cluster. Below is a break down of how we can solve it mathematically (feel free to skip it).

The objective function is:

$$J = \sum_{i=1}^{m} \sum_{k=1}^{K} w_{ik} \left\| x^i - \mu_k \right\|^2 \tag{6.1}$$

where wik=1 for data point xi if it belongs to cluster k; otherwise, wik=0. Also, μk is the centroid of xi's cluster.

It's a minimization problem of two parts. We first minimize J w.r.t. wik and treat μk fixed. Then we minimize J w.r.t. μk and treat wik fixed. Technically speaking, we differentiate J w.r.t. wik first and update cluster assignments (*E-step*). Then we differentiate J w.r.t. μk and recompute the centroids after the cluster assignments from previous step (*M-step*). Therefore, E-step is:

$$\frac{\partial J}{\partial w_{ik}} = \sum_{i=1}^{m} \sum_{k=1}^{K} \|x^i - \mu_k\|^2$$

$$\Rightarrow w_{ik} = \begin{cases} 1 & \text{if } k = argmin_j \|x^i - \mu_j\|^2 \\ 0 & \text{otherwise.} \end{cases}$$

(6.2)

In other words, assign the data point xi to the closest cluster judged by its sum of squared distance from cluster's centroid.

And M-step is:

$$\frac{\partial J}{\partial \mu_k} = 2 \sum_{i=1}^{m} w_{ik}(x^i - \mu_k) = 0$$

$$\Rightarrow \mu_k = \frac{\sum_{i=1}^{m} w_{ik} x^i}{\sum_{i=1}^{m} w_{ik}}$$

(6.3)

Which translates to recomputing the centroid of each cluster to reflect the new assignments.

Few things to note here:

- Since clustering algorithms including kmeans use distance-based measurements to determine the similarity between data points, it's recommended to standardize the data to have a mean of zero and a standard deviation of one since almost always the features in any dataset would have different units of measurements such as age vs income.
- Given kmeans iterative nature and the random initialization of centroids at the start of the algorithm, different initializations may lead to different clusters since kmeans algorithm may *stuck in a local optimum and may not converge to global optimum*. Therefore, it's recommended to run the algorithm using different initializations of centroids and pick the results of the run that that yielded the lower sum of squared distance.
- Assignment of examples isn't changing is the same thing as no change in within-cluster variation:

$$\frac{1}{m_k} \sum_{i=1}^{m_k} \|x^i - \mu_{c^k}\|^2 \tag{6.4}$$

Applications

kmeans algorithm is very popular and used in a variety of applications such as market segmentation, document clustering, image segmentation and image compression, etc. [13]. The goal usually when we undergo a cluster analysis is either:

1. Get a meaningful intuition of the structure of the data we're dealing with.
2. Cluster-then-predict where different models will be built for different subgroups if we believe there is a wide variation in the behaviors of different subgroups. An example of that is clustering patients into different subgroups and build a model for each subgroup to predict the probability of the risk of having heart attack.

Clustering on two cases:

- Geyser eruptions segmentation (2D dataset).
- Image compression.

Advantages of k-means

1. Relatively simple to implement.
2. Scales to large data sets.
3. Guarantees convergence.
4. Can warm-start the positions of centroids.
5. Easily adapts to new examples.
6. Generalizes to clusters of different shapes and sizes, such as elliptical clusters.

Disadvantages of k-means

1. Choosing manually.
2. Being dependent on initial values.
3. Clustering data of varying sizes and density.

4. Clustering outliers.
5. Scaling with number of dimensions.

Segment 1 - K-means method

Setting up for clustering analysis

```
In [2]: import numpy as np
        import pandas as pd

        import matplotlib.pyplot as plt

        import sklearn
        from sklearn.cluster import KMeans
        from mpl_toolkits.mplot3d import Axes3D
        from sklearn.preprocessing import scale
        import sklearn.metrics as sm
        from sklearn import datasets
        from sklearn.metrics import confusion_matrix, classification_report
```

```
In [3]: %matplotlib inline
        plt.figure(figsize=(7,4))
```

```
Out[3]: <matplotlib.figure.Figure at 0xc76e4e0>

        <matplotlib.figure.Figure at 0xc76e4e0>
```

```
In [4]: iris = datasets.load_iris()

        X = scale(iris.data)
        y = pd.DataFrame(iris.target)
        variable_names = iris.feature_names
        X[0:10,]
```

```
Out[4]: array([[-0.90068117,  1.03205722, -1.3412724 , -1.31297673],
               [-1.14301691, -0.1249576 ,  1.3412724 , -1.31297673],
               [-1.38535265,  0.33784833, -1.39813811, -1.31297673],
               [-1.50652052,  0.10644536, -1.2844067 , -1.31297673],
               [-1.02184904,  1.26346019, -1.3412724 , -1.31297673],
               [-0.53717756,  1.95766909, -1.17067529, -1.05003079],
               [-1.50652052,  0.80065426, -1.3412724 , -1.18150376],
               [-1.02184904,  0.80065426, -1.2844067 , -1.31297673],
               [-1.74885626, -0.35636057, -1.3412724 , -1.31297673],
               [-1.14301691,  0.10644536, -1.2844067 , -1.4444497 ]])
```

Building and running your model

```
In [5]: clustering = KMeans(n_clusters=3, random_state=5)

        clustering.fit(X)
```

```
Out[5]: KMeans(copy_x=True, init='k-means++', max_iter=300, n_clusters=3, n_init=10,
        n_jobs=1, precompute_distances='auto', random_state=5, tol=0.0001,
        verbose=0)
```

Plotting your model outputs

```
In [7]:  iris_df = pd.DataFrame(iris.data)
         iris_df.columns = ['Sepal_Length', 'Sepal_Width', 'Petal_Length', 'Petal_Width']
         y.columns = ['Targets']
```

```
In [8]:  color_theme = np.array(['darkgray', 'lightsalmon', 'powderblue'])

         plt.subplot(1,2,1)
         plt.scatter(x=iris_df.Petal_Length,y=iris_df.Petal_Width, c=color_theme[iris.target], s=50)
         plt.title('Ground Truth Classification')

         plt.subplot(1,2,2)
         plt.scatter(x=iris_df.Petal_Length,y=iris_df.Petal_Width, c=color_theme[clustering.labels_], s=50)
         plt.title('K-Means Classification')
```

```
Out[8]:  <matplotlib.text.Text at 0xcca8160>
```

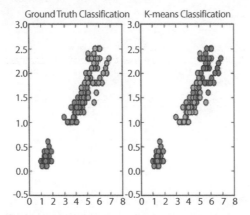

```
In [9]:  relabel = np.choose(clustering.labels_, [2, 0, 1]).astype(np.int64)
         plt.subplot(1,2,1)
         plt.scatter(x=iris_df.Petal_Length,y=iris_df.Petal_Width, c=color_theme[iris.target], s=50)
         plt.title('Ground Truth Classification')

         plt.subplot(1,2,2)
         plt.scatter(x=iris_df.Petal_Length,y=iris_df.Petal_Width, c=color_theme[relabel], s=50)
         plt.title('K-Means Classification')
```

```
Out[9]:  <matplotlib.text.Text at 0xcd8bf60>
```

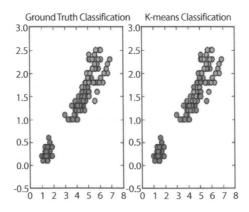

Evaluate your clustering results

```
In [10]: print(classification_report(y, relabel))
```

```
                precision    recall   f1-score    support

            0        1.00      1.00       1.00         50
            1        0.74      0.78       0.76         50
            2        0.77      0.72       0.74         50

avg / total          0.83      0.83       0.83        150
```

6.2   Hierarchial Methods

A **Hierarchical clustering** method works via grouping data into a tree of clusters. Hierarchical clustering begins by treating every data points as a separate cluster. Then, it repeatedly executes the subsequent steps:

1. Identify the 2 clusters which can be closest together, and
2. Merge the 2 maximum comparable clusters. We need to continue these steps until all the clusters are merged together.

In Hierarchical Clustering, the aim is to produce a hierarchical series of nested clusters. A diagram called **Dendrogram** (A Dendrogram is a tree-like diagram that statistics the sequences of merges or splits) graphically represents this hierarchy and is an inverted tree that describes the order in which factors are merged (bottom-up view) or cluster are break up (top-down view).

The basic method to generate hierarchical clustering are:

1. **Agglomerative:**
   Initially consider every data point as an **individual** Cluster and at every step, **merge** the nearest pairs of the cluster. (It is a bottom-up method). At first everydata set set is considered as individual entity or cluster. At every iteration, the clusters merge with different clusters until one cluster is formed.
2. **Divisive:**
   We can say that the Divisive Hierarchical clustering is precisely the **opposite** of the Agglomerative Hierarchical clustering. In Divisive Hierarchical clustering, we take into account all of the data points as a single cluster and in every iteration, we separate the data points from the clusters which aren't comparable. In the end, we are left with N clusters.

Working of Dendrogram in Hierarchical clustering

The dendrogram is a tree-like structure that is mainly used to store each step as a memory that the HC algorithm performs. In the dendrogram plot, the Y-axis shows the Euclidean distances between the data points, and the x-axis shows all the data points of the given dataset.

The working of the dendrogram can be explained using the below diagram:

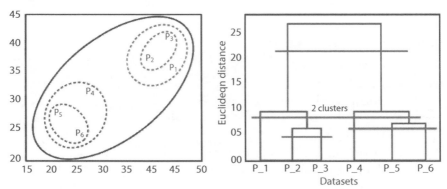

In the above diagram, the left part is showing how clusters are created in agglomerative clustering, and the right part is showing the corresponding dendrogram.

- As we have discussed above, firstly, the datapoints P2 and P3 combine together and form a cluster, correspondingly a dendrogram is created, which connects P2 and P3 with a rectangular shape. The hight is decided according to the Euclidean distance between the data points.
- In the next step, P5 and P6 form a cluster, and the corresponding dendrogram is created. It is higher than of previous, as the Euclidean distance between P5 and P6 is a little bit greater than the P2 and P3.
- Again, two new dendrograms are created that combine P1, P2, and P3 in one dendrogram, and P4, P5, and P6, in another dendrogram.
- At last, the final dendrogram is created that combines all the data points together.

We can cut the dendrogram tree structure at any level as per our requirement.

Applications of Hierarchical Clustering

1. US Senator Clustering through Twitter
2. Charting Evolution through Phylogenetic Trees
3. Tracking Viruses through Phylogenetic Trees

Advantages of Hierarchical Clustering

1. No apriori information about the number of clusters required.
2. Easy to implement and gives best result in some cases.

Disadvantages Of Hierarchical Clustering

1. Algorithm can never undo what was done previously.
2. Time complexity of at least O(n^2 log n) is required, where 'n' is the number of data points.
3. Based on the type of distance matrix chosen for merging different algorithms can suffer with one or more of the following:
   i) Sensitivity to noise and outliers
   ii) Breaking large clusters
   iii) Difficulty handling different sized clusters and convex shapes
4. No objective function is directly minimized
5. Sometimes it is difficult to identify the correct number of clusters by the dendogram.

Segment 2 - Hierarchial methods

Setting up for clustering analysis

```
In [1]:  import numpy as np
         import pandas as pd

         import scipy
         from scipy.cluster.hierarchy import dendrogram, linkage
         from scipy.cluster.hierarchy import fcluster
         from scipy.cluster.hierarchy import cophenet
         from scipy.spatial.distance import pdist

         import matplotlib.pyplot as plt
         from pylab import rcParams
         import seaborn as sb

         import sklearn
         from sklearn.cluster import AgglomerativeClustering
         import sklearn.metrics as sm
```

```
In [2]: np.set_printoptions(precision=4, suppress=True)
        plt.figure(figsize=(10, 3))
        %matplotlib inline
        plt.style.use('seaborn-whitegrid')
```

```
In [4]: address = 'C:/Users/Lillian Pierson/Desktop/Exercise Files/Ch06/06_02/mtcars.csv'
        cars = pd.read_csv(address)
        cars.columns = ['car_names','mpg','cyl','disp', 'hp', 'drat', 'wt', 'qsec', 'vs', 'am', 'gear', 'carb']

        X = cars.ix[:,(1,3,4,6)].values

        y = cars.ix[:,(9)].values
```

Decision tree models with CART

Machine Learning has been one of the most rapidly advancing topics to study in the field of Artificial Intelligence. There are a lot of algorithms under Machine Learning that have specifically gained popularity due to their transparent nature. One of them is the Decision Tree algorithm, popularly known as the Classification and Regression Trees (CART) algorithm.

The CART algorithm is a type of classification algorithm that is required to build a decision tree on the basis of Gini's impurity index. It is a basic machine learning algorithm and provides a wide variety of use cases. A statistician named Leo Breiman coined the phrase to describe Decision Tree algorithms that may be used for classification or regression predictive modeling issues.

CART is an umbrella word that refers to the following types of decision trees:

- **Classification Trees:** When the target variable is continuous, the tree is used to find the "class" into which the target variable is most likely to fall.
- **Regression trees:** These are used to forecast the value of a continuous variable.

Understanding Decision Tree

A decision Tree is a technique used for predictive analysis in the fields of statistics, data mining, and machine learning. The predictive model here is the decision tree and it is employed to progress from observations about an item that is represented by branches and finally concludes at the item's target value, which is represented in the leaves. Because of their readability and simplicity, decision trees are among the most popular machine learning methods.

The structure of a decision tree consists of three main parts: Root nodes, Internal Nodes and Leaf Nodes.

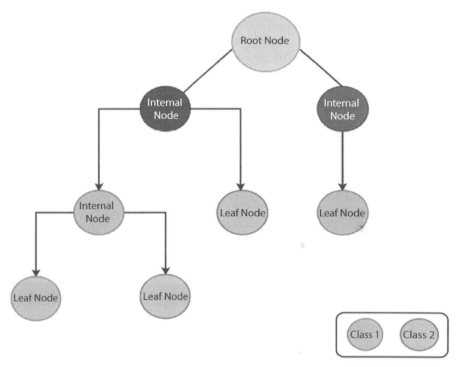

As shown in the diagram, the first node or the Root node is the training data set, followed by the internal node and leaf node. The internal node acts as the decision-making node, as this is the point at which the node divides further based on the best feature of the sub-group. The final node or the leaf node is the one that holds the decision.

CART Algorithm

In the decision tree, the nodes are split into subnodes on the basis of a threshold value of an attribute. The CART algorithm does that by searching for the best homogeneity for the subnodes, with the help of the Gini Index criterion.

The root node is taken as the training set and is split into two by considering the best attribute and threshold value. Further, the subsets are also split using the same logic. This continues till the last pure sub-set is found in the tree or the maximum number of leaves possible in that growing tree. This is also known as Tree Pruning.

Calculating Gini Index:

$$GI = \sum_{i=0}^{c} P_i(1 - P_i)$$

Which can be written as:

$$GI = 1 - \sum_{i=0}^{c} P_i^2$$

The formula of Gini Index
Here, c is the total number of classes and P is the probability of class i.

CART models from Data:

CART models are formed by picking input variables and evaluating split points on those variables until an appropriate tree is produced, according to Machine Learning Mastery.

Let us look at the steps required to create a Decision Tree using the CART algorithm:

- **Greedy Algorithm:**
  The input variables and the split points are selected through a greedy algorithm. Constructing a binary decision tree is a technique of splitting up the input space. A predetermined ending condition, such as a minimum number of training examples given to each leaf node of the tree, is used to halt tree building.

  The input space is divided using the Greedy approach. This is known as recursive binary splitting. This is a numerical method in which all of the values are aligned and several split points are tried and assessed using a cost function, with the split with the lowest cost being chosen.

  The cost function that is reduced to determine split points for regression predictive modeling problems is the sum squared error across all training samples that lie inside the rectangle:

  sum(y – p)^2

Here, y is the output of the training sample, and p is the estimated output for the rectangle.

The Gini index function is used for classification, and it indicates how "pure" the leaf nodes are. The formula for this is:

$$G = sum(pk * (1 - pk))$$

Here, G is the Gini index, pk is the proportion of training instances with class k in the rectangle.

- **Stopping Criterion:**

As it works its way down the tree with the training data, the recursive binary splitting method described above must know when to stop splitting.

The most frequent halting method is to utilize a minimum amount of training data allocated to each leaf node. If the count is less than a certain threshold, the split is rejected and the node is considered the last leaf node.

The number of training members is adjusted according to the dataset. It specifies how exact the tree will be to the training data.

- **Tree pruning:**

A decision tree's complexity is defined as the number of splits in the tree. Trees with fewer branches are recommended. They are simple to grasp and less prone to cluster the data.

Working through each leaf node in the tree and evaluating the effect of deleting it using a hold-out test set is the quickest and simplest pruning approach. Only leaf nodes are eliminated if the total cost function for the complete test set decreases. When no additional improvements can be achieved, then no more nodes should be removed.

More advanced pruning approaches, such as cost complexity pruning (also known as weakest link pruning), can be applied, in which a learning parameter (alpha) is used to determine whether nodes can be eliminated depending on the size of the sub-tree.

- **Data preparation for CART algorithm:**

No special data preparation is required for the CART algorithm.

Advantages of CART algorithm

1. The CART algorithm is nonparametric, thus it does not depend on information from a certain sort of distribution.
2. The CART algorithm combines both testings with a test data set and cross-validation to more precisely measure the goodness of fit.
3. CART allows one to utilize the same variables many times in various regions of the tree. This skill is capable of revealing intricate interdependencies between groups of variables.
4. Outliers in the input variables have no meaningful effect on CART.
5. One can loosen halting restrictions to allow decision trees to overgrow and then trim the tree down to its ideal size. This method reduces the likelihood of missing essential structure in the data set by terminating too soon.
6. To choose the input set of variables, CART can be used in combination with other prediction algorithms.

Disadvantage of CART algorithm:

1. A small change in the data can cause a large change in the structure of the decision tree causing instability.
2. For a Decision tree sometimes calculation can go far more complex compared to other algorithms.
3. Decision tree often involves higher time to train the model.
4. Decision tree training is relatively expensive as the complexity and time has taken are more.
5. The Decision Tree algorithm is inadequate for applying regression and predicting continuous values.

Using scipy to generate dendrograms

```
In [7]:  Z = linkage(X, 'ward')
```

```
In [8]:  dendrogram(Z, truncate_mode='lastp', p=12, leaf_rotation=45., leaf_font_size=15., show_contracted=True)

         plt.title('Truncated Hierarchical Clustering Dendrogram')
         plt.xlabel('Cluster Size')
         plt.ylabel('Distance')

         plt.axhline(y=500)
         plt.axhline(y=150)
         plt.show()
```

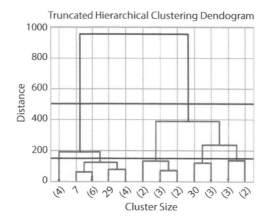

Generating hierarchical clusters

```
In [13]: k=2

         Hclustering = AgglomerativeClustering(n_clusters=k, affinity='euclidean', linkage='ward')
         Hclustering.fit(X)

         sm.accuracy_score(y, Hclustering.labels_)
Out[13]: 0.78125
```

```
In [14]: Hclustering = AgglomerativeClustering(n_clusters=k, affinity='euclidean', linkage='complete')
         Hclustering.fit(X)

         sm.accuracy_score(y, Hclustering.labels_)
Out[14]: 0.4375
```

```
In [15]: Hclustering = AgglomerativeClustering(n_clusters=k, affinity='euclidean', linkage='average')
         Hclustering.fit(X)

         sm.accuracy_score(y, Hclustering.labels_)
Out[15]: 0.78125
```

```
In [16]: Hclustering = AgglomerativeClustering(n_clusters=k, affinity='manhattan', linkage='average')
         Hclustering.fit(X)

         sm.accuracy_score(y, Hclustering.labels_)
Out[16]: 0.71875
```

6.3 Instance-Based Learning w/k-Nearest Neighbor

Instance-based learning

The Machine Learning systems which are categorized as instance-based learning are the systems that learn the training examples by heart and then generalizes to new instances based on some similarity measure [13]. It is called instance-based because it builds the hypotheses from the training instances [14]. It is also known as memory-based learning or lazy-learning. The time complexity of this algorithm depends upon the size of training data. The worst-case time complexity of this algorithm is O (n), where n is the number of training instances.

For example, If we were to create a spam filter with an instance-based learning algorithm, instead of just flagging emails that are already marked as spam emails, our spam filter would be programmed to also flag emails that are very similar to them. This requires a measure of resemblance between two emails. A similarity measure between two emails could be the same sender or the repetitive use of the same keywords or something else.

Advantages:

1. Instead of estimating for the entire instance set, local approximations can be made to the target function.
2. This algorithm can adapt to new data easily, one which is collected as we go.

Disadvantages:

1. Classification costs are high
2. Large amount of memory required to store the data, and each query involves starting the identification of a local model from scratch.

Some of the instance-based learning algorithms are :

1. K Nearest Neighbor (KNN)
2. Self-Organizing Map (SOM)
3. Learning Vector Quantization (LVQ)
4. Locally Weighted Learning (LWL)

K-Nearest Neighbor (KNN)

- K-Nearest Neighbour is one of the simplest Machine Learning algorithms based on Supervised Learning technique.
- K-NN algorithm assumes the similarity between the new case/data and available cases and put the new case into the category that is most similar to the available categories.

- K-NN algorithm stores all the available data and classifies a new data point based on the similarity. This means when new data appears then it can be easily classified into a well suite category by using K- NN algorithm.
- K-NN algorithm can be used for Regression as well as for Classification but mostly it is used for the Classification problems.
- K-NN is a **non-parametric algorithm**, which means it does not make any assumption on underlying data.
- It is also called a **lazy learner algorithm** because it does not learn from the training set immediately instead it stores the dataset and at the time of classification, it performs an action on the dataset.
- KNN algorithm at the training phase just stores the dataset and when it gets new data, then it classifies that data into a category that is much similar to the new data.
- **Example:** Suppose, we have an image of a creature that looks similar to cat and dog, but we want to know either it is a cat or dog. So for this identification, we can use the KNN algorithm, as it works on a similarity measure. Our KNN model will find the similar features of the new data set to the cats and dogs images and based on the most similar features it will put it in either cat or dog category.

KNN Classifier

Input value   Predicted Output

Why do we need a K-NN Algorithm?

Suppose there are two categories, i.e., Category A and Category B, and we have a new data point x1, so this data point will lie in which of these categories. To solve this type of problem, we need a K-NN algorithm. With the help of K-NN, we can easily identify the category or class of a particular dataset. Consider the below diagram:

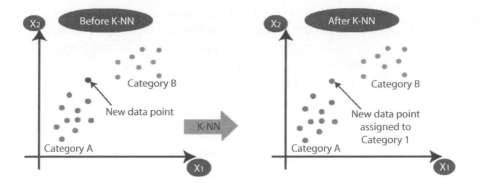

How does K-NN work?

The K-NN working can be explained on the basis of the below algorithm:

- **Step-1:** Select the number K of the neighbors
- **Step-2:** Calculate the Euclidean distance of **K number of neighbors**
- **Step-3:** Take the K nearest neighbors as per the calculated Euclidean distance.
- **Step-4:** Among these k neighbors, count the number of the data points in each category.
- **Step-5:** Assign the new data points to that category for which the number of the neighbor is maximum.
- **Step-6:** Our model is ready.

Suppose we have a new data point and we need to put it in the required category. Consider the below image:

- Firstly, we will choose the number of neighbors, so we will choose the k=5.

- Next, we will calculate the **Euclidean distance** between the data points. The Euclidean distance is the distance between two points, which we have already studied in geometry. It can be calculated as:

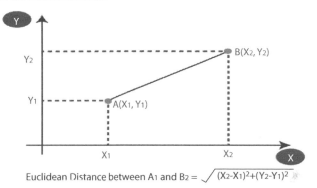

Euclidean Distance between A₁ and B₂ = $\sqrt{(X_2-X_1)^2+(Y_2-Y_1)^2}$

- By calculating the Euclidean distance we got the nearest neighbors, as three nearest neighbors in category A and two nearest neighbors in category B. Consider the below image:

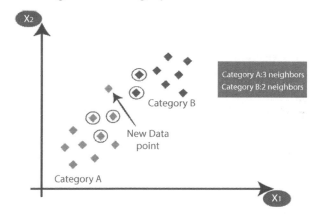

- As we can see the 3 nearest neighbors are from category A, hence this new data point must belong to category A.

How to select the value of K in the K-NN Algorithm?

Below are some points to remember while selecting the value of K in the K-NN algorithm:

- There is no particular way to determine the best value for "K", so we need to try some values to find the best out of them. The most preferred value for K is 5.

- A very low value for K such as K=1 or K=2, can be noisy and lead to the effects of outliers in the model.
- Large values for K are good, but it may find some difficulties.

Applications of KNN

1. Text mining
2. Agriculture
3. Finance
4. Medical
5. Facial recognition
6. Recommendation systems (Amazon, Hulu, Netflix, etc)

Advantages of KNN Algorithm:

- It is simple to implement.
- It is robust to the noisy training data
- It can be more effective if the training data is large.

Disadvantages of KNN Algorithm:

- Always needs to determine the value of K which may be complex some time.
- The computation cost is high because of calculating the distance between the data points for all the training samples.

Segment 3 - Instance-based learning w/ k-Nearest Neighbor

Setting up for classification analysis

```
In [2]: import numpy as np
        import pandas as pd
        import scipy

        import matplotlib.pyplot as plt
        from pylab import rcParams

        import urllib

        import sklearn
        from sklearn.neighbors import KNeighborsClassifier
        from sklearn import neighbors
        from sklearn import preprocessing
        from sklearn.cross_validation import train_test_split
        from sklearn import metrics
```

```
In [3]:  np.set_printoptions(precision=4, suppress=True)
         %matplotlib inline
         rcParams['figure.figsize'] = 7, 4
         plt.style.use('seaborn-whitegrid')
```

Splitting your data into test and training datasets

```
In [4]:  address = 'C:/Users/Lillian Pierson/Desktop/Exercise Files/Ch06/06_03/mtcars.csv'
         cars = pd.read_csv(address)
         cars.columns = ['car_names','mpg','cyl','disp', 'hp', 'drat', 'wt', 'qsec', 'vs', 'am', 'gear', 'carb']

         X_prime = cars.ix[:,(1,3,4,6)].values

         y = cars.ix[:,9].values
```

```
In [5]:  X = preprocessing.scale(X_prime)
```

```
In [7]:  X_train, X_test, y_train, y_test = train_test_split(X, y, test_size=.33, random_state=17)
```

Building and training your model with training data

```
In [9]:  clf = neighbors.KNeighborsClassifier()

         clf.fit(X_train, y_train)
         print(clf)

         KNeighborsClassifier(algorithm='auto', leaf_size=30, metric='minkowski',
                   metric_params=None, n_jobs=1, n_neighbors=5, p=2,
                   weights='uniform')
```

Evaluating your model's predictions against the test dataset

```
In [13]: y_expect = y_test
         y_pred = clf.predict(X_test)

         print(metrics.classification_report(y_expect, y_pred))

                      precision    recall  f1-score   support

                   0       0.71      1.00      0.83         5
                   1       1.00      0.67      0.80         6

         avg / total       0.87      0.82      0.82        11
```

References

1. Driver and Kroeber (1932). "Quantitative Expression of Cultural Relationships". University of California Publications in American Archaeology and Ethnology. Quantitative Expression of Cultural Relationships: 211–256 – via http://dpg.lib.berkeley.edu.
2. Zubin, Joseph (1938). "A technique for measuring like-mindedness". The Journal of Abnormal and Social Psychology. 33 (4): 508–516. doi:10.1037/h0055441. ISSN 0096-851X.
3. Tryon, Robert C. (1939). Cluster Analysis: Correlation Profile and Orthometric (factor) Analysis for the Isolation of Unities in Mind and Personality. Edwards Brothers.
4. Cattell, R. B. (1943). "The description of personality: Basic traits resolved into clusters". Journal of Abnormal and Social Psychology. 38 (4): 476–506. doi:10.1037/h0054116.
5. Estivill-Castro, Vladimir (20 June 2002). "Why so many clustering algorithms – A Position Paper". ACM SIGKDD Explorations Newsletter. 4 (1): 65–75.
6. https://www.javatpoint.com/clustering-in-machine-learning#:~:text=Clustering%20or%20cluster%20analysis%20is,consisting%20of%20similar%20data%20points.
7. https://www.geeksforgeeks.org/clustering-in-machine-learning/
8. https://machinelearningmastery.com/clustering-algorithms-with-python/
9. https://www.analyticsvidhya.com/blog/2016/11/an-introduction-to-clustering-and-different-methods-of-clustering/
10. Prakash K.B. Content extraction studies using total distance algorithm, 2017, Proceedings of the 2016 2nd International Conference on Applied and Theoretical Computing and Communication Technology, iCATccT 2016, 10.1109/ICATCCT.2016.7912085
11. Prakash K.B. Mining issues in traditional indian web documents,2015, Indian Journal of Science and Technology, 8(32), 10.17485/ijst/2015/v8i1/77056
12. Prakash K.B., Rajaraman A., Lakshmi M. Complexities in developing multilingual on-line courses in the Indian context, 2017, Proceedings of the 2017 International Conference On Big Data Analytics and Computational Intelligence, ICBDACI 2017, 8070860, 339-342, 10.1109/ICBDACI.2017.8070860
13. Prakash K.B., Kumar K.S., Rao S.U.M. Content extraction issues in online web education, 2017,Proceedings of the 2016 2nd International Conference on Applied and Theoretical Computing and Communication Technology, iCATccT 2016, 7912086, 680-685, 10.1109/ICATCCT.2016.7912086
14. Prakash K.B., Rajaraman A., Perumal T., Kolla P. Foundations to frontiers of big data analytics, 2016, Proceedings of the 2016 2nd International Conference on Contemporary Computing and Informatics, IC3I 2016, 7917968,242-247, 10.1109/IC3I.2016.7917968

Network Analysis with NetworkX

Association Rules Models with Apriori

Apriori [1] is an algorithm for frequent item set mining and association rule learning over relational databases. It proceeds by identifying the frequent individual items in the database and extending them to larger and larger item sets as long as those item sets appear sufficiently often in the database [1]. The frequent item sets determined by Apriori can be used to determine association rules which highlight general trends in the database: this has applications in domains such as market basket analysis [2].

The Apriori algorithm was proposed by Agrawal and Srikant in 1994. Apriori is designed to operate on databases containing transactions (for example, collections of items bought by customers, or details of a website frequentation or IP addresses [2]). Other algorithms are designed for finding association rules in data having no transactions (Winepi and Minepi), or having no timestamps (DNA sequencing). Each transaction is seen as a set of items (an itemset).

Given athreshold, the Apriori algorithm identifies the item sets which are subsets of at least transactions in the database.

Apriori uses a "bottom up" approach, where frequent subsets are extended one item at a time (a step known as candidate generation), and groups of candidates are tested against the data. The algorithm terminates when no further successful extensions are found.

Apriori uses breadth-first search and a Hash tree structure to count candidate item setsefficiently. It generates candidate item sets of length from item sets of length. Then it prunes the candidates which have an infrequent sub pattern. According to the downward closure lemma, the candidate set contains all frequent-length item sets. After that, it scans the transaction database to determine frequent item sets among the candidates.

Kolla Bhanu Prakash. Data Science Handbook: A Practical Approach, (157–172) © 2022 Scrivener Publishing LLC

The pseudo code for the algorithm is given below for a transaction database, and a support threshold of. Usual set theoretic notation is employed, though note that is a multiset. is the candidate set for level. At each step, the algorithm is assumed to generate the candidate sets from the large item sets of the preceding level, heeding the downward closure lemma. accesses a field of the data structure that represents candidate set, which is initially assumed to be zero. Many details are omitted below, usually the most important part of the implementation is the data structure used for storing the candidate sets, and counting their frequencies.

Apriori (T, ε)
$L_1 \leftarrow$ {large 1 - itemsets}
$k \leftarrow 2$
while L_{k-1} **is not** empty
    $C_k \leftarrow$ Apriori_gen (L_{k-1}, k)
for transactions t **in** T
        $D_t \leftarrow \{c \text{ in } C_k : c \subseteq t\}$
for candidates c **in** D_t
            count $[c] \leftarrow$ count $[c] + 1$

$L_k \leftarrow \{c \text{ in } C_k : \text{count } [c] \geq \varepsilon\}$
$k \leftarrow k + 1$

return Union (L_k)

Apriori_gen (L, k)
    result $\leftarrow$ list ()
for all $p \subseteq L, q \subseteq L$ **where** $p_1 = q_1, p_2 = q_2, ..., p_{k-2} = q_{k-2}$ and $p_{k-1} < q_{k-1}$
        $c = p \cup \{q_{k-1}\}$
if $u \subseteq c$ **for all** u **in** L
        result.add (c)
return result

Advantages of the Apriori algorithm

1. It is an easy-to-implement and easy-to-understand algorithm.
2. It can be used on large itemsets.

Disadvantages of the Apriori Algorithm

1. Sometimes, it may need to find a large number of candidate rules which can be computationally expensive.
2. Calculating support is also expensive because it has to go through the entire database.

7.1   Working with Graph Objects

Segment 2 - Working with Graph Objects

```
In [1]: ! pip install networkx
```

```
Requirement already satisfied (use --upgrade to upgrade): networkx in c:\program files\anaconda2\lib\site-pack
ages
Requirement already satisfied (use --upgrade to upgrade): decorator>=3.4.0 in c:\program files\anaconda2\lib\s
ite-packages (from networkx)
```

```
You are using pip version 8.1.2, however version 9.0.1 is available.
You should consider upgrading via the 'python -m pip install --upgrade pip' command.
```

```
In [2]: import numpy as np
        import pandas as pd

        import matplotlib.pyplot as plt
        from pylab import rcParams
        import seaborn as sb

        import networkx as nx
```

```
In [3]: %matplotlib inline
        rcParams['figure.figsize'] = 5, 4
        sb.set_style('whitegrid')
```

Creating Graph Objects

```
In [4]: G = nx.Graph()
        nx.draw(G)
```

```
In [5]: G.add_node(1)
        nx.draw(G)
```

```
In [6]: G.add_nodes_from([2,3,4,5,6,8,9,12,15,16])
        nx.draw(G)
```

In [7]:
```
G.add_edges_from([(2,4),(2,6),(2,8),(2,12),(2,16),(3,6),(3,9),  (3,12),(3,15),(4,8),(4,12),(4,16),(6,12),(6,16)])
nx.draw(G)
```

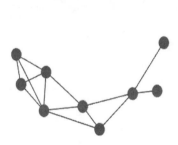

The Basics about Drawing Graph Objects

In [8]:
```
nx.draw_circular(G)
```

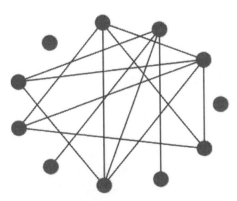

```
In [9]: nx.draw_spring(G)
```

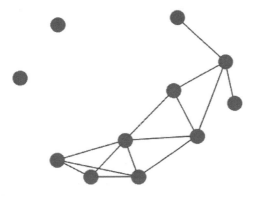

Labeling and Coloring Your Graph Plots

```
In [10]: nx.draw_circular(G, node_color='bisque', with_labels=True)
```

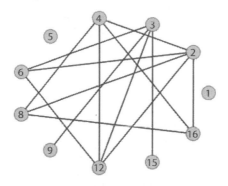

```
In [11]: G.remove_node(1)
         nx.draw_circular(G, node_color='bisque', with_labels=True)
```

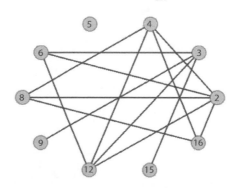

Identifying Graph Properties

In [12]:
```
sum_stats = nx.info(G)
print sum_stats
```

```
Name:
Type: Graph
Number of nodes: 10
Number of edges: 14
Average degree:   2.8000
```

In [13]:
```
print nx.degree(G)
```

```
{2: 5, 3: 4, 4: 4, 5: 0, 6: 3, 8: 3, 9: 1, 12: 4, 15: 1, 16: 3}
```

Using Graph Generators

In [14]:
```
G = nx.complete_graph(25)
nx.draw(G, node_color='bisque', with_labels=True)
```

In [15]:
```
G = nx.gnc_graph(7, seed=25)
nx.draw(G, node_color='bisque', with_labels=True)
```

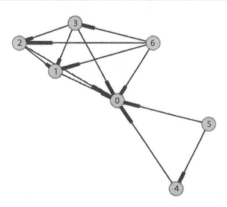

```
In [16]: ego_G = nx.ego_graph(G, 3, radius=5)
         nx.draw(G, node_color='bisque', with_labels=True)
```

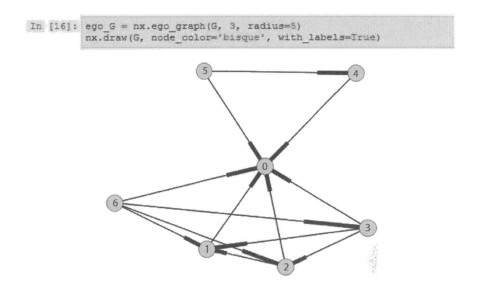

7.2   Simulating a Social Network (ie; Directed Network Analysis)

Neural Networks with a Perceptron

In the Artificial Neural Network(ANN), the perceptron is a convenient model of a biological neuron, it was the early algorithm of binary classifiers in supervised machine learning. The purpose behind the designing of the perceptron model was to incorporate visual inputs, organizing subjects or captions into one of two classes and dividing classes through a line [3, 4].

Classification is one most important elements of machine learning, especially in image transformation [5]. Machine learning algorithms exploit various means of processing to identify and analyze patterns [6]. Proceed with classification tasks, the perceptron algorithms analyze classes and patterns in order to attain the linear separation between the various class of objects and correspond patterns obtained from numerical or visual input data [7].

What is the Perceptron Model, Precisely?

Talking in reference to the history of the perceptron model, it was first developed at Cornell Aeronautical Laboratory, United States, in 1957 for machine-implemented image recognition. The machine was first ever created artificial neural networks [8].

At the same time, the perceptron algorithm was expected to be the most notable innovation of artificial intelligence, it was surrounded with high hopes but technical constraints step out the door that turns out with the conclusion that single-layered perceptron model only applicable for the classes which are linearly separable [9].

Later on, discovered that multi-layered perceptron algorithms enabled us to classify non linearly separable groups [10].

Till now, you must have got the core idea of studying the perceptron model, let's move one step closer to target, **kinds of perceptron models;**

1. Single-layered perceptron model, and
2. Multi-layered perceptron model.

Defining them in deep!!!

1. **Single-layered perceptron model**

    A single-layer perceptron model includes a feed-forward network depends on a threshold transfer function in its model [11]. It is the easiest type of artificial neural network that able to analyze only linearly separable objects with binary outcomes (target) i.e. 1, and 0.

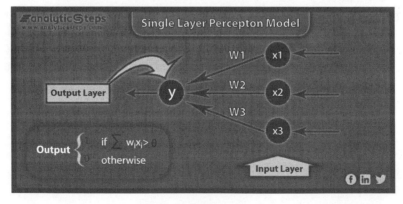

Single-Layered Perceptron Model

    If you talk about the functioning of the single-layered perceptron model, its algorithm doesn't have previous information, so initially, weights are allocated inconstantly, then the algorithm adds up all the weighted inputs, if the added value is more than some pre-determined value (or, threshold value) then single-layered perceptron is stated as activated and delivered output as +1 [12].

In simple words, multiple input values feed up to the perceptron model, model executes with input values, and if the estimated value is the same as the required output, then the model performance is found out to be satisfied, therefore weights demand no changes. In fact, if the model doesn't meet the required result then few changes are made up in weights to minimize errors [13].

2. **Multi-layered perceptron model**

A multi-layered perceptron model has a structure similar to a single-layered perceptron model with more number of hidden layers. It is also termed as a **Backpropagation algorithm**. It executes in two stages; the **forward stage** and the **backward stages** [14].

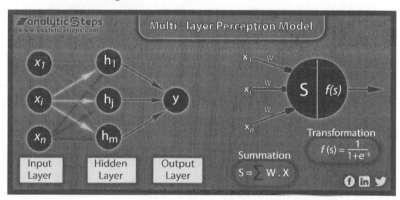

Multi-Layered Perceptron Model

In the forward stage, activation functions are originated from the input layer to the output layer, and in the backward stage, the error between the actual observed value and demanded given value is originated backward in the output layer for modifying weights and bias values.

In simple terms, multi-layered perceptron can be treated as a network of numerous artificial neurons overhead varied layers, the activation function is no longer linear, instead, non-linear activation functions such as Sigmoid functions, TanH, ReLU activation Functions, etc are deployed for execution [15].

Applications

- Classification.
- Encode Database (Multilayer Perceptron).
- Monitor Access Data (Multilayer Perceptron).

Advantages

- Neural networks are flexible and can be used for both regression and classification problems. Any data which can be made numeric can be used in the model, as neural network is a mathematical model with approximation functions.
- Neural networks are good to model with nonlinear data with large number of inputs; for example, images. It is reliable in an approach of tasks involving many features. It works by splitting the problem of classification into a layered network of simpler elements.
- Once trained, the predictions are pretty fast.
- Neural networks can be trained with any number of inputs and layers.
- Neural networks work best with more data points.

Disdvantages

- Neural networks are black boxes, meaning we cannot know how much each independent variable is influencing the dependent variables.
- It is computationally very expensive and time consuming to train with traditional CPUs.
- Neural networks depend a lot on training data. This leads to the problem of over-fitting and generalization. The mode relies more on the training data and may be tuned to the data.

Segment 3 - Simulating a Social Network (ie; Directed Network Analysis)

```
In [1]:  import numpy as np
         import pandas as pd

         import networkx as nx

         import matplotlib.pyplot as plt
         from pylab import rcParams
         import seaborn as sb
```

```
In [2]:  %matplotlib inline
         rcParams['figure.figsize'] = 5, 4
         sb.set_style('whitegrid')
```

Generating a Graph Object and Edgelist

```
In [3]:  DG = nx.gn_graph(7, seed=25)

         for line in nx.generate_edgelist(DG, data=False): print(line)
         1 0
         2 0
         3 2
         4 3
         5 0
         6 4
```

Assigning Attributes to Nodes

```
In [4]:  print DG.node[0]

         {}
```

```
In [5]:  DG.node[0]['name'] = 'Alice'
```

```
In [6]:  print DG.node[0]

         {'name': 'Alice'}
```

```
In [7]:  DG.node[1]['name'] = 'Bob'
         DG.node[2]['name'] = 'Claire'
         DG.node[3]['name'] = 'Dennis'
         DG.node[4]['name'] = 'Esther'
         DG.node[5]['name'] = 'Frank'
         DG.node[6]['name'] = 'George'
```

```
In [10]:  DG.add_nodes_from([(0,{'age':25}),(1,{'age':31}),(2,{'age':18}),(3,{'age':47}),(4,{'age':22}),
                             (5,{'age':23}),(6,{'age':50})])
          print DG.node[0]

          {'age': 25, 'name': 'Alice'}
```

```
In [11]:  DG.node[0]['gender'] = 'f'
          DG.node[1]['gender'] = 'm'
          DG.node[2]['gender'] = 'f'
          DG.node[3]['gender'] = 'm'
          DG.node[4]['gender'] = 'f'
          DG.node[5]['gender'] = 'm'
          DG.node[6]['gender'] = 'm'
```

Visualize Your Network Graph

```
In [13]:  nx.draw_circular(DG, node_color='bisque', with_labels=True)
```

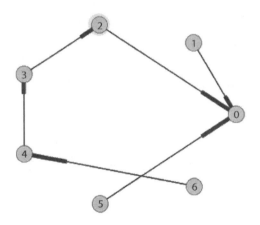

```
In [14]:  labeldict = {0: 'Alice',1:'Bob',2:'Claire',3:'Dennis',4:'Esther',5:'Frank',6:'George'}
          nx.draw_circular(DG, labels=labeldict, node_color='bisque', with_labels=True)
```

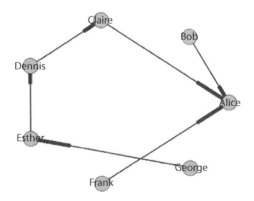

```
In [15]: G = DG.to_undirected()
```

```
In [16]: nx.draw_spectral(G, labels=labeldict, node_color='bisque', with_labels=True)
```

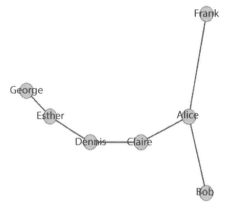

7.3   Analyzing a Social Network

Segment 4 - Analyzing a Social Network

```
In [1]: import numpy as np
        import pandas as pd

        import matplotlib.pyplot as plt
        from pylab import rcParams
        import seaborn as sb

        import networkx as nx
```

```
In [2]: %matplotlib inline
        rcParams['figure.figsize'] = 5, 4
        sb.set_style('whitegrid')
```

```
In [3]: DG = nx.gn_graph(7, seed = 25)

        for line in nx.generate_edgelist(DG, data=False):
            print(line)

        DG.node[0]['name'] = 'Alice'
        DG.node[1]['name'] = 'Bob'
        DG.node[2]['name'] = 'Claire'
        DG.node[3]['name'] = 'Dennis'
        DG.node[4]['name'] = 'Esther'
        DG.node[5]['name'] = 'Frank'
        DG.node[6]['name'] = 'George'
```

```
1 0
2 0
3 2
4 3
5 0
6 4
```

In [4]: `G = DG.to_undirected()`

In [5]: `print nx.info(DG)`

```
Name: gn_graph(7)
Type: DiGraph
Number of nodes: 7
Number of edges: 6
Average in degree:   0.8571
Average out degree:   0.8571
```

Considering Degrees in a Social Network

In [6]: `DG.degree()`

Out[6]: `{0: 3, 1: 1, 2: 2, 3: 2, 4: 2, 5: 1, 6: 1}`

Identifying Successor Nodes

In [7]: `nx.draw_circular(DG, node_color='bisque', with_labels=True)`

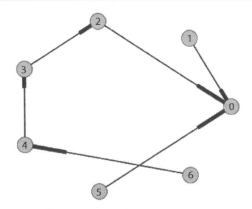

```
In [8]: DG.successors(3)
Out[8]: [2]


In [9]: DG.neighbors(4)
Out[9]: [3]


In [10]: G.neighbors(4)
Out[10]: [3, 6]
```

References

1. Piatetsky-Shapiro, Gregory (1991), Discovery, analysis, and presentation of strong rules, in Piatetsky-Shapiro, Gregory; and Frawley, William J.; eds., Knowledge Discovery in Databases, AAAI/MIT Press, Cambridge, MA.
2. Agrawal, R.; Imieliński, T.; Swami, A. (1993). "Mining association rules between sets of items in large databases". Proceedings of the 1993 ACM SIGMOD international conference on Management of data - SIGMOD '93. p. 207. CiteSeerX 10.1.1.40.6984. doi:10.1145/170035.170072. ISBN 978-0897915922. S2CID 490415.
3. Garcia, Enrique (2007). "Drawbacks and solutions of applying association rule mining in learning management systems" (PDF). Sci2s.
4. "Data Mining Techniques: Top 5 to Consider". Precisely. 2021-11-08. Retrieved 2021-12-10.
5. "16 Data Mining Techniques: The Complete List - Talend". Talend - A Leader in Data Integration & Data Integrity. Retrieved 2021-12-10.
6. "What are Association Rules in Data Mining (Association Rule Mining)?". SearchBusinessAnalytics. Retrieved 2021-12-10.
7. "Drawbacks and solutions of applying association rule mining in learning management systems". ResearchGate. Retrieved 2021-12-10.
8. Tan, Pang-Ning; Michael, Steinbach; Kumar, Vipin (2005). "Chapter 6. Association Analysis: Basic Concepts and Algorithms" (PDF). Introduction to Data Mining. Addison-Wesley. ISBN 978-0-321-32136-7.
9. Jian Pei; Jiawei Han; Lakshmanan, L.V.S. (2001). "Mining frequent itemsets with convertible constraints". Proceedings 17th International Conference on Data Engineering. pp. 433–442. CiteSeerX 10.1.1.205.2150. doi:10.1109/ICDE.2001.914856. ISBN 978-0-7695-1001-9. S2CID 1080975.

10. Agrawal, Rakesh; and Srikant, Ramakrishnan; Fast algorithms for mining association rules in large databases Archived 2015-02-25 at the Wayback Machine, in Bocca, Jorge B.; Jarke, Matthias; and Zaniolo, Carlo; editors, Proceedings of the 20th International Conference on Very Large Data Bases (VLDB), Santiago, Chile, September 1994, pages 487-499

11. Prakash K.B. Content extraction studies using total distance algorithm, 2017, Proceedings of the 2016 2nd International Conference on Applied and Theoretical Computing and Communication Technology, iCATccT 2016, 10.1109/ICATCCT.2016.7912085

12. Prakash K.B. Mining issues in traditional indian web documents, 2015, Indian Journal of Science and Technology, 8(32), 10.17485/ijst/2015/v8i1/77056

13. Prakash K.B., Rajaraman A., Lakshmi M. Complexities in developing multilingual on-line courses in the Indian context, 2017, Proceedings of the 2017 International Conference On Big Data Analytics and Computational Intelligence, ICBDACI 2017, 8070860, 339-342, 10.1109/ICBDACI.2017.8070860

14. Prakash K.B., Kumar K.S., Rao S.U.M. Content extraction issues in online web education, 2017, Proceedings of the 2016 2nd International Conference on Applied and Theoretical Computing and Communication Technology, iCATccT 2016, 7912086, 680-685, 10.1109/ICATCCT.2016.7912086

15. Prakash K.B., Rajaraman A., Perumal T., Kolla P. Foundations to frontiers of big data analytics, 2016, Proceedings of the 2016 2nd International Conference on Contemporary Computing and Informatics, IC3I 2016, 7917968, 242-247, 10.1109/IC3I.2016.7917968

Basic Algorithmic Learning

8.1 Linear Regression

In the most simple words, **Linear Regression** is the supervised Machine Learning model in which the **model finds the best fit linear line between the independent and dependent variable** i.e it finds the linear relationship between the dependent and independent variable [1].

Linear Regression is of two types: **Simple and Multiple. Simple Linear Regression** is where only one independent variable is present and the model has to find the linear relationship of it with the dependent variable [2].

Whereas, In **Multiple Linear Regression** there are more than one independent variables for the model to find the relationship [3].

Equation of Simple Linear Regression, where bo is the intercept, b1 is coefficient or slope, x is the independent variable and y is the dependent variable [4].

$$y = b_o + b_1 x$$

Equation of Multiple Linear Regression, where bo is the intercept, $b_1, b_2, b_3, b_4 \ldots, b_n$ are coefficients or slopes of the independent variables $x_1, x_2, x_3, x_4 \ldots, x_n$ and y is the dependent variable [5].

$$y = b_o + b_1 x_1 + b_2 x_2 + b_3 x_3 \ldots + b_n x_n$$

A Linear Regression model's main aim is to find the best fit linear line and the optimal values of intercept and coefficients such that the error is minimized. Error is the difference between the actual value and Predicted value and the goal is to reduce this difference [6].

Let's understand this with the help of a diagram.

Kolla Bhanu Prakash. Data Science Handbook: A Practical Approach, (173–196) © 2022 Scrivener Publishing LLC

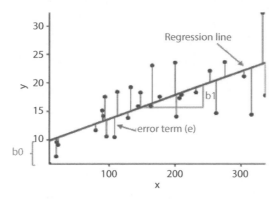

In the above diagram,

- x is our dependent variable which is plotted on the x-axis and y is the dependent variable which is plotted on the y-axis.
- Black dots are the data points i.e the actual values.
- b_o is the intercept which is 10 and b_1 is the slope of the x variable.
- The blue line is the best fit line predicted by the model i.e the predicted values lie on the blue line.

The vertical distance between the data point and the regression line is known as error or residual. Each data point has one residual and the sum of all the differences is known as **the Sum of Residuals/Errors [7].**

Mathematical Approach:

Residual/Error = Actual values – Predicted Values
Sum of Residuals/Errors = Sum(Actual- Predicted Values)
Square of Sum of Residuals/Errors = (Sum(Actual- Predicted Values))^2
i.e

$$\sum e_i^2 = \sum (Y_i - \hat{Y}_i)^2$$

Assumptions of Linear Regression

The basic assumptions of Linear Regression are as follows:

1. **Linearity**
   It states that the dependent variable Y should be linearly related to independent variables. This assumption can be checked by plotting a scatter plot between both variables.

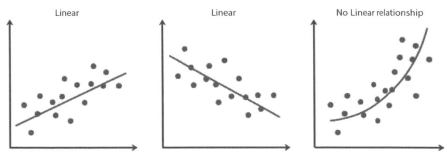

Linear   Linear   No Linear relationship

Copyright 2014. Laerd Statistics.

2. Normality

The X and Y variables should be normally distributed. Histograms, KDE plots, Q-Q plots can be used to check the Normality assumption.

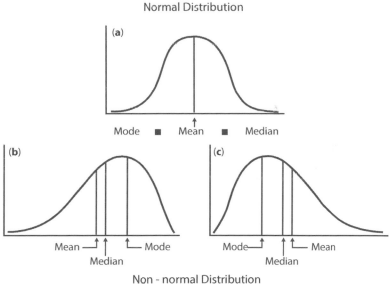

Normal Distribution

(a)

Mode ■ Mean ■ Median

(b)

(c)

Mean — Mode   Mode — Mean

Median   Median

Non - normal Distribution

Negatively Skewed   Positively Skewed

3. Homoscedasticity

The variance of the error terms should be constant i.e the spread of residuals should be constant for all values of X. This assumption can be checked by plotting a residual plot. If the assumption is violated then the points will form a funnel shape otherwise they will be constant.

Residuals that show an increasing trend

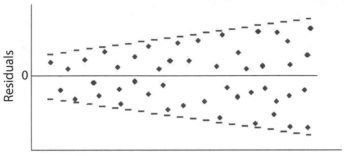

Residuals that show a decreasing trend

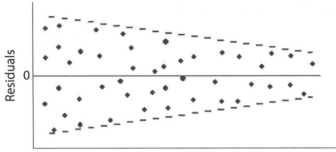

Constant variance

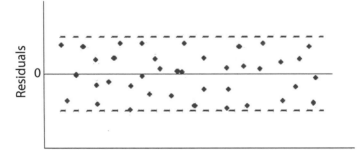

4. Independence/No Multicollinearity

The variables should be independent of each other i.e no correlation should be there between the independent variables. To check the assumption, we can use a correlation matrix or VIF score. If the VIF score is greater than 5 then the variables are highly correlated [8].

In the below image, a high correlation is present between x5 and x6 variables.

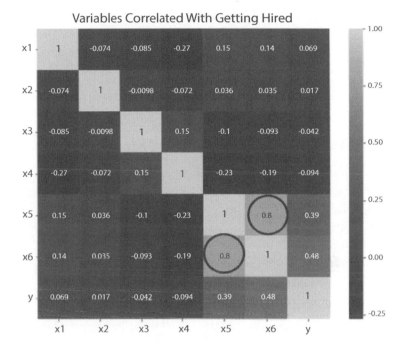

5. The **error terms should be normally distributed**. Q-Q plots and Histograms can be used to check the distribution of error terms.

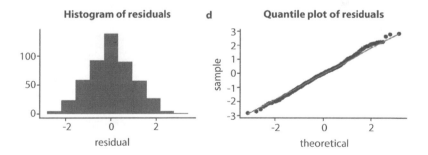

6. **No Autocorrelation**

   The error terms should be independent of each other. Autocorrelation can be tested using the Durbin Watson test. The null hypothesis assumes that there is no autocorrelation. The value of the test lies between 0 to 4. If the value of the test is 2 then there is no autocorrelation [9].

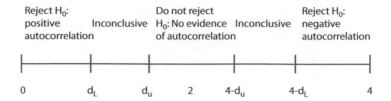

How to deal with the Violation of any of the Assumption

The Violation of the assumptions leads to a decrease in the accuracy of the model therefore the predictions are not accurate and error is also high. **For example,** if the Independence assumption is violated then the relationship between the independent and dependent variable can not be determined precisely [10].

There are various methods are techniques available to deal with the violation of the assumptions. Let's discuss some of them below.

Violation of Normality Assumption of Variables or Error Terms

To treat this problem, we can transform the variables to the normal distribution using various transformation functions such as log transformation, Reciprocal, or Box-Cox Transformation [11]. All the functions are discussed in this article of mine: How to transform into Normal Distribution

Violation of MultiCollineraity Assumption

It can be dealt with by:

- Doing nothing (if there is no major difference in the accuracy)
- Removing some of the highly correlated independent variables.
- Deriving a new feature by linearly combining the independent variables, such as adding them together or performing some mathematical operation.
- Performing an analysis designed for highly correlated variables, such as principal components analysis [12].

Evaluation Metrics for Regression Analysis

To understand the performance of the Regression model performing model evaluation is necessary. Some of the Evaluation metrics used for Regression analysis are:

1. R squared or Coefficient of Determination

The most commonly used metric for model evaluation in regression analysis is R squared. It can be defined as a Ratio of variation to the Total Variation. The value of R squared lies between 0 to 1, the value closer to 1 the better the model [13].

$$R^2 = 1 - \frac{SS_{RES}}{SS_{TOT}} = \frac{\sum_i (y_i - \hat{y}_i)^2}{\sum_i (y_i - \overline{y}_i)^2}$$

where SSRES is the Residual Sum of squares and SSTOT is the Total Sum of squares

2. Adjusted R squared

It is the improvement to R squared. The problem/drawback with R2 is that as the features increase, the value of R2 also increases which gives the illusion of a good model. So the Adjusted R2 solves the drawback of R2. It only considers the features which are important for the model and shows the real improvement of the model. Adjusted R2 is always lower than R2.

$$R^2 \text{adjusted} = 1 - \frac{(1 - R^2)(N - 1)}{N - p - 1}$$

where

R^2 = sample R-square
p = Number of predictors
N = Total sample size.

3. Mean Squared Error (MSE)

Another Common metric for evaluation is Mean squared error which is the mean of the squared difference of actual vs predicted values [14].

$$MSE = \frac{1}{n} \sum \underbrace{\left(y - \breve{y}\right)^2}_{\substack{\text{The square of the difference} \\ \text{between actual and} \\ \text{predicted}}}$$

4. Root Mean Squared Error (RMSE)

It is the root of MSE i.e Root of the mean difference of Actual and Predicted values. RMSE penalizes the large errors whereas MSE doesn't [15].

$$\text{RMSE} = \sqrt{\frac{1}{n}\sum_{i=1}^{n}(y_i - \hat{y}_i)^2}$$

Segment 1 - Linear Regression

```
In [1]:  import numpy as np
         import pandas as pd

         import matplotlib.pyplot as plt
         from pylab import rcParams
         import seaborn as sb

         import sklearn
         from sklearn.linear_model import LinearRegression
         from sklearn.preprocessing import scale
         from collections import Counter
```

```
In [3]:  %matplotlib inline
         rcParams['figure.figsize'] = 5, 4
         sb.set_style('whitegrid')
```

(Multiple) linear regression on the enrollment data

In **Multiple Linear Regression** there are more than one independent variables for the model to find the relationship.

Equation of Multiple Linear Regression, where bo is the intercept, $b_1, b_2, b_3, b_4 \ldots, b_n$ are coefficients or slopes of the independent variables $x_1, x_2, x_3, x_4 \ldots, x_n$ and y is the dependent variable.

$$y = b_o + b_1 x_1 + b_2 x_2 + b_3 x_3 \ldots + b_n x_n$$

(Multiple) linear regression on the enrollment data

In [8]:
```
address = 'C:/Users/Lillian Pierson/Desktop/Exercise Files/Ch08/08_01/enrollment_forecast.csv'
enroll = pd.read_csv(address)
enroll.columns = ['year','roll','unem', 'hgrad', 'inc']
enroll.head()
```

Out[8]:

	year	roll	unem	hgrad	inc
0	1	5501	8.1	9552	1923
1	2	5945	7.0	9680	1961
2	3	6629	7.3	9731	1979
3	4	7556	7.5	11666	2030
4	5	8716	7.0	14675	2112

In [9]: sb.pairplot(enroll)

Out[9]: <seaborn.axisgrid.PairGrid at 0x13686710>

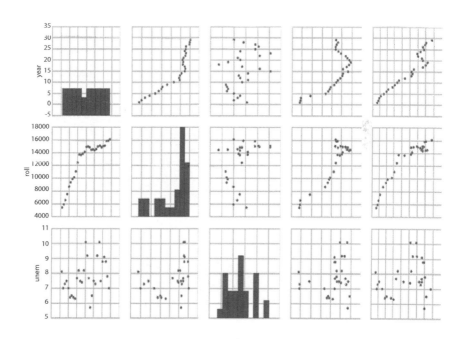

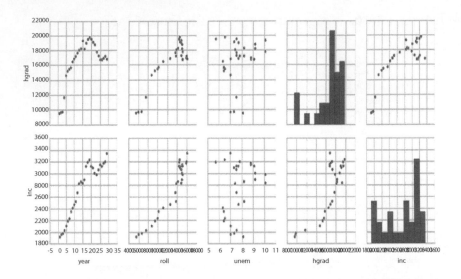

```
In [10]:  print enroll.corr()

                 year       roll       unem      hgrad        inc
          year   1.000000   0.900934   0.378305   0.670300   0.944287
          roll   0.900934   1.000000   0.391344   0.890294   0.949876
          unem   0.378305   0.391344   1.000000   0.177376   0.282310
          hgrad  0.670300   0.890294   0.177376   1.000000   0.820089
          inc    0.944287   0.949876   0.282310   0.820089   1.000000
```

```
In [12]:  enroll_data = enroll.ix[:,(2,3)].values
          enroll_target = enroll.ix[:,1].values
          enroll_data_names = ['unem', 'hgrad']

          X, y = scale(enroll_data), enroll_target
```

Checking for missing values

```
In [13]:  missing_values = X==np.NAN
          X[missing_values == True]
```

```
Out[13]:  array([], dtype=float64)
```

```
In [14]:  LinReg = LinearRegression(normalize=True)

          LinReg.fit(X,y)

          print LinReg.score(X,y)

          0.848881266613
```

8.2   Logistic Regression

Logistic regression is a statistical analysis method used to predict a data value based on prior observations of a data set. Logistic regression has become an important tool in the discipline of machine learning. The approach allows an algorithm being used in a machine learning application to classify incoming data based on historical data. As more relevant data comes in, the algorithm should get better at predicting classifications within data sets. Logistic regression can also play a role in data preparation activities by allowing data sets to be put into specifically predefined buckets during the extract, transform, load (ETL) process in order to stage the information for analysis.

A logistic regression model predicts a dependent data variable by analyzing the relationship between one or more existing independent variables. For example, a logistic regression could be used to predict whether a political candidate will win or lose an election or whether a high school student will be admitted to a particular college.

The resulting analytical model can take into consideration multiple input criteria. In the case of college acceptance, the model could consider factors such as the student's grade point average, SAT score and number of extracurricular activities. Based on historical data about earlier outcomes involving the same input criteria, it then scores new cases on their probability of falling into a particular outcome category.

Purpose and Examples of Logistic Regression

Logistic regression is one of the most commonly used machine learning algorithms for binary classification problems, which are problems with two class values, including predictions such as "this or that," "yes or no" and "A or B."

The purpose of logistic regression is to estimate the probabilities of events, including determining a relationship between features and the probabilities of particular outcomes.

One example of this is predicting if a student will pass or fail an exam when the number of hours spent studying is provided as a feature and the variables for the response has two values: pass and fail.

Organizations can use insights from logistic regression outputs to enhance their business strategies so they can achieve their business goals, including reducing expenses or losses and increasing ROI in marketing campaigns, for example.

An e-commerce company that mails expensive promotional offers to customers would like to know whether a particular customer is likely to respond to the offers or not. For example, they'll want to know whether that consumer will be a "responder" or a "non responder." In marketing, this is called *propensity to respond modeling*.

Likewise, a credit card company develops a model to decide whether to issue a credit card to a customer or not will try to predict whether the customer is going to default or not on the credit card based on such characteristics as annual income, monthly credit card payments and number of defaults. In banking parlance, this is known as *default propensity modeling*.

Uses of Logistic Regression

Logistic regression has become particularly popular in online advertising, enabling marketers to predict the likelihood of specific website users who will click on particular advertisements as a yes or no percentage.

Logistic regression can also be used in:

- Healthcare to identify risk factors for diseases and plan preventive measures.
- Weather forecasting apps to predict snowfall and weather conditions.
- Voting apps to determine if voters will vote for a particular candidate.
- Insurance to predict the chances that a policy holder will die before the term of the policy expires based on certain criteria, such as gender, age and physical examination.
- Banking to predict the chances that a loan applicant will default on a loan or not, based on annual income, past defaults and past debts.

Logistic Regression vs. Linear Regression

The main difference between logistic regression and linear regression is that logistic regression provides a constant output, while linear regression provides a continuous output.

In logistic regression, the outcome, such as a dependent variable, only has a limited number of possible values. However, in linear regression, the outcome is continuous, which means that it can have any one of an infinite number of possible values.

Logistic regression is used when the response variable is categorical, such as yes/no, true/false and pass/fail. Linear regression is used when the response variable is continuous, such as number of hours, height and weight.

For example, given data on the time a student spent studying and that student's exam scores, logistic regression and linear regression can predict different things.

With logistic regression predictions, only specific values or categories are allowed. Therefore, logistic regression can predict whether the student passed or failed. Since linear regression predictions are continuous, such as numbers in a range, it can predict the student's test score on a scale of 0-100.

Advantages of Logistic Regression

1. Logistic regression is easier to implement, interpret, and very efficient to train.
2. It makes no assumptions about distributions of classes in feature space.
3. It can easily extend to multiple classes (multinomial regression) and a natural probabilistic view of class predictions.
4. It not only provides a measure of how appropriate a predictor (coefficient size) is, but also its direction of association (positive or negative).
5. It is very fast at classifying unknown records.
6. Good accuracy for many simple data sets and it performs well when the dataset is linearly separable.
7. It can interpret model coefficients as indicators of feature importance.
8. Logistic regression is less inclined to over-fitting but it can overfit in high dimensional datasets .One may consider Regularization (L1 and L2) techniques to avoid over-fitting in these scenarios.

Disadvantages of Logistic Regression

1. If the number of observations is lesser than the number of features, Logistic Regression should not be used, otherwise, it may lead to overfitting.
2. It constructs linear boundaries.

3. The major limitation of Logistic Regression is the assumption of linearity between the dependent variable and the independent variables.
4. It can only be used to predict discrete functions. Hence, the dependent variable of Logistic Regression is bound to the discrete number set.
5. Non-linear problems can't be solved with logistic regression because it has a linear decision surface. Linearly separable data is rarely found in real-world scenarios.
6. Logistic Regression requires average or no multicollinearity between independent variables.
7. It is tough to obtain complex relationships using logistic regression. More powerful and compact algorithms such as Neural Networks can easily outperform this algorithm.
8. In Linear Regression independent and dependent variables are related linearly. But Logistic Regression needs that independent variables are linearly related to the log odds (log(p/(1-p)).

Segment 2 - Logistic Regression

```
In [1]: import numpy as np
        import pandas as pd
        from pandas import Series, DataFrame

        import scipy
        from scipy.stats import spearmanr

        import matplotlib.pyplot as plt
        from pylab import rcParams
        import seaborn as sb

        import sklearn
        from sklearn.preprocessing import scale
        from sklearn.linear_model import LogisticRegression
        from sklearn.cross_validation import train_test_split
        from sklearn import metrics
        from sklearn import preprocessing
```

```
In [2]: %matplotlib inline
        rcParams['figure.figsize'] = 5, 4
        sb.set_style('whitegrid')
```

Logistic Regression on mtcars

```
In [3]: address = 'C:/Users/Lillian Pierson/Desktop/Exercise Files/Ch08/08_02/mtcars.csv'
        cars = pd.read_csv(address)
        cars.columns = ['car_names','mpg','cyl','disp', 'hp', 'drat', 'wt', 'qsec', 'vs', 'am', 'gear', 'carb']
        cars.head()
```

Out[3]:

	car_names	mpg	cyl	disp	hp	drat	wt	qsec	vs	am	gear	carb
0	Mazda RX4	21.0	6	160.0	110	3.90	2.620	16.46	0	1	4	4
1	Mazda RX4 Wag	21.0	6	160.0	110	3.90	2.875	17.02	0	1	4	4
2	Datsun 710	22.8	4	108.0	93	3.85	2.320	18.61	1	1	4	1
3	Hornet 4 Drive	21.4	6	258.0	110	3.08	3.215	19.44	1	0	3	1
4	Hornet Sportabout	18.7	8	360.0	175	3.15	3.440	17.02	0	0	3	2

```
In [4]: cars_data = cars.ix[:,(5,11)].values
        cars_data_names = ['drat','carb']

        y = cars.ix[:,9].values
```

Checking for Independence between Features

```
In [5]: sb.regplot(x='drat', y='carb', data=cars, scatter=True)
Out[5]: <matplotlib.axes._subplots.AxesSubplot at 0xc375898>
```

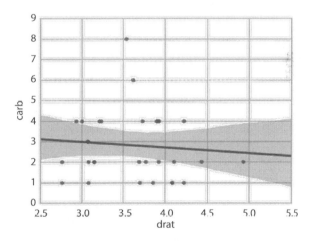

```
In [6]: drat = cars['drat']
        carb = cars['carb']

        spearmanr_coefficient, p_value = spearmanr(drat, carb)
        print 'Spearman Rank Correlation Coefficient %0.3f' % (spearmanr_coefficient)

        Spearman Rank Correlation Coefficient -0.125
```

Checking for Missing Values

```
In [7]:  cars.isnull().sum()
```
```
Out[7]:  car_names     0
         mpg           0
         cyl           0
         disp          0
         hp            0
         drat          0
         wt            0
         qsec          0
         vs            0
         am            0
         gear          0
         carb          0
         dtype: int64
```

Checking that your Target is Binary or Ordinal

```
In [8]:  sb.countplot(x='am', data=cars, palette='hls')
```
```
Out[8]:  <matplotlib.axes._subplots.AxesSubplot at 0xc64e080>
```

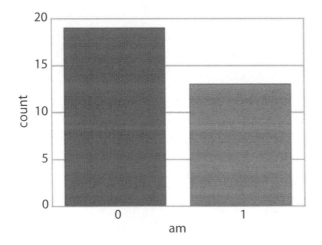

Checking that your Dataset size is Sufficient

```
In [9]: cars.info()
```

```
<class 'pandas.core.frame.DataFrame'>
RangeIndex: 32 entries, 0 to 31
Data columns (total 12 columns):
car_names    32 non-null object
mpg          32 non-null float64
cyl          32 non-null int64
disp         32 non-null float64
hp           32 non-null int64
drat         32 non-null float64
wt           32 non-null float64
qsec         32 non-null float64
vs           32 non-null int64
am           32 non-null int64
gear         32 non-null int64
carb         32 non-null int64
dtypes: float64(5), int64(6), object(1)
memory usage: 3.1+ KB
```

Deploying and Evaluating your Model

```
In [10]: X = scale(cars_data)
```

```
In [11]: LogReg = LogisticRegression()

         LogReg.fit(X,y)
         print LogReg.score(X,y)
```

```
         0.8125
```

```
In [12]: y_pred = LogReg.predict(X)
         from sklearn.metrics import classification_report
         print(classification_report(y, y_pred))
```

	precision	recall	f1-score	support
0	0.88	0.79	0.83	19
1	0.73	0.85	0.79	13
avg / total	0.82	0.81	0.81	32

8.3   Naive Bayes Classifiers

What is a Classifier?

A classifier is a machine learning model that is used to discriminate different objects based on certain features.

Principle of Naive Bayes Classifier:

A Naive Bayes classifier is a probabilistic machine learning model that's used for classification task. The crux of the classifier is based on the Bayes theorem.

Bayes Theorem:

$$P(A|B) = \frac{P(B|A)P(A)}{P(B)}$$

Using Bayes theorem, we can find the probability of **A** happening, given that **B** has occurred. Here, **B** is the evidence and **A** is the hypothesis. The assumption made here is that the predictors/features are independent. That is presence of one particular feature does not affect the other. Hence it is called naive.

Example:

Let us take an example to get some better intuition. Consider the problem of playing golf. The dataset is represented as below.

	OUTLOOK	TEMPERATURE	HUMIDITY	WINDY	PLAY GOLF
0	Rainy	Hot	High	False	No
1	Rainy	Hot	High	False	No
2	Overcast	Hot	High	False	Yes
3	Sunny	Mild	High	False	Yes
4	Sunny	Cool	Normal	False	Yes
5	Sunny	Cool	Normal	True	No
6	Overcast	Cool	Normal	True	Yes
7	Rainy	Mild	High	False	No
8	Rainy	Cool	Normal	False	Yes
9	Sunny	Mild	Normal	False	Yes
10	Rainy	Mild	Normal	True	
11	Overcast	Mild	High	True	Yes
12	Overcast	Hot	Normal	False	Yes
13	Sunny	Mild	High	True	No

We classify whether the day is suitable for playing golf, given the features of the day. The columns represent these features and the rows represent individual entries. If we take the first row of the dataset, we can observe that is not suitable for playing golf if the outlook is rainy, temperature is hot, humidity is high and it is not windy. We make two assumptions here, one as stated above we consider that these predictors are independent. That is, if the temperature is hot, it does not necessarily mean that the humidity is high. Another assumption made here is that all the predictors have an equal effect on the outcome. That is, the day being windy does not have more importance in deciding to play golf or not.

According to this example, Bayes theorem can be rewritten as:

$$P(y|X) = \frac{P(X|y)P(y)}{P(X)}$$

The variable **y** is the class variable(play golf), which represents if it is suitable to play golf or not given the conditions. Variable **X** represent the parameters/features.

X is given as,

$$X = (x_1, x_2, x_3, \ldots., x_n)$$

Here x_1,x_2....x_n represent the features, i.e they can be mapped to outlook, temperature, humidity and windy. By substituting for **X** and expanding using the chain rule we get,

$$P(y|x_1,\ldots,x_n) = \frac{P(x_1|y)P(x_2|y)\ldots P(x_n|y)P(y)}{P(x_1)P(x_2)\ldots P(x_n)}$$

Now, you can obtain the values for each by looking at the dataset and substitute them into the equation. For all entries in the dataset, the denominator does not change, it remain static. Therefore, the denominator can be removed and a proportionality can be introduced.

$$P(y|x_1,\ldots,x_n) \propto P(y)\prod_{i=1}^{n} P(x_i|y)$$

In our case, the class variable(**y**) has only two outcomes, yes or no. There could be cases where the classification could be multivariate. Therefore, we need to find the class **y** with maximum probability.

$$y = argmax_y P(y) \prod_{i=1}^{n} P(x_i|y)$$

Using the above function, we can obtain the class, given the predictors.

Types of Naive Bayes Classifier:

Multinomial Naive Bayes:

This is mostly used for document classification problem, i.e whether a document belongs to the category of sports, politics, technology etc. The features/predictors used by the classifier are the frequency of the words present in the document.

Bernoulli Naive Bayes:

This is similar to the multinomial naive bayes but the predictors are boolean variables. The parameters that we use to predict the class variable take up only values yes or no, for example if a word occurs in the text or not.

Gaussian Naive Bayes:

When the predictors take up a continuous value and are not discrete, we assume that these values are sampled from a gaussian distribution.

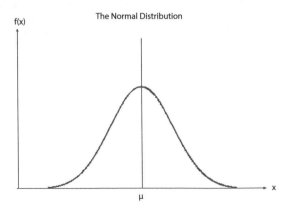

Gaussian Distribution (Normal Distribution)

Since the way the values are present in the dataset changes, the formula for conditional probability changes to,

$$P(x_i|y) = \frac{1}{\sqrt{2\pi\sigma_y^2}} exp\left(-\frac{(x_i - \mu_y)^2}{2\sigma_y^2}\right)$$

Applications of Naive Bayes Algorithm

As you must've noticed, this algorithm offers plenty of advantages to its users. That's why it has a lot of applications in various sectors too. Here are some applications of Naive Bayes algorithm:

- As this algorithm is fast and efficient, you can use it to make real-time predictions.
- This algorithm is popular for multi-class predictions. You can find the probability of multiple target classes easily by using this algorithm.
- Email services (like Gmail) use this algorithm to figure out whether an email is a spam or not. This algorithm is excellent for spam filtering.
- Its assumption of feature independence, and its effectiveness in solving multi-class problems, makes it perfect for performing Sentiment Analysis. Sentiment Analysis refers to the identification of positive or negative sentiments of a target group (customers, audience, etc.)
- Collaborative Filtering and the Naive Bayes algorithm work together to build recommendation systems. These systems use data mining and machine learning to predict if the user would like a particular resource or not.

Advantages of Naive Bayes

- This algorithm works very fast and can easily predict the class of a test dataset.
- You can use it to solve multi-class prediction problems as it's quite useful with them.
- Naive Bayes classifier performs better than other models with less training data if the assumption of independence of features holds.
- If you have categorical input variables, the Naive Bayes algorithm performs exceptionally well in comparison to numerical variables.

Disadvantages of Naive Bayes

- If your test data set has a categorical variable of a category that wasn't present in the training data set, the Naive Bayes model will assign it zero probability and won't be able to make any predictions in this regard. This phenomenon is called 'Zero Frequency,' and you'll have to use a smoothing technique to solve this problem.
- This algorithm is also notorious as a lousy estimator. So, you shouldn't take the probability outputs of 'predict_proba' too seriously.
- It assumes that all the features are independent. While it might sound great in theory, in real life, you'll hardly find a set of independent features.

Segment 3 - Naive Bayes Classifiers

```
In [1]:  import numpy as np
         import pandas as pd

         import urllib

         import sklearn
         from sklearn.naive_bayes import BernoulliNB
         from sklearn.naive_bayes import GaussianNB
         from sklearn.naive_bayes import MultinomialNB
         from sklearn.cross_validation import train_test_split
         from sklearn import metrics
         from sklearn.metrics import accuracy_score
```

Naive Bayes

Using Naive Bayes to Predict Spam

```
In [2]:  url = "https://archive.ics.uci.edu/ml/machine-learning-databases/spambase/spambase.data"
         raw_data = urllib.urlopen(url)
         dataset = np.loadtxt(raw_data, delimiter=",")
         print dataset[0]

         [  0.     0.64   0.64   0.     0.32   0.     0.     0.     0.
            0.     0.     0.64   0.     0.     0.     0.32   0.
            1.29   1.93   0.     0.96   0.     0.     0.     0.     0.
            0.     0.     0.     0.     0.     0.     0.     0.     0.
            0.     0.     0.     0.     0.     0.     0.     0.     0.
            0.     0.     0.     0.     0.     0.     0.     0.778
            0.     0.     3.756 61.   278.     1.  ]
```

```
In [3]:  X = dataset[:,0:48]

         y = dataset[:, -1]
```

```
In [5]:  X_train, X_test, y_train, y_test = train_test_split(X, y, test_size=.33, random_state=17)
```

```
In [10]:  BernNB = BernoulliNB(binarize=True)
          BernNB.fit(X_train, y_train)
          print(BernNB)

          y_expect = y_test
          y_pred = BernNB.predict(X_test)
          print accuracy_score(y_expect, y_pred)
```

```
BernoulliNB(alpha=1.0, binarize=True, class_prior=None, fit_prior=True)
0.855826201448
```

```
In [11]:  MultiNB = MultinomialNB()

          MultiNB.fit(X_train, y_train)
          print(MultiNB)

          y_pred = MultiNB.predict(X_test)
          print accuracy_score(y_expect, y_pred)
```

```
MultinomialNB(alpha=1.0, class_prior=None, fit_prior=True)
0.873601053325
```

```
In [12]:  GausNB = GaussianNB()
          GausNB.fit(X_train, y_train)
          print(GausNB)

          y_pred = GausNB.predict(X_test)
          print accuracy_score(y_expect, y_pred)
```

```
GaussianNB()
0.813034891376
```

```
In [13]:  BernNB = BernoulliNB(binarize=0.1)
          BernNB.fit(X_train, y_train)
          print(BernNB)

          y_expect = y_test
          y_pred = BernNB.predict(X_test)
          print accuracy_score(y_expect, y_pred)
```

```
BernoulliNB(alpha=1.0, binarize=0.1, class_prior=None, fit_prior=True)
0.895325872284
```

References

1. Domingos, Pedro; Pazzani, Michael (1997). "On the optimality of the simple Bayesian classifier under zero-one loss". Machine Learning. 29 (2/3): 103–137. doi:10.1023/A:1007413511361.

2. Webb, G. I.; Boughton, J.; Wang, Z. (2005). "Not So Naive Bayes: Aggregating One-Dependence Estimators". Machine Learning. 58 (1): 5–24. doi:10.1007/s10994-005-4258-6.

3. Mozina, M.; Demsar, J.; Kattan, M.; Zupan, B. (2004). Nomograms for Visualization of Naive Bayesian Classifier (PDF). Proc. PKDD-2004. pp. 337–348.

4. Maron, M. E. (1961). "Automatic Indexing: An Experimental Inquiry". Journal of the ACM. 8 (3): 404–417. doi:10.1145/321075.321084. hdl:2027/uva.x030748531. S2CID 6692916.

5. Minsky, M. (1961). Steps toward Artificial Intelligence. Proc. IRE. 49. pp. 8–30.

6. Cohen, J., Cohen P., West, S.G., & Aiken, L.S. (2003). Applied multiple regression/correlation analysis for the behavioral sciences. (2nd ed.) Hillsdale, NJ: Lawrence Erlbaum Associates

7. Charles Darwin. The Variation of Animals and Plants under Domestication. (1868) (Chapter XIII describes what was known about reversion in Galton's time. Darwin uses the term "reversion".)

8. Draper, N.R.; Smith, H. (1998). Applied Regression Analysis (3rd ed.). John Wiley. ISBN 978-0-471-17082-2.

9. Francis Galton. "Regression Towards Mediocrity in Hereditary Stature," Journal of the Anthropological Institute, 15:246-263 (1886). (Facsimile at: [1])

10. Robert S. Pindyck and Daniel L. Rubinfeld (1998, 4h ed.). Econometric Models and Economic Forecasts, ch. 1 (Intro, incl. appendices on Σ operators & derivation of parameter est.) & Appendix 4.3 (mult. regression in matrix form).

11. Prakash K.B. Content extraction studies using total distance algorithm, 2017, Proceedings of the 2016 2nd International Conference on Applied and Theoretical Computing and Communication Technology, iCATccT 2016, 10.1109/ICATCCT.2016.7912085

12. Prakash K.B. Mining issues in traditional indian web documents, 2015, Indian Journal of Science and Technology,8(32), 10.17485/ijst/2015/v8i1/77056

13. Prakash K.B., Rajaraman A., Lakshmi M. Complexities in developing multi-lingual on-line courses in the Indian context, 2017, Proceedings of the 2017 International Conference On Big Data Analytics and Computational Intelligence, ICBDACI 2017, 8070860, 339-342, 10.1109/ICBDACI.2017.8070860

14. Prakash K.B., Kumar K.S., Rao S.U.M. Content extraction issues in online web education, 2017, Proceedings of the 2016 2nd International Conference on Applied and Theoretical Computing and Communication Technology, iCATccT 2016, 7912086, 680-685, 10.1109/ICATCCT.2016.7912086

15. Prakash K.B., Rajaraman A., Perumal T., Kolla P. Foundations to frontiers of big data analytics, 2016, Proceedings of the 2016 2nd International Conference on Contemporary Computing and Informatics, IC3I 2016, 7917968, 242-247, 10.1109/IC3I.2016.7917968

Web-Based Data Visualizations with Plotly

9.1 Collaborative Analytics

Collaborative analytics is part of the broader movement in analytics to approach BI from a community-driven perspective. It uses a combination of business intelligence software and collaboration tools to allow a broad spectrum of people in an organization- (and beyond) to participate in data analytics.

Collaborative analytics emphasizes the problem-solving process, correctly identifying that data analysis that generates the most valuable insights doesn't happen in a vacuum. Without the input of people who have a thorough understanding of the industry, are talking with customers, working on product development, managing production, etc., data analysts are operating without context.

What collaborative analytics includes

Functionally, collaborative analytics includes a variety of elements. It involves collaboration around the discovery, creation, sharing, and use of data assets. For example, a sales leader may realize that a particular dataset in the organization's CRM would be valuable for a particular use, recommending to the data team that they make that data available in the analytics tool. Collaborative analytics also works the other direction — data teams make business users aware of endorsed datasets and the data resources available and how to best use them. This "best use" education may involve a formal training program on data skills, or it may happen on an informal basis, as needed. More likely, it's a mix of both.

While human minds are an indispensable part of collaborative analytics, the process also makes use of AI. Much of AI's potential when it comes to knowledge sharing remains to be realized, but current capabilities are valuable, including improving community exposure and streamlining

Kolla Bhanu Prakash. Data Science Handbook: A Practical Approach, (197–220) © 2022 Scrivener Publishing LLC

processes. AI's ability to do things like identify similar datasets in a warehouse, encourage joins, and prompt users to try different visualizations to reveal trends more effectively dramatically improves a company's proficiency with collaborative analytics.

Tool capabilities that enable collaboration

What does collaborative analytics software look like in action? There are a few capabilities that facilitate the process.

- **Team workspaces** — Team workspaces governed by permissions and controls that ensure security allow employees with teams and across teams to collaborate.
- **Reusable workflows** — Datasets used and analyses conducted by one team are able to be saved and reused by others.
- **Single source of truth** — Data is centralized and available via a single access point, ensuring that everyone is using the same version of the data.
- **Chat** — Built-in or API-integrated collaboration tools allow team members to ask questions, make comments, and tag others for feedback.
- **Visual, collaborative data modeling** — A visual approach to data modeling allows business users to participate without writing code. Schemas and tables are available for all users to explore, and business users can create or contribute to new data models and add their input to existing datasets.

What's holding companies back from being community-driven

Although most organizations aspire to be collaborative, the reality is that roadblocks are preventing full adoption. Here's what holding companies back and what they can do to remove these roadblocks.

Most popular BI tools weren't built to be collaborative
While many legacy tools have bolted-on analytics collaboration functionality, they haven't been built from the ground up with collaboration in mind. This results in clunky or complicated user experiences that, in practice, end up preventing business users from being as involved as they want to (and

should be). To implement collaborative analytics well, you need a tool that has an easy-to-use UX that enables all types of people to explore data, not just those with SQL knowledge.

Many newer tools that aim to be collaborative only offer limited access to business users

Even many solutions that were built with collaboration tools as foundational features don't offer business users the ability to ask unique questions, or explore reports with set parameters. True collaboration is limited to those with technical skills on the data team. There's no ability for business users to participate in data modeling or conduct queries beyond a limited, pre-designed sandbox where they are second-class data citizens.

Some organizations aren't taking advantage of cloud data warehouse capabilities that enable collaborative analytics

In order to implement collaborative analytics, you must have the right infrastructure in place with the right capabilities. Modern cloud data warehouses like Snowflake and Google BigQuery can store massive amounts of data, scale to meet analytical demands of entire organizations, and make it possible to centralize company data for holistic analysis. They are a requirement for any company seriously considering a collaborative and community-driven approach to analytics.

Many organizations aren't using an A&BI solution that enables a community-driven approach with protective governance

Opening up data access, exploration, and analysis without compromising security demands a modernized approach to data governance. To be truly community-driven, your analytics and BI solution must make data accessible and approachable for everyone while upholding strict compliance and security standards.

Benefits of a collaborative approach to analytics & BI

We've established that you need the right tools in order to truly achieve collaboration. But implementing tools is always a bit of work and requires resources. Is collaborative analytics worth it? Here are a few of the many benefits that provide a strong answer of "yes."

Discovery of available data

Data sources and datasets can easily remain undiscovered or be overlooked without someone pointing them out to the larger team. When a broad spectrum of people serving a variety of roles is involved in the data analytics process, an organization is able to identify and share all its valuable data and put it to use.

Better use of available data

Companies sit on a treasure trove of data. But 73% of it goes unused for analytics. When all the data relevant to a given question is brought to bear, collaborative teams can make better use of the data. Those on the data team can endorse the most relevant and accurate data, and business users understand the nuances of meaning that can be derived from it.

Fuller use of domain experts' knowledge

When domain experts are limited to static dashboards built by the data team, the organization allows much of their knowledge to go to waste. These domain experts can ask more meaningful follow-up questions due to their on-the-ground understanding of the situation that's the subject of the inquiry. Organizations are already paying for this knowledge — with collaborative analytics, they're able to maximize their investment.

More accurate answers to the "why" questions

Data teams' expertise lies in the areas of data sourcing, processing, modeling, and analytics. They aren't typically talking to the customers, working with the product, or spending time observing the production line. For this reason, they're extremely adept at identifying trends and issues, but they often don't know what questions to ask to find out why trends and issues are happening. They are, of course, able to narrow down the "why" possibilities. But past a certain point, their analysis is guesswork. They need input from those with domain expertise, who are seeing and hearing things that aren't showing up in the data.

At times, this input can save a company from making costly errors. For example, an analyst may discover that sales have dropped in a particular region of the country while all other regions remain strong. Without input from the territory manager, the real cause will remain unknown. The company could waste millions of dollars rectifying a "problem" that doesn't exist — only to discover that the drop was due to a different problem that requires another outlay of cash in order to solve the issue.

Faster speed to insight

The faster you can collaborate and bring all knowledge and perspectives to bear, the faster your speed to insight. Yes, a certain level of collaboration can happen without the appropriate tools and processes. But often, companies that "win" are those who are able to move quickly — before competitors. And in cases where insights are necessary to solve problems, speed can mean significant cost savings.

Generate curiosity and encourage people to look for new insights

Another major benefit is that collaborative analytics encourages curiosity. When domain experts have the ability to participate and their input is taken into account, they're motivated to look for new insights on their own. This tendency is of great value to an organization, as the company is able to innovate and move in ways it wouldn't be able to otherwise.

What to look for in collaborative analytics & BI software

Because many collaborative analytics tools are limited in their collaborative functionality, you'll want to do your research before committing to one. Here's what to look for in collaborative BI software to ensure you experience the benefits that a community-driven approach has to offer.

Full set of collaboration tools

Look for team workspaces that allow users to collaborate on analysis as individual teams and share data with other teams in the organization. Be sure that business users can easily build on each other's work and share insights using connected tools that they already use in their everyday workflows, such as Slack and email.

Robust permissions and security features

Be sure that business users won't be hindered from fully making use of the tool in the name of security. Robust permissions and security features, alongside a balanced data governance program, allow the people who should have access to fully explore and use the tool.

Collaboration in exploration

Your collaborative analytics tool should be built with both technical and business users in mind. Technical users should be able to easily perform all their tasks in the tool. At the same time, business users should be able to experience an intuitive interface based on popular non-technical tools like Microsoft Office to explore data, create their own visualizations, contribute their perspectives, and work as equals with the data team. Your tool should allow anyone to do a deep-dive series of queries — a capability that Sigma excels in.

Reusable datasets and analyses

An essential part of collaboration is the ability to build on the work of others. Your collaborative analytics tool should allow you to reuse datasets and analyses that other teams have already added and created.

Collaborative data modeling

Before business users can make use of data, it must be modeled. Ideally, business users will collaborate with technical users on the modeling process, and for this purpose, visual data modeling capability is a must. Collaboration in a central location using a visual format that anyone can understand ensures that business users aren't modeling data on their desktops using the Excel program installed on their hard drive, while at the same time keeping data democratized.

How to build a collaborative analytics culture

While tools are important, they're not enough. A 2019 survey by NewVantage Partners revealed that 95% of executives said their difficulty in becoming data-driven is a result of cultural challenges around data. You can have all the best tools, from a modern cloud data warehouse to the best collaborative analytics platform, and still fail to experience the benefits of collaboration.

Beyond the tools, you need a collaborative analytics culture that encourages users to view one another with respect, to value a variety of perspectives, and to take advantage of their ability to uncover the "whys" behind the trends. Here are the primary steps you'll need to take to build a collaborative analytics culture.

Emphasize the benefits of collaborative analytics

Showing your people just how collaborative analytics can benefit not only the company at large but also each of their teams will go a long way in generating buy-in. When team members understand the value of collaboration, they'll be motivated to contribute and to seek the contributions of others.

Break down silos between departments

The default style of most organizations is for departments to operate independently, in silos. This is such a norm that it has become the target of jokes.

To build a collaborative analytics culture, you'll need to disrupt this pattern. To do this, you'll need to communicate your vision for collaboration, open up cross-departmental communications, hold cross-functional trainings, and put other measures in place designed to build trust between departments. 95% of executives said cultural challenges hindered their ability to become data-driven.

Promote diversity of perspectives

One of the most important tasks involved in building a culture of collaboration is to promote diversity. Help everyone to understand just why other perspectives are so valuable. Point to the success of other organizations using collaboration to reach their goals. Everyone in the organization should receive a loud and clear message that each individual perspective is valued.

Encourage curiosity

Truly data-driven teams run on curiosity. They're constantly asking the "why" questions — and following up with additional "why" questions. Encourage both your data team and your domain experts to get curious and explore data to satisfy their curiosity and generate valuable insights in the process.

Build a balanced data governance program

Data democratization doesn't have to look like the Wild West. A data governance framework that simultaneously makes data accessible while minimizing risk will ensure that people don't fear collaboration. The need for data governance is nothing new, and best practices have remained fairly consistent. Snowflake's Chief Data Evangelist, Kent Graziano, aptly says, "What might be surprising to many people is that data governance best practices have existed for a couple of decades. The questions have already been answered. We now need to force ourselves into the discipline of following those best practices."

Democratize access to data

Finally, a collaborative analytics culture depends on democratized access to data. As long as an organization restricts data access to the technical elite, domain experts will not feel that their voice is valued in the data conversation. Yes, security measures must be put in place, and processes must be followed. But business users should be able to easily use your data analytics tool — and in a broader capacity than simply making comments in a chat function and viewing pre-designed dashboards.

Community-driven analytics is the future

Due to the invaluable benefits of collaborative analytics, many organizations are in a race to become more community-driven. As the research shows, the majority of those companies that are not yet taking advantage of collaborative analytics processes are planning to implement collaborative analytics in the future. Only 11% of companies say they don't plan to follow the collaborative path.

To start seeing the benefits that community-driven analytics offers and compete with organizations that are, you'll need to start building your collaborative capabilities and culture now.

Advantages

- **Data analytics helps an organization make better decisions**
  Lot of times decisions within organizations are made more on gut feel rather than facts and data. One of the reasons for this could be lack of access to quality data that can help with better decision making. Analytics can help with transforming the data that is available into valuable information for executives so that better decisions can be made. This can be a source of competitive advantage if fewer poor decisions are made since poor decisions can have a negative impact on a number of areas including company growth and profitability.

- **Increase the efficiency of the work**

  Analytics can help analyse large amounts of data quickly and display it in a formulated manner to help achieve specific organizational goals. It encourages a culture of efficiency and teamwork by allowing the managers to share the insights from the analytics results to the employees. The gaps and improvement areas within a company become evident and actions can be taken to increase the overall efficiency of the workplace thereby increasing productivity [1].

- **The analytics keeps you updated of your customer behavioural changes**

  In today's world, customers have a lot of choices. If organizations are not tuned to customer desires and expectations, they can soon find themselves in a downward spiral. Customers tend to change their minds as they are continuously exposed to new information in this era of digitization. With vast amount of customer data, it is practically impossible for organizations to make senses of all the changes in customer perception data without using the power of analytics. Analytics gives you insights into how your target market thinks and if there is any change. Hence, being aware of shift in customer behaviour can provide a decisive advantage to companies so that they can react faster to the market changes [2].

- **Personalization of products and services**

  Gone are the days where a company could sell a standard set of products and services to customers. Customers crave products and services that can meet their individual needs. Analytics can help companies keep track of what kind of service, product, or content is preferred by the customer and then show the recommendations based on their preferences. For example, in social media, we usually see what we like to see, all of this is made possible due to the data collection and analytics that companies do. Data analytics can help provide targeted services to customers based on their individual requirements [3].

- **Improving quality of products and services**

  Data analytics can help with enhancing the user experience by detecting and correcting errors or avoiding non-value-added tasks. For example, self-learning systems can use data to understand the way customers are interacting with the tools and make appropriate changes to improve user experience. In addition, data analytics can help with automated data cleansing and improving the quality of data and consecutively benefiting both customers and organizations [4].

Disadvantages

- **Lack of alignment within teams**
  There is a lack of alignment between different teams or departments within an organization. Data analytics may be done by a select set of team members and the analysis done may be shared with a limited set of executives. However, the insights generated by these teams are either of not much value or are having limited impact on organizational metrics. This could be due to a "silos" way of working with each team only using their existing processes disconnected from other departments. The analytics team should be focussed on answering the right questions for the business and the results generated by data analytics teams needs to be properly communicated to the right employees to drive the right set of actions and behaviours so that it can have an positive impact on the organization [5].
- **Lack of commitment and patience**
  Analytics solutions are not difficult to implement, however, they are costly, and the ROI is not immediate. Especially, if existing data is not available, it may take time to put processes and procedures in place to start collecting the data. By nature, the analytics models improve accuracy over time and require dedication to implement the solution. Since the business users do not see results immediately, they sometimes lose interest which results in loss of trust and the models fail. When an organization decides to implement data analytics methods, there needs to be a feedback loop and mechanism in place to understand what is working and what is not, and corrective actions are required to fix things that are broken. Without this closed loop system, senior management may decide that analytics is not working or much valuable and may abandon the entire exercise [6].
- **Low quality of data**
  One of the biggest limitations of data analytics is lack of access to quality data. It is possible that companies already have access to a lot of data, but the question is do they have the right data that they need? A top down approach is required

where the business questions that need to be answered need to be known first and what data is required to answer these questions can then be determined. In some cases, data may have been collected for historical reasons may not be suitable to answer the questions that we ask today. At other times, even though we have the right metrics that we are collecting data on, the quality of the data collection may be poor. There can be instances where adequate data is not available or is missing for proper analytics to be done. As they say, garbage-in garbage-out. If the data quality is poor, the decision made by using this data is also going to be poor. Hence, actions must be taken to fix the quality of the data before it can be effectively used within organizations [7].

- **Privacy concerns**
  Sometimes, data collection might breach the privacy of the customers as their information such as purchases, online transactions, and subscriptions are available to companies whose services they are using. Some companies might exchange those datasets with other companies for mutual benefit. Certain data collected can also be used against a person, country, or community. Organizations need to be cautious of what sort of data they are collecting from customers and ensure the security and confidentiality of the data. Only the data required for the analysis needs to be captured and if there is sensitive data, it needs to be anonymized so that sensitive data is protected. Data breaches can cause customers to lose trust in the organizations which may result in a negative impact on the organization [8].
- **Complexity & Bias**
  Some of the analytics tools developed by companies are more like a black box model [9]. What is inside the black box is not clear or the logic the system uses to learn from data and create a model is not readily evident [10]. For example, a neural network model that learns from various scenarios to decide who should be given a loan and who should be rejected. The usage of these tools may be easy but the logic of how decisions are made is not clear to anyone within the company [11]. If companies are not careful and a poor quality data set is used to train the model, there may be hidden biases in the decisions made by these systems which may not be readily evident and organizations may be breaking the law by discriminating against race, gender, sex, age etc. [12].

9.2 Basic Charts

Setting up to use Plotly within Jupyter

```
In [1]: ! pip install Plotly
```
```
Requirement already satisfied (use --upgrade to upgrade): Plotly in c:\program files\anaconda2\lib\site-packag
es
Requirement already satisfied (use --upgrade to upgrade): requests in c:\program files\anaconda2\lib\site-pack
ages (from Plotly)
Requirement already satisfied (use --upgrade to upgrade): pytz in c:\program files\anaconda2\lib\site-packages
(from Plotly)
Requirement already satisfied (use --upgrade to upgrade): six in c:\program files\anaconda2\lib\site-packages
(from Plotly)

You are using pip version 8.1.2, however version 9.0.1 is available.
You should consider upgrading via the 'python -m pip install --upgrade pip' command.
```

```
In [2]: ! pip install cufflinks
```
```
Requirement already satisfied (use --upgrade to upgrade): cufflinks in c:\program files\anaconda2\lib\site-pac
kages
Requirement already satisfied (use --upgrade to upgrade): plotly>=1.7.6 in c:\program files\anaconda2\lib\site
-packages (from cufflinks)
Requirement already satisfied (use --upgrade to upgrade): colorlover>=0.2 in c:\program files\anaconda2\lib\si
te-packages (from cufflinks)
Requirement already satisfied (use --upgrade to upgrade): pandas in c:\program files\anaconda2\lib\site-packag
es (from cufflinks)
Requirement already satisfied (use --upgrade to upgrade): requests in c:\program files\anaconda2\lib\site-pack
ages (from plotly>=1.7.6->cufflinks)
Requirement already satisfied (use --upgrade to upgrade): pytz in c:\program files\anaconda2\lib\site-packages
(from plotly>=1.7.6->cufflinks)
Requirement already satisfied (use --upgrade to upgrade): six in c:\program files\anaconda2\lib\site-packages
(from plotly>=1.7.6->cufflinks)
Requirement already satisfied (use --upgrade to upgrade): python-dateutil in c:\program files\anaconda2\lib\si
te-packages (from pandas->cufflinks)
Requirement already satisfied (use --upgrade to upgrade): numpy>=1.7.0 in c:\program files\anaconda2\lib\site-
packages (from pandas->cufflinks)

You are using pip version 8.1.2, however version 9.0.1 is available.
You should consider upgrading via the 'python -m pip install --upgrade pip' command.
```

```python
In [3]: import numpy as np
        import pandas as pd

        import cufflinks as cf

        import plotly.plotly as py
        import plotly.tools as tls
        import plotly.graph_objs as go
```

```python
In [ ]: tls.set_credentials_file(username='bigdatagal', api_key='b4TEVwSkwDzEJOHT9g5X')
```

Creating line charts

A very basic line chart

```python
In [6]: a = np.linspace(start=0, stop=36, num=36)

        np.random.seed(25)
        b = np.random.uniform(low=0.0, high=1.0, size=36)

        trace = go.Scatter(x=a, y=b)

        data = [trace]

        py.iplot(data, filename='basic-line-chart')
```

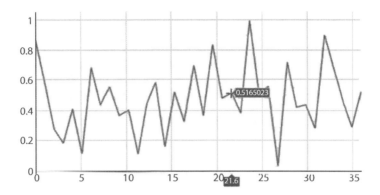

A line chart with more than one variable plotted

```
In [6]: x = [1,2,3,4,5,6,7,8,9]
        y = [1,2,3,4,0,4,3,2,1]
        z = [10,9,8,7,6,5,4,3,2,1]

        trace0 = go.Scatter(x=x, y=y, name='List Object', line = dict(width=5))
        trace1 = go.Scatter(x=x, y=z, name='List Object 2', line = dict(width=10,))

        data = [trace0, trace1]

        layout = dict(title='Double Line Chart', xaxis= dict(title='x-axis'), yaxis= dict(title='y-axis'))
        print layout

        {'yaxis': {'title': 'y-axis'}, 'xaxis': {'title': 'x-axis'}, 'title': 'Double Line Chart'}
```

```
In [7]: fig = dict(data=data, layout=layout)
        print fig

        {'layout': {'yaxis': {'title': 'y-axis'}, 'xaxis': {'title': 'x-axis'}, 'title': 'Double Line Chart'}, 'data':
        [{'y': [1, 2, 3, 4, 0, 4, 3, 2, 1], 'x': [1, 2, 3, 4, 5, 6, 7, 8, 9], 'line': {'width': 5}, 'type': 'scatter',
        'name': 'List Object'}, {'y': [10, 9, 8, 7, 6, 5, 4, 3, 2, 1], 'x': [1, 2, 3, 4, 5, 6, 7, 8, 9], 'line': {'wid
        th': 10}, 'type': 'scatter', 'name': 'List Object 2'}]}
```

```
In [2]: py.iplot(fig, filename='styled-line-chart')
```

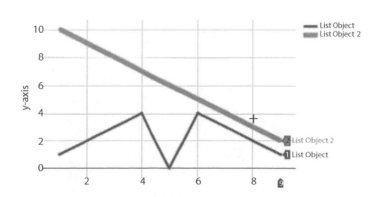

A line chart from a pandas dataframe

```
In [9]: address = 'C:/Users/Lillian Pierson/Desktop/Exercise Files/Ch09/09_01/mtcars.csv'
        cars = pd.read_csv(address)
        cars.columns = ['car_names','mpg','cyl','disp', 'hp', 'drat', 'wt', 'qsec', 'vs', 'am', 'gear', 'carb']

        df = cars[['cyl', 'wt','mpg']]

        layout = dict(title = 'Chart From Pandas DataFrame', xaxis= dict(title='x-axis'), yaxis= dict(title='y-axis'))

        df.iplot(filename='cf-simple-line-chart', layout=layout)
```

Chart From Pandas DataFrame

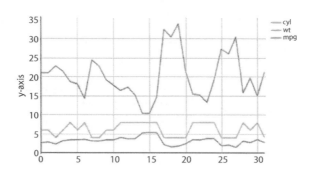

Creating bar charts

```
In [17]: data = [go.Bar(x=[1,2,3,4,5,6,7,8,9,10],y=[1,2,3,4,0.5,4,3,2,1])]
         print data

         [{'y': [1, 2, 3, 4, 0.5, 4, 3, 2, 1], 'x': [1, 2, 3, 4, 5, 6, 7, 8, 9, 10], 'type': 'bar'}]
```

```
In [18]: layout = dict(title='Simple Bar Chart',
                       xaxis = dict(title='x-axis'),
                       yaxis = dict(title='y-axis'))
         py.iplot(data, filename='basic-bar-chart', layout=layout)
```

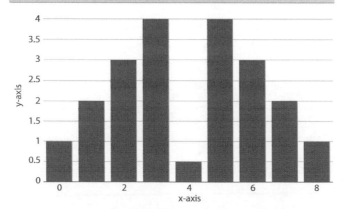

In [19]:
```
color_theme = dict(color=['rgba(169,169,169,1)', 'rgba(255,160,122,1)','rgba(176,224,230,1)', 'rgba(255,228,196,
                    'rgba(189,183,107,1)', 'rgba(188,143,143,1)','rgba(221,160,221,1)'])
print color_theme
```

```
{'color': ['rgba(169,169,169,1)', 'rgba(255,160,122,1)', 'rgba(176,224,230,1)', 'rgba(255,228,196,1)', 'rgba(1
89,183,107,1)', 'rgba(188,143,143,1)', 'rgba(221,160,221,1)']}
```

In [21]:
```
trace0 = go.Bar(x=[1,2,3,4,5,6,7], y=[1,2,3,4,0.5,3,1], marker=color_theme)
data = [trace0]
layout = go.Layout(title='Custom Colors')
fig = go.Figure(data=data, layout=layout)

py.iplot(fig, filename='color-bar-chart')
```

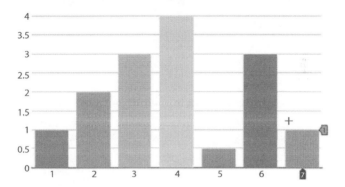

Creating pie charts

In [22]:
```
fig = {'data':[{'labels': ['bicycle', 'motorbike','car','van', 'stroller'],
                'values': [1, 2, 3, 4, 0.5],'type': 'pie'}],
       'layout': {'title': 'Simple Pie Chart'}}
py.iplot(fig)
```

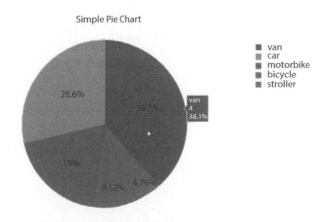

9.3   Statistical Charts

Setting up to use Plotly within Jupyter

```
In [3]: import numpy as np
        import pandas as pd

        import cufflinks as cf

        import plotly.plotly as py
        import plotly.tools as tls
        import plotly.graph_objs as go

        import sklearn
        from sklearn.preprocessing import StandardScaler
```

```
In [4]: tls.set_credentials_file(username='bigdatagal', api_key='hvginfgvwe')
```

Creating histograms

Make a histogram from a pandas Series object

```
In [1]: address = 'C:/Users/Lillian Pierson/Desktop/Exercise Files/Ch09/09_02/mtcars.csv'
        cars = pd.read_csv(address)
        cars.columns = ['car_names','mpg','cyl','disp', 'hp', 'drat', 'wt', 'qsec', 'vs', 'am', 'gear', 'carb']

        mpg = cars.mpg

        mpg.iplot(kind='histogram', filename='simple-histogram-chart')
```

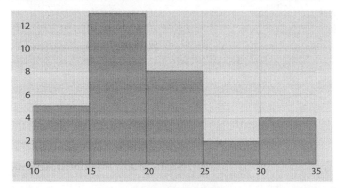

```
In [7]: cars_data = cars.ix[:,(1,3,4)].values

        cars_data_std = StandardScaler().fit_transform(cars_data)

        cars_select = pd.DataFrame(cars_data_std)
        cars_select.columns = ['mpg', 'disp', 'hp']

        cars_select.iplot(kind='histogram', filename='multiple-histogram-chart')
```

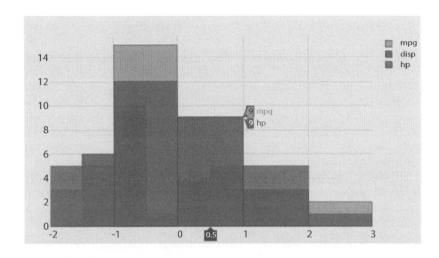

In [8]: `cars_select.iplot(kind='histogram', subplots=True, filename='subplot-histograms')`

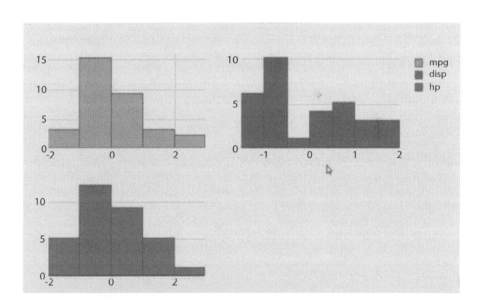

In [9]: `cars_select.iplot(kind='histogram', subplots=True, shape=(3,1), filename='subplot-histograms')`

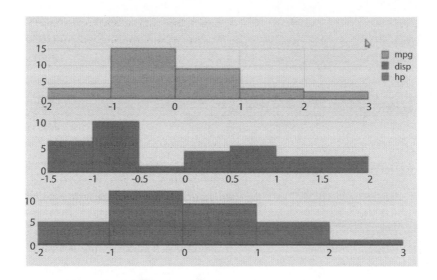

```
In [10]: cars_select.iplot(kind='histogram', subplots=True, shape=(1, 3), filename='subplot-histograms')
```

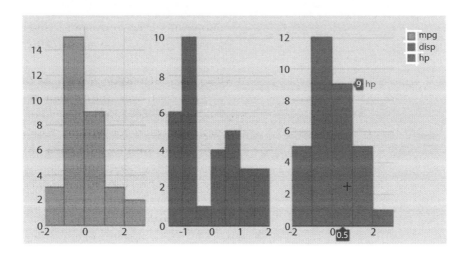

Creating box plots

```
In [2]: cars_select.iplot(kind='box', filename='box-plots')
```

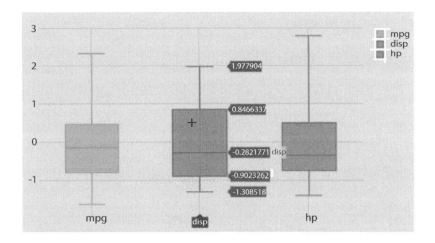

Creating scatter plots

```
In [19]: fig = {'data':[{'x':cars_select.mpg, 'y':cars_select.disp, 'mode':'markers','name':'mpg'},
                  {'x':cars_select.hp, 'y':cars_select.disp,'mode':'markers', 'name':'hp'}]
               , 'layout':{'xaxis':{'title':''}, 'yaxis':{'title':'Standardized Displacement'}}}
         py.iplot(fig, filename='grouped-scatter-plot')
```

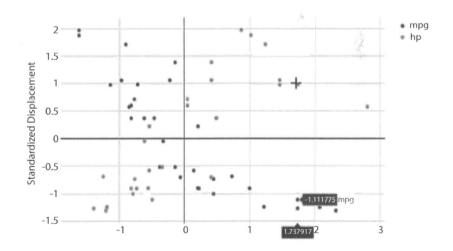

9.4 Plotly Maps

Setting up to use Plotly within Jupyter

```
In [9]:  import numpy as np
         import pandas as pd

         import plotly.plotly as py
         import plotly.tools as tls
```

```
In [10]:  tls.set_credentials_file(username='bigdatagal', api_key='hvginfgvwe')
```

Generating Choropleth maps

```
In [11]:  address = 'C:/Users/Lillian Pierson/Desktop/Exercise Files/Ch09/09_03/States.csv'
          states = pd.read_csv(address)
          states.columns = ['code','region','pop','satv', 'satm', 'percent', 'dollars', 'pay']
          states.head()
```

Out[11]:

	code	region	pop	satv	satm	percent	dollars	pay
0	AL	ESC	4041	470	514	8	3.648	27
1	AK	PAC	550	438	476	42	7.887	43
2	AZ	MTN	3665	445	497	25	4.231	30
3	AR	WSC	2351	470	511	6	3.334	23
4	CA	PAC	29760	419	484	45	4.826	39

```
In [18]:  states['text'] = 'SATv '+states['satv'].astype(str) + 'SATm '+states['satm'].astype(str) +'<br>'+\
          'State '+states['code']

          data = [dict(type='choropleth', autocolorscale=False, locations = states['code'], z= states['dollars'], location
          data
```

```
Out[19]:  [{'autocolorscale': False,
            'colorbar': {'title': 'thousand dollars'},
            'colorscale': 'custom-colorscale',
            'locationmode': 'USA-states',
            'locations': 0    AL
            1     AK
            2     AZ
            3     AR
            4     CA
            5     CO
            6     CN
            7     DE
            8     DC
            9     FL
            10    GA
            11    HI
            12    ID
            13    IL
            14    IN
```

```
In [19]: layout = dict(title='State Spending on Public Education, in $k/student',
                       geo = dict(scope='usa', projection=dict(type='albers usa'), showlakes = True, lakecolor = 'rgb(66,
         layout
```

```
Out[19]: {'geo': {'lakecolor': 'rgb(66,165,245)',
          'projection': {'type': 'albers usa'},
          'scope': 'usa',
          'showlakes': True},
          'title': 'State Spending on Public Education, in $k/student'}
```

```
In [20]: fig = dict(data=data, layout=layout)

         py.iplot(fig, filename='d3-choropleth-map')
```

State Spending on Public Education, in $k/student

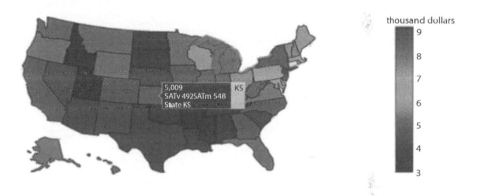

Segment 3 - Plotly maps

Setting up to use Plotly within Jupyter

```
In [9]: import numpy as np
        import pandas as pd

        import plotly.plotly as py
        import plotly.tools as tls
```

```
In [10]: tls.set_credentials_file(username='bigdatagal', api_key='hvginfgvwe')
```

Generating Choropleth maps

```
In [11]:  address = 'C:/Users/Lillian Pierson/Desktop/Exercise Files/Ch09/09_03/States.csv'
          states = pd.read_csv(address)
          states.columns = ['code','region','pop','satv', 'satm', 'percent', 'dollars', 'pay']
          states.head()
```

Out[11]:

	code	region	pop	satv	satm	percent	dollars	pay
0	AL	ESC	4041	470	514	8	3.848	27
1	AK	PAC	550	438	476	42	7.887	43
2	AZ	MTN	3665	445	497	25	4.231	30
3	AR	WSC	2351	470	511	6	3.334	23
4	CA	PAC	29760	419	484	45	4.826	39

```
In [18]:  states['text'] = 'SATv '+states['satv'].astype(str) + 'SATm '+states['satm'].astype(str) +'<br>'+\
          'State '+states['code']

          data = [dict(type='choropleth', autocolorscale=False, locations = states['code'], z= states['dollars'], location
          data
```

```
Out[18]:  [{'autocolorscale': False,
            'colorbar': {'title': 'thousand dollars'},
            'colorscale': 'custom-colorscale',
            'locationmode': 'USA-states',
            'locations': 0    AL
            1     AK
            2     AZ
            3     AR
            4     CA
            5     CO
            6     CN
            7     DE
            8     DC
            9     FL
            10    GA
            11    HI
            12    ID
            13    IL
            14    IN
```

```
In [19]:  layout = dict(title='State Spending on Public Education, in $k/student',
                   geo = dict(scope='usa', projection=dict(type='albers usa'), showlakes = True, lakecolor = 'rgb(66,
          layout
```

```
Out[19]:  {'geo': {'lakecolor': 'rgb(66,165,245)',
            'projection': {'type': 'albers usa'},
            'scope': 'usa',
            'showlakes': True},
           'title': 'State Spending on Public Education, in $k/student'}
```

```
In [20]:  fig = dict(data=data, layout=layout)

          py.iplot(fig, filename='d3-choropleth-map')
```

Generating point maps

```
In [21]:  address = 'C:/Users/Lillian Pierson/Desktop/Exercise Files/Ch09/09_03/snow_inventory.csv'
          snow = pd.read_csv(address)
          snow.columns = ['stn_id', 'lat', 'long', 'elev', 'code']

          snow_sample = snow.sample(n=200, random_state=25, axis=0)
          snow_sample.head
```

	stn_id	lat	long	elev	code
4479	USC00406292	36.4739	-81.8033	736.1	TN
2678	USC00237398	38.6856	-90.5231	137.2	MO
2902	USC00252820	40.0739	-97.1669	411.5	NE
2128	USC00170833	46.4283	-67.8442	128.0	ME
2138	USC00172878	47.2386	-68.6136	185.9	ME

```
data = [dict(type='scattergeo', locationmode='USA-states', lon= snow_sample['long'], lat = snow_sample['lat'],
        marker = dict(size=12, autocolorscale=False, colorscale='custom-colorscale', color = snow_sample['elev'],
            colorbar=dict(title = 'Elevation (m)')))]

layout = dict(title='NOAA Weather Snowfall Station Elevations', colorbar= True,
        geo = dict(scope='usa', projection= dict(type='albers usa'), showland=True, landcolor= "rgb(250,250,250)",
            subunitcolor = "rgb(217,217,217)", countrycolor = "rgb(217,217,217)", countrywidth = 0.5, subunitwidth =

fig = dict(data=data, layout=layout)

py.iplot(fig, validate=False, filename='d3-elevation')
```

References

1. Cleveland, William S. (1993). Visualizing Data. Hobart Press. ISBN 0-9634884-0-6.
2. Evergreen, Stephanie (2016). Effective Data Visualization: The Right Chart for the Right Data. Sage. ISBN 978-1-5063-0305 5.
3. Healy, Kieran (2019). Data Visualization: A Practical Introduction. Princeton: Princeton University Press. ISBN 978-0-691-18161-5.
4. Post, Frits H.; Nielson, Gregory M.; Bonneau, Georges-Pierre (2003). Data Visualization: The State of the Art. New York: Springer. ISBN 978-1-4613-5430-7.

5. Rosling, H.; Rosling, O.; Rosling Rönnlund, A. (2018). Factfulness: Ten Reasons We're Wrong About the World – and Why Things Are Better Than You Think. Flatiron Books. p. 288. ISBN 9781250123817.
6. Wilke, Claus O. (2018). Fundamentals of Data Visualization. O'Reilly. ISBN 978-1-4920-3108-6.
7. Wilkinson, Leland (2012). Grammar of Graphics. New York: Springer. ISBN 978-1-4419-2033-1.
8. Prakash K.B. Content extraction studies using total distance algorithm, 2017, Proceedings of the 2016 2nd International Conference on Applied and Theoretical Computing and Communication Technology, iCATccT 2016, 10.1109/ICATCCT.2016.7912085
9. Prakash K.B. Mining issues in traditional indian web documents, 2015, Indian Journal of Science and Technology, 8(32), 10.17485/ijst/2015/v8i1/77056
10. Prakash K.B., Rajaraman A., Lakshmi M. Complexities in developing multilingual on-line courses in the Indian context, 2017, Proceedings of the 2017 International Conference On Big Data Analytics and Computational Intelligence, ICBDACI 2017, 8070860, 339-342, 10.1109/ICBDACI.2017.8070860
11. Prakash K.B., Kumar K.S., Rao S.U.M. Content extraction issues in online web education, 2017, Proceedings of the 2016 2nd International Conference on Applied and Theoretical Computing and Communication Technology, iCATccT 2016, 7912086, 680-685, 10.1109/ICATCCT.2016.7912086
12. Prakash K.B., Rajaraman A., Perumal T., Kolla P. Foundations to frontiers of big data analytics, 2016, Proceedings of the 2016 2nd International Conference on Contemporary Computing and Informatics, IC3I 2016, 7917968,242-247, 10.1109/IC3I.2016.7917968

Web Scraping with Beautiful Soup

Web scraping is an automatic method to obtain large amounts of data from websites. Most of this data is unstructured data in an HTML format which is then converted into structured data in a spreadsheet or a database so that it can be used in various applications [1]. There are many different ways to perform web scraping to obtain data from websites. these include using online services, particular API's or even creating your code for web scraping from scratch. Many large websites, like Google, Twitter, Facebook, StackOverflow, etc. have API's that allow you to access their data in a structured format [2]. This is the best option, but there are other sites that don't allow users to access large amounts of data in a structured form or they are simply not that technologically advanced. In that situation, it's best to use Web Scraping to scrape the website for data [3].

Web scraping requires two parts, namely the **crawler** and the **scraper**. The crawler is an artificial intelligence algorithm that browses the web to search for the particular data required by following the links across the internet [4]. The scraper, on the other hand, is a specific tool created to extract data from the website. The design of the scraper can vary greatly according to the complexity and scope of the project so that it can quickly and accurately extract the data [5].

How Web Scrapers Work?

Web Scrapers can extract all the data on particular sites or the specific data that a user wants. Ideally, it's best if you specify the data you want so that the web scraper only extracts that data quickly [6]. For example, you might want to scrape an Amazon page for the types of juicers available, but you might only want the data about the models of different juicers and not the customer reviews [7].

So, when a web scraper needs to scrape a site, first the URLs are provided. Then it loads all the HTML code for those sites and a more advanced

Kolla Bhanu Prakash. Data Science Handbook: A Practical Approach, (221–256) © 2022 Scrivener Publishing LLC

scraper might even extract all the CSS and Javascript elements as well. Then the scraper obtains the required data from this HTML code and outputs this data in the format specified by the user. Mostly, this is in the form of an Excel spreadsheet or a CSV file, but the data can also be saved in other formats, such as a JSON file.

Different Types of Web Scrapers

Web Scrapers can be divided on the basis of many different criteria, including Self-built or Pre-built Web Scrapers, Browser extension or Software Web Scrapers, and Cloud or Local Web Scrapers.

You can have **Self-built Web Scrapers** but that requires advanced knowledge of programming. And if you want more features in your Web Scraper, then you need even more knowledge. On the other hand, pre-built **Web Scrapers** are previously created scrapers that you can download and run easily. These also have more advanced options that you can customize [8].

Browser extensions Web Scrapers are extensions that can be added to your browser. These are easy to run as they are integrated with your browser, but at the same time, they are also limited because of this. Any advanced features that are outside the scope of your browser are impossible to run on Browser extension Web Scrapers. But **Software Web Scrapers** don't have these limitations as they can be downloaded and installed on your computer. These are more complex than Browser web scrapers, but they also have advanced features that are not limited by the scope of your browser [9].

Cloud Web Scrapers run on the cloud, which is an off-site server mostly provided by the company that you buy the scraper from. These allow your computer to focus on other tasks as the computer resources are not required to scrape data from websites. **Local Web Scrapers**, on the other hand, run on your computer using local resources. So, if the Web scrapers require more CPU or RAM, then your computer will become slow and not be able to perform other tasks [10].

Applications of Web Scraping

Web Scraping has multiple applications across various industries. Let's check out some of these now!

1. **Price Monitoring**
   Web Scraping can be used by companies to scrap the product data for their products and competing products as well to see how it impacts their pricing strategies. Companies can use this data to fix the optimal pricing for their products so that they can obtain maximum revenue.
2. **Market Research**
   Web scraping can be used for market research by companies. High-quality web scraped data obtained in large volumes can be very helpful for companies in analyzing consumer trends and understanding which direction the company should move in the future.
3. **News Monitoring**
   Web scraping news sites can provide detailed reports on the current news to a company. This is even more essential for companies that are frequently in the news or that depend on daily news for their day to day functioning. After all, news reports can make or break a company in a single day!
4. **Sentiment Analysis**
   If companies want to understand the general sentiment for their products among their consumers, then Sentiment Analysis is a must. Companies can use web scraping to collect data from social media websites such as Facebook and Twitter as to what the general sentiment about their products is. This will help them in creating products that people desire and moving ahead of their competition [11].
5. **Email Marketing**
   Companies can also use Web scraping for email marketing. They can collect Email ID's from various sites using web scraping and then send bulk promotional and marketing Emails to all the people owning these Email ID's.

Advantages of Web Scraping

The most prominent advantages of web scraping services have been elaborated in the points below:

1. Low Costs
2. Easy Implementation

3. Accelerated Processes With Low Maintenance
4. Accurate Results

Disadvantages of Web Scraping

The major disadvantages of web scraping services have been elaborated in the following points:

1. Difficult To Analyze Scraping Processes
2. The Analysis Is Important Before Extracting Data
3. The Time Factor
4. Data Protection And Speed Issues

Working with objects

```
In [1]: ! pip install BeautifulSoup

        Requirement already satisfied (use --upgrade to upgrade): BeautifulSoup in c:\program files\anaconda2\lib\site
        -packages

        You are using pip version 8.1.2, however version 9.0.1 is available.
        You should consider upgrading via the 'python -m pip install --upgrade pip' command.

In [2]: from bs4 import BeautifulSoup
```

10.1   The BeautifulSoup Object

```
In [3]: html_doc = '''
        <html><head><title>Best Books</title></head>
        <body>
        <p class='title'><b>DATA SCIENCE FOR DUMMIES</b></p>

        <p class='description'>Jobs in data science abound, but few people have the data science skills needed to fill t
        <br><br>
        Edition 1 of this book:
              <br>
        <ul>
          <li>Provides a background in data science fundamentals before moving on to working with relational databases a
          <li>Details different data visualization techniques that can be used to showcase and summarize your data</li>
          <li>Explains both supervised and unsupervised machine learning, including regression, model validation, and cl
          <li>Includes coverage of big data processing tools like MapReduce, Hadoop, Storm, and Spark</li>
          </ul>
        <br><br>
        What to do next:
        <br>
        <a href='http://www.data-mania.com/blog/books-by-lillian-pierson/' class = 'preview' id='link 1'>See a preview o
        <a href='http://www.data-mania.com/blog/data-science-for-dummies-answers-what-is-data-science/' class = 'preview
        <a href='http://bit.ly/Data-Science-For-Dummies' class = 'preview' id='link 3'>buy the book!</a>
        </p>

        <p class='description'>...</p>
        '''
```

```
In [5]:  soup = BeautifulSoup(html_doc, 'html.parser')
         print(soup)
```

```
<html><head><title>Best Books</title></head>
<body>
<p class="title"><b>DATA SCIENCE FOR DUMMIES</b></p>
<p class="description">Jobs in data science abound, but few people have the data science skills needed to fill
these increasingly important roles in organizations. Data Science For Dummies is the pe
<br><br>
Edition 1 of this book:
        <br>
<ul>
<li>Provides a background in data science fundamentals before moving on to working with relational databases a
nd unstructured data and preparing your data for analysis</li>
<li>Details different data visualization techniques that can be used to showcase and summarize your data</li>
<li>Explains both supervised and unsupervised machine learning, including regression, model validation, and cl
ustering techniques</li>
<li>Includes coverage of big data processing tools like MapReduce, Hadoop, Storm, and Spark</li>
</ul>
<br><br>
What to do next:
<br>
<a class="preview" href="http://www.data-mania.com/blog/books-by-lillian-pierson/" id="link 1">See a preview o
f the book</a>,
<a class="preview" href="http://www.data-mania.com/blog/data-science-for-dummies-answers-what-is-data-science
/" id="link 2">get the free pdf download,</a> and then
<a class="preview" href="http://bit.ly/Data-Science-For-Dummies" id="link 3">buy the book!</a>
</br></br></br></br></br></br></p>
<p class="description">...</p>
</body></html>
```

```
In [7]:  print soup.prettify()[0:350]
```

```
<html>
 <head>
  <title>
   Best Books
  </title>
 </head>
 <body>
  <p class="title">
   <b>
    DATA SCIENCE FOR DUMMIES
   </b>
  </p>
  <p class="description">
   Jobs in data science abound, but few people have the data science skills needed to fill these increasingly
important roles in organizations. Data Science For Dummies is the pe
   <br>
```

Tag objects

Working with names

```
In [8]:  soup = BeautifulSoup('<b body="description"">Product Description</b>', 'html')
         tag=soup.b
         type(tag)

C:\Program Files\Anaconda2\lib\site-packages\bs4\__init__.py:181: UserWarning: No parser was explicitly specif
ied, so I'm using the best available HTML parser for this system ("lxml"). This usually isn't a problem, but i
f you run this code on another system, or in a different virtual environment, it may use a different parser an
d behave differently.

The code that caused this warning is on line 174 of the file C:\Program Files\Anaconda2\lib\runpy.py. To get r
id of this warning, change code that looks like this:

 BeautifulSoup([your markup])

to this:

 BeautifulSoup([your markup], "lxml")

  markup_type=markup_type))
```

```
Out[8]:  bs4.element.Tag
```

```
In [9]: print tag
```

```
<b body="description">Product Description</b>
```

```
In [10]: tag.name
```

```
Out[10]: 'b'
```

```
In [11]: tag.name = 'bestbooks'
         tag
```

```
Out[11]: <bestbooks body="description">Product Description</bestbooks>
```

```
In [12]: tag.name
```

```
Out[12]: 'bestbooks'
```

Working with attributes

```
In [13]: tag['body']
```

```
Out[13]: 'description'
```

```
In [14]: tag.attrs
```

```
Out[14]: {'body': 'description'}
```

```
In [15]: tag['id'] = 3
         tag.attrs
```

```
Out[15]: {'body': 'description', 'id': 3}
```

```
In [16]: tag
```

```
Out[16]: <bestbooks body="description" id="3">Product Description</bestbooks>
```

```
In [17]: del tag['body']
         del tag['id']
         tag
```

```
Out[17]: <bestbooks>Product Description</bestbooks>
```

```
In [18]: tag.attrs
```

```
Out[18]: {}
```

Using tags to navigate a tree

```
In [19]: html_doc = '''
         <html><head><title>Best Books</title></head>
         <body>
         <p class='title'><b>DATA SCIENCE FOR DUMMIES</b></p>

         <p class='description'>Jobs in data science abound, but few people have the data science skills needed to fill t
         <br><br>
         Edition 1 of this book:
              <br>
         <ul>
           <li>Provides a background in data science fundamentals before moving on to working with relational databases a
           <li>Details different data visualization techniques that can be used to showcase and summarize your data</li>
           <li>Explains both supervised and unsupervised machine learning, including regression, model validation, and cl
           <li>Includes coverage of big data processing tools like MapReduce, Hadoop, Storm, and Spark</li>
         </ul>
         <br><br>
         What to do next:
         <br>
         <a href="http://www.data-mania.com/blog/books-by-lillian-pierson/" class = 'preview' id="link 1">See a preview o
         <a href="http://www.data-mania.com/blog/data-science-for-dummies-answers-what-is-data-science/" class = 'preview
         <a href="http://bit.ly/Data-Science-For-Dummies" class = 'preview' id="link 3">buy the book!</a>
         </p>

         <p class='description'>...</p>
         '''
         soup = BeautifulSoup(html_doc, 'html.parser')
```

```
In [20]: soup.head
```
```
Out[20]: <head><title>Best Books</title></head>
```

```
In [21]: soup.title
```
```
Out[21]: <title>Best Books</title>
```

```
In [22]: soup.body.b
```
```
Out[22]: <b>DATA SCIENCE FOR DUMMIES</b>
```

```
In [23]: soup.body
```
```
Out[23]: <body>\n<p class="title"><b>DATA SCIENCE FOR DUMMIES</b></p>\n<p class="description">Jobs in data science abou
         nd, but few people have the data science skills needed to fill these increasingly important roles in organizat
         ions. Data Science For Dummies is the pe\n<br><br>\nEdition 1 of this book:\n        <br>\n<ul>\n<li>Provides
         a background in data science fundamentals before moving on to working with relational databases and unstructur
         ed data and preparing your data for analysis</li>\n<li>Details different data visualization techniques that ca
         n be used to showcase and summarize your data</li>\n<li>Explains both supervised and unsupervised machine lear
         ning, including regression, model validation, and clustering techniques</li>\n<li>Includes coverage of big dat
         a processing tools like MapReduce, Hadoop, Storm, and Spark</li>\n</ul>\n<br><br>\nWhat to do next:\n<br>\n<a
         class="preview" href="http://www.data-mania.com/blog/books-by-lillian-pierson/" id="link 1">See a preview of t
         he book</a>,\n<a class="preview" href="http://www.data-mania.com/blog/data-science-for-dummies-answers-what-is
         -data-science/" id="link 2">get the free pdf download,</a> and then\n<a class="preview" href="http://bit.ly/Da
         ta-Science-For-Dummies" id="link 3">buy the book!</a>\n</br></br></br></br></br></br></p>\n<p class="descripti
         on">...</p>\n</body>
```

```
In [24]: soup.ul
```
```
Out[24]: <ul>\n<li>Provides a background in data science fundamentals before moving on to working with relational datab
         ases and unstructured data and preparing your data for analysis</li>\n<li>Details different data visualization
         techniques that can be used to showcase and summarize your data</li>\n<li>Explains both supervised and unsuper
         vised machine learning, including regression, model validation, and clustering techniques</li>\n<li>Includes c
         overage of big data processing tools like MapReduce, Hadoop, Storm, and Spark</li>\n</ul>
```

```
In [25]: soup.a
```
```
Out[25]: <a class="preview" href="http://www.data-mania.com/blog/books-by-lillian-pierson/" id="link 1">See a preview o
         f the book</a>
```

10.2   Exploring NavigableString Objects

In [13]:
```python
from bs4 import BeautifulSoup
```

The BeautifulSoup object

In [14]:
```python
soup = BeautifulSoup('<b body="description">Product description</b>')
```

NavigableString objects

In [15]:
```python
tag= soup.b
type(tag)
```

Out[15]: **bs4.element.Tag**

In [16]:
```python
tag.name
```

Out[16]: **'b'**

In [17]:
```python
tag.string
```

Out[17]: u'Product description'

In [19]:
```python
type(tag.string)
```

Out[19]: **bs4.element.NavigableString**

```
In [20]: nav_string = tag.string
         nav_string

Out[20]: u'Product description'

In [21]: nav_string.replace_with('Null')
         tag.string

Out[21]: u'Null'
```

Working with NavigableString objects

```
In [22]: html_doc = '''
<html><head><title>Best Books</title></head>
<body>
<p class="title"><b>DATA SCIENCE FOR DUMMIES</b></p>

<p class="description">Jobs in data science abound, but few people have the data science skills needed to fill t
<br><br>
Edition 1 of this book:
        <br>
    <ul>
      <li>Provides a background in data science fundamentals before moving on to working with relational databases a
      <li>Details different data visualization techniques that can be used to showcase and summarize your data</li>
      <li>Explains both supervised and unsupervised machine learning, including regression, model validation, and cl
      <li>Includes coverage of big data processing tools like MapReduce, Hadoop, Storm, and Spark</li>
    </ul>
<br><br>
What to do next:
<br>
<a href='http://www.data-mania.com/blog/books-by-lillian-pierson/' class = 'preview' id='link 1'>See a preview o
<a href='http://www.data-mania.com/blog/data-science-for-dummies-answers-what-is-data-science/' class = 'preview
<a href='http://bit.ly/Data-Science-For-Dummies' class = 'preview' id='link 3'>buy the book'</a>
</p>

<p class="description">...</p>
'''
soup = BeautifulSoup(html_doc, 'html.parser')
```

```
In [23]: for string in soup.stripped_strings: print(repr(string))
u'Best Books'
u'DATA SCIENCE FOR DUMMIES'
u'Jobs in data science abound, but few people have the data science skills needed to fill these increasingly i
mportant roles in organizations. Data Science For Dummies is the pe'
u'Edition 1 of this book:'
u'Provides a background in data science fundamentals before moving on to working with relational databases and
unstructured data and preparing your data for analysis'
u'Details different data visualization techniques that can be used to showcase and summarize your data'
u'Explains both supervised and unsupervised machine learning, including regression, model validation, and clus
tering techniques'
u'Includes coverage of big data processing tools like MapReduce, Hadoop, Storm, and Spark'
u'What to do next:'
u'See a preview of the book'
u','
u'get the free pdf download,'
u'and then'
u'buy the book!'
u'...'
```

```
In [24]:  title_tag = soup.title
          title_tag

Out[24]:  <title>Best Books</title>


In [25]:  title_tag.parent

Out[25]:  <head><title>Best Books</title></head>


In [26]:  title_tag.string

Out[26]:  u'Best Books'


In [27]:  title_tag.string.parent

Out[27]:  <title>Best Books</title>
```

DATA SCIENCE FOR DUMMIES

Jobs in data science abound, but few people have the data science skills needed to fill these increasingly important roles in organizations. Data Science For Dummies is the pe

Edition 1 of this book:

- Provides a background in data science fundamentals before moving on to working with relational databases and unstructured data and preparing your data for analysis
- Details different data visualization techniques that can be used to showcase and summarize your data
- Explains both supervised and unsupervised machine learning, including regression, model validation, and clustering techniques
- Includes coverage of big data processing tools like MapReduce, Hadoop, Storm, and Spark

What to do next:
See a preview of the book, get the free pdf download, and then buy the book!

10.3   Data Parsing

```
In [1]:  import pandas as pd

         from bs4 import BeautifulSoup

         import re
```

```
In [2]: r = '''
        <html><head><title>Best Books</title></head>
        <body>
        <p class='title'><b>DATA SCIENCE FOR DUMMIES</b></p>

        <p class='description'>Jobs in data science abound, but few people have the data science skills needed to fill t
        <br><br>
        Edition 1 of this book:
                <br>
          <ul>
           <li>Provides a background in data science fundamentals before moving on to working with relational databases a
            <li>Details different data visualization techniques that can be used to showcase and summarize your data</li>
            <li>Explains both supervised and unsupervised machine learning, including regression, model validation, and cl
            <li>Includes coverage of big data processing tools like MapReduce, Hadoop, Storm, and Spark</li>
          </ul>
        <br><br>
        What to do next:
        <br>
        <a href='http://www.data-mania.com/blog/books-by-lillian-pierson/' class = 'preview' id='link 1'>See a preview o
        <a href='http://www.data-mania.com/blog/data-science-for-dummies-answers-what-is-data-science/' class = 'preview
        <a href='http://bit.ly/Data-Science-For-Dummies' class = 'preview' id='link 3'>buy the book!</a>
        </p>

        <p class='description'>...</p>
        '''
```

```
In [3]: soup = BeautifulSoup(r, 'lxml')
        type(soup)
```

```
Out[3]: bs4.BeautifulSoup
```

Parsing your data

```
In [4]: print soup.prettify()[0:100]
```

```
<html>
 <head>
  <title>
   Best Books
  </title>
 </head>
 <body>
  <p class="title">
   <b>
    DA
```

Getting data from a parse tree

```
In [5]: text_only = soup.get_text()
        print(text_only)
```

```
Best Books

DATA SCIENCE FOR DUMMIES
Jobs in data science abound, but few people have the data science skills needed to fill these increasingly imp
ortant roles in organizations. Data Science For Dummies is the pe

Edition 1 of this book:


Provides a background in data science fundamentals before moving on to working with relational databases and u
nstructured data and preparing your data for analysis
Details different data visualization techniques that can be used to showcase and summarize your data
Explains both supervised and unsupervised machine learning, including regression, model validation, and cluste
ring techniques
Includes coverage of big data processing tools like MapReduce, Hadoop, Storm, and Spark


What to do next:

See a preview of the book,
get the free pdf download, and then
buy the book!
...
```

Searching and retrieving data from a parse tree

Retrieving tags by filtering with name arguments

```
In [6]: soup.find_all("li")
```

Out[6]: [<li>Provides a background in data science fundamentals before moving on to working with relational databases and unstructured data and preparing your data for analysis</li>,
<li>Details different data visualization techniques that can be used to showcase and summarize your data</li>,
<li>Explains both supervised and unsupervised machine learning, including regression, model validation, and c lustering techniques</li>,
<li>Includes coverage of big data processing tools like MapReduce, Hadoop, Storm, and Spark</li>]

Retrieving tags by filtering with keyword arguments

```
In [8]: soup.find_all(id="link 3")
```

Out[8]: [<a class="preview" href="http://bit.ly/Data-Science-For-Dummies" id="link 3">buy the book!</a>]

Retrieving tags by filtering with string arguments

```
In [11]: soup.find_all('ul')
```

Out[11]: [<ul>\n<li>Provides a background in data science fundamentals before moving on to working with relational data bases and unstructured data and preparing your data for analysis</li>\n<li>Details different data visualizatio n techniques that can be used to showcase and summarize your data</li>\n<li>Explains both supervised and unsup ervised machine learning, including regression, model validation, and clustering techniques</li>\n<li>Includes coverage of big data processing tools like MapReduce, Hadoop, Storm, and Spark</li>\n</ul>]

Retrieving tags by filtering with list objects

```
In [12]: soup.find_all(['ul', 'b'])
```

Out[12]: [DATA SCIENCE FOR DUMMIES,
<ul>\n<li>Provides a background in data science fundamentals before moving on to working with relational data bases and unstructured data and preparing your data for analysis</li>\n<li>Details different data visualizatio n techniques that can be used to showcase and summarize your data</li>\n<li>Explains both supervised and unsup ervised machine learning, including regression, model validation, and clustering techniques</li>\n<li>Includes coverage of big data processing tools like MapReduce, Hadoop, Storm, and Spark</li>\n</ul>]

Retrieving tags by filtering with regular expressions

```
In [13]: l = re.compile('l')
         for tag in soup.find_all(l): print(tag.name)

         html
         title
         ul
         li
         li
         li
         li
```

Retrieving tags by filtering with a Boolean value

```
In [14]: for tag in soup.find_all(True): print(tag.name)

         html
         head
         title
         body
         p
         b
         p
         br
         br
         br
         ul
         li
         li
         li
         li
         br
         br
         br
         a
         a
         a
         p
```

Retrieving weblinks by filtering with string objects

```
In [16]: for link in soup.find_all('a'): print(link.get('href'))

         http://www.data-mania.com/blog/books-by-lillian-pierson/
         http://www.data-mania.com/blog/data-science-for-dummies-answers-what-is-data-science/
         http://bit.ly/Data-Science-For-Dummies
```

Retrieving strings by filtering with regular expressions

```
In [17]: soup.find_all(string=re.compile("data"))

Out[17]: [u'Jobs in data science abound, but few people have the data science skills needed to fill these increasingly
         important roles in organizations. Data Science For Dummies is the pe\n',
          u'Provides a background in data science fundamentals before moving on to working with relational databases an
         d unstructured data and preparing your data for analysis',
          u'Details different data visualization techniques that can be used to showcase and summarize your data',
          u'Includes coverage of big data processing tools like MapReduce, Hadoop, Storm, and Spark']
```

10.4   Web Scraping

```
In [1]: from bs4 import BeautifulSoup
        import urllib
        import re
```

```
In [2]: r = urllib.urlopen('https://analytics.usa.gov').read()
        soup = BeautifulSoup(r, "lxml")
        type(soup)
```

Out[2]: bs4.BeautifulSoup

Scraping a webpage and saving your results

```
In [3]: print soup.prettify()[:100]
```

```
<!DOCTYPE html>
<html lang="en">
 <!-- Initalize title and data source variables -->
 <head>
  <!--
```

```
In [4]: for link in soup.find_all('a'): print(link.get('href'))
```

```
/
#explanation
https://analytics.usa.gov/data/
data/
#top-pages-realtime
#top-pages-7-days
#top-pages-30-days
https://analytics.usa.gov/data/live/all-pages-realtime.csv
https://analytics.usa.gov/data/live/top-domains-30-days.csv
https://www.digitalgov.gov/services/dap/
https://www.digitalgov.gov/services/dap/common-questions-about-dap-faq/#part-4
https://support.google.com/analytics/answer/2763052?hl=en
https://analytics.usa.gov/data/live/second-level-domains.csv
https://analytics.usa.gov/data/live/sites.csv
mailto:DAP@support.digitalgov.gov
https://github.com/GSA/analytics.usa.gov
https://github.com/18F/analytics-reporter
https://github.com/GSA/analytics.usa.gov/issues
mailto:DAP@support.digitalgov.gov
https://analytics.usa.gov/data/
```

```
In [6]: for link in soup.findAll('a', attrs={'href': re.compile("^http")}): print link
```

```
<a href="https://analytics.usa.gov/data/">Data</a>
<a href="https://analytics.usa.gov/data/live/all-pages-realtime.csv">Download the full dataset.</a>
<a href="https://analytics.usa.gov/data/live/top-domains-30-days.csv">Download the full dataset.</a>
<a class="external-link" href="https://www.digitalgov.gov/services/dap/">Digital Analytics Program</a>
<a class="external-link" href="https://www.digitalgov.gov/services/dap/common-questions-about-dap-faq/#part-4"
>does not track individuals</a>
<a class="external-link" href="https://support.google.com/analytics/answer/2763052?hl=en">anonymizes the IP ad
dresses</a>
<a class="external-link" href="https://analytics.usa.gov/data/live/second-level-domains.csv">400 executive bra
nch government domains</a>
<a class="external-link" href="https://analytics.usa.gov/data/live/sites.csv">about 5000 total websites</a>
<a class="external-link" href="https://github.com/GSA/analytics.usa.gov">code for this website</a>
<a class="external-link" href="https://github.com/18F/analytics-reporter">code behind the data collection</a>
<a class="external-link" href="https://github.com/GSA/analytics.usa.gov/issues">open an issue on GitHub</a>
<a href="https://analytics.usa.gov/data/">download the data here.</a>
```

```
In [17]: file = open('parsed_data.txt', 'wb')
         for link in soup.findAll('a', attrs={'href': re.compile("^http")}):
             soup_link = str(link)
             print soup_link
             file.write(soup_link)
         file.flush()
         file.close()
```

```
<a href="https://analytics.usa.gov/data/">Data</a>
<a href="https://analytics.usa.gov/data/live/all-pages-realtime.csv">Download the full dataset.</a>
<a href="https://analytics.usa.gov/data/live/top-domains-30-days.csv">Download the full dataset.</a>
<a class="external-link" href="https://www.digitalgov.gov/services/dap/">Digital Analytics Program</a>
<a class="external-link" href="https://www.digitalgov.gov/services/dap/common-questions-about-dap-faq/#part-4"
>does not track individuals</a>
<a class="external-link" href="https://support.google.com/analytics/answer/2763052?hl=en">anonymizes the IP ad
dresses</a>
<a class="external-link" href="https://analytics.usa.gov/data/live/second-level-domains.csv">400 executive bra
nch government domains</a>
<a class="external-link" href="https://analytics.usa.gov/data/live/sites.csv">about 5000 total websites</a>
<a class="external-link" href="https://github.com/GSA/analytics.usa.gov">code for this website</a>
<a class="external-link" href="https://github.com/18F/analytics-reporter">code behind the data collection</a>
<a class="external-link" href="https://github.com/GSA/analytics.usa.gov/issues">open an issue on GitHub</a>
<a href="https://analytics.usa.gov/data/">download the data here.</a>
```

```
In [19]: %pwd
```

Out[19]: u'C:\\Users\\Lillian Pierson\\Desktop\\Exercise Files\\Ch10\\10_04'

10.5   Ensemble Models with Random Forests

Ensemble Learning algorithms

Ensemble learning algorithms are **meta-algorithms** that combine several machine learning algorithms into one predictive model in order to decrease variance, bias or improve predictions.

The algorithm can be any machine learning algorithm such as logistic regression, decision tree, etc. These models, when used as inputs of ensemble methods, are called "**base models**".

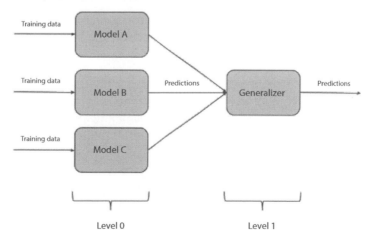

Ensemble learning

Ensemble methods usually produce more accurate solutions than a single model would. This has been the case in a number of machine learning competitions, where the winning solutions used ensemble methods. In the popular Netflix Competition, the winner used an ensemble method to implement a powerful collaborative filtering algorithm. Another example is KDD 2009 where the winner also used ensemble methods.

Ensemble algorithms or methods can be divided into two groups:

- **Sequential ensemble methods** — where the base learners are generated sequentially (e.g. AdaBoost). The basic motivation of sequential methods is to **exploit the dependence between the base learners.** The overall performance can be boosted by weighing previously mislabeled examples with higher weight.
- **Parallel ensemble methods** — where the base learners are generated in parallel (e.g. Random Forest). The basic motivation of parallel methods is to **exploit independence between the base learners** since the error can be reduced dramatically by averaging.

Most ensemble methods use a single base learning algorithm to produce homogeneous base learners, i.e. learners of the same type, leading to homogeneous ensembles.

There are also some methods that use heterogeneous learners, i.e. learners of different types, leading to heterogeneous ensembles. In order for ensemble methods to be more accurate than any of its individual members, the base learners have to be as accurate as possible and as diverse as possible.

What is the Random Forest algorithm?

Random forest is a supervised ensemble learning algorithm that is used for both classifications as well as regression problems. But however, it is mainly used for classification problems. As we know that a forest is made up of trees and more trees mean more robust forest. Similarly, the random forest algorithm creates decision trees on data samples and then gets the prediction from each of them and finally selects the best solution by means of voting. It is an ensemble method that is better than a single decision tree because it reduces the over-fitting by averaging the result [12].

Blue

As per majority voting, the final result is 'Blue'.

The fundamental concept behind random forest is a simple but powerful one — **the wisdom of crowds.**

"A large number of relatively uncorrelated models(trees) operating as a committee will outperform any of the individual constituent models."

The low correlation between models is the key.

The reason why Random forest produces exceptional results is that the trees protect each other from their individual errors. While some trees may be wrong, many others will be right, so as a group the trees are able to move in the correct direction.

Why the name "Random"?

Two key concepts that give it the name random:

1. A random sampling of training data set when building trees.
2. Random subsets of features considered when splitting nodes.

How is Random Forest ensuring Model diversity?

Random forest ensures that the behavior of each individual tree is not too correlated with the behavior of any other tree in the model by using the following two methods:

- Bagging or Bootstrap Aggregation
- Random feature selection

Bagging or Bootstrap Aggregation

Decision trees are very sensitive to the data they are trained on, small changes to the training data set can result in a significantly different tree structure. The random forest takes advantage of this by allowing each individual tree to **randomly sample from the dataset with replacement**, resulting in different trees. This process is called Bagging.

Note that with bagging we are not subsetting the training data into smaller chunks and training each tree on a different chunk. Rather, if we have a sample of size **N**, we are still feeding each tree a training set of size **N**. But instead of the original training data, we take a random sample of size **N** with replacement.

For example — If our training data is [1,2,3,4,5,6], then we might give one of our trees the list [1,2,2,3,6,6] and we can give another tree a list [2,3,4,4,5,6]. Notice that the lists are of length **6** and some elements are repeated in the randomly selected training data we can give to our tree (because we sample with replacement).

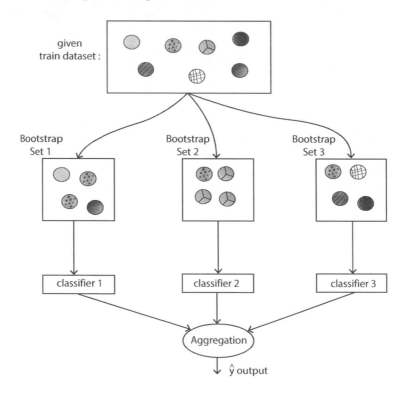

Bagging

The above figure shows how random samples are taken from the dataset with replacement.

Random feature selection

In a normal decision tree, when it is time to split a node, we consider every possible feature and pick the one that produces the most separation between the observations in the left node vs right node. In contrast, each tree in a random forest can pick only from a random subset of features. This forces even more variation amongst the trees in the model and ulti-mately results in low correlation across trees and more diversification.

So in random forest, we end up with trees that are trained on different sets of data and also use different features to make decisions.

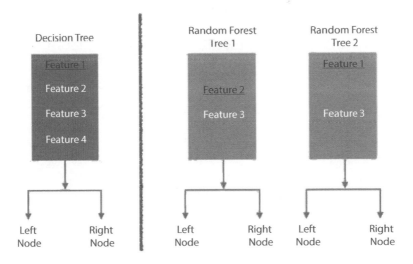

Random feature selection by different trees in random forest.

And finally, uncorrelated trees have created that buffer and predict each other from their respective errors.

Random Forest creation pseudocode:

1. Randomly select "**k**" features from total "**m**" features where **k << m**

2. Among the "**k**" features, calculate the node "**d**" using the best split point
3. Split the node into **daughter nodes** using the **best split**
4. Repeat the 1 **to 3** steps until "l" number of nodes has been reached
5. Build forest by repeating steps 1 **to 4** for "n" number times to create **"n" number of trees.**

Random Forest classifier Building in Scikit-learn

In this section, we are going to build a Gender Recognition classifier using the Random Forest algorithm from the voice dataset. The idea is to identify a voice as male or female, based upon the acoustic properties of the voice and speech. The dataset consists of 3,168 recorded voice samples, collected from male and female speakers. The voice samples are pre-processed by acoustic analysis in R using the seewave and tuneR packages, with an analyzed frequency range of 0hz-280hz.

The dataset can be downloaded from kaggle.

The goal is to create a Decision tree and Random Forest classifier and compare the accuracy of both the models. The following are the steps that we will perform in the process of model building:

1. Importing Various Modules and Loading the Dataset
2. Exploratory Data Analysis (EDA)
3. Outlier Treatment
4. Feature Engineering
5. Preparing the Data
6. Model building
7. Model optimization

So let us start.

Step-1: Importing Various Modules and Loading the Dataset

```
# Ignore the warnings
import warnings
warnings.filterwarnings('always')
warnings.filterwarnings('ignore')# data visualisation and manipulation-
import numpy as np
import pandas as pd
```

```
import matplotlib.pyplot as plt
from matplotlib import style
import seaborn as sns
import missingno as msno#configure
# sets matplotlib to inline and displays graphs below the corressponding
cell.
%matplotlib inline
style.use('fivethirtyeight')
sns.set(style='whitegrid',color_codes=True)#import the necessary modelling
algos.
from sklearn.ensemble import RandomForestClassifier
from sklearn.tree import DecisionTreeClassifier

#model selection
from sklearn.model_selection import train_test_split
from sklearn.model_selection import KFold
from sklearn.metrics import accuracy_score,precision_score
from sklearn.model_selection import GridSearchCV#preprocess.
from sklearn.preprocessing import MinMaxScaler,StandardScaler
```

Now load the dataset.

```
train=pd.read_csv("../RandomForest/voice.csv")df=train.copy()
```

Step-2: Exploratory Data Analysis (EDA)

```
df.head(10)
```

Q25	Q75	IQR	skew	kurt	sp.ent	sfm	...	centroid	meanfun	minfun	maxfun	meandom	mindom	maxdom	dfrange	modindx	label
.015071	0.090193	0.075122	12.863462	274.402906	0.893369	0.491918	...	0.059781	0.084279	0.015702	0.275862	0.007812	0.007812	0.007812	0.000000	0.000000	male
.019414	0.092866	0.073252	22.423285	634.613855	0.892193	0.513724	...	0.066009	0.107937	0.015826	0.250000	0.009014	0.007812	0.054688	0.046875	0.052632	male
.008701	0.131908	0.123207	30.757155	1024.927705	0.846389	0.478905	...	0.077316	0.098706	0.015656	0.271186	0.007990	0.007812	0.015825	0.007812	0.046512	male
.096582	0.207955	0.111374	1.232831	4.177296	0.963322	0.727232	...	0.151228	0.088965	0.017798	0.250000	0.201497	0.007812	0.562500	0.554688	0.247119	male
.078720	0.206045	0.127325	1.101174	4.333713	0.971955	0.783568	...	0.135120	0.106398	0.016931	0.266667	0.712812	0.007812	5.484375	5.476562	0.208274	male
.067958	0.209592	0.141634	1.932562	8.308896	0.963181	0.738207	...	0.132786	0.110102	0.017112	0.253906	0.280222	0.007812	2.726562	2.718750	0.125160	male
.092899	0.205718	0.112819	1.530643	5.987498	0.967573	0.762638	...	0.150762	0.105945	0.026230	0.266667	0.479620	0.007812	5.312500	5.304688	0.123992	male
.110532	0.231962	0.121430	1.397156	4.766611	0.959255	0.719858	...	0.160514	0.093052	0.017758	0.144144	0.301339	0.007812	0.539062	0.531250	0.283937	male
.088206	0.208587	0.120381	1.099746	4.070284	0.970723	0.770992	...	0.142239	0.096729	0.017957	0.250000	0.336476	0.015825	2.164062	2.156250	0.148272	male
.075580	0.201957	0.126377	1.190368	4.787310	0.975246	0.804505	...	0.134329	0.105881	0.019300	0.262295	0.340366	0.015825	4.695312	4.679688	0.089920	male
.101430	0.216740	0.115310	0.979442	3.974223	0.965249	0.733893	...	0.157021	0.088894	0.022089	0.117647	0.460227	0.007812	2.812500	2.804688	0.200000	male

Dataset
The following acoustic properties of each voice are measured and included within our data:

- **meanfreq**: mean frequency (in kHz)
- **sd**: standard deviation of the frequency
- **median**: median frequency (in kHz)
- **Q25**: first quantile (in kHz)
- **Q75**: third quantile (in kHz)
- **IQR**: interquartile range (in kHz)
- **skew**: skewness
- **kurt**: kurtosis
- **sp.ent**: spectral entropy
- **sfm**: spectral flatness
- **mode**: mode frequency
- **centroid**: frequency centroid
- **peakf**: peak frequency (the frequency with the highest energy)
- **meanfun**: the average of fundamental frequency measured across an acoustic signal
- **minfun**: minimum fundamental frequency measured across an acoustic signal
- **maxfun**: maximum fundamental frequency measured across an acoustic signal
- **meandom**: the average of dominant frequency measured across an acoustic signal
- **mindom**: minimum of dominant frequency measured across an acoustic signal
- **maxdom**: maximum of dominant frequency measured across an acoustic signal
- **dfrange**: the range of dominant frequency measured across an acoustic signal
- **modindx**: modulation index which is calculated as the accumulated absolute difference between adjacent measurements of fundamental frequencies divided by the frequency range
- **label**: male or female

```
df.shape
```

Note that we have 3168 voice samples and for each sample, 20 different acoustic properties are recorded. Finally, the 'label' column is the target variable which we have to predict which is the gender of the person.

Now our next step is handling the missing values.

```
# check for null values.
df.isnull().any()
```

```
                    meanfreq      False
                    sd            False
                    median        False
                    Q25           False
                    Q75           False
                    IQR           False
                    skew          False
                    kurt          False
                    sp.ent        False
                    sfm           False
                    mode          False
                    centroid      False
                    meanfun       False
                    minfun        False
                    maxfun        False
                    meandom       False
                    mindom        False
                    maxdom        False
                    dfrange       False
                    modindx       False
                    label         False
```

No missing values in our dataset.

Now I will perform the univariate analysis. Note that since all of the features are 'numeric' the most reasonable way to plot them would either be a 'histogram' or a 'boxplot'.

Also, univariate analysis is useful for outlier detection. Hence besides plotting a boxplot and a histogram for each column or feature, I have written a small utility function that tells the remaining no. of observations for each feature if we remove its outliers.

To detect the outliers I have used the standard 1.5 InterQuartileRange (IQR) rule which states that any observation lesser than 'first quartile — 1.5 IQR' or greater than 'third quartile +1.5 IQR' is an outlier.

```
def calc_limits(feature):
    q1,q3=df[feature].quantile([0.25,0.75])
    iqr=q3-q1
    rang=1.5*iqr
    return(q1-rang,q3+rang)
```

```
def plot(feature):
    fig,axes=plt.subplots(1,2)
    sns.boxplot(data=df,x=feature,ax=axes[0])
    sns.distplot(a=df[feature],ax=axes[1],color='#ff4125')
    fig.set_size_inches(15,5)

    lower,upper = calc_limits(feature)
    l=[df[feature] for i in df[feature] if i>lower and i<upper]
    print("Number of data points remaining if outliers removed : ",len(l))
```

Let us plot the first feature i.e. meanfreq.

```
plot('meanfreq')
```

Number of data points remaining if outliers removed : 3104

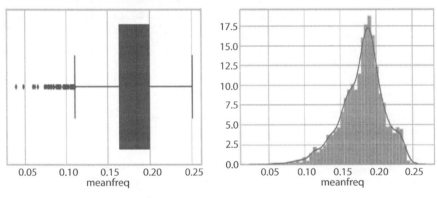

Inferences made from the above plots —

1. First of all, note that the values are in compliance with that observed from describing the method data frame.
2. Note that we have a couple of outliers w.r.t. to 1.5 quartile rule (represented by a 'dot' in the box plot). Removing these data points or outliers leaves us with around 3104 values.
3. Also, from the distplot that the distribution seems to be a bit -ve skewed hence we can normalize to make the distribution a bit more symmetric.
4. lastly, note that a left tail distribution has more outliers on the side below to q1 as expected and a right tail has above the q3.

Similar inferences can be made by plotting other features also, I have plotted some, you guys can check for all.

Number of data points remaing if outliers removed : 3158

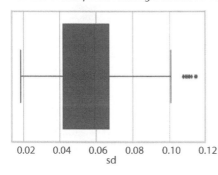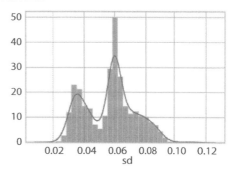

Number of data points remaining if outliers removed : 3059

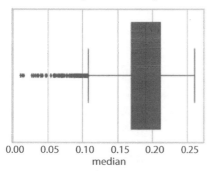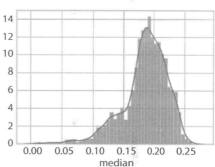

Number of data points remaining if outliers removed : 3059

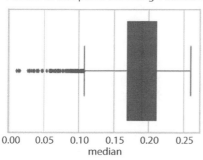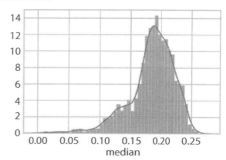

Number of data points remaining if outliers removed : 3168

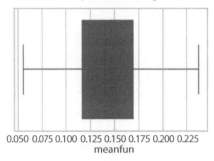 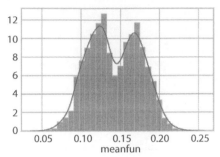

Now plot and count the target variable to check if the target class is balanced or not.

```
sns.countplot(data=df,x='label')
df['label'].value_counts()
```

female 1584
male 1584
Name: label, dtype: int64

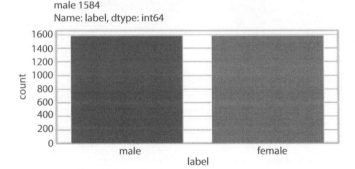

Plot for Target variable

We have the equal number of observations for the 'males' and the 'females' class hence it is a balanced dataset and we don't need to do anything about it.

Now I will perform Bivariate analysis to analyze the correlation between different features. To do it I have plotted a 'heat map' which clearly visualizes the correlation between different features.

```
temp = []
for i in df.label:
  if i == 'male':
    temp.append(1)
  else:
```

```
    temp.append(0)

df['label'] = temp

#corelation matrix.

cor_mat= df[:].corr()

mask = np.array(cor_mat)

mask[np.tril_indices_from(mask)] = False

fig=plt.gcf()

fig.set_size_inches(23,9)

sns.heatmap(data=cor_mat,mask=mask,square=True,annot=True,
cbar=True)
```

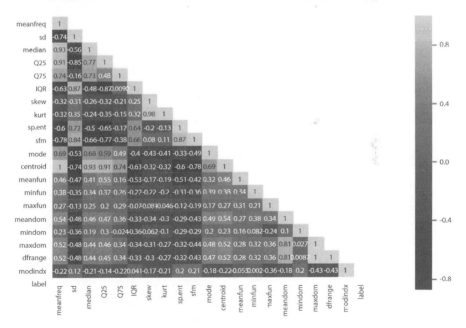

Heatmap
Inferences made from above heatmap plot—

1. Mean frequency is moderately related to label.
2. IQR and label tend to have a strong positive correlation.

3. Spectral entropy is also quite highly correlated with the label while sfm is moderately related with label.
4. skewness and kurtosis aren't much related to label.
5. meanfun is highly negatively correlated with the label.
6. Centroid and median have a high positive correlation expected from their formulae.
7. Also, meanfreq and centroid are exactly the same features as per formulae and so are thevalues. Hence their correlation is perfect 1. In this case, we can drop any of that column. Note that centroid in general has a high degree of correlation with most of the other features so I'm going to drop centroid column.
8. sd is highly positively related to sfm and so is sp.ent to sd.
9. kurt and skew are also highly correlated.
10. meanfreq is highly related to the median as well as Q25.
11. IQR is highly correlated to sd.
12. Finally, self relation ie of a feature to itself is equal to 1 as expected.

Note that we can drop some highly correlated features as they add redundancy to the model but let us keep all the features for now. In the case of highly correlated features, we can use dimensionality reduction techniques like Principal Component Analysis(PCA) to reduce our feature space.

```
df.drop('centroid',axis=1,inplace=True)
```

Step-3: Outlier Treatment
Here we have to deal with the outliers. Note that we discovered the potential outliers in the **'univariate analysis'** section. Now to remove those outliers we can either remove the corresponding data points or impute them with some other statistical quantity like median (robust to outliers) etc.

For now, I shall be removing all the observations or data points that are an outlier to 'any' feature. Doing so substantially reduces the dataset size.

```
# removal of any data point which is an outlier for any fetaure.
for col in df.columns:
    lower,upper=calc_limits(col)
    df = df[(df[col] >lower) & (df[col]<upper)]df.shape
```

Note that the new shape is (1636, 20), we are left with 20 features.

Step-4: Feature Engineering

Here I have dropped some columns which according to my analysis proved to be less useful or redundant.

```
temp_df=df.copy()temp_df.drop(['skew','kurt','mindom','maxdom'],
axis=1,inplace=True) # only one of maxdom and dfrange.
temp_df.head(10)
```

meanfreq	sd	median	Q25	Q75	IQR	sp.ent	sfm	mode	meanfun	minfun	maxfun	meandom	dfrange	modindx	label
0.151228	0.072111	0.158011	0.096582	0.207955	0.111374	0.963322	0.727232	0.083878	0.088965	0.017798	0.250000	0.201497	0.554688	0.247119	1
0.135120	0.079146	0.124656	0.078720	0.208045	0.127325	0.971955	0.783568	0.104261	0.106398	0.016931	0.266667	0.712812	5.476562	0.208274	1
0.132786	0.079557	0.119090	0.067958	0.209592	0.141634	0.963181	0.738307	0.112555	0.110132	0.017112	0.253968	0.298222	2.718750	0.125160	1
0.150762	0.074463	0.160106	0.092899	0.205718	0.112819	0.967573	0.762638	0.086197	0.105945	0.026230	0.266667	0.479620	5.304688	0.123992	1
0.142239	0.078018	0.138587	0.088206	0.208587	0.120381	0.970723	0.770992	0.219103	0.096729	0.017957	0.250000	0.336476	2.156250	0.148272	1
0.190846	0.065790	0.207951	0.132280	0.244357	0.112076	0.938546	0.538810	0.050129	0.113323	0.017544	0.275862	1.434115	6.312500	0.254780	1
0.168346	0.074121	0.145618	0.115756	0.239824	0.124068	0.934523	0.559742	0.060033	0.083484	0.015717	0.231884	0.146563	3.117188	0.059537	1
0.181015	0.074369	0.169299	0.128673	0.254175	0.125502	0.915284	0.475317	0.059957	0.098643	0.016145	0.275862	0.209844	3.687500	0.059940	1
0.175659	0.071652	0.144192	0.131058	0.256527	0.125469	0.876749	0.403910	0.134411	0.132726	0.016563	0.226571	0.257812	0.640625	0.203437	1
0.174826	0.071533	0.146471	0.123529	0.247059	0.123529	0.875392	0.436706	0.120000	0.124685	0.016754	0.250000	0.799006	4.164062	0.205816	1

Filtered dataset

Now let us create some new features. I have done two new things here. Firstly I have made 'meanfreq', 'median' and 'mode' to comply with the standard relation **3Median=2Mean +Mode**. For this, I have adjusted values in the 'median' column as shown below. You can alter values in any of the other columns say the 'meanfreq' column.

```
temp_df['meanfreq']=temp_df['meanfreq'].apply(lambda x:x*2)
temp_df['median']=temp_df['meanfreq']+temp_df['mode']
temp_df['median']=temp_df['median'].apply(lambda  x:x/3)sns.boxplot
(data=temp_df,y='median',x='label') # seeing the new 'median' against
the 'label'
```

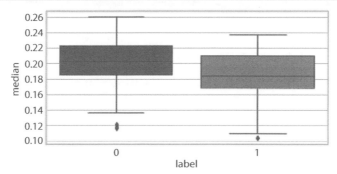

The second new feature that I have added is a new feature to measure the 'skewness'.

For this, I have used the 'Karl Pearson Coefficient' which is calculated as
Coefficient = (Mean — Mode)/StandardDeviation
You can also try some other coefficient also and see how it compared
with the target i.e. the 'label' column.

```
temp_df['pear_skew']=temp_df['meanfreq']-temp_df['mode']
temp_df['pear_skew']=temp_df['pear_skew']/temp_df['sd']
temp_df.head(10)sns.boxplot(data=temp_df,y='pear_skew',x='label')
```

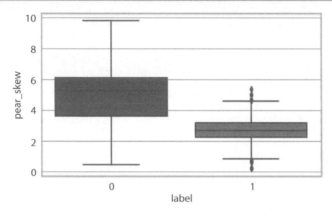

Step-5: Preparing the Data

The first thing that we'll do is normalize all the features or basically we'll
perform feature scaling to get all the values in a comparable range.

```
scaler=StandardScaler()
scaled_df=scaler.fit_transform(temp_df.drop('label',axis=1))
X=scaled_df
Y=df['label'].as_matrix()
```

Next split your data into train and test set.

```
x_train,x_test,y_train,y_test=train_test_split(X,Y,test_size=0.20,
random_state=42)
```

Step-6: Model building

Now we'll build two classifiers, decision tree, and random forest and compare the accuracies of both of them.

```
models=[RandomForestClassifier(),
DecisionTreeClassifier()]model_names=['RandomForestClassifier',
'DecisionTree']acc=[]
```

```
d={}for model in range(len(models)):
   clf=models[model]
   clf.fit(x_train,y_train)
   pred=clf.predict(x_test)
   acc.append(accuracy_score(pred,y_test))


d={'Modelling Algo':model_names,'Accuracy':acc}
```

Put the accuracies in a data frame.

```
acc_frame=pd.DataFrame(d)
acc_frame
```

	Modelling Algo	Accuracy
0	RandomForestClassifier	0.981707
1	DecisionTree	0.939024

Plot the accuracies:

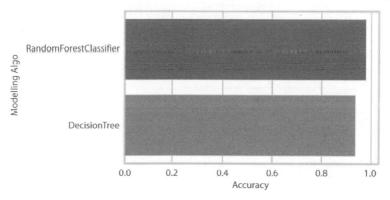

As we have seen, just by using the default parameters for both of our models, the random forest classifier outperformed the decision tree classifier(as expected).

Step-7: Parameter Tuning with GridSearchCV
Lastly, let us also tune our random forest classifier using GridSearchCV.

```
param_grid = {
   'n_estimators': [200, 500],
   'max_features': ['auto', 'sqrt', 'log2'],
   'max_depth' : [4,5,6,7,8],
   'criterion' :['gini', 'entropy']
```

```
}
CV_rfc = GridSearchCV(estimator=RandomForestClassifier(), param_
grid=param_grid, scoring='accuracy', cv= 5)

CV_rfc.fit(x_train, y_train)
```

```
GridSearchCV(cv=5, error_score='raise-deprecating',
        estimator=RandomForestClassifier(bootstrap=True, class_weight=None,
                                criterion='gini', max_depth=None,
                                max_features='auto',
                                max_leaf_nodes=None,
                                min_impurity_decrease=0.0,
                                min_impurity_split=None,
                                min_samples_leaf=1,
                                min_samples_split=2,
                                min_weight_fraction_leaf=0.0,
                                n_estimators='warn', n_jobs=None,
                                oob_score=False,
                                random_state=None, verbose=0,
                                warm_start=False),
        iid='warn', n_jobs=None,
        param_grid={'criterion': ['gini', 'entropy'],
                    'max_depth': [4, 5, 6, 7, 8],
                    'max_features': ['auto', 'sqrt', 'log2'],
                    'n_estimators': [200, 500]},
        pre_dispatch='2*n_jobs', refit=True, return_train_score=False,
        scoring='accuracy', verbose=0)
```

```
print("Best score : ",CV_rfc.best_score_)
print("Best Parameters : ",CV_rfc.best_params_)
print("Precision Score:",precision_score(CV_rfc.predict(x_test),y_test))
```

```
Best score :  0.981651376146789
Best Parameters :  {'criterion': 'entropy', 'max_depth': 6, 'max_features': 'auto', 'n_estimators': 500}
Precision Score :  0.9836709677419355
```

After hyperparameter optimization as we can see the results are pretty good :)
If you want you can also check the Importance of each feature.

```
df1 = pd.DataFrame.from_records(x_train)
tmp = pd.DataFrame({'Feature': df1.columns, 'Feature importance':
clf_rf.feature_importances_})
tmp = tmp.sort_values(by='Feature importance',ascending=False)
plt.figure(figsize = (7,4))
plt.title('Features importance',fontsize=14)
s = sns.barplot(x='Feature',y='Feature importance',data=tmp)
s.set_xticklabels(s.get_xticklabels(),rotation=90)
plt.show()
```

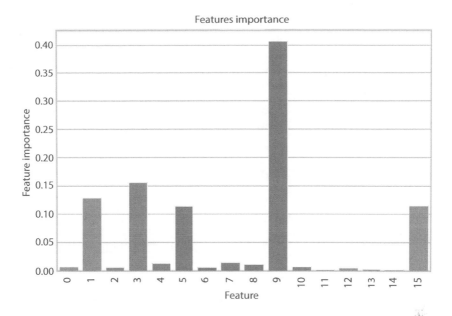

Advantages of Random Forest

1. Random Forest is based on the bagging algorithm and uses Ensemble Learning technique. It creates as many trees on the subset of the data and combines the output of all the trees. In this way it reduces overfitting problem in decision trees and also reduces the variance and therefore improves the accuracy [13].
2. Random Forest can be used to solve both classification as well as regression problems.
3. Random Forest works well with both categorical and continuous variables.
4. Random Forest can automatically handle missing values.
5. No feature scaling required: No feature scaling (standardization and normalization) required in case of Random Forest as it uses rule based approach instead of distance calculation.
6. Handles non-linear parameters efficiently: Non linear parameters don't affect the performance of a Random Forest unlike curve based algorithms. So, if there is high non-linearity between the independent variables, Random Forest may outperform as compared to other curve basedalgorithms.
7. Random Forest can automatically handle missing values.

8. Random Forest is usually robust to outliers and can handle them automatically.
9. Random Forest algorithm is very stable. Even if a new data point is introduced in the dataset, the overall algorithm is not affected much since the new data may impact one tree, but it is very hard for it to impact all the trees.
10. Random Forest is comparatively less impacted by noise.

Disadvantages of Random Forest

1. **Complexity:** Random Forest creates a lot of trees (unlike only one tree in case of decision tree) and combines their outputs. By default, it creates 100 trees in Python sklearn library. To do so, this algorithm requires much more computational power and resources. On the other hand decision tree is simple and does not require so much computational resources.

2. **Longer Training Period:** Random Forest require much more time to train as compared to decision trees as it generates a lot of trees (instead of one tree in case of decision tree) and makes decision on the majority of votes.

References

1. FindDataLab.com (2020-06-09). "Can You Still Perform Web Scraping With The New CNIL Guidelines?". Medium. Retrieved 2020-07-05.
2. Song, Ruihua; Microsoft Research (Sep 14, 2007). "Joint Optimization of Wrapper Generation and Template Detection" (PDF). The 13th International Conference on Knowledge Discovery and Data Mining: 894.
3. Roush, Wade (2012-07-25). "Diffbot Is Using Computer Vision to Reinvent the Semantic Web". www.xconomy.com. Retrieved 2013-03-15.
4. Neuburger, Jeffrey D (5 December 2014). "QVC Sues Shopping App for Web Scraping That Allegedly Triggered Site Outage". The National Law Review. Proskauer Rose LLP. Retrieved 5 November 2015.
5. https://www.geeksforgeeks.org/what-is-web-scraping-and-how-to-use-it/
6. https://www.zyte.com/learn/what-is-web-scraping/
7. https://www.imperva.com/learn/application-security/web-scraping-attack/
8. https://realpython.com/beautiful-soup-web-scraper-python/

9. Prakash K.B. Content extraction studies using total distance algorithm, 2017, Proceedings of the 2016 2nd International Conference on Applied and Theoretical Computing and Communication Technology, iCATccT 2016, 10.1109/ICATCCT.2016.7912085
10. Prakash K.B. Mining issues in traditional indian web documents,2015, Indian Journal of Science and Technology, 8(32), 10.17485/ijst/2015/v8i1/77056
11. Prakash K.B., Rajaraman A., Lakshmi M. Complexities in developing multilingual on-line courses in the Indian context, 2017, Proceedings of the 2017 International Conference On Big Data Analytics and Computational Intelligence, ICBDACI 2017, 8070860, 339-342, 10.1109/ICBDACI.2017.8070860
12. Prakash K.B., Kumar K.S., Rao S.U.M. Content extraction issues in online web education, 2017, Proceedings of the 2016 2nd International Conference on Applied and Theoretical Computing and Communication Technology, iCATccT 2016, 7912086,680-685,10.1109/ICATCCT.2016.7912086
13. Prakash K.B., Rajaraman A., Perumal T., Kolla P. Foundations to frontiers of big data analytics, 2016, Proceedings of the 2016 2nd International Conference on Contemporary Computing and Informatics, IC3I 2016, 7917968, 242-247, 10.1109/IC3I.2016.7917968

DATA SCIENCE PROJECTS

11

Covid19 Detection and Prediction

```
In [0]:  from google.colab import drive
         drive.mount('/gdrive')
         %cd /gdrive/My Drive/cvd
```

```
In [0]:  import numpy as np
         import pandas as pd
         import datetime as dt
         import sklearn
         from scipy import stats
         from sklearn import preprocessing
         from sklearn.model_selection import GridSearchCV
         from sklearn.ensemble import RandomForestClassifier
         from sklearn.ensemble import AdaBoostClassifier
         from sklearn.model_selection import train_test_split
         from sklearn.metrics import recall_score as rs
         from sklearn.metrics import precision_score as ps
         from sklearn.metrics import f1_score as fm
         from sklearn.metrics import log_loss

         encoder = preprocessing.LabelEncoder()
```

Kolla Bhanu Prakash. Data Science Handbook: A Practical Approach, (259–276) © 2022 Scrivener
Publishing LLC

```
In [0]:  data = pd.read_csv('data.csv')
         data = data.drop('id',axis=1)
         data = data.fillna(np.nan,axis=0)
         data['location'] = encoder.fit_transform(data['location'].astype(str))
         data['country'] = encoder.fit_transform(data['country'].astype(str))
         data['gender'] = encoder.fit_transform(data['gender'].astype(str))
         data[['symptom1']] = encoder.fit_transform(data['symptom1'].astype(str))
         data[['symptom2']] = encoder.fit_transform(data['symptom2'].astype(str))
         data[['symptom3']] = encoder.fit_transform(data['symptom3'].astype(str))
         data[['symptom4']] = encoder.fit_transform(data['symptom4'].astype(str))
         data[['symptom5']] = encoder.fit_transform(data['symptom5'].astype(str))
         data[['symptom6']] = encoder.fit_transform(data['symptom6'].astype(str))
```

```
In [0]:  data['sym_on'] = pd.to_datetime(data['sym_on'])
         data['hosp_vis'] = pd.to_datetime(data['hosp_vis'])
         data['sym_on']= data['sym_on'].map(dt.datetime.toordinal)
         data['hosp_vis']= data['hosp_vis'].map(dt.datetime.toordinal)
         data['diff_sym_hos']= data['hosp_vis'] - data['sym_on']
```

```
In [0]:  data['diff_symp_hos'] = data['hosp_vis']-data['sym_on']
```

```
In [0]:  data = data.drop(['sym_on','hosp_vis'],axis=1)
```

```
In [0]:  print(data.dtypes)
```

```
In [0]:  import matplotlib.pyplot as plt
         def counter2(colname1,colname2):
           colname1 = pd.Series(colname1)
           colname2 = pd.Series(colname2)
           count1 = 0
           for i in range(min([colname1.size,colname2.size])):
             if(colname1[i]==1 and colname2[i]==1):
               count1 = count1+1
           return count1

         def counter1(colname):
           colname1 = pd.Series(colname)
           count = 0
           for i in range(colname1.size):
             if(colname1[i]==1):
               count = count+1
           return count
```

```
In [0]:  fwuh = counter1(data['from_wuhan'])
         vwuh = counter1(data['vis_wuhan'])
```

```
In [0]:  print(counter1(data['death']))
         print(counter2(data['from_wuhan'],data['death']))
         print(counter2(data['vis_wuhan'],data['death']))
```

```
In [0]:  import matplotlib.pyplot as plt

         plt.bar(['From Wuhan','Visiting Wuhan'],[counter2(data['death'],data['from_wuhan']),counter2(data['death'],data['vis_wuhan'])],color=
         'green')
         plt.title('Patient Deaths')
         plt.xlabel('Patients\' Native Place')
         plt.ylabel('Number of Deaths')
         plt.plot([counter2(data['death'],data['from_wuhan']),counter2(data['death'],data['vis_wuhan'])],color='red')
         plt.show()
```

```
In [0]:  plt.bar(['From Wuhan','Visiting Wuhan'],[counter2(data['recov'],data['from_wuhan']),counter2(data['recov'],data['vis_wuhan'])],color=
         'purple')
         plt.title('Recovered Patients')
         plt.xlabel('Patients\' Native Place')
         plt.ylabel('Number of Patients Recovered')
         plt.plot([counter2(data['recov'],data['from_wuhan']),counter2(data['recov'],data['vis_wuhan'])],color='blue')
         plt.show()
```

```
In [0]:  tdata = pd.read_csv('train.csv')
         print(tdata.head())
```

```
In [0]:  tdata = pd.read_csv('train.csv')
         tdata = tdata.drop('id',axis=1)
         tdata = tdata.fillna(np.nan,axis=0)
         tdata['age'] = tdata['age'].fillna(value=tdata['age'].mean())
         tdata['location'] = encoder.fit_transform(tdata['location'].astype(str))
         tdata['country'] = encoder.fit_transform(tdata['country'].astype(str))
         tdata['gender'] = encoder.fit_transform(tdata['gender'].astype(str))
         tdata[['symptom1']] = encoder.fit_transform(tdata['symptom1'].astype(str))
         tdata[['symptom2']] = encoder.fit_transform(tdata['symptom2'].astype(str))
         tdata[['symptom3']] = encoder.fit_transform(tdata['symptom3'].astype(str))
         tdata[['symptom4']] = encoder.fit_transform(tdata['symptom4'].astype(str))
         tdata[['symptom5']] = encoder.fit_transform(tdata['symptom5'].astype(str))
         tdata[['symptom6']] = encoder.fit_transform(tdata['symptom6'].astype(str))
```

```
In [0]:  tdata['sym_on'] = pd.to_datetime(tdata['sym_on'])
         tdata['hosp_vis'] = pd.to_datetime(tdata['hosp_vis'])
         tdata['sym_on']= tdata['sym_on'].map(dt.datetime.toordinal)
         tdata['hosp_vis']= tdata['hosp_vis'].map(dt.datetime.toordinal)
         tdata['diff_sym_hos']= tdata['hosp_vis'] - tdata['sym_on']
```

```
In [0]:  tdata = tdata.drop(['sym_on','hosp_vis'],axis=1)
```

```
In [0]:  print(tdata)
```

```
In [0]:  print(tdata.isna().sum())
```

```
In [0]:  from sklearn.metrics import recall_score as rs
         from sklearn.metrics import precision_score as ps
         from sklearn.metrics import f1_score as fs
         from sklearn.metrics import balanced_accuracy_score as bas
         from sklearn.metrics import confusion_matrix as cm
```

```
In [0]:  rf = RandomForestClassifier(bootstrap=True, ccp_alpha=0.0, class_weight=None,
                            criterion='gini', max_depth=2, max_features='auto',
                            max_leaf_nodes=None, max_samples=None,
                            min_impurity_decrease=0.0, min_impurity_split=None,
                            min_samples_leaf=2, min_samples_split=2,
                            min_weight_fraction_leaf=0.0, n_estimators=100,
                            n_jobs=None, oob_score=False, random_state=None,
                            verbose=0, warm_start=False)
         classifier = AdaBoostClassifier(rf,50,0.01,'SAMME.R',10)
```

```
In [0]:  X = tdata[['location','country','gender','age','vis_wuhan','from_wuhan','symptom1','symptom2','symptom3','symptom4','symptom5','symp
         om6','diff_sym_hos']]
         Y = tdata['death']
```

```
In [0]:  X_train, X_test, Y_train, Y_test = train_test_split(X,Y,test_size=0.2,random_state=0)
         classifier.fit(X_train,np.array(Y_train).reshape(Y_train.shape[0],1))
```

```
In [0]:  pred = np.array(classifier.predict(X_test))

         recall = rs(Y_test,pred)
         precision = ps(Y_test,pred)
         f1 = fs(Y_test,pred)
         ma = classifier.score(X_test,Y_test)
```

```
In [0]:  print('*** Evaluation metrics for test dataset ***\n')
         print('Recall Score: ',recall)
         print('Precision Score: ',precision)
         print('F1 Score: ',f1)
         print('Accuracy: ',ma)
         a = pd.DataFrame(Y_test)
         a['pred']= classifier.predict(X_test)
         print('\n\tTable 3\n')
         print(a.head())
```

```
*** Evaluation metrics for test dataset ***

Recall Score:  0.75
Precision Score:  1.0
F1 Score:  0.8571428571428571
Accuracy:  0.9333333333333333

        Table 3

      death  pred
130       0     0
203       0     0
170       1     0
66        0     0
181       0     0
```

```
In [0]:  print(pd.DataFrame({'Val':Y_test,'Pred':classifier.predict(X_test)}))
```

```
In [0]:  X1 = tdata[['location','country','gender','age','vis_wuhan','from_wuhan','symptom1','symptom2','symptom3','symptom4','symptom5','symp
         tom6','diff_sym_hos']]
         Y1 = tdata['death']
         classifier1 = RandomForestClassifier()

         n_estimators = [100,200,300,400,500]
         max_depth = [1,2,5,6]
         min_samples_split = [1,2,6,7]
         min_samples_leaf = [2,3,4,5]

         params_grid = {'n_estimators':n_estimators,'max_depth':max_depth,'min_samples_split':min_samples_split,'min_samples_leaf':min_samples
         _leaf}

         gridder = GridSearchCV(estimator=classifier1,param_grid=params_grid,n_jobs=-1,cv=5,verbose=5 )
         gridder.fit(X1,np.array(Y1).reshape(Y1.shape[0],))
```

```
Fitting 5 folds for each of 320 candidates, totalling 1600 fits
[Parallel(n_jobs=-1)]: Using backend LokyBackend with 2 concurrent workers.
[Parallel(n_jobs=-1)]: Done 24 tasks      | elapsed:    2.8s
[Parallel(n_jobs=-1)]: Done 97 tasks      | elapsed:   24.3s
[Parallel(n_jobs=-1)]: Done 180 tasks     | elapsed:   50.6s
[Parallel(n_jobs=-1)]: Done 306 tasks     | elapsed:  1.5min
[Parallel(n_jobs=-1)]: Done 468 tasks     | elapsed:  2.3min
[Parallel(n_jobs=-1)]: Done 666 tasks     | elapsed:  3.2min
[Parallel(n_jobs=-1)]: Done 900 tasks     | elapsed:  4.4min
[Parallel(n_jobs=-1)]: Done 1170 tasks    | elapsed:  5.9min
[Parallel(n_jobs=-1)]: Done 1476 tasks    | elapsed:  7.3min
[Parallel(n_jobs=-1)]: Done 1600 out of 1600 | elapsed:  8.0min finished
/usr/local/lib/python3.6/dist-packages/sklearn/model_selection/_search.py:739: DataConversionWarning: A column-vector y was passed wh
en a 1d array was expected. Please change the shape of y to (n_samples,), for example using ravel().
  self.best_estimator_.fit(X, y, **fit_params)
```

```
Out[0]:  GridSearchCV(cv=5, error_score=nan,
                      estimator=RandomForestClassifier(bootstrap=True, ccp_alpha=0.0,
                                                       class_weight=None,
                                                       criterion='gini', max_depth=None,
                                                       max_features='auto',
                                                       max_leaf_nodes=None,
                                                       max_samples=None,
                                                       min_impurity_decrease=0.0,
                                                       min_impurity_split=None,
                                                       min_samples_leaf=1,
                                                       min_samples_split=2,
                                                       min_weight_fraction_leaf=0.0,
                                                       n_estimators=100, n_jobs=None,
                                                       oob_score=False,
                                                       random_state=None, verbose=0,
                                                       warm_start=False),
                      iid='deprecated', n_jobs=-1,
                      param_grid={'max_depth': [1, 2, 5, 6],
                                  'min_samples_leaf': [2, 3, 4, 5],
                                  'min_samples_split': [1, 2, 6, 7],
                                  'n_estimators': [100, 200, 300, 400, 500]},
                      pre_dispatch='2*n_jobs', refit=True, return_train_score=False,
                      scoring=None, verbose=5)
```

```
In [0]:  print(gridder.best_estimator_)
```

```
RandomForestClassifier(bootstrap=True, ccp_alpha=0.0, class_weight=None,
                       criterion='gini', max_depth=2, max_features='auto',
                       max_leaf_nodes=None, max_samples=None,
                       min_impurity_decrease=0.0, min_impurity_split=None,
                       min_samples_leaf=2, min_samples_split=2,
                       min_weight_fraction_leaf=0.0, n_estimators=100,
                       n_jobs=None, oob_score=False, random_state=None,
                       verbose=0, warm_start=False)
```

```
In [0]:  !ls
```

```
data.csv   test.xlsx   train.csv
```

```
In [0]:  udata = pd.read_excel('test.xlsx')
         udata = udata.drop('id',axis=1)
```

```
In [0]:   print(udata.columns)
```

```
Index(['location', 'country', 'gender', 'age', 'sym_on', 'hosp_vis',
       'vis_wuhan', 'from_wuhan', 'symptom1', 'symptom2', 'symptom3',
       'symptom4', 'symptom5', 'symptom6'],
      dtype='object')
```

```
In [0]:   udata = udata.fillna(np.nan,axis=0)
          udata['age'] = udata['age'].fillna(value=udata['age'].mean())
          udata['from_wuhan'] = udata['from_wuhan'].fillna(value=0)
          udata['from_wuhan'] = udata['from_wuhan'].astype(int)
          udata['location'] = encoder.fit_transform(udata['location'].astype(str))
          udata['country'] = encoder.fit_transform(udata['country'].astype(str))
          udata['gender'] = encoder.fit_transform(udata['gender'].astype(str))
          udata[['symptom1']] = encoder.fit_transform(udata['symptom1'].astype(str))
          udata[['symptom2']] = encoder.fit_transform(udata['symptom2'].astype(str))
          udata[['symptom3']] = encoder.fit_transform(udata['symptom3'].astype(str))
          udata[['symptom4']] = encoder.fit_transform(udata['symptom4'].astype(str))
          udata[['symptom5']] = encoder.fit_transform(udata['symptom5'].astype(str))
          udata[['symptom6']] = encoder.fit_transform(udata['symptom6'].astype(str))
```

```
In [0]:   print(udata['from_wuhan'].mode())
```

```
0    0
dtype: int64
```

```
In [0]:   udata['sym_on'] = pd.to_datetime(udata['sym_on'])
          udata['hosp_vis'] = pd.to_datetime(udata['hosp_vis'])
          udata['sym_on']= udata['sym_on'].map(dt.datetime.toordinal)
          udata['hosp_vis']= udata['hosp_vis'].map(dt.datetime.toordinal)
          udata['diff_sym_hos']= udata['hosp_vis'] - udata['sym_on']
```

```
In [0]:   print(udata['from_wuhan'].unique())
```

```
[0 1]
```

```
In [0]:   print(udata.dtypes)
```

```
location        int64
country         int64
gender          int64
age             float64
sym_on          int64
hosp_vis        int64
vis_wuhan       int64
from_wuhan      int64
symptom1        int64
symptom2        int64
symptom3        int64
symptom4        int64
symptom5        int64
symptom6        int64
diff_sym_hos    int64
dtype: object
```

```
In [0]:   udata = udata[['location','country','gender','age','vis_wuhan','from_wuhan','symptom1','symptom2','symptom3','symptom4','symptom5','symptom6','diff_sym_hos']]
          udata['result'] = classifier.predict(udata)
```

```
In [0]: print(udata['result'])
```

```
        0      1
        1      0
        2      0
        3      0
        4      0
              ..
        858    1
        859    0
        860    0
        861    0
        862    0
        Name: result, Length: 863, dtype: int64
```

```
In [0]: !cd '/gdrive/My Drive/cvd'
```

```
In [0]: udata.to_csv('/gdrive/My Drive/cvd/final.csv')
```

```
1   # importing the required libraries
2   import pandas as pd
3   # Visualisation libraries
4   import matplotlib.pyplot as plt
5   %matplotlib inline
6   import seaborn as sns
7   import plotly.express as px
8   import plotly.graph_objects as go
9   import folium
10  from folium import plugins
11  # Manipulating the default plot size
12  plt.rcParams['figure.figsize'] = 10, 12
13  # Disable warnings
14  import warnings
15  warnings.filterwarnings('ignore')
```

```
1   # Reading the datasets
2   df= pd.read_excel('/content/Covid cases in India.xlsx')
3   df_india = df.copy()
4   df
```

	S. No.	Name of State / UT	Total Confirmed cases (Indian National)	Total Confirmed cases (Foreign National)	Cured	Death
0	1	Andhra Pradesh	9		0	0	0
1	2	Bihar	3		0	0	1
2	3	Chhattisgarh	1		0	0	0
3	4	Delhi	30		1	6	1
4	5	Gujarat	32		1	0	1
5	6	Haryana	14		14	11	0
6	7	Himachal Pradesh	3		0	0	1
7	8	Karnataka	41		0	3	1
8	9	Kerala	101		8	4	0
9	10	Madhya Pradesh	9		0	0	0
10	11	Maharashtra	98		3	0	2

```
1   # Coordinates of India States and Union Territories
2   India_coord = pd.read_excel('/content/Indian Coordinates.xlsx')
3   #Day by day data of India, Korea, Italy and Wuhan
4   dbd_India = pd.read_excel('/content/per_day_cases.xlsx',parse_dates=True, sheet
5   dbd_Italy = pd.read_excel('/content/per_day_cases.xlsx',parse_dates=True, sheet
6   dbd_Korea = pd.read_excel('/content/per_day_cases.xlsx',parse_dates=True, sheet
7   dbd_Wuhan = pd.read_excel('/content/per_day_cases.xlsx',parse_dates=True, sheet
```

```
1   df.drop(['S. No.'],axis=1,inplace=True)
2   df['Total cases'] = df['Total Confirmed cases (Indian National)'] + df['Total C
3   total_cases = df['Total cases'].sum()
4   print('Total number of confirmed COVID 2019 cases across India till date (22nd
```

```
1   df.style.background_gradient(cmap='Reds')
```

	Name of State / UT	Total Confirmed cases (Indian National)	Total Confirmed cases (Foreign National)	Cured	Death	Total cases
0	Andhra Pradesh	9	0	0	0	9
1	Bihar	3	0	0	1	3
2	Chhattisgarh	1	0	0	0	1
3	Delhi	30	1	6	1	31
4	Gujarat	32	1	0	1	33
5	Haryana	14	14	11	0	28
6	Himachal Pradesh	3	0	0	1	3
7	Karnataka	41	0	3	1	41
8	Kerala	101	8	4	0	109
9	Madhya Pradesh	9	0	0	0	9
10	Maharashtra	98	3	0	2	101

```
1   #Total Active  is the Total cases - (Number of death + Cured)
2   df['Total Active'] = df['Total cases'] - (df['Death'] + df['Cured'])
3   total_active = df['Total Active'].sum()
4   print('Total number of active COVID 2019 cases across India:', total_active)
5   Tot_Cases = df.groupby('Name of State / UT')['Total Active'].sum().sort_values(
6   Tot_Cases.style.background_gradient(cmap='Reds')
```

	Total Active
Name of State / UT	
Kerala	105
Maharashtra	99
Karnataka	37
Telengana	34
Gujarat	32
Rajasthan	29
Punjab	28
Uttar Pradesh	24
Delhi	24
Tamil Nadu	17
Haryana	17
Ladakh	13
Madhya Pradesh	9
Andhra Pradesh	9
West Bengal	8
Chandigarh	7
Jammu and Kashmir	6

```
1   df_full = pd.merge(India_coord,df,on='Name of State / UT')
2   map = folium.Map(location=[20, 70], zoom_start=4,tiles='Stamenterrain')
3   for lat, lon, value, name inzip(df_full['Latitude'], df_full['Longitude'], df_f
4       folium.CircleMarker([lat, lon], radius=value*0.8, popup = ('<strong>State</
5   ''<strong>Total Cases</strong>: ' + str(value) + '
6   '),color='red',fill_color='red',fill_opacity=0.3 ).add_to(map)
7   map
```

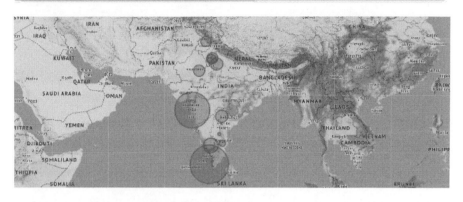

```
1   f, ax = plt.subplots(figsize=(12, 8))
2   data = df_full[['Name of State / UT','Total cases','Cured','Death']]
3   data.sort_values('Total cases',ascending=False,inplace=True)
4   sns.set_color_codes("pastel")
5   sns.barplot(x="Total cases", y="Name of State / UT", data=data,label="Total", c
6   sns.set_color_codes("muted")
7   sns.barplot(x="Cured", y="Name of State / UT", data=data, label="Cured", color='
```

```
1   # Add a legend and informative axis label
2   ax.legend(ncol=2, loc="lower right", framcon=True)
3   ax.set(xlim=(0, 35), ylabel="",xlabel="Cases")
4   sns.despine(left=True, bottom=True)
```

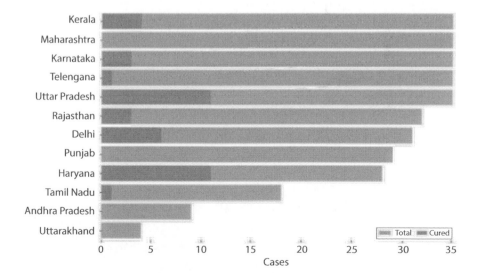

```
1   #This cell's code is required when you are working with plotly on colab
2   import plotly
3   plotly.io.renderers.default = 'colab'
```

```
1   # Rise of COVID-19 cases in India
2   fig = go.Figure()
3   fig.add_trace(go.Scatter(x=dbd_India['Date'], y = dbd_India['Total Cases'], mo
4   fig.update_layout(title_text='Trend of Coronavirus Cases in India (Cumulative
5   fig.show()
```

```
1   import plotly.express as px
2   fig = px.bar(dbd_India, x="Date", y="New Cases", barmode='group', height=400)
3   fig.update_layout(title_text='Coronavirus Cases in India on daily basis',plot_
4   fig.show()
```

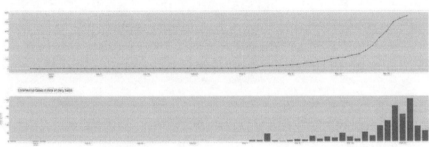

```
1    # import plotly.express as px
2    fig = px.bar(dbd_India, x="Date", y="Total Cases", color='Total Cases', orient
3              title='Confirmed Cases in India', color_discrete_sequence = px.co
4    '''Colour Scale for plotly
5    <a href="https://plot.ly/python/builtin-colorscales/">https://plot.ly/python/b
6    '''
7    fig.update_layout(plot_bgcolor='rgb(230, 230, 230)')
8    fig.show()
9    fig = px.bar(dbd_Italy, x="Date", y="Total Cases", color='Total Cases', orient
10             title='Confirmed Cases in Italy', color_discrete_sequence = px.co
11   fig.update_layout(plot_bgcolor='rgb(230, 230, 230)')
12   fig.show()
13   fig = px.bar(dbd_Korea, x="Date", y="Total Cases", color='Total Cases', orient
14             title='Confirmed Cases in South Korea', color_discrete_sequence =
15   fig.update_layout(plot_bgcolor='rgb(230, 230, 230)')
16   fig.show()
17   fig = px.bar(dbd_Wuhan, x="Date", y="Total Cases", color='Total Cases', orient
18             title='Confirmed Cases in Wuhan', color_discrete_sequence = px.co
19   fig.update_layout(plot_bgcolor='rgb(230, 230, 230)')
20   fig.show()
```

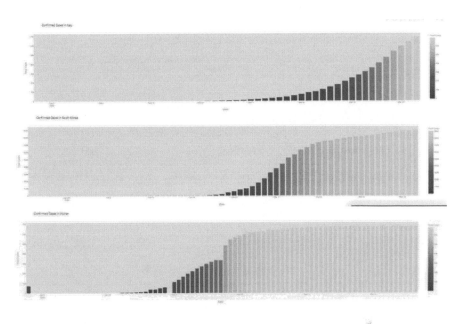

```
1    # import plotly.graph_objects as go
2    from plotly.subplots import make_subplots
3    fig = make_subplots(
4        rows=2, cols=2,
5        specs=[[{}, {}],
6               [{"colspan": 2}, None]],
7        subplot_titles=("S.Korea","Italy", "India","Wuhan"))
8    fig.add_trace(go.Bar(x=dbd_Korea['Date'], y=dbd_Korea['Total Cases'],
9                         marker=dict(color=dbd_Korea['Total Cases'], coloraxis="col
10   fig.add_trace(go.Bar(x=dbd_Italy['Date'], y=dbd_Italy['Total Cases'],
11                        marker=dict(color=dbd_Italy['Total Cases'], coloraxis="col
12   fig.add_trace(go.Bar(x=dbd_India['Date'], y=dbd_India['Total Cases'],
13                        marker=dict(color=dbd_India['Total Cases'], coloraxis="col
14   # fig.add_trace(go.Bar(x=dbd_Wuhan['Date'], y=dbd_Wuhan['Total Cases'],
15   #                      marker=dict(color=dbd_Wuhan['Total Cases'], coloraxis="c
16   fig.update_layout(coloraxis=dict(colorscale='Bluered_r'), showlegend=False,tit
17   fig.update_layout(plot_bgcolor='rgb(230, 230, 230)')
18   fig.show()
```

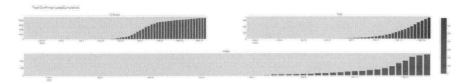

```
1  # import plotly.graph_objects as go
2  title = 'Main Source for News'
3  labels = ['S.Korea', 'Italy', 'India']
4  colors = ['rgb(122,128,0)', 'rgb(255,0,0)', 'rgb(49,130,189)']
5  mode_size = [10, 10, 12]
6  line_size = [1, 1, 8]
7  fig = go.Figure()
8  fig.add_trace(go.Scatter(x=dbd_Korea['Days after surpassing 100 cases'],
9                     y=dbd_Korea['Total Cases'],mode='lines',
10                    name=labels[0],
11                    line=dict(color=colors[0], width=line_size[0]),
12                    connectgaps=True))
13 fig.add_trace(go.Scatter(x=dbd_Italy['Days after surpassing 100 cases'],
14                    y=dbd_Italy['Total Cases'],mode='lines',
15                    name=labels[1],
16                    line=dict(color=colors[1], width=line_size[1]),
17                    connectgaps=True))
18 fig.add_trace(go.Scatter(x=dbd_India['Days after surpassing 100 cases'],
19                    y=dbd_India['Total Cases'],mode='lines',
20                    name=labels[2],
21                    line=dict(color=colors[2], width=line_size[2]),
22                    connectgaps=True))
23 annotations = []
24 annotations.append(dict(xref='paper', yref='paper', x=0.5, y=-0.1,
25                         xanchor='center', yanchor='top',
26                         text='Days after crossing 100 cases ',
27                         font=dict(family='Arial',
28                                   size=12,
29                                   color='rgb(150,150,150)'),
30                         showarrow=False))
31 fig.update_layout(annotations=annotations,plot_bgcolor='white',yaxis_title='C
32 fig.show()
```

```
1  df = pd.read_csv('/content/covid_19_clean_complete.csv',parse_dates=['Date'])
2  df.rename(columns={'ObservationDate':'Date', 'Country/Region':'Country'}, inpla
3  df_confirmed = pd.read_csv("/content/time_series_covid19_confirmed_global.csv")
4  df_recovered = pd.read_csv("/content/time_series_covid19_recovered_global.csv")
5  df_deaths = pd.read_csv("/content/time_series_covid19_deaths_global.csv")
6  df_confirmed.rename(columns={'Country/Region':'Country'}, inplace=True)
7  df_recovered.rename(columns={'Country/Region':'Country'}, inplace=True)
8  df_deaths.rename(columns={'Country/Region':'Country'}, inplace=True)
9  df_deaths.head()
```

```
1  df2 = df.groupby(["Date", "Country", "Province/State"])[['Date', 'Province/Stat
2  df2.head()
```

```
1  #Overall worldwide Confirmed/ Deaths/ Recovered cases
2  df.groupby('Date').sum().head()
```

```
1   confirmed = df.groupby('Date').sum()['Confirmed'].reset_index()
2   deaths = df.groupby('Date').sum()['Deaths'].reset_index()
3   recovered = df.groupby('Date').sum()['Recovered'].reset_index()
```

```
1   fig = go.Figure()
2   #Plotting datewise confirmed cases
3   fig.add_trace(go.Scatter(x=confirmed['Date'], y=confirmed['Confirmed'], mode='l
4   fig.add_trace(go.Scatter(x=deaths['Date'], y=deaths['Deaths'], mode='lines+mark
5   fig.add_trace(go.Scatter(x=recovered['Date'], y=recovered['Recovered'], mode='l
6   fig.update_layout(title='Worldwide NCOVID-19 Cases', xaxis_tickfont_size=14,yax
7   fig.show()
```

```
1   from fbprophet import Prophet
2   confirmed = df.groupby('Date').sum()['Confirmed'].reset_index()
3   deaths = df.groupby('Date').sum()['Deaths'].reset_index()
4   recovered = df.groupby('Date').sum()['Recovered'].reset_index()
```

```
1   confirmed.columns = ['ds','y']
2   #confirmed['ds'] = confirmed['ds'].dt.date
3   confirmed['ds'] = pd.to_datetime(confirmed['ds'])
4   confirmed.tail()
```

	ds	y
57	2020-03-19	242708.0
58	2020-03-20	272166.0
59	2020-03-21	304524.0
60	2020-03-22	335955.0
61	2020-03-23	336004.0

```
1   m = Prophet(interval_width=0.95)
2   m.fit(confirmed)
3   future = m.make_future_dataframe(periods=7)
4   future.tail()
```

```
1   #predicting the future with date, and upper and lower limit of y value
2   forecast = m.predict(future)
3   forecast[['ds', 'yhat', 'yhat_lower', 'yhat_upper']].tail()
```

```
1 | confirmed_forecast_plot = m.plot(forecast)
```

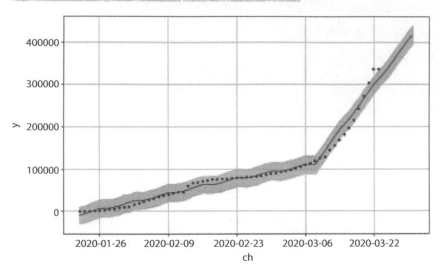

```
1 | confirmed_forecast_plot =m.plot_components(forecast)
```

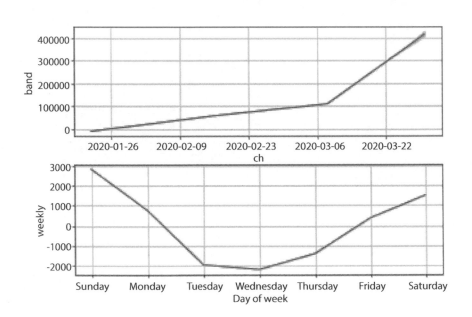

```
1   deaths.columns = ['ds','y']
2   deaths['ds'] = pd.to_datetime(deaths['ds'])
3   m = Prophet(interval_width=0.95)
4   m.fit(deaths)
5   future = m.make_future_dataframe(periods=7)
6   future.tail()
```

```
1   forecast = m.predict(future)
2   forecast[['ds', 'yhat', 'yhat_lower', 'yhat_upper']].tail()
```

```
1   deaths_forecast_plot = m.plot(forecast)
```

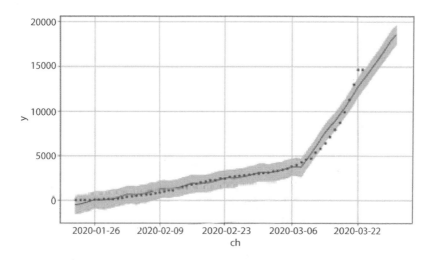

```
1   deaths_forecast_plot = m.plot_components(forecast)
```

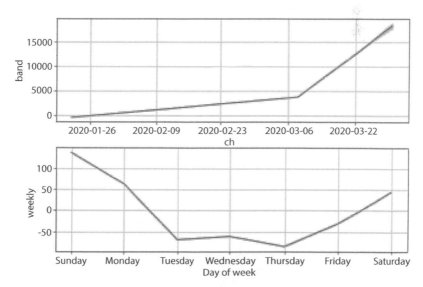

```
1  │  recovered.columns = ['ds','y']
2  │  recovered['ds'] = pd.to_datetime(recovered['ds'])
3  │  m = Prophet(interval_width=0.95)
4  │  m.fit(recovered)
5  │  future = m.make_future_dataframe(periods=7)
6  │  future.tail()
7  │
8  │
9  │  forecast = m.predict(future)
10 │  forecast[['ds', 'yhat', 'yhat_lower', 'yhat_upper']].tail()
11 │
12 │
13 │  recovered_forecast_plot = m.plot(forecast)
```

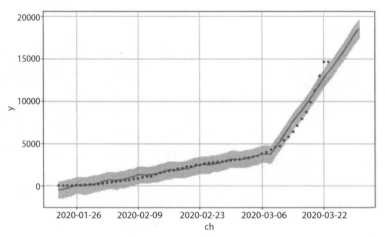

```
1 │  recovered_forecast_plot = m.plot_components(forecast)
```

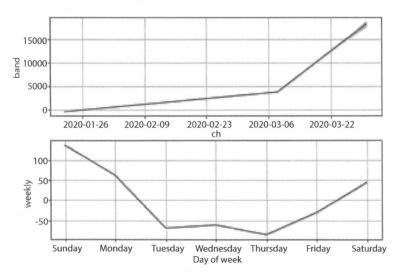

Bibliography

1. https://www.edureka.co/blog/covid-19-outbreak-prediction-using-machine-learning/
2. "Symptoms of Coronavirus". U.S. Centers for Disease Control and Prevention (CDC). 13 May 2020.
3. "Q&A on coronaviruses (COVID-19)". World Health Organization (WHO). 17 April 2020.
4. "COVID-19 vaccines". World Health Organization (WHO). Retrieved 3 March 2021.

```
#Intialization of Program. by Importing various LIbraries
import numpy as np
import matplotlib.pyplot as plt
# here we are working on Tensorflow version 2.1.0 so we need to write
tensorflow.keras.
#keras is in built function in Tensorflow.
import os
import tensorflow as tf
from tensorflow.keras.preprocessing.image import ImageDataGenerator
from tensorflow.keras.layers import Dense, Input, Dropout,Flatten, Conv2D
from tensorflow.keras.layers import BatchNormalization, Activation,
MaxPooling2D
from tensorflow.keras.models import Model, Sequential
from tensorflow.keras.optimizers import Adam
from tensorflow.keras.callbacks import ModelCheckpoint, ReduceLROnPlateau
from tensorflow.keras.utils import plot_model
from IPython.display import SVG, Image
```

```
# For checking out that how many images are available in the train set we
can use import OS
for types in os.listdir("F:/JetBrains/goeduhub training/PROJECTDATA
1/train_set/"):
    print(str(len(os.listdir("F:/JetBrains/goeduhub training/PROJECTDATA
1/train_set/"+ types)))+" "+ types+' images')
```

Kolla Bhanu Prakash. Data Science Handbook: A Practical Approach, (277–284) © 2022 Scrivener
Publishing LLC

```
917 Pepper__bell__Bacterial_spot images
1402 Pepper__bell__healthy images
927 Potato___Early_blight images
127 Potato__healthy images
919 Potato___Late_blight images
1523 Tomato_Bacterial_spot images
666 Tomato_Early_blight images
1198 Tomato_healthy images
1816 Tomato_Late_blight images
671 Tomato_Leaf_Mold images
1166 Tomato_Septoria_leaf_spot images
1094 Tomato_Spider_mites_Two_spotted_spider_mite images
1035 Tomato__Target_Spot images
286 Tomato__Tomato_mosaic_virus images
2475 Tomato__Tomato_YellowLeaf__Curl_Virus images
```

```
# Complete Dataset images can be loaded using ImageDataGenerator function
img_size=48
batch_size=64
datagen_train=ImageDataGenerator(horizontal_flip=True)
train_generator=datagen_train.flow_from_directory("F:/JetBrains/goeduhub
training/PROJECTDATA 1/train_set",
target_size=(img_size,img_size),
batch_size=batch_size,
class_mode='categorical',
shuffle=True)


datagen_test=ImageDataGenerator(horizontal_flip=True)
validation_generator=datagen_test.flow_from_directory("F:/JetBrains
/goeduhub training/PROJECTDATA 1/test_data",
target_size=(img_size,img_size),
batch_size=batch_size,
class_mode='categorical',
shuffle=True)
```

```
Found 16222 images belonging to 15 classes.
Found 1254 images belonging to 15 classes.
```

```
detection=Sequential()

#convolutional layer-1
detection.add(Conv2D(64,(3,3),padding='same',input_shape=(48,48,3)))
detection.add(BatchNormalization())
detection.add(Activation('relu'))
detection.add(MaxPooling2D(pool_size=(2,2)))
detection.add(Dropout(0.25))

#2 -convolutional layer-2
detection.add(Conv2D(128,(5,5),padding='same'))
detection.add(BatchNormalization())
detection.add(Activation('relu'))
detection.add(MaxPooling2D(pool_size=(2,2)))
detection.add(Dropout(0.25))

#3 -convolutional layer-3
detection.add(Conv2D(256,(3,3),padding='same'))
detection.add(BatchNormalization())
detection.add(Activation('relu'))
detection.add(MaxPooling2D(pool_size=(2,2)))
detection.add(Dropout(0.25))

#4 -convolutional layer-4
detection.add(Conv2D(512,(3,3),padding='same'))
detection.add(BatchNormalization())
detection.add(Activation('relu'))
detection.add(MaxPooling2D(pool_size=(2,2)))
detection.add(Dropout(0.25))
```

```
#5 -convolutional layer-5
detection.add(Conv2D(512,(3,3),padding='same'))
detection.add(BatchNormalization())
detection.add(Activation('relu'))
detection.add(MaxPooling2D(pool_size=(2,2)))
detection.add(Dropout(0.25))

detection.add(Flatten())
detection.add(Dense(256))
detection.add(BatchNormalization())
detection.add(Activation('relu'))
detection.add(Dropout(0.25))

detection.add(Dense(512))
detection.add(BatchNormalization())
detection.add(Activation('relu'))
detection.add(Dropout(0.25)

detection.add(Dense(15,activation='softmax'))
optimum=Adam(lr=0.005)
#lr-learning rate
detection.compile(optimizer=optimum,loss='categorical_crossentropy',metrics=
['accuracy'])

detection.summary()
```

```
Model: "sequential"
Layer (type)                    Output Shape          Param #
conv2d (Conv2D)                 (None, 48, 48, 64)    1792
batch_normalization (BatchNo    (None, 48, 48, 64)    256
activation (Activation)         (None, 48, 48, 64)    0
max_pooling2d (MaxPooling2D)    (None, 24, 24, 64)    0
dropout (Dropout)               (None, 24, 24, 64)    0
conv2d_1 (Conv2D)               (None, 24, 24, 128)   204928
batch_normalization_1 (Batch    (None, 24, 24, 128)   512
activation_1 (Activation)       (None, 24, 24, 128)   0
max_pooling2d_1 (MaxPooling2    (None, 12, 12, 128)   0
dropout_1 (Dropout)             (None, 12, 12, 128)   0
conv2d_2 (Conv2D)               (None, 12, 12, 256)   295168
batch_normalization_2 (Batch    (None, 12, 12, 256)   1024
activation_2 (Activation)       (None, 12, 12, 256)   0
max_pooling2d_2 (MaxPooling2    (None, 6, 6, 256)     0
dropout_2 (Dropout)             (None, 6, 6, 256)     0
conv2d_3 (Conv2D)               (None, 6, 6, 512)     1180160
batch_normalization_3 (Batch    (None, 6, 6, 512)     2048
```

```
ephocs=10
steps_per_epoch=train_generator.n//train_generator.batch_size
steps_per_epoch
validation_steps=validation_generator.n//validation_generator.batch_size
validation_steps
detection.fit(x=train_generator,
                steps_per_epoch=steps_per_epoch,
                epochs=ephocs,
                validation_data=validation_generator,
                validation_steps=validation_steps)
detection.save('Plant_Disease_Detection.h5')
```

```
Epoch 1/10
250/250 [==============================] - 170s 679ms/step - loss: 0.6594 - accuracy: 0.6087 - val_loss: 0.5875 - val_accuracy: 0.6421
Epoch 2/10
250/250 [==============================] - 61s 244ms/step - loss: 0.5757 - accuracy: 0.6970 - val_loss: 0.5773 - val_accuracy: 0.7266
Epoch 3/10
250/250 [==============================] - 64s 257ms/step - loss: 0.5069 - accuracy: 0.7501 - val_loss: 0.7142 - val_accuracy: 0.7414
Epoch 4/10
250/250 [==============================] - 116s 464ms/step - loss: 0.4514 - accuracy: 0.7829 - val_loss: 0.4798 - val_accuracy: 0.7444
Epoch 5/10
250/250 [==============================] - 171s 683ms/step - loss: 0.3952 - accuracy: 0.8207 - val_loss: 0.6178 - val_accuracy: 0.7515
Epoch 6/10
250/250 [==============================] - 122s 487ms/step - loss: 0.3391 - accuracy: 0.8537 - val_loss: 0.8423 - val_accuracy: 0.7551
Epoch 7/10
250/250 [==============================] - 117s 468ms/step - loss: 0.2545 - accuracy: 0.8930 - val_loss: 0.5112 - val_accuracy: 0.7444
Epoch 8/10
250/250 [==============================] - 115s 458ms/step - loss: 0.1828 - accuracy: 0.9293 - val_loss: 0.3916 - val_accuracy: 0.7550
Epoch 9/10
250/250 [==============================] - 117s 469ms/step - loss: 0.1161 - accuracy: 0.9609 - val_loss: 0.7551 - val_accuracy: 0.7490
Epoch 10/10
250/250 [==============================] - 115s 459ms/step - loss: 0.0740 - accuracy: 0.9771 - val_loss: 0.3719 - val_accuracy: 0.7525
```

```
from tensorflow.keras.models import load_model
Detection=load_model('Plant_Disease_Detection.h5')
from tensorflow.keras.preprocessing import image
import numpy as np
import matplotlib.pyplot as plt
import cv2
test_img=image.load_img("F:/JetBrains/goeduhub training/PROJECTDATA
1/test_data/Tomato_healthy/0d515778-61ef-4f0b-ab54-75607c80220f___RS_HL
9745.jpg",target_size=(48,48))
plt.imshow(test_img)
test_img=image.img_to_array(test_img)
test_img=np.expand_dims(test_img,axis=0)
result=Detection.predict(test_img)
a=result.argmax()
# print('a:',a)
classes=train_generator.class_indices
# print(classes)
# print(len(classes))
category=[]
for i in classes:
        category.append(i)
```

```
for i in range(len(classes)):
        if(i==a):
                output=category[i]
output
```

Tomato_healthy

```
from tensorflow.keras.models import load_model
Detection=load_model('Plant_Disease_Detection.h5')
from tensorflow.keras.preprocessing import image
import matplotlib.pyplot as plt
import numpy as np
import cv2
test_img=image.load_img("F:/JetBrains/goeduhub training/PROJECTDATA
1/test_data/Pepper__bell___healthy/1dd1b153-8ded-439f-8c9e-
c9970c67e642___JR_HL 8163.jpg",target_size=(48,48))
plt.imshow(test_img)
test_img=image.img_to_array(test_img)
test_img=np.expand_dims(test_img,axis=0)
result=Detection.predict(test_img)
a=result.argmax()
# print('a',a)
classes=train_generator.class_indices
category=[]
for i in classes:
        category.append(i)
for i in range(len(classes)):
        if(i==a):
                output=category[i]
output
```

Pepper_bell__healthy

Bibliography

1. https://www.goeduhub.com/10519/project-leaf-disease-detection-and-recognition-using-cnn
2. https://www.frontiersin.org/articles/10.3389/fpls.2016.01419/full
3. D. Al-Bashish, M. Braik, S. Bani-Ahmad,Detection and classification of leaf diseases using Kmeans-based segmentation and neural-networks-based classification, Inform Technol J, 10 (2011), pp. 267-275
4. G. Wang, Y. Sun, and J. Wang, "Automatic image-based plant disease severity estimation using deep learning," Computational Intelligence and Neuroscience, vol. 2017, Article ID 2917536, 8 pages, 2017.
5. A. Kamilaris and F. X. Prenafeta-Boldú, "Deep learning in agriculture: a survey," Computers and Electronics in Agriculture, vol. 147, pp. 70–90, 2018.

Brain Tumor Detection with Data Science

```
#Intialization of Program. by Importing various LIbraries
import numpy as np
import matplotlib.pyplot as plt
# here we are working on Tensorflow version 2.1.0 so we need to write
tensorflow.keras.
#keras is in built function in Tensorflow.
import os
import tensorflow as tf
from tensorflow.keras.preprocessing.image import ImageDataGenerator
from tensorflow.keras.layers import Dense, Input, Dropout,Flatten, Conv2D
from tensorflow.keras.layers import BatchNormalization, Activation,
MaxPooling2D
from tensorflow.keras.models import Model, Sequential
from tensorflow.keras.optimizers import Adam
from tensorflow.keras.callbacks import ModelCheckpoint, ReduceLROnPlateau
from tensorflow.keras.utils import plot_model
from IPython.display import SVG, Image
```

```
# For checking out that how many images are available in the train set we
can use import OS
for types in os.listdir("F:/JetBrains/goeduhub training/PROJECTDATA
1/train_set/"):
    print(str(len(os.listdir("F:/JetBrains/goeduhub training/PROJECTDATA
1/train_set/"+ types)))+" "+ types+' images')
```

```python
import pandas as pd
import numpy as np
import seaborn as sns
import matplotlib.pyplot as plt
import cv2
from skimage import io
import tensorflow as tf
from tensorflow.python.keras import Sequential
from tensorflow.keras import layers, optimizers
from tensorflow.keras.applications.resnet50 import ResNet50
from tensorflow.keras.layers import *
from tensorflow.keras.models import Model
from tensorflow.keras.callbacks import EarlyStopping, ModelCheckpoint
from tensorflow.keras import backend as K
from sklearn.preprocessing import StandardScaler
%matplotlib inline
```

```python
# data containing path to Brain MRI and their corresponding mask
brain_df = pd.read_csv('/Healthcare AI Datasets/Brain_MRI/data_mask.csv')
```

```python
brain_df.info()
```

```
<class 'pandas.core.frame.DataFrame'>
RangeIndex: 3929 entries, 0 to 3928
Data columns (total 4 columns):
 #   Column      Non-Null Count  Dtype
---  ------      --------------  -----
 0   patient_id  3929 non-null   object
 1   image_path  3929 non-null   object
 2   mask_path   3929 non-null   object
 3   mask        3929 non-null   int64
dtypes: int64(1), object(3)
memory usage: 122.9+ KB
```

```python
brain_df.head(5)
```

	patient_id	image_path	mask_path	mask
0	TCGA_CS_5395_19981004	TCGA_CS_5395_19981004/TCGA_CS_5395_19981004_1.tif	TCGA_CS_5395_19981004/TCGA_CS_5395_19981004_1_...	0
1	TCGA_CS_5395_19981004	TCGA_CS_4944_20010208/TCGA_CS_4944_20010208_1.tif	TCGA_CS_4944_20010208/TCGA_CS_4944_20010208_1_...	0
2	TCGA_CS_5395_19981004	TCGA_CS_4941_19960909/TCGA_CS_4941_19960909_1.tif	TCGA_CS_4941_19960909/TCGA_CS_4941_19960909_1_...	0
3	TCGA_CS_5395_19981004	TCGA_CS_4943_20000902/TCGA_CS_4943_20000902_1.tif	TCGA_CS_4943_20000902/TCGA_CS_4943_20000902_1_...	0
4	TCGA_CS_5395_19981004	TCGA_CS_5396_20010302/TCGA_CS_5396_20010302_1.tif	TCGA_CS_5396_20010302/TCGA_CS_5396_20010302_1_...	0

```
brain_df['mask'].value_counts()
```

```
0    2556
1    1373
Name: mask, dtype: int64
```

```
image = cv2.imread(brain_df.image_path[1301])
plt.imshow(image)
```

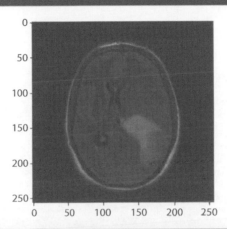

```
image1 = cv2.imread(brain_df.mask_path[1301])
plt.imshow(image1)
```

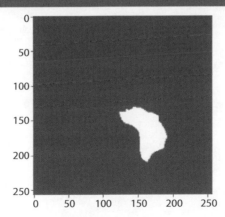

```
cv2.imread(brain_df.mask_path[1301]).max()
```

Output: 255

```
cv2.imread(brain_df.mask_path[1301]).min()
```

Output: 0

```
count = 0
fig, axs = plt.subplots(12, 3, figsize = (20, 50))
for i in range(len(brain_df)):
  if brain_df['mask'][i] ==1 and count <5:
    img = io.imread(brain_df.image_path[i])
    axs[count][0].title.set_text('Brain MRI')
    axs[count][0].imshow(img)

    mask = io.imread(brain_df.mask_path[i])
    axs[count][1].title.set_text('Mask')
    axs[count][1].imshow(mask, cmap = 'gray')

    img[mask == 255] = (255, 0, 0) #Red color
    axs[count][2].title.set_text('MRI with Mask')
    axs[count][2].imshow(img)
    count+=1

fig.tight_layout()
```

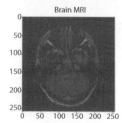
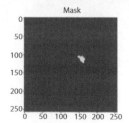
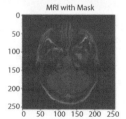

```python
# Drop the patient id column
brain_df_train = brain_df.drop(columns = ['patient_id'])
brain_df_train.shape
```

```python
brain_df_train['mask'] = brain_df_train['mask'].apply(lambda x: str(x))
brain_df_train.info()
```

```
<class 'pandas.core.frame.DataFrame'>
RangeIndex: 3929 entries, 0 to 3928
Data columns (total 3 columns):
 #   Column      Non-Null Count  Dtype
---  ------      --------------  -----
 0   image_path  3929 non-null   object
 1   mask_path   3929 non-null   object
 2   mask        3929 non-null   object
dtypes: object(3)
memory usage: 92.2+ KB
```

```python
# split the data into train and test data
from sklearn.model_selection import train_test_split
train, test = train_test_split(brain_df_train, test_size = 0.15)
```

```python
# create an image generator
from keras_preprocessing.image import ImageDataGenerator

#Create a data generator which scales the data from 0 to 1 and makes validation split of 0.15
datagen = ImageDataGenerator(rescale=1./255., validation_split = 0.15)

train_generator=datagen.flow_from_dataframe(
dataframe=train,
directory= './',
x_col='image_path',
y_col='mask',
subset="training",
batch_size=16,
shuffle=True,
class_mode="categorical",
target_size=(256,256))

valid_generator=datagen.flow_from_dataframe(
dataframe=train,
```

```python
directory= './',
x_col='image_path',
y_col='mask',
subset="validation",
batch_size=16,
shuffle=True,
class_mode="categorical",
target_size=(256,256))
```

```
# Create a data generator for test images
test_datagen=ImageDataGenerator(rescale=1./255.)

test_generator=test_datagen.flow_from_dataframe(
dataframe=test,
directory= './',
x_col='image_path',
y_col='mask',
batch_size=16,
shuffle=False,
class_mode='categorical',
target_size=(256,256))
```

```
# Get the ResNet50 base model (Transfer Learning)
basemodel = ResNet50(weights = 'imagenet', include_top = False, input_tensor = Input(shape=(256,
basemodel.summary()
```

```
Model: "resnet50"
```

Layer (type)	Output Shape	Param #	Connected to
input_1 (InputLayer)	[(None, 256, 256, 3)	0	
conv1_pad (ZeroPadding2D)	(None, 262, 262, 3)	0	input_1[0][0]
conv1_conv (Conv2D)	(None, 128, 128, 64)	9472	conv1_pad[0][0]
conv1_bn (BatchNormalization)	(None, 128, 128, 64)	256	conv1_conv[0][0]
conv1_relu (Activation)	(None, 128, 128, 64)	0	conv1_bn[0][0]
pool1_pad (ZeroPadding2D)	(None, 130, 130, 64)	0	conv1_relu[0][0]
pool1_pool (MaxPooling2D)	(None, 64, 64, 64)	0	pool1_pad[0][0]
conv2_block1_1_conv (Conv2D)	(None, 64, 64, 64)	4160	pool1_pool[0][0]

```
# freeze the model weights
for layer in basemodel.layers:
  layers.trainable = False
```

```
headmodel = basemodel.output
headmodel = AveragePooling2D(pool_size = (4,4))(headmodel)
headmodel = Flatten(name= 'flatten')(headmodel)
headmodel = Dense(256, activation = "relu")(headmodel)
headmodel = Dropout(0.3)(headmodel)
headmodel = Dense(256, activation = "relu")(headmodel)
headmodel = Dropout(0.3)(headmodel)
headmodel = Dense(256, activation = "relu")(headmodel)
headmodel = Dropout(0.3)(headmodel)
headmodel = Dense(2, activation = 'softmax')(headmodel)

model = Model(inputs = basemodel.input, outputs = headmodel)
model.summary()
```

```
average_pooling2d (AveragePooli  (None, 2, 2, 2048)     0        conv5_block3_out[0][0]

flatten (Flatten)                (None, 8192)           0        average_pooling2d[0][0]

dense (Dense)                    (None, 256)            2097408  flatten[0][0]

dropout (Dropout)                (None, 256)            0        dense[0][0]

dense_1 (Dense)                  (None, 256)            65792    dropout[0][0]

dropout_1 (Dropout)              (None, 256)            0        dense_1[0][0]

dense_2 (Dense)                  (None, 256)            65792    dropout_1[0][0]

dropout_2 (Dropout)              (None, 256)            0        dense_2[0][0]

dense_3 (Dense)                  (None, 2)              514      dropout_2[0][0]
==================================================================================
```

```python
# compile the model
model.compile(loss = 'categorical_crossentropy', optimizer='adam', metrics= ["accuracy"])
```

```python
# use early stopping to exit training if validation loss is not decreasing even after certain ep
earlystopping = EarlyStopping(monitor='val_loss', mode='min', verbose=1, patience=20)

# save the model with least validation loss
checkpointer = ModelCheckpoint(filepath="classifier-resnet-weights.hdf5", verbose=1, save_best_o
```

```python
model.fit(train_generator, steps_per_epoch= train_generator.n // 16, epochs = 1, validation_data
```

```python
# make prediction
test_predict = model.predict(test_generator, steps = test_generator.n // 16, verbose =1)

# Obtain the predicted class from the model prediction
predict = []
for i in test_predict:
  predict.append(str(np.argmax(i)))
predict = np.asarray(predict)
```

```python
# Obtain the accuracy of the model
from sklearn.metrics import accuracy_score

accuracy = accuracy_score(original, predict)
accuracy
```

```
0.9826388888888888
```

```python
from sklearn.metrics import classification_report
report = classification_report(original, predict, labels = [0,1])
print(report)
```

```
              precision    recall  f1-score   support

           0       0.98      0.99      0.99       365
           1       0.99      0.97      0.98       211

   micro avg       0.98      0.98      0.98       576
   macro avg       0.98      0.98      0.98       576
weighted avg       0.98      0.98      0.98       576
```

```
# Get the dataframe containing MRIs which have masks associated with them.
brain_df_mask = brain_df[brain_df['mask'] == 1]
brain_df_mask.shape
```

Output: (1373, 4)

```
from sklearn.model_selection import train_test_split
X_train, X_val = train_test_split(brain_df_mask, test_size=0.15)
X_test, X_val = train_test_split(X_val, test_size=0.5)
```

```
train_ids = list(X_train.image_path)
train_mask = list(X_train.mask_path)

val_ids = list(X_val.image_path)
val_mask= list(X_val.mask_path)

# Utilities file contains the code for custom data generator
from utilities import DataGenerator

# create image generators
training_generator = DataGenerator(train_ids,train_mask)
validation_generator = DataGenerator(val_ids,val_mask)
```

```
def resblock(X, f):

  # make a copy of input
  X_copy = X

  X = Conv2D(f, kernel_size = (1,1) ,strides = (1,1),kernel_initializer ='he_normal')(X)
  X = BatchNormalization()(X)
  X = Activation('relu')(X)

  X = Conv2D(f, kernel_size = (3,3), strides =(1,1), padding = 'same', kernel_initializer ='he_
  X = BatchNormalization()(X)

  X_copy = Conv2D(f, kernel_size = (1,1), strides =(1,1), kernel_initializer ='he_normal')(X_c
  X_copy = BatchNormalization()(X_copy)

  # Adding the output from main path and short path together
  X = Add()([X,X_copy])
  X = Activation('relu')(X)

  return X
```

```
def upsample_concat(x, skip):
  x = UpSampling2D((2,2))(x)
  merge = Concatenate()([x, skip])

  return merge
```

```python
input_shape = (256,256,3)

# Input tensor shape
X_input = Input(input_shape)

# Stage 1
conv1_in = Conv2D(16,3,activation= 'relu', padding = 'same', kernel_initializer ='he_normal')(X_
conv1_in = BatchNormalization()(conv1_in)
conv1_in = Conv2D(16,3,activation= 'relu', padding = 'same', kernel_initializer ='he_normal')(co
conv1_in = BatchNormalization()(conv1_in)
pool_1 = MaxPool2D(pool_size = (2,2))(conv1_in)

# Stage 2
conv2_in = resblock(pool_1, 32)
pool_2 = MaxPool2D(pool_size = (2,2))(conv2_in)
```

```python
# Stage 3
conv3_in = resblock(pool_2, 64)
pool_3 = MaxPool2D(pool_size = (2,2))(conv3_in)

# Stage 4
conv4_in = resblock(pool_3, 128)
pool_4 = MaxPool2D(pool_size = (2,2))(conv4_in)

# Stage 5 (Bottle Neck)
conv5_in = resblock(pool_4, 256)

# Upscale stage 1
up_1 = upsample_concat(conv5_in, conv4_in)
up_1 = resblock(up_1, 128)

# Upscale stage 2
up_2 = upsample_concat(up_1, conv3_in)
up_2 = resblock(up_2, 64)
```

```python
# Upscale stage 3
up_3 = upsample_concat(up_2, conv2_in)
up_3 = resblock(up_3, 32)

# Upscale stage 4
up_4 = upsample_concat(up_3, conv1_in)
up_4 = resblock(up_4, 16)

# Final Output
output = Conv2D(1, (1,1), padding = "same", activation = "sigmoid")(up_4)

model_seg = Model(inputs = X_input, outputs = output )
```

```
# use early stopping to exit training if validation loss is not decreasing even after certain ep
earlystopping = EarlyStopping(monitor='val_loss', mode='min', verbose=1, patience=20)

# save the best model with lower validation loss
checkpointer = ModelCheckpoint(filepath="ResUNet-weights.hdf5", verbose=1, save_best_only=True)

model_seg.fit(training_generator, epochs = 1, validation_data = validation_generator, callbacks
```

```
from utilities import prediction

# making prediction
image_id, mask, has_mask = prediction(test, model, model_seg)
```

```
# creating a dataframe for the result
df_pred = pd.DataFrame({'image_path': image_id,'predicted_mask': mask,'has_mask': has_mask})

# Merge the dataframe containing predicted results with the original test data.
df_pred = test.merge(df_pred, on = 'image_path')
df_pred.head()
```

	image_path	mask_path	mask	predicted_mask	has_mask
0	TCGA_HT_8106_19970727/TCGA_HT_8106_19970727_7.tif	TCGA_HT_8106_19970727/TCGA_HT_8106_19970727_7_...	0	No mask	0
1	TCGA_CS_5396_20010302/TCGA_CS_5396_20010302_7.tif	TCGA_CS_5396_20010302/TCGA_CS_5396_20010302_7_...	0	No mask	0
2	TCGA_DU_6399_19830416/TCGA_DU_6399_19830416_30...	TCGA_DU_6399_19830416/TCGA_DU_6399_19830416_30...	1	[[[8.8394046e-07], [2.956604e-06], [1.1406702...	1
3	TCGA_DU_7294_19890104/TCGA_DU_7294_19890104_8.tif	TCGA_DU_7294_19890104/TCGA_DU_7294_19890104_8_...	0	No mask	0
4	TCGA_HT_7602_19951103/TCGA_HT_7602_19951103_18...	TCGA_HT_7602_19951103/TCGA_HT_7602_19951103_18...	0	No mask	0

```
count = 0
fig, axs = plt.subplots(10, 5, figsize=(30, 50))
for i in range(len(df_pred)):
  if df_pred['has_mask'][i] == 1 and count < 5:
    # read the images and convert them to RGB format
    img = io.imread(df_pred.image_path[i])
    img = cv2.cvtColor(img, cv2.COLOR_BGR2RGB)
    axs[count][0].title.set_text("Brain MRI")
    axs[count][0].imshow(img)

    # Obtain the mask for the image
    mask = io.imread(df_pred.mask_path[i])
    axs[count][1].title.set_text("Original Mask")
    axs[count][1].imshow(mask)

    # Obtain the predicted mask for the image
    predicted_mask = np.asarray(df_pred.predicted_mask[i])[0].squeeze().round()
    axs[count][2].title.set_text("AI Predicted Mask")
    axs[count][2].imshow(predicted_mask)
```

```
# Apply the mask to the image 'mask==255'
img[mask == 255] = (255, 0, 0)
axs[count][3].title.set_text("MRI with Original Mask (Ground Truth)")
axs[count][3].imshow(img)

img_ = io.imread(df_pred.image_path[i])
img_ = cv2.cvtColor(img_, cv2.COLOR_BGR2RGB)
img_[predicted_mask == 1] = (0, 255, 0)
axs[count][4].title.set_text("MRI with AI Predicted Mask")
axs[count][4].imshow(img_)
count += 1

fig.tight_layout()
```

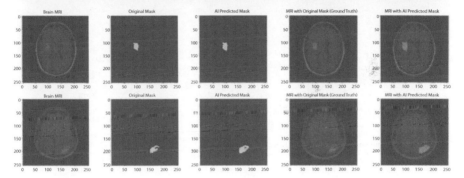

Bibliography

1. https://www.analyticsvidhya.com/blog/2021/06/brain-tumor-detection-and-localization-using-deep-learning-part-1/
2. https://www.analyticsvidhya.com/blog/2021/06/brain-tumor-detection-and-localization-using-deep-learning-part-2/
3. https://www.kaggle.com/ahmedhamada0/brain-tumor-detection
4. https://towardsdatascience.com/building-a-brain-tumor-classification-app-e9a0eb9f068

Color Detection with Python

```
1.    pip install opencv-python numpy pandas
```

```
1.    import argparse
2.
3.    ap = argparse.ArgumentParser()
4.    ap.add_argument('-i', '--image', required=True, help="Image Path")
5.    args = vars(ap.parse_args())
6.    img_path = args['image']
7.    #Reading image with opencv
8.    img = cv2.imread(img_path)
```

```
1.    #Reading csv file with pandas and giving names to each column
2.    index=["color","color_name","hex","R","G","B"]
3.    csv = pd.read_csv('colors.csv', names=index, header=None)
```

```
1.    cv2.namedWindow('image')
2.    cv2.setMouseCallback('image',draw_function)
```

```
1.    def draw_function(event, x,y,flags,param):
2.        if event == cv2.EVENT_LBUTTONDBLCLK:
3.            global b,g,r,xpos,ypos, clicked
4.            clicked = True
5.            xpos = x
6.            ypos = y
7.            b,g,r = img[y,x]
8.            b = int(b)
9.            g = int(g)
10.           r = int(r)
```

```
1.    def getColorName(R,G,B):
2.        minimum = 10000
3.        for i in range(len(csv)):
4.            d = abs(R- int(csv.loc[i,"R"])) + abs(G- int(csv.loc[i,"G"]))+
      abs(B- int(csv.loc[i,"B"]))
5.            if(d<=minimum):
6.                minimum = d
7.                cname = csv.loc[i,"color_name"]
8.        return cname
```

Kolla Bhanu Prakash. Data Science Handbook: A Practical Approach, (297–300) © 2022 Scrivener Publishing LLC

```
1.    while(1):
2.        cv2.imshow("image",img)
3.        if (clicked):
4.            #cv2.rectangle(image, startpoint, endpoint, color, thickness) -1
      thickness fills rectangle entirely
5.            cv2.rectangle(img, (20,20), (750,60), (b,g,r), -1)
6.
7.            #Creating text string to display ( Color name and RGB values )
8.            text = getColorName(r,g,b) + ' R='+ str(r) + ' G='+ str(g) + '
      B='+ str(b)

9.
10.           #cv2.putText(img,text,start,font(0-7), fontScale, color,
      thickness, lineType, (optional bottomLeft bool) )
11.           cv2.putText(img, text,(50,50),2,0.8,(255,255,255),2,cv2.LINE_AA)
12.       #For very light colours we will display text in black colour
13.           if(r+g+b>=600):
14.               cv2.putText(img, text,(50,50),2,0.8,(0,0,0),2,cv2.LINE_AA)
15.
16.           clicked=False
17.
18.       #Break the loop when user hits 'esc' key
19.       if cv2.waitKey(20) & 0xFF ==27:
20.           break
21.
22.    cv2.destroyAllWindows()
```

```
1.    python color_detection.py -i <add your image path here>
```

```
color_detection.py - D:\datafiles project\color detection\color_detection.py (3.6.0)
File  Edit  Format  Run  Options  Window  Help
import cv2
import numpy as np
import pandas as pd
import argparse

#Creating argument parser to take image path from command line
ap = argparse.ArgumentParser()
ap.add_argument('-i', '--image', required=True, help="Image Path")
args = vars(ap.parse_args())
img_path = args['image']

#Reading the image with opencv
img = cv2.imread(img_path)

#declaring global variables (are used later on)
clicked = False
r = g = b = xpos = ypos = 0

#Reading csv file with pandas and giving names to each column
index=["color","color_name","hex","R","G","B"]
csv = pd.read_csv('colors.csv', names=index, header=None)
```

```
#function to calculate minimum distance from all colors and get the most matching color
def getColorName(R,G,B):
    minimum = 10000
    for i in range(len(csv)):
        d = abs(R- int(csv.loc[i,"R"])) + abs(G- int(csv.loc[i,"G"]))+ abs(B- int(csv.loc[i,"B"]))
        if(d<=minimum):
            minimum = d
            cname = csv.loc[i,"color_name"]
    return cname

#function to get x,y coordinates of mouse double click
def draw_function(event, x,y,flags,param):
    if event == cv2.EVENT_LBUTTONDBLCLK:
        global b,g,r,xpos,ypos, clicked
        clicked = True
        xpos = x
        ypos = y
        b,g,r = img[y,x]
        b = int(b)
        g = int(g)
        r = int(r)

cv2.namedWindow('image')
cv2.setMouseCallback('image',draw_function)

while(1):

    cv2.imshow("image",img)
    if (clicked):

        #cv2.rectangle(image, startpoint, endpoint, color, thickness)-1 fills entire rectangle
        cv2.rectangle(img,(20,20), (750,60), (b,g,r), -1)

        #Creating text string to display( Color name and RGB values )
        text = getColorName(r,g,b) + ' R='+ str(r) +  ' G='+ str(g) + ' B='+ str(b)

        #cv2.putText(img,text,start,font(0-7),fontScale,color,thickness,lineType )
        cv2.putText(img, text, (50,50),2,0.8,(255,255,255),2,cv2.LINE_AA)

        #For very light colours we will display text in black colour
        if(r+g+b>=600):
            cv2.putText(img, text, (50,50),2,0.8,(0,0,0),2,cv2.LINE_AA)

        clicked=False

    #Break the loop when user hits 'esc' key
    if cv2.waitKey(20) & 0xFF ==27:
        break

cv2.destroyAllWindows()
```

Bibliography

1. https://data-flair.training/blogs/project-in-python-colour-detection/
2. https://www.geeksforgeeks.org/multiple-color-detection-in-real-time-using-python-opencv/
3. https://www.geeksforgeeks.org/detection-specific-colorblue-using-opencv-python/

Detecting Parkinson's Disease

```
1.   pip install numpy pandas sklearn xgboost
```

```
1.   C:\Users\DataFlair>jupyter lab
```

```python
[1]: #DataFlair - Make necessary imports
     import numpy as np
     import pandas as pd
     import os, sys
     from sklearn.preprocessing import MinMaxScaler
     from xgboost import XGBClassifier
     from sklearn.model_selection import train_test_split
     from sklearn.metrics import accuracy_score
```

```python
[3]: #DataFlair - Get the features and labels
     features=df.loc[:,df.columns!='status'].values[:,1:]
     labels=df.loc[:,'status'].values
```

```python
[4]: #DataFlair - Get the count of each label (0 and 1) in labels
     print(labels[labels==1].shape[0], labels[labels==0].shape[0])

     147 48
```

```python
[5]: #DataFlair - Scale the features to between -1 and 1
     scaler=MinMaxScaler((-1,1))
     x=scaler.fit_transform(features)
     y=labels
```

```python
[6]: #DataFlair - Split the dataset
     x_train,x_test,y_train,y_test=train_test_split(x, y, test_size=0.2, random_state=7)
```

Kolla Bhanu Prakash. Data Science Handbook: A Practical Approach, (301–302) © 2022 Scrivener Publishing LLC

```
[7]:  #DataFlair - Train the model
      model=XGBClassifier()
      model.fit(x_train,y_train)
```

```
[7]:  XGBClassifier(base_score=0.5, booster='gbtree', colsample_bylevel=1,
                    colsample_bynode=1, colsample_bytree=1, gamma=0,
                    learning_rate=0.1, max_delta_step=0, max_depth=3,
                    min_child_weight=1, missing=None, n_estimators=100, n_jobs=1,
                    nthread=None, objective='binary:logistic', random_state=0,
                    reg_alpha=0, reg_lambda=1, scale_pos_weight=1, seed=None,
                    silent=None, subsample=1, verbosity=1)
```

```
[8]:  # DataFlair - Calculate the accuracy
      y_pred=model.predict(x_test)
      print(accuracy_score(y_test, y_pred)*100)
```

```
      94.87179487179486
```

Bibliography

1. https://data-flair.training/blogs/python-machine-learning-project-detecting-parkinson-disease/
2. Sveinbjornsdottir S (October 2016). "The clinical symptoms of Parkinson's disease". Journal of Neurochemistry. 139 (Suppl 1): 318–24. doi:10.1111/jnc.13691. PMID 27401947.
3. Carroll WM (2016). International Neurology. John Wiley & Sons. p. 188. ISBN 978-1118777367.
4. Kalia LV, Lang AE (August 2015). "Parkinson's disease". Lancet. 386 (9996): 896–912. doi:10.1016/s0140-6736(14)61393-3. PMID 25904081. S2CID 5502904.
5. Ferri FF (2010). "Chapter P". Ferri's differential diagnosis : a practical guide to the differential diagnosis of symptoms, signs, and clinical disorders (2nd ed.). Philadelphia, PA: Elsevier/Mosby. ISBN 978-0323076999.
6. Macleod AD, Taylor KS, Counsell CE (November 2014). "Mortality in Parkinson's disease: a systematic review and meta-analysis". Movement Disorders. 29 (13): 1615–22. doi:10.1002/mds.25898. PMID 24821648.

16

Sentiment Analysis

```
library(tidytext)
sentiments
```

word <chr>	sentiment <chr>
ache	negative
ached	negative
aches	negative
achey	negative
achievable	positive
achievement	positive
achievements	positive
achievible	positive
aching	negative
acrid	negative

61-70 of 6,786 rows   Previous 1 … 5 6 **7** 8 9 … 100 Next

```
got_sentiments("bing")
```

word <chr>	sentiment <chr>
2-faces	negative
abnormal	negative
abolish	negative
abominable	negative
abominably	negative
abominate	negative
abomination	negative
abort	negative
aborted	negative
aborts	negative

1-10 of 6,786 rows   Previous **1** 2 3 4 5 6 … 100 Next

```
library(janeaustenr)
library(stringr)
library(tidytext)

tidy_data <- austen_books() %>%
  group_by(book) %>%
  mutate(linenumber = row_number(),
         chapter = cumsum(str_detect(text, regex("^chapter [\\divxlc]",
                                      ignore_case = TRUE)))) %>%
  ungroup() %>%
  unnest_tokens(word, text)
```

Kolla Bhanu Prakash. *Data Science Handbook: A Practical Approach*, (303–306) © 2022 Scrivener Publishing LLC

```
positive_senti <- get_sentiments("bing") %>%
  filter(sentiment == "positive")

tidy_data %>%
  filter(book == "Emma") %>%
  semi_join(positive_senti) %>%
  count(word, sort = TRUE)
```

```
Joining, by = "word"
```

word	n
<chr>	<int>
well	401
good	359
great	264
like	200
better	173
enough	129
happy	125
love	117
pleasure	115
right	92

1-10 of 668 rows   Previous **1** 2 3 4 5 6 … 67 Next

```
library(tidyr)
bing <- get_sentiments("bing")
Emma_sentiment <- tidy_data %>%
  inner_join(bing) %>%
  count(book = "Emma" , index = linenumber %/% 80, sentiment) %>%
  spread(sentiment, n, fill = 0) %>%
  mutate(sentiment = positive - negative)
```

```
library(ggplot2)

ggplot(Emma_sentiment, aes(index, sentiment, fill = book)) +
  geom_bar(stat = "identity", show.legend = TRUE) +
  facet_wrap(~book, ncol = 2, scales = "free_x")
```

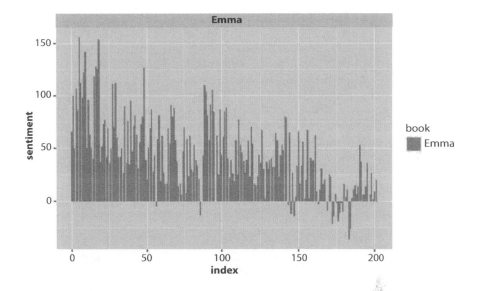

```
counting_words <- tidy_data %>%
  inner_join(bing) %>%
  count(word, sentiment, sort = TRUE)
```

```
Joining, by = "word"
```

Hide

```
head(counting_words)
```

word	sentiment	n
<chr>	<chr>	<int>
miss	negative	1855
well	positive	1523
good	positive	1380
great	positive	981
like	positive	725
better	positive	639

6 rows

```
counting_words %>%
  filter(n > 150) %>%
  mutate(n = ifelse(sentiment == "negative", -n, n)) %>%
  mutate(word = reorder(word, n)) %>%
  ggplot(aes(word, n, fill = sentiment))+
  geom_col() +
  coord_flip() +
  labs(y = "Sentiment Score")
```

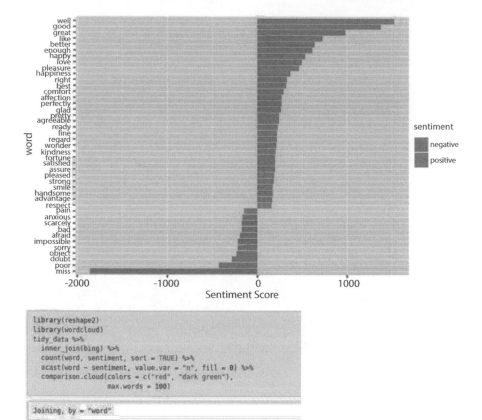

```
library(reshape2)
library(wordcloud)
tidy_data %>%
  inner_join(bing) %>%
  count(word, sentiment, sort = TRUE) %>%
  acast(word ~ sentiment, value.var = "n", fill = 0) %>%
  comparison.cloud(colors = c("red", "dark green"),
                   max.words = 100)
```

```
Joining, by = "word"
```

Bibliography

1. https://data-flair.training/blogs/data-science-r-sentiment-analysis-project/
2. Hamborg, Felix; Donnay, Karsten (2021). "NewsMTSC: A Dataset for (Multi-) Target-dependent Sentiment Classification in Political News Articles". "Proceedings of the 16th Conference of the European Chapter of the Association for Computational Linguistics: Main Volume"
3. Vong Anh Ho, Duong Huynh-Cong Nguyen, Danh Hoang Nguyen, Linh Thi-Van Pham, Duc-Vu Nguyen, Kiet Van Nguyen, Ngan Luu-Thuy Nguyen. "Emotion Recognition for Vietnamese Social Media Text". In Proceedings of the 2019 International Conference of the Pacific Association for Computational Linguistics (PACLING 2019), Hanoi, Vietnam (2019).

Road Lane Line Detection

1. Imports:

```
1.   import matplotlib.pyplot as plt
2.
3.   import numpy as np
4.   import cv2
5.   import os
6.   import matplotlib.image as mpimg
7.   from moviepy.editor import VideoFileClip
8.   import math
```

2. Apply frame masking and find region of interest:

```
1.   def interested_region(img, vertices):
2.       if len(img.shape) > 2:
3.           mask_color_ignore = (255,) * img.shape[2]
4.       else:
5.           mask_color_ignore = 255
6.
7.       cv2.fillPoly(np.zeros_like(img), vertices, mask_color_ignore)
8.       return cv2.bitwise_and(img, np.zeros_like(img))
```

3. Conversion of pixels to a line in Hough Transform space:

```
1.   def hough_lines(img, rho, theta, threshold, min_line_len, max_line_gap):
2.       lines = cv2.HoughLinesP(img, rho, theta, threshold, np.array([]),
     minLineLength=min_line_len, maxLineGap=max_line_gap)
3.       line_img = np.zeros((img.shape[0], img.shape[1], 3), dtype=np.uint8)
4.       lines_drawn(line_img,lines)
5.       return line_img
```

Kolla Bhanu Prakash. *Data Science Handbook: A Practical Approach*, (307–316) © 2022 Scrivener
Publishing LLC

4. Create two lines in each frame after Hough transform:

```
1.    def lines_drawn(img, lines, color=[255, 0, 0], thickness=6):
2.        global cache
3.        global first_frame
4.        slope_l, slope_r = [],[]
5.        lane_l,lane_r = [],[]
6.
7.        α =0.2
8.        for line in lines:
9.            for x1,y1,x2,y2 in line:
10.               slope = (y2-y1)/(x2-x1)
11.               if slope > 0.4:
12.                   slope_r.append(slope)
13.                   lane_r.append(line)
14.               elif slope < -0.4:
15.                   slope_l.append(slope)
16.                   lane_l.append(line)
17.           img.shape[0] = min(y1,y2,img.shape[0])
18.       if((len(lane_l) == 0) or (len(lane_r) == 0)):
19.           print ('no lane detected')
20.           return 1
21.       slope_mean_l = np.mean(slope_l,axis =0)
22.       slope_mean_r = np.mean(slope_r,axis =0)
23.       mean_l = np.mean(np.array(lane_l),axis=0)
24.       mean_r = np.mean(np.array(lane_r),axis=0)
25.
26.       if ((slope_mean_r == 0) or (slope_mean_l == 0 )):
27.           print('dividing by zero')
28.           return 1
29.
30.       x1_l = int((img.shape[0] - mean_l[0][1] - (slope_mean_l * mean_l[0]
      [0]))/slope_mean_l)
31.       x2_l = int((img.shape[0] - mean_l[0][1] - (slope_mean_l * mean_l[0]
      [0]))/slope_mean_l)
32.       x1_r = int((img.shape[0] - mean_r[0][1] - (slope_mean_r * mean_r[0]
      [0]))/slope_mean_r)
33.       x2_r = int((img.shape[0] - mean_r[0][1] - (slope_mean_r * mean_r[0]
      [0]))/slope_mean_r)
34.
35.
```

```
36.        if x1_l > x1_r:
37.            x1_l = int((x1_l+x1_r)/2)
38.            x1_r = x1_l
39.            y1_l = int((slope_mean_l * x1_l ) + mean_l[0][1] - (slope_mean_l *
       mean_l[0][0]))
40.            y1_r = int((slope_mean_r * x1_r ) + mean_r[0][1] - (slope_mean_r *
       mean_r[0][0]))
41.            y2_l = int((slope_mean_l * x2_l ) + mean_l[0][1] - (slope_mean_l *
       mean_l[0][0]))
42.            y2_r = int((slope_mean_r * x2_r ) + mean_r[0][1] - (slope_mean_r *
       mean_r[0][0]))
43.        else:
44.            y1_l = img.shape[0]
45.            y2_l = img.shape[0]
46.            y1_r = img.shape[0]
47.            y2_r = img.shape[0]
48.
49.        present_frame =
       np.array([x1_l,y1_l,x2_l,y2_l,x1_r,y1_r,x2_r,y2_r],dtype ="float32")
50.
51.        if first_frame == 1:
52.            next_frame = present_frame
53.            first_frame = 0
54.        else :
55.            prev_frame = cache
56.            next_frame = (1-α)*prev_frame+α*present_frame
57.
58.        cv2.line(img, (int(next_frame[0]), int(next_frame[1])),
       (int(next_frame[2]),int(next_frame[3])), color, thickness)
59.        cv2.line(img, (int(next_frame[4]), int(next_frame[5])),
       (int(next_frame[6]),int(next_frame[7])), color, thickness)
60.
61.        cache = next_frame
```

5. Process each frame of video to detect lane:

```
1.    def weighted_img(img, initial_img, α=0.8, β=1., λ=0.):
2.        return cv2.addWeighted(initial_img, α, img, β, λ)
3.
4.
```

```
5.   def process_image(image):
6.
7.       global first_frame
8.
9.       gray_image = cv2.cvtColor(image, cv2.COLOR_BGR2GRAY)
10.      img_hsv = cv2.cvtColor(image, cv2.COLOR_RGB2HSV)
11.
12.
13.      lower_yellow = np.array([20, 100, 100], dtype = "uint8")
14.      upper_yellow = np.array([30, 255, 255], dtype="uint8")
15.
16.      mask_yellow = cv2.inRange(img_hsv, lower_yellow, upper_yellow)
17.      mask_white = cv2.inRange(gray_image, 200, 255)
18.      mask_yw = cv2.bitwise_or(mask_white, mask_yellow)
19.      mask_yw_image = cv2.bitwise_and(gray_image, mask_yw)
20.
21.      gauss_gray= cv2.GaussianBlur(mask_yw_image, (5, 5), 0)
22.
23.      canny_edges=cv2.Canny(gauss_gray, 50, 150)
24.
25.      imshape = image.shape
26.      lower_left = [imshape[1]/9,imshape[0]]
27.      lower_right = [imshape[1]-imshape[1]/9,imshape[0]]
28.      top_left = [imshape[1]/2-imshape[1]/8,imshape[0]/2+imshape[0]/10]
29.      top_right = [imshape[1]/2+imshape[1]/8,imshape[0]/2+imshape[0]/10]
30.      vertices =
      [np.array([lower_left,top_left,top_right,lower_right],dtype=np.int32)]
31.      roi_image = interested_region(canny_edges, vertices)
32.
33.      theta = np.pi/180
34.
35.      line_image = hough_lines(roi_image, 4, theta, 30, 100, 180)
36.      result = weighted_img(line_image, image, α=0.8, β=1., λ=0.)
37.      return result
```

6. Clip the input video to frames and get the resultant output video file:

```
1.   first_frame = 1
2.   white_output = '__path_to_output_file__'
3.   clip1 = VideoFileClip("__path_to_input_file__")
4.   white_clip = clip1.fl_image(process_image)
5.   white_clip.write_videofile(white_output, audio=False)
```

Code for Lane Line Detection Project GUI:

```
1.   import tkinter as tk
2.   from tkinter import *
3.   import cv2
4.   from PIL import Image, ImageTk
5.   import os
6.   import numpy as np
7.
8.
9.   global last_frame1
10.  last_frame1 = np.zeros((480, 640, 3), dtype=np.uint8)
11.  global last_frame2
12.  last_frame2 = np.zeros((480, 640, 3), dtype=np.uint8)
13.  global cap1
14.  global cap2
15.  cap1 = cv2.VideoCapture("path_to_input_test_video")
16.  cap2 = cv2.VideoCapture("path_to_resultant_lane_detected_video")
17.
18.  def show_vid():
19.      if not cap1.isOpened():
20.          print("cant open the camera1")
21.      flag1, frame1 = cap1.read()
22.      frame1 = cv2.resize(frame1,(400,500))
23.      if flag1 is None:
24.          print ("Major error!")
25.      elif flag1:
26.          global last_frame1
27.          last_frame1 = frame1.copy()
28.          pic = cv2.cvtColor(last_frame1, cv2.COLOR_BGR2RGB)
29.          img = Image.fromarray(pic)
30.          imgtk = ImageTk.PhotoImage(image=img)
31.          lmain.imgtk = imgtk
32.          lmain.configure(image=imgtk)
33.          lmain.after(10, show_vid)
34.
35.
36.  def show_vid2():
37.      if not cap2.isOpened():
38.          print("cant open the camera2")
39.      flag2, frame2 = cap2.read()
40.      frame2 = cv2.resize(frame2,(400,500))
41.      if flag2 is None:
42.          print ("Major error2!")
43.      elif flag2:
44.          global last_frame2
45.          last_frame2 = frame2.copy()
46.          pic2 = cv2.cvtColor(last_frame2, cv2.COLOR_BGR2RGB)
47.          img2 = Image.fromarray(pic2)
48.          img2tk = ImageTk.PhotoImage(image=img2)
49.          lmain2.img2tk = img2tk
50.          lmain2.configure(image=img2tk)
51.          lmain2.after(10, show_vid2)
52.
```

```
53.  if __name__ == '__main__':
54.      root=tk.Tk()
55.      lmain = tk.Label(master=root)
56.      lmain2 = tk.Label(master=root)
57.
58.      lmain.pack(side = LEFT)
59.      lmain2.pack(side = RIGHT)
60.      root.title("Lane-line detection")
61.      root.geometry("900x700+100+10")
62.      exitbutton = Button(root, text='Quit',fg="red",command=
     root.destroy).pack(side = BOTTOM,)
63.      show_vid()
64.      show_vid2()
65.      root.mainloop()
66.      cap.release()
```

jupyter gui.py✔ 06/26/2020

File   Edit   View   Language

```
1  import tkinter as tk
2  from tkinter import *
3  import cv2
4  from PIL import Image, ImageTk
5  import os
6  import numpy as np
7
8
9  global last_frame1                              #creating global        variable
10 last_frame1 = np.zeros((480, 640, 3), dtype=np.uint8)
11 global last_frame2                              #creating global     variable
12 last_frame2 = np.zeros((480, 640, 3), dtype=np.uint8)
13 global cap1
14 global cap2
15 cap1 = cv2.VideoCapture("./input2.mp4")
16 cap2 = cv2.VideoCapture("./output2.mp4")
17
18 def show_vid():
19     if not cap1.isOpened():
20         print("cant open the camera1")
21     flag1, frame1 = cap1.read()
22     frame1 = cv2.resize(frame1,(600,500))
23     if flag1 is None:
24         print ("Major error!")
25     elif flag1:
26         global last_frame1
27         last_frame1 = frame1.copy()
28         pic = cv2.cvtColor(last_frame1, cv2.COLOR_BGR2RGB)
29         img = Image.fromarray(pic)
30         imgtk = ImageTk.PhotoImage(image=img)
31         lmain.imgtk = imgtk
32         lmain.configure(image=imgtk)
33         lmain.after(10, show_vid)
34
--
```

```
def show_vid2():
    if not cap2.isOpened():
        print("cant open the camera2")
    flag2, frame2 = cap2.read()
    frame2 = cv2.resize(frame2,(600,500))
    if flag2 is None:
        print ("Major error2!")
    elif flag2:
        global last_frame2
        last_frame2 = frame2.copy()
        pic2 = cv2.cvtColor(last_frame2, cv2.COLOR_BGR2RGB)
        img2 = Image.fromarray(pic2)
        img2tk = ImageTk.PhotoImage(image=img2)
        lmain2.img2tk = img2tk
        lmain2.configure(image=img2tk)
        lmain2.after(10, show_vid2)
```

```python
if __name__ == '__main__':
    root=tk.Tk()
    img = ImageTk.PhotoImage(Image.open("logo.png"))
    heading = Label(root,image=img, text="Lane-Line Detection")
    # heading.configure(background='#CDCDCD',foreground='#364156')
    heading.pack()
    heading2=Label(root,text="Lane-Line Detection",pady=20, font=('arial',45,'bold'))
    heading2.configure(foreground='#364156')
    heading2.pack()
    lmain = tk.Label(master=root)
    lmain2 = tk.Label(master=root)

    lmain.pack(side = LEFT)
    lmain2.pack(side = RIGHT)
    root.title("Lane-line detection")
    root.geometry("1250x900+100+10")

exitbutton = Button(root, text='Quit',fg="red",command=    root.destroy).pack(side = BOTTOM,)
show_vid()
show_vid2()
root.mainloop()
cap.release()
```

jupyter main.py 06/26/2020

File   Edit   View   Language

```python
1   import matplotlib.pyplot as plt
2
3   import numpy as np
4   import cv2
5   import os
6   import matplotlib.image as mpimg
7   from moviepy.editor import VideoFileClip
8   import math
9
10  def interested_region(img, vertices):
11      if len(img.shape) > 2:
12          mask_color_ignore = (255,) * img.shape[2]
13      else:
14          mask_color_ignore = 255
15
16      cv2.fillPoly(np.zeros_like(img), vertices, mask_color_ignore)
17      return cv2.bitwise_and(img, mask)
18
19  def lines_drawn(img, lines, color=[255, 0, 0], thickness=6):
20      global cache
21      global first_frame
22      slope_l, slope_r = [],[]
23      lane_l,lane_r = [],[]
24
25      α =0.2
26
27
28      for line in lines:
29          for x1,y1,x2,y2 in line:
30              slope = (y2-y1)/(x2-x1)
31              if slope > 0.4:
32                  slope_r.append(slope)
33                  lane_r.append(line)
34              elif slope < -0.4:
35                  slope_l.append(slope)
36                  lane_l.append(line)
37      #2
38      img.shape[0] = min(y1,y2,img.shape[0])
39
40      # to prevent errors in challenge video from dividing by zero
41      if((len(lane_l) == 0) or (len(lane_r) == 0)):
42          print ('no lane detected')
43          return 1
44
```

```
45      #3
46      slope_mean_l = np.mean(slope_l,axis =0)
47      slope_mean_r = np.mean(slope_r,axis =0)
48      mean_l = np.mean(np.array(lane_l),axis=0)
49      mean_r = np.mean(np.array(lane_r),axis=0)
50
51      if ((slope_mean_r == 0) or (slope_mean_l == 0 )):
52          print('dividing by zero')
53          return 1
54
55      x1_l = int((img.shape[0] - mean_l[0][1] - (slope_mean_l * mean_l[0][0]))/slope_mean_l)
56      x2_l = int((img.shape[0] - mean_l[0][1] - (slope_mean_l * mean_l[0][0]))/slope_mean_l)
57      x1_r = int((img.shape[0] - mean_r[0][1] - (slope_mean_r * mean_r[0][0]))/slope_mean_r)
58      x2_r = int((img.shape[0] - mean_r[0][1] - (slope_mean_r * mean_r[0][0]))/slope_mean_r)
59
60      #6
61      if x1_l > x1_r:
62          x1_l = int((x1_l+x1_r)/2)
63          x1_r = x1_l
64          y1_l = int((slope_mean_l * x1_l ) + mean_l[0][1] - (slope_mean_l * mean_l[0][0]))
65          y1_r = int((slope_mean_r * x1_r ) + mean_r[0][1] - (slope_mean_r * mean_r[0][0]))
66          y2_l = int((slope_mean_l * x2_l ) + mean_l[0][1] - (slope_mean_l * mean_l[0][0]))
67          y2_r = int((slope_mean_r * x2_r ) + mean_r[0][1] - (slope_mean_r * mean_r[0][0]))
68      else:
69          y1_l = img.shape[0]
70          y2_l = img.shape[0]
71          y1_r = img.shape[0]
72          y2_r = img.shape[0]
73
74      present_frame = np.array([x1_l,y1_l,x2_l,y2_l,x1_r,y1_r,x2_r,y2_r],dtype ="float32")
75
76      if first_frame == 1:
77          next_frame = present_frame
78          first_frame = 0
79      else :
80          prev_frame = cache
81          next_frame = (1-α)*prev_frame+α*present_frame
82
83      cv2.line(img, (int(next_frame[0]), int(next_frame[1])), (int(next_frame[2]),int(next_frame[3])), color, thickness)
84      cv2.line(img, (int(next_frame[4]), int(next_frame[5])), (int(next_frame[6]),int(next_frame[7])), color, thickness)
85
86      cache = next_frame
87
88  def hough_lines(img, rho, theta, threshold, min_line_len, max_line_gap):
89      lines = cv2.HoughLinesP(img, rho, theta, threshold, np.array([]), minLineLength=min_line_len,
90  maxLineGap=max_line_gap)
91      line_img = np.zeros((img.shape[0], img.shape[1], 3), dtype=np.uint8)
92      lines_drawn(line_img,lines)
93      return line_img
94
95  def weighted_img(img, initial_img, α=0.8, β=1., λ=0.):
96      return cv2.addWeighted(initial_img, α, img, β, λ)
97
98
99  def process_image(image):
100
101      global first_frame
102
103      gray_image = cv2.cvtColor(image, cv2.COLOR_RGB2GRAY)
104      img_hsv = cv2.cvtColor(image, cv2.COLOR_RGB2HSV)
105
106
107      lower_yellow = np.array([20, 100, 100], dtype = "uint8")
108      upper_yellow = np.array([30, 255, 255], dtype="uint8")
109
110      mask_yellow = cv2.inRange(img_hsv, lower_yellow, upper_yellow)
111      mask_white = cv2.inRange(gray_image, 200, 255)
112      mask_yw = cv2.bitwise_or(mask_white, mask_yellow)
113      mask_yw_image = cv2.bitwise_and(gray_image, mask_yw)
114
115      gauss_gray= cv2.GaussianBlur(mask_yw_image, (5, 5), 0)
116
117
118      canny_edges=cv2.Canny(gauss_gray, 50, 150)
119
120      imshape = image.shape
121      lower_left = [imshape[1]/9,imshape[0]]
122      lower_right = [imshape[1]-imshape[1]/9,imshape[0]]
123      top_left = [imshape[1]/2-imshape[1]/8,imshape[0]/2+imshape[0]/10]
124      top_right = [imshape[1]/2+imshape[1]/8,imshape[0]/2+imshape[0]/10]
125      vertices = [np.array([lower_left,top_left,top_right,lower_right],dtype=np.int32)]
126      roi_image = interested_region(canny_edges, vertices)
127
128      theta = np.pi/180
129
130      line_image = hough_lines(roi_image, 4, theta, 30, 100, 180)
131      result = weighted_img(line_image, image, α=0.8, β=1., λ=0.)
132      return result
133
```

Bibliography

1. https://data-flair.training/blogs/road-lane-line-detection/

Fake News Detection

```
pip install numpy pandas sklearn
```

```
C:\Users\DataFlair>jupyter lab
```

```
[1]: #DataFlair - Make necessary imports
     import numpy as np
     import pandas as pd
     import itertools
     from sklearn.model_selection import train_test_split
     from sklearn.feature_extraction.text import TfidfVectorizer
     from sklearn.linear_model import PassiveAggressiveClassifier
     from sklearn.metrics import accuracy_score, confusion_matrix
```

```
[2]: #Read the data
     df=pd.read_csv('D:\\DataFlair\\news.csv')

     #Get shape and head
     df.shape
     df.head()
```

	Unnamed: 0	title	text	label
0	8476	You Can Smell Hillary's Fear	Daniel Greenfield, a Shillman Journalism Fello...	FAKE
1	10294	Watch The Exact Moment Paul Ryan Committed Pol...	Google Pinterest Digg Linkedin Reddit Stumbleu...	FAKE
2	3608	Kerry to go to Paris in gesture of sympathy	U.S. Secretary of State John F. Kerry said Mon...	REAL
3	10142	Bernie supporters on Twitter erupt in anger ag...	— Kaydee King (@KaydeeKing) November 9, 2016 T...	FAKE
4	875	The Battle of New York Why This Primary Matters	It's primary day in New York and front-runners...	REAL

```
[3]: #DataFlair - Get the Labels
     labels=df.label
     labels.head()
```

```
[3]: 0    FAKE
     1    FAKE
     2    REAL
     3    FAKE
     4    REAL
     Name: label, dtype: object
```

```
[4]: #DataFlair - Split the dataset
     x_train,x_test,y_train,y_test=train_test_split(df['text'], labels, test_size=0.2, random_state=7)
```

```
[5]:  #DataFlair - Initialize a TfidfVectorizer
      tfidf_vectorizer=TfidfVectorizer(stop_words='english', max_df=0.7)

      #DataFlair - Fit and transform train set, transform test set
      tfidf_train=tfidf_vectorizer.fit_transform(x_train)
      tfidf_test=tfidf_vectorizer.transform(x_test)
```

```
[6]:  #DataFlair - Initialize a PassiveAggressiveClassifier
      pac=PassiveAggressiveClassifier(max_iter=50)
      pac.fit(tfidf_train,y_train)

      #DataFlair - Predict on the test set and calculate accuracy
      y_pred=pac.predict(tfidf_test)
      score=accuracy_score(y_test,y_pred)
      print(f'Accuracy: {round(score*100,2)}%')

      Accuracy: 92.82%
```

```
[7]:  #DataFlair - Build confusion matrix
      confusion_matrix(y_test,y_pred, labels=['FAKE','REAL'])

[7]:  array([[589,  49],
             [ 42, 587]], dtype=int64)
```

Bibliography

1. https://data-flair.training/blogs/advanced-python-project-detecting-fake-news/

Speech Emotion Recognition

```
1.   C:\Users\DataFlair>jupyter lab
```

```
1.   pip install librosa soundfile numpy sklearn pyaudio
```

```
Python 3.7.3 (default, Apr 24 2019, 15:29:51) [MSC v.1915 64 bit (AMD64)]
Type "copyright", "credits" or "license" for more information
IPython 7.6.1 -- An enhanced Interactive Python. Type '?' for help.
```

```python
#DataFlair - Make necessary imports
import librosa
import soundfile
import os, glob, pickle
import numpy as np
from sklearn.model_selection import train_test_split
from sklearn.neural_network import MLPClassifier
from sklearn.metrics import accuracy_score
```

```python
[2]: #DataFlair - Extract features (mfcc, chroma, mel) from a sound file
     def extract_feature(file_name, mfcc, chroma, mel):
         with soundfile.SoundFile(file_name) as sound_file:
             X = sound_file.read(dtype="float32")
             sample_rate=sound_file.samplerate
             if chroma:
                 stft=np.abs(librosa.stft(X))
             result=np.array([])
             if mfcc:
                 mfccs=np.mean(librosa.feature.mfcc(y=X, sr=sample_rate, n_mfcc=40).T, axis=0)
                 result=np.hstack((result, mfccs))
             if chroma:
                 chroma=np.mean(librosa.feature.chroma_stft(S=stft, sr=sample_rate).T,axis=0)
                 result=np.hstack((result, chroma))
             if mel:
                 mel=np.mean(librosa.feature.melspectrogram(X, sr=sample_rate).T,axis=0)
                 result=np.hstack((result, mel))
         return result
```

```python
[3]: #DataFlair - Emotions in the RAVDESS dataset
     emotions={
         '01':'neutral',
         '02':'calm',
         '03':'happy',
         '04':'sad',
         '05':'angry',
         '06':'fearful',
         '07':'disgust',
         '08':'surprised'
     }

     #DataFlair - Emotions to observe
     observed_emotions=['calm', 'happy', 'fearful', 'disgust']
```

Kolla Bhanu Prakash. Data Science Handbook: A Practical Approach, (319–322) © 2022 Scrivener Publishing LLC

his PC › Local Disk (D:) › DataFlair › ravdess data ›

Name	Date modified	Type
Actor_01	9/4/2019 12:14 PM	File folder
Actor_02	9/4/2019 12:14 PM	File folder
Actor_03	9/4/2019 12:14 PM	File folder
Actor_04	9/4/2019 12:14 PM	File folder
Actor_05	9/4/2019 12:14 PM	File folder
Actor_06	9/4/2019 12:14 PM	File folder
Actor_07	9/4/2019 12:14 PM	File folder
Actor_08	9/4/2019 12:14 PM	File folder
Actor_09	9/4/2019 12:14 PM	File folder
Actor_10	9/4/2019 12:14 PM	File folder
Actor_11	9/4/2019 12:14 PM	File folder
Actor_12	9/4/2019 12:14 PM	File folder
Actor_13	9/4/2019 12:14 PM	File folder
Actor_14	9/4/2019 12:14 PM	File folder
Actor_15	9/4/2019 12:14 PM	File folder
Actor_16	9/4/2019 12:14 PM	File folder
Actor_17	9/4/2019 12:14 PM	File folder
Actor_18	9/4/2019 12:14 PM	File folder
Actor_19	9/4/2019 12:14 PM	File folder
Actor_20	9/4/2019 12:14 PM	File folder
Actor_21	9/4/2019 12:14 PM	File folder
Actor_22	9/4/2019 12:14 PM	File folder
Actor_23	9/4/2019 12:14 PM	File folder
Actor_24	9/4/2019 12:14 PM	File folder

his PC › Local Disk (D:) › DataFlair › ravdess data › Actor_01

Name	#	Title	Co
03-01-01-01-01-01-01			
03-01-01-01-01-02-01			
03-01-01-01-02-01-01			
03-01-01-01-02-02-01			
03-01-02-01-01-01-01			
03-01-02-01-01-02-01			
03-01-02-01-02-01-01			

```
[4]:  #DataFlair - Load the data and extract features for each sound file
      def load_data(test_size=0.2):
          x,y=[],[]
          for file in glob.glob("D:\\DataFlair\\ravdess data\\Actor_*\\*.wav"):
              file_name=os.path.basename(file)
              emotion=emotions[file_name.split("-")[2]]
              if emotion not in observed_emotions:
                  continue
              feature=extract_feature(file, mfcc=True, chroma=True, mel=True)
              x.append(feature)
              y.append(emotion)
          return train_test_split(np.array(x), y, test_size=test_size, random_state=9)
```

```
[5]:  #DataFlair - Split the dataset
      x_train,x_test,y_train,y_test=load_data(test_size=0.25)
```

```
[6]:  #DataFlair - Get the shape of the training and testing datasets
      print((x_train.shape[0], x_test.shape[0]))

      (576, 192)
```

```
[7]:  #DataFlair - Get the number of features extracted
      print(f'Features extracted: {x_train.shape[1]}')

      Features extracted: 180
```

```
[8]:  #DataFlair - Initialize the Multi Layer Perceptron Classifier
      model=MLPClassifier(alpha=0.01, batch_size=256, epsilon=1e-08, hidden_layer_sizes=(300,), learning_rate='adaptive', max_iter=500)
```

```
[9]:  #DataFlair - Train the model
      model.fit(x_train,y_train)
```

```
[9]:  MLPClassifier(activation='relu', alpha=0.01, batch_size=256, beta_1=0.9,
                    beta_2=0.999, early_stopping=False, epsilon=1e-08,
                    hidden_layer_sizes=(300,), learning_rate='adaptive',
                    learning_rate_init=0.001, max_iter=500, momentum=0.9,
                    n_iter_no_change=10, nesterovs_momentum=True, power_t=0.5,
                    random_state=None, shuffle=True, solver='adam', tol=0.0001,
                    validation_fraction=0.1, verbose=False, warm_start=False)
```

```
[10]: #DataFlair - Predict for the test set
      y_pred=model.predict(x_test)
```

```
[11]: #DataFlair - Calculate the accuracy of our model
      accuracy=accuracy_score(y_true=y_test, y_pred=y_pred)

      #DataFlair - Print the accuracy
      print("Accuracy: {:.2f}%".format(accuracy*100))

      Accuracy: 72.40%
```

Bibliography

1. https://data-flair.training/blogs/python-mini-project-speech-emotion-recognition/
2. Kleine-Cosack, Christian (October 2006). "Recognition and Simulation of Emotions" (PDF). The introduction of emotion to computer science was done by Pickard (sic) who created the field of affective computing.
3. Neiberg, D; Elenius, K; Laskowski, K (2006). "Emotion recognition in spontaneous speech using GMMs" (PDF). Proceedings of Interspeech.
4. Yacoub, Sherif; Simske, Steve; Lin, Xiaofan; Burns, John (2003). "Recognition of Emotions in Interactive Voice Response Systems". Proceedings of Eurospeech: 729–732.

20

Gender and Age Detection with Data Science

Steps to Develop Age and Gender Detection Project

1. Transferring the information

```
1  import os
2  from google.colab import drive
3  drive.mount('/content/drive')
4
5  os.chdir('/content/drive/MyDrive/TechVidvan')
```

2. Import the fundamental libraries for stacking and survey information:

Numpy: for working with the information, cleaning it, arranging it in the necessary way and erasing immaterial information.
Pandas: for perusing the dataset csv documents.
Matplotlib: for plotting the charts and showing pictures within the colab console alongside seaborn.
Opencv and PIL: for working with pictures resizing it, formating it for the model and stuff.

```
1  import numpy as np
2  import pandas as pd
3  import matplotlib.pyplot as plt
4  import seaborn as sns
5  import cv2
6  from PIL import Image
```

Kolla Bhanu Prakash. Data Science Handbook: A Practical Approach, (323–340) © 2022 Scrivener Publishing LLC

3. Peruse the Data

```
1   #load data
2   fold0 = pd.read_csv("AdienceBenchmarkGenderAndAgeClassification/fold_0_data.txt"
        ,sep = "\t" )
3   fold1 = pd.read_csv("AdienceBenchmarkGenderAndAgeClassification/fold_1_data.txt"
        ,sep = "\t")
4   fold2 = pd.read_csv("AdienceBenchmarkGenderAndAgeClassification/fold_2_data.txt"
        ,sep = "\t")
5   fold3 = pd.read_csv("AdienceBenchmarkGenderAndAgeClassification/fold_3_data.txt"
        ,sep = "\t")
6   fold4 = pd.read_csv("AdienceBenchmarkGenderAndAgeClassification/fold_4_data.txt"
        ,sep = "\t")
```

```
1   total_data = pd.concat([fold0, fold1, fold2, fold3, fold4], ignore_index=True)
2   print(total_data.shape)
3   total_data.info()
```

```
(19370, 12)
<class 'pandas.core.frame.DataFrame'>
RangeIndex: 19370 entries, 0 to 19369
Data columns (total 12 columns):
 #   Column              Non-Null Count  Dtype
---  ------              --------------  -----
 0   user_id             19370 non-null  object
 1   original_image      19370 non-null  object
 2   face_id             19370 non-null  int64
 3   age                 19370 non-null  object
 4   gender              18591 non-null  object
 5   x                   19370 non-null  int64
 6   y                   19370 non-null  int64
 7   dx                  19370 non-null  int64
 8   dy                  19370 non-null  int64
 9   tilt_ang            19370 non-null  int64
 10  fiducial_yaw_angle  19370 non-null  int64
 11  fiducial_score      19370 non-null  int64
dtypes: int64(8), object(4)
memory usage: 1.8+ MB
```

Print the best 5 records from the dataframeusing.head() work, confirming the information structure.

```
1  total_data.head()
```

	user_id	original_image	face_id	age	gender	x	y	dx	dy	tilt_ang	fiducial_yaw_angle	fiducial_score
0	30601258@N03	10399646885_67c7d20df9_o.jpg	1	(25, 32)	f	0	414	1086	1383	-115	30	17
1	30601258@N03	10424815813_e94629b1ec_o.jpg	2	(25, 32)	m	301	105	640	641	0	0	94
2	30601258@N03	10437979845_5985be4b26_o.jpg	1	(25, 32)	f	2395	876	771	771	175	-30	74
3	30601258@N03	10437979845_5985be4b26_o.jpg	3	(25, 32)	m	752	1255	484	485	180	0	47
4	30601258@N03	11816644924_075c3d8d59_o.jpg	2	(25, 32)	m	175	80	769	768	-75	0	34

Plot a visual chart for orientation esteems. This will imagine the difference in information just as outline of what the orientation information holds.

```
1  #bar chart
2  gender = ['f','m','u']
3  plt.bar(gender, total_data.gender.value_counts(), align='center', alpha=0.5)
4  plt.show()
```

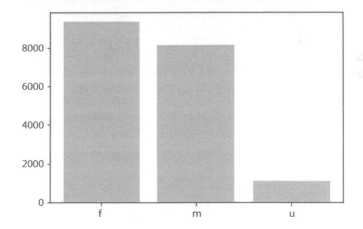

4. Import the essential modules for model structure

```
1  import tensorflow as tf
2  from keras.models import Sequential
3  from keras.layers import Conv2D, MaxPooling2D, Activation, Dropout, Flatten,
       Dense, Dropout, LayerNormalization
4  from keras.preprocessing.image import ImageDataGenerator, img_to_array, load_img
```

```
1  path = "AdienceBenchmarkGenderAndAgeClassification/faces/"+total_data.user_id
       .loc[0]+"/coarse_tilt_aligned_face."+str(total_data.face_id.loc[0])+"."
       +total_data.original_image.loc[0]
2  img = load_img(path)
3  plt.imshow(img)
4  plt.show()
```

5. Utilize the important information and guide them

```
1  imp_data = total_data[['age', 'gender', 'x', 'y', 'dx', 'dy']].copy()
2  imp_data.info()
3
4  img_path = []
5  for row in total_data.iterrows():
6      path = "AdienceBenchmarkGenderAndAgeClassification/faces/"+row[1].user_id+"
           /coarse_tilt_aligned_face."+str(row[1].face_id)+"."+row[1]
           .original_image
7      img_path.append(path)
8
9  imp_data['img_path'] = img_path
10 imp_data.head()
```

```
[→  <class 'pandas.core.frame.DataFrame'>
    RangeIndex: 19370 entries, 0 to 19369
    Data columns (total 6 columns):
     #   Column  Non-Null Count  Dtype
    ---  ------  --------------  -----
     0   age     19370 non-null  object
     1   gender  18591 non-null  object
     2   x       19370 non-null  int64
     3   y       19370 non-null  int64
     4   dx      19370 non-null  int64
     5   dy      19370 non-null  int64
    dtypes: int64(4), object(2)
    memory usage: 908.1+ KB
```

	age	gender	x	y	dx	dy	img_path
0	(25, 32)	f	0	414	1086	1383	AdienceBenchmarkGenderAndAgeClassification/fac...
1	(25, 32)	m	301	105	640	641	AdienceBenchmarkGenderAndAgeClassification/fac...
2	(25, 32)	f	2395	876	771	771	AdienceBenchmarkGenderAndAgeClassification/fac...

```
1  age_mapping = [('(0, 2)', '0-2'), ('2', '0-2'), ('3', '0-2'), ('(4, 6)', '4-6'),
       ('(8, 12)', '8-13'), ('13', '8-13'), ('22', '15-20'), ('(8, 23)', '15-20'),
       ('23', '25-32'), ('(15, 20)', '15-20'), ('(25, 32)', '25-32'), ('(27, 32)',
       '25-32'), ('32', '25-32'), ('34', '25-32'), ('29', '25-32'), ('(38, 42)',
       '38-43'), ('35', '38-43'), ('36', '38-43'), ('42', '48-53'), ('45', '38-43'
       ), ('(38, 43)', '38-43'), ('(38, 42)', '38-43'), ('(38, 48)', '48-53'),
       ('46', '48-53'), ('(48, 53)', '48-53'), ('55', '48-53'), ('56', '48-53'), ('
       (60, 100)', '60+'), ('57', '60+'), ('58', '60+')]
2
3  age_mapping_dict = {each[0]: each[1] for each in age_mapping}
4  drop_labels = []
5  for idx, each in enumerate(imp_data.age):
6      if each == 'None':
7          drop_labels.append(idx)
8      else:
9          imp_data.age.loc[idx] = age_mapping_dict[each]
10
11 imp_data = imp_data.drop(labels=drop_labels, axis=0) #droped None values
12 imp_data.age.value_counts(dropna=False)
```

```
/usr/local/lib/python3.7/dist-packages/pandas/core/indexing.py:670: SettingWithCopyWarni
A value is trying to be set on a copy of a slice from a DataFrame

See the caveats in the documentation: https://pandas.pydata.org/pandas-docs/stable/user
  iloc._setitem_with_indexer(indexer, value)
25-32    5296
38-43    2776
0-2      2509
8-13     2292
4-6      2140
15-20    1792
48-53     916
60+       901
Name: age, dtype: int64
```

```
1  imp_data = imp_data.dropna()
2  clean_data = imp_data[imp_data.gender != 'u'].copy()
3  clean_data.info()
```

```
<class 'pandas.core.frame.DataFrame'>
Int64Index: 17452 entries, 0 to 19345
Data columns (total 7 columns):
 #   Column    Non-Null Count   Dtype
---  ------    --------------   -----
 0   age       17452 non-null   object
 1   gender    17452 non-null   object
 2   x         17452 non-null   int64
 3   y         17452 non-null   int64
 4   dx        17452 non-null   int64
 5   dy        17452 non-null   int64
 6   img_path  17452 non-null   object
dtypes: int64(4), object(3)
memory usage: 1.1+ MB
```

```
1  gender_to_label_map = {
2      'f' : 0,
3      'm' : 1
4  }
5
6  clean_data['gender'] = clean_data['gender'].apply(lambda g:
       gender_to_label_map[g])
7  clean_data.head()
```

	age	gender	x	y	dx	dy	img_path
0	25-32	0	0	414	1086	1383	AdienceBenchmarkGenderAndAgeClassification/fac...
1	25-32	1	301	105	640	641	AdienceBenchmarkGenderAndAgeClassification/fac...
2	25-32	0	2395	876	771	771	AdienceBenchmarkGenderAndAgeClassification/fac...

```
1   age_to_label_map = {
2       '0-2'   :0,
3       '4-6'   :1,
4       '8-13'  :2,
5       '15-20' :3,
6       '25-32' :4,
7       '38-43' :5,
8       '48-53' :6,
9       '60+'   :7
10  }
11
12  clean_data['age'] = clean_data['age'].apply(lambda age: age_to_label_map[age])
13  clean_data.head()
```

	age	gender	x	y	dx	dy	img_path
0	4	0	0	414	1086	1383	AdienceBenchmarkGenderAndAgeClassification/fac...
1	4	1	301	105	640	641	AdienceBenchmarkGenderAndAgeClassification/fac...
2	4	0	2395	876	771	771	AdienceBenchmarkGenderAndAgeClassification/fac...
3	4	1	752	1255	484	485	AdienceBenchmarkGenderAndAgeClassification/fac...
4	4	1	175	80	769	768	AdienceBenchmarkGenderAndAgeClassification/fac...

```
1   X = clean_data[['img_path']]
2   y = clean_data[['gender']]
3   from sklearn.model_selection import train_test_split
4   X_train, X_test, y_train, y_test = train_test_split(X, y, test_size=0.3, random_state=42)
5
6   print('Train data shape {}'.format(X_train.shape))
7   print('Test data shape {}'.format(X_test.shape))
8
9   train_images = []
10  test_images = []
11
12  for row in X_train.iterrows():
13      image = Image.open(row[1].img_path)
14      image = image.resize((227, 227))  # Resize the image
15      data = np.asarray(image)
16      train_images.append(data)
17
18  for row in X_test.iterrows():
19      image = Image.open(row[1].img_path)
20      image = image.resize((227, 227))  # Resize the image
21      data = np.asarray(image)
22      test_images.append(data)
23
24  train_images = np.asarray(train_images)
25  test_images = np.asarray(test_images)
26
27  print('Train images shape {}'.format(train_images.shape))
28  print('Test images shape {}'.format(test_images.shape))
```

6. Orientation Model

```
1   model = Sequential()
2   model.add(Conv2D(input_shape=(227, 227, 3), filters=96, kernel_size=(7, 7),
        strides=4, padding='valid', activation='relu'))
3   model.add(MaxPooling2D(pool_size=(2,2),strides=(2,2)))
4   model.add(LayerNormalization())
5   model.add(Conv2D(filters=256, kernel_size=(5, 5), strides=1, padding='same',
        activation='relu'))
6   model.add(MaxPooling2D(pool_size=(2,2),strides=(2,2)))
7   model.add(LayerNormalization())
8   model.add(Conv2D(filters=256, kernel_size=(3, 3), strides=1, padding='same',
        activation='relu'))
9   model.add(MaxPooling2D(pool_size=(2,2),strides=(2,2)))
10  model.add(LayerNormalization())
11
12  model.add(Flatten())
13  model.add(Dense(units=512, activation='relu'))
14  model.add(Dropout(rate=0.25))
15  model.add(Dense(units=512, activation='relu'))
16  model.add(Dropout(rate=0.25))
17  model.add(Dense(units=2, activation='softmax'))
18
19  model.summary()
```

```
Model: "sequential"
```

Layer (type)	Output Shape	Param #
conv2d (Conv2D)	(None, 56, 56, 96)	14208
max_pooling2d (MaxPooling2D)	(None, 28, 28, 96)	0
layer_normalization (LayerNo	(None, 28, 28, 96)	192
conv2d_1 (Conv2D)	(None, 28, 28, 256)	614656
max_pooling2d_1 (MaxPooling2	(None, 14, 14, 256)	0
layer_normalization_1 (Layer	(None, 14, 14, 256)	512
conv2d_2 (Conv2D)	(None, 14, 14, 256)	590080
max_pooling2d_2 (MaxPooling2	(None, 7, 7, 256)	0
layer_normalization_2 (Layer	(None, 7, 7, 256)	512
flatten (Flatten)	(None, 12544)	0
dense (Dense)	(None, 512)	6423040
dropout (Dropout)	(None, 512)	0
dense_1 (Dense)	(None, 512)	262656
dropout_1 (Dropout)	(None, 512)	0
dense_2 (Dense)	(None, 2)	1026

```
Total params: 7,906,882
Trainable params: 7,906,882
Non-trainable params: 0
```

7. Train the model

```
1  callback = tf.keras.callbacks.EarlyStopping(monitor='loss', patience=3) #
     Callback for earlystopping
2  model.compile(optimizer='adam', loss=tf.keras.losses
     .SparseCategoricalCrossentropy(from_logits=True), metrics=['accuracy'])
3  history = model.fit(train_images, y_train, batch_size=32, epochs=25,
     validation_data=(test_images, y_test), callbacks=[callback])
4
5  print("+++++++++++++++++++++++++++++++++++++++++++++++++++++++++++++++++++++++
     +++++++++++++++++++++++++++++++++++++++++++++++++")
6
7  model.save('gender_mode125.h5')
```

```
Epoch 1/25
382/382 [==============================] - 11s 27ms/step - loss: 0.6899 - accuracy: 0.5414 - val_loss: 0.6925 - val_accuracy: 0.5241
Epoch 2/25
382/382 [==============================] - 10s 26ms/step - loss: 0.6909 - accuracy: 0.5360 - val_loss: 0.6926 - val_accuracy: 0.5241
Epoch 3/25
382/382 [==============================] - 10s 26ms/step - loss: 0.6910 - accuracy: 0.5345 - val_loss: 0.6922 - val_accuracy: 0.5241
Epoch 4/25
382/382 [==============================] - 10s 26ms/step - loss: 0.6905 - accuracy: 0.5370 - val_loss: 0.6927 - val_accuracy: 0.5241
Epoch 5/25
382/382 [==============================] - 10s 26ms/step - loss: 0.6900 - accuracy: 0.5404 - val_loss: 0.6926 - val_accuracy: 0.5241
Epoch 6/25
382/382 [==============================] - 10s 27ms/step - loss: 0.6895 - accuracy: 0.5419 - val_loss: 0.6922 - val_accuracy: 0.5241
Epoch 7/25
382/382 [==============================] - 10s 27ms/step - loss: 0.6901 - accuracy: 0.5402 - val_loss: 0.6925 - val_accuracy: 0.5241
Epoch 8/25
382/382 [==============================] - 10s 27ms/step - loss: 0.6894 - accuracy: 0.5447 - val_loss: 0.6921 - val_accuracy: 0.5241
Epoch 9/25
382/382 [==============================] - 10s 27ms/step - loss: 0.6899 - accuracy: 0.5426 - val_loss: 0.6922 - val_accuracy: 0.5241
Epoch 10/25
382/382 [==============================] - 10s 27ms/step - loss: 0.6909 - accuracy: 0.5340 - val_loss: 0.6930 - val_accuracy: 0.5241
Epoch 11/25
382/382 [==============================] - 10s 27ms/step - loss: 0.6891 - accuracy: 0.5452 - val_loss: 0.6923 - val_accuracy: 0.5241
++++++++++++++++++++++++++++++++++++++++++++++++++++++++++++++++++++++++++++++++++++++++++++++++++++++++++++++
```

```
1  test_loss, test_acc = model.evaluate(test_images, y_test, verbose=2)
2  print(test_acc)
```

8. Make preparing and testing split for age information

```
1  X = clean_data[['img_path']]
2  y = clean_data[['age']]
3  from sklearn.model_selection import train_test_split
4  X_train, X_test, y_train, y_test = train_test_split(X, y, test_size=0.3, random_state=42)
5
6  print('Train data shape {}'.format(X_train.shape))
7  print('Test data shape {}'.format(X_test.shape))
8
9  train_images = []
10 test_images = []
11
12 for row in X_train.iterrows():
13     image = Image.open(row[1].img_path)
14     image = image.resize((227, 227))   # Resize the image
15     data = np.asarray(image)
16     train_images.append(data)
17
18 for row in X_test.iterrows():
19     image = Image.open(row[1].img_path)
20     image = image.resize((227, 227))   # Resize the image
21     data = np.asarray(image)
22     test_images.append(data)
23
24 train_images = np.asarray(train_images)
25 test_images = np.asarray(test_images)
26
27 print('Train images shape {}'.format(train_images.shape))
28 print('Test images shape {}'.format(test_images.shape))
```

9. Age Model

```
1   model = Sequential()
2   model.add(Conv2D(input_shape=(227, 227, 3), filters=96, kernel_size=(7, 7), strides=4,
        padding='valid', activation='relu'))
3   model.add(MaxPooling2D(pool_size=(2,2),strides=(2,2)))
4   model.add(LayerNormalization())
5   model.add(Conv2D(filters=256, kernel_size=(5, 5), strides=1, padding='same', activation
        ='relu'))
6   model.add(MaxPooling2D(pool_size=(2,2),strides=(2,2)))
7   model.add(LayerNormalization())
8   model.add(Conv2D(filters=256, kernel_size=(3, 3), strides=1, padding='same', activation
        ='relu'))
9   model.add(MaxPooling2D(pool_size=(2,2),strides=(2,2)))
10  model.add(LayerNormalization())
11
12  model.add(Flatten())
13  model.add(Dense(units=512, activation='relu'))
14  model.add(Dropout(rate=0.25))
15  model.add(Dense(units=512, activation='relu'))
16  model.add(Dropout(rate=0.25))
17  model.add(Dense(units=8, activation='softmax'))
18
19  model.summary()
```

```
Model: "sequential_1"
```

Layer (type)	Output Shape	Param #
conv2d_3 (Conv2D)	(None, 56, 56, 96)	14208
max_pooling2d_3 (MaxPooling2	(None, 28, 28, 96)	0
layer_normalization_3 (Layer	(None, 28, 28, 96)	192
conv2d_4 (Conv2D)	(None, 28, 28, 256)	614656
max_pooling2d_4 (MaxPooling2	(None, 14, 14, 256)	0
layer_normalization_4 (Layer	(None, 14, 14, 256)	512
conv2d_5 (Conv2D)	(None, 14, 14, 256)	590080
max_pooling2d_5 (MaxPooling2	(None, 7, 7, 256)	0
layer_normalization_5 (Layer	(None, 7, 7, 256)	512
flatten_1 (Flatten)	(None, 12544)	0
dense_3 (Dense)	(None, 512)	6423040
dropout_2 (Dropout)	(None, 512)	0
dense_4 (Dense)	(None, 512)	262656
dropout_3 (Dropout)	(None, 512)	0
dense_5 (Dense)	(None, 8)	4104

```
Total params: 7,909,960
Trainable params: 7,909,960
Non-trainable params: 0
```

```
1  callback = tf.keras.callbacks.EarlyStopping(monitor='loss', patience=3)
   # callback for earlystopping
2  model.compile(optimizer='adam', loss=tf.keras.losses
     .SparseCategoricalCrossentropy(from_logits=True), metrics
     =['accuracy'])
3  history = model.fit(train_images, y_train, batch_size=32, epochs=50,
     validation_data=(test_images, y_test), callbacks=[callback])
4
5  model.save('age_model50.h5')
6
7  test_loss, test_acc = model.evaluate(test_images, y_test, verbose=2)
8  print(test_acc)
```

Induction on the prepared model

```
1  import keras
2  import json
3  import sys
4  import tensorflow as tf
5  from keras.layers import Input
6  import numpy as np
7  import argparse
8  from wide_resnet import WideResNet
9  from keras.utils.data_utils import get_file
10 import face_recognition
```

```
1  gender_model = tf.keras.models.load_model('weights.hdf5')
2  gender_model.summary()
```

```
1  age_map=[['0-2'],['4-6'],['8-13'],['15-20'],['25-32'],['38-43'],['48
   -63'],['60+']]
```

```
1  def detect_face(self):
2      cap=cv2.VideoCapture(0)
3      while True:
4          grb,frame=cap.read()
5          gray = cv2.cvtColor(frame, cv2.COLOR_BGR2GRAY)
6          if not grb:
7              break
```

```
1  face_locations = face_recognition.face_locations(frame)
2  print(face_locations)
3  if(face_locations==[]):
4      cv2.imshow('Gender and age', frame)
5      if cv2.waitKey(1) == 27:
6          break
```

```
1  else:
2      cv2.rectangle(frame, (face_locations[0][3], face_locations[0][0]),
          (face_locations[0][1], face_locations[0][2]), (255, 200, 0), 2)
3      img=frame[face_locations[0][0]-25: face_locations[0][2]+25,
          face_locations[0][3]-25: face_locations[0][1]+25]
```

```
1   # predict ages and genders of the detected faces
2   img2= cv2.resize(img, (64, 64))
3   img2=np.array([img2]).reshape((1, 64,64,3))
4   results = self.model.predict(img2)
```

```
1   predicted_genders = results[0]
2   gen="F" if predicted_genders[0][0] > 0.5 else "M"
3   ages = np.arange(0, 101).reshape(101, 1)
4   predicted_ages = results[1].dot(ages).flatten()
```

```
1   pred=""
2   pred=str(int(predicted_ages[0]))+" "+str(gen)
3   print(pred)
4   cv2.putText(frame, pred,(face_locations[0][3],face_locations[0][0]) ,
        cv2.FONT_HERSHEY_SIMPLEX,0.7, (2, 255, 255), 2)
```

```
1            cv2.imshow('Gender and age', frame)
2            if cv2.waitKey(1) == 27:
3                break
4   cap.release()
5   cv2.destroyAllWindows()
6   # When everything is done, release the capture
```

Age & Gender Detection Project Output

Bibliography

1. https://techvidvan.com/tutorials/gender-age-detection-ml-keras-opencv-cnn/

21

Diabetic Retinopathy

```
In [2]:   from scipy import misc
          from PIL import Image
          from skimage import exposure
          from sklearn import svm

          import scipy
          from math import sqrt,pi
          from numpy import exp
          from matplotlib import pyplot as plt
          import numpy as np
          import glob
          import matplotlib.pyplot as pltss
          import cv2
          from matplotlib import cm
          import pandas as pd
          from math import pi, sqrt
          import pywt
```

```
In [103]:  img_counting_cols=600
           immatrix=[]
           im_unpre = []
           fimage_path = Image.open("C:\Users\Rohan\Desktop\Diabetic_Retinopathy\diaretdb1_v_1_1\diaretdb1_v_1_1\resources\images\ddb1_fundusimages\image0")
           fimagp = scid.imread(fimage_path)

           for i in range(1,90):
               img_pt = r"C:\Users\Rohan\Desktop\Diabetic_Retinopathy\diaretdb1_v_1_1\diaretdb1_v_1_1\resources\images\ddb1_fundusimages\image"
               if i < 10:
                   img_pt = img_pt + "00" + str(i) + ".png"
               else:
                   img_pt = img_pt + "0" + str(i)+ ".png"

               img = cv2.imread(img_pt)
               im_unpre.append(np.array(img).flatten())
               img_gray = cv2.cvtColor(img, cv2.COLOR_BGR2GRAY)
               equ = cv2.equalizeHist(img_gray)
               immatrix.append(np.array(equ).flatten())
               fces = np.hstack((img_gray,equ))
```

```
In [4]:   np.shape(np.array(equ).flatten())
```

```
Out[4]:   (1728000,)
```

```
In [111]:  np.shape(immatrix)
           np.shape(equ)
           plt.imshow(immatrix[78].reshape((1152,1500)),cmap='gray')
           plt.show()
```

In [6]:
```
imm_dwt = []
for equ in immatrix:
    equ = equ.reshape((1152,1500))
    coeffs = pywt.dwt2(equ, 'haar')
    equ2 = pywt.idwt2(coeffs, 'haar')
    imm_dwt.append(np.array(equ2).flatten())
```

Visualising a random image

In [7]:
```
np.shape(imm_dwt)
np.shape(equ2)
plt.imshow(imm_dwt[78].reshape((1152,1500)),cmap='gray')
plt.show()
```

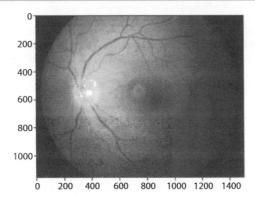

```
In [27]: def _filter_kernel_mf_fdog(L, sigma, t = 3, mf = True):
             dim_y = int(L)
             dim_x = 2 * int(t * sigma)
             arr = np.zeros((dim_y, dim_x), 'f')

             ctr_x = dim_x / 2
             ctr_y = int(dim_y / 2.)

             # an un-natural way to set elements of the array
             # to their x coordinate.
             # x's are actually columns, so the first dimension of the iterator is used
             it = np.nditer(arr, flags=['multi_index'])
             while not it.finished:
                 arr[it.multi_index] = it.multi_index[1] - ctr_x
                 it.iternext()

             two_sigma_sq = 2 * sigma * sigma
             sqrt_w_pi_sigma = 1. / (sqrt(2 * pi) * sigma)
             if not mf:
                 sqrt_w_pi_sigma = sqrt_w_pi_sigma / sigma ** 2

             #@vectorize(['float32(float32)'], target='cpu')
             def k_fun(x):
                 return sqrt_w_pi_sigma * exp(-x * x / two_sigma_sq)

             #@vectorize(['float32(float32)'], target='cpu')
             def k_fun_derivative(x):
                 return -x * sqrt_w_pi_sigma * exp(-x * x / two_sigma_sq)

             if mf:
                 kernel = k_fun(arr)
                 kernel = kernel - kernel.mean()
             else:
                 kernel = k_fun_derivative(arr)

             # return the "convolution" kernel for filter2D
             return cv2.flip(kernel, -1)


def show_images(images,titles=None, scale=1.3):
    """Display a list of images"""
    n_ims = len(images)
    if titles is None: titles = ['(%d)' % i for i in range(1,n_ims + 1)]
    fig = plt.figure()
    n = 1
    for image,title in zip(images,titles):
        a = fig.add_subplot(1,n_ims,n) # Make subplot
        if image.ndim == 2: # Is image grayscale?
            plt.imshow(image, cmap = cm.Greys_r)
        else:
            plt.imshow(cv2.cvtColor(image, cv2.COLOR_RGB2BGR))
        a.set_title(title)
        plt.axis("off")
        n += 1
    fig.set_size_inches(np.array(fig.get_size_inches(), dtype=np.float) * n_ims / scale)
    plt.show()


def gaussian_matched_filter_kernel(L, sigma, t = 3):
    '''
    K =  1/(sqrt(2 * pi) * sigma ) * exp(-x^2/2sigma^2), |y| <= L/2, |x| < s * t
    '''
    return _filter_kernel_mf_fdog(L, sigma, t, True)

#Creating a matched filter bank using the kernel generated from the above functions
def createMatchedFilterBank(K, n = 12):
    rotate = 180 / n
    center = (K.shape[1] / 2, K.shape[0] / 2)
    cur_rot = 0
    kernels = [K]

    for i in range(1, n):
        cur_rot += rotate
        r_mat = cv2.getRotationMatrix2D(center, cur_rot, 1)
        k = cv2.warpAffine(K, r_mat, (K.shape[1], K.shape[0]))
        kernels.append(k)
```

```
    return kernels

#Given a filter bank, apply them and record maximum response

def applyFilters(im, kernels):

    images = np.array([cv2.filter2D(im, -1, k) for k in kernels])
    return np.max(images, 0)


gf = gaussian_matched_filter_kernel(20, 5)
bank_gf = createMatchedFilterBank(gf, 4)

imm_gauss = []
for equ2 in imm_dwt:
    equ2 = equ2.reshape((1152,1500))
    equ3 = applyFilters(equ2,bank_gf)
    imm_gauss.append(np.array(equ3).flatten())
```

```
In [30]:  # the array ranges from 0 - 89
          np.shape(imm_gauss)
          plt.imshow(imm_gauss[78].reshape((1152,1500)),cmap='gray')
          plt.show()
```

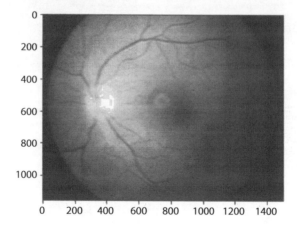

```
In [8]:  def createMatchedFilterBank():
             filters = []
             ksize = 31
             for theta in np.arange(0, np.pi, np.pi / 16):
                 kern = cv2.getGaborKernel((ksize, ksize), 6, theta,12, 0.37, 0, ktype=cv2.CV_32F)
                 kern /= 1.5*kern.sum()
                 filters.append(kern)
             return filters

         def applyFilters(im, kernels):
             images = np.array([cv2.filter2D(im, -1, k) for k in kernels])
             return np.max(images, 0)

         bank_gf = createMatchedFilterBank()
         #equx=equ3
         #equ3 = applyFilters(equ2,bank_gf)
         imm_gauss2 = []
         for equ2 in imm_dwt:
             equ2 = equ2.reshape((1152,1500))
             equ3 = applyFilters(equ2,bank_gf)
             imm_gauss2.append(np.array(equ3).flatten())
```

```
In [40]:  # the array ranges from 0 - 89
          np.shape(imm_gauss2)
          plt.imshow(imm_gauss2[20].reshape((1152,1500)),cmap='gray')
          plt.show()
```

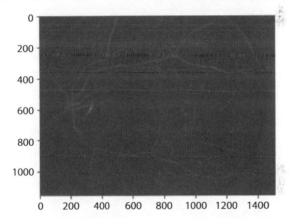

```
In [128]:  # the array ranges from 0 - 89
           np.shape(imm_gauss2)
           plt.imshow(imm_gauss2[1].reshape((1152,1500)),cmap='gray')
           plt.show()
```

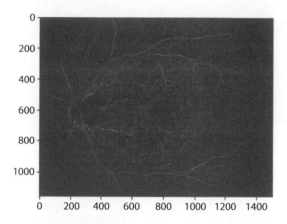

In [38]:
```
e_ = equ3
np.shape(e_)
e_=e_.reshape((-1,3))
np.shape(e_)
```

Out[38]: (576000, 3)

In [ ]:
```
img = equ3
Z = img.reshape((-1,3))

# convert to np.float32
Z = np.float32(Z)

k=cv2.KMEANS_PP_CENTERS

# define criteria, number of clusters(K) and apply kmeans()
criteria = (cv2.TERM_CRITERIA_EPS + cv2.TERM_CRITERIA_MAX_ITER, 10, 1.0)
K = 2
ret,label,center=cv2.kmeans(Z,K,None,criteria,10,k)

# Now convert back into uint8, and make original image
center = np.uint8(center)
res = center[label.flatten()]
res2 = res.reshape((img.shape))
```

```
In [10]:  imm_kmean = []
          for equ3 in imm_gauss2:
              img = equ3.reshape((1152,1500))
              Z = img.reshape((-1,3))

              # convert to np.float32
              Z = np.float32(Z)

              k=cv2.KMEANS_PP_CENTERS


              # define criteria, number of clusters(K) and apply kmeans()
              criteria = (cv2.TERM_CRITERIA_EPS + cv2.TERM_CRITERIA_MAX_ITER, 10, 1.0)
              K = 2
              ret,label,center=cv2.kmeans(Z,K,None,criteria,10,k)

              # Now convert back into uint8, and make original image
              center = np.uint8(center)
              res = center[label.flatten()]
              res2 = res.reshape((img.shape))
              imm_kmean.append(np.array(res2).flatten())
```

```
In [113]:  # the array ranges from 0 - 89
           np.shape(imm_kmean)
           plt.imshow(imm_kmean[78].reshape((1152,1500)),cmap="gray")
           plt.show()
```

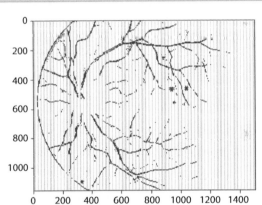

```
In [42]:  from sklearn.svm import SVC
          clf = SVC()
```

```
In [64]:  Y = np.ones(89)
```

```
In [65]:  Y[1]=Y[5]=Y[7]=Y[17]=Y[6]=0
```

```
In [66]:  clf.fit(imm_kmean, Y)
```

```
Out[66]:  SVC(C=1.0, cache_size=200, class_weight=None, coef0=0.0,
              decision_function_shape=None, degree=3, gamma='auto', kernel='rbf',
              max_iter=-1, probability=False, random_state=None, shrinking=True,
              tol=0.001, verbose=False)
```

```
In [72]:  y_pred = clf.predict(imm_kmean)
```

```
In [1]:  k = [1,3,4,9,10,11,13,14,20,22,24,25,26,27,28,29,35,36,38,42,53,55,57,64,70,79,84,86]
```

```
In [3]:  k = k-np.ones(len(k))
```

```
In [87]:  k
```

```
Out[87]:  array([  0.,    2.,    3.,    8.,    9.,   10.,   12.,   13.,   19.,   21.,   23.,
                  24.,   25.,   26.,   27.,   28.,   34.,   35.,   37.,   41.,   52.,   54.,
                  56.,   63.,   69.,   78.,   83.,   85.])
```

```
In [92]:  k =[int(x) for x in k]
```

```
In [93]:  k
```

```
Out[93]:  [0,
           2,
           3,
           8,
           9,
           10,
           12,
           13,
           19,
           21,
           23,
           24,
           25,
           26,
           27,
           28,
           34,
           35,
           37,
           41,
           52,
           54,
           56,
           63,
           69,
           78,
           83,
           85]
```

```
In [98]:  imm_train = []
          y_train = []
          k.append(5)
          k.append(7)
          for i in k:
              imm_train.append(imm_kmean[i])
              y_train.append(Y[i])
```

```
In [99]:  y_train

Out[99]:  [1.0,
           1.0,
           1.0,
           1.0,
           1.0,
           1.0,
           1.0,
           1.0,
           1.0,
           1.0,
           1.0,
           1.0,
           1.0,
           1.0,
           1.0,
           1.0,
           1.0,
           1.0,
           1.0,
           1.0,
           1.0,
           1.0,
           1.0,
           1.0,
           1.0,
           1.0,
           1.0,
           1.0,
           1.0,
           0.0,
           0.0]
```

```
In [100]:  clf.fit(imm_train, y_train)

Out[100]:  SVC(C=1.0, cache_size=200, class_weight=None, coef0=0.0,
               decision_function_shape=None, degree=3, gamma='auto', kernel='rbf',
               max_iter=-1, probability=False, random_state=None, shrinking=True,
               tol=0.001, verbose=False)
```

```
In [101]:  y_pred = clf.predict(imm_kmean)

In [102]:  accuracy_score(Y,y_pred)
Out[102]:  0.9662921348314607


In [114]:  from sklearn.neighbors import KNeighborsClassifier

In [115]:  neigh = KNeighborsClassifier(n_neighbors=3)

In [116]:  neigh.fit(imm_train, y_train)
Out[116]:  KNeighborsClassifier(algorithm='auto', leaf_size=30, metric='minkowski',
                   metric_params=None, n_jobs=1, n_neighbors=3, p=2,
                   weights='uniform')

In [117]:  y_pred2=neigh.predict(imm_kmean)

In [119]:  neigh.score(imm_kmean,Y)
Out[119]:  0.9438202247191011
```

Bibliography

1. https://github.com/rsk97/Diabetic-Retinopathy-Detection/blob/master/ Diabetic_retinopathy_detection.ipynb
2. Pardianto G (2005). "Understanding diabetic retinopathy". Mimbar Ilmiah Oftalmologi Indonesia. 2: 65–6.
3. Tarr JM, Kaul K, Chopra M, Kohner EM, Chibber R (2013). "Pathophysiology of diabetic retinopathy". ISRN Ophthalmology. 2013: 343560.
4. Bek T (2010). "Experimental Approaches to Diabetic Retinopathy – Front Diabetes" (PDF). In Hammes HP, Porta M (eds.). Clinical Presentations and Pathological Correlates of Retinopathy. Karger.com. 20. Basel. pp. 1–19.

Driver Drowsiness Detection in Python

```
1.   for (x,y,w,h) in faces:
2.        cv2.rectangle(frame, (x,y), (x+w, y+h), (100,100,100), 1 )
```

```
1.   l_eye = frame[ y : y+h, x : x+w ]
```

```
1.   cv2.putText(frame, "Open", (10, height-20), font, 1, (255,255,255), 1,
     cv2.LINE_AA )
```

Kolla Bhanu Prakash. Data Science Handbook: A Practical Approach, (351–356) © 2022 Scrivener Publishing LLC

```
1.    import cv2
2.    import os
3.    from keras.models import load_model
4.    import numpy as np
5.    from pygame import mixer
6.    import time
7.
8.    mixer.init()
9.    sound = mixer.Sound('alarm.wav')
10.
11.    face = cv2.CascadeClassifier('haar cascade
      files\haarcascade_frontalface_alt.xml')
12.    leye = cv2.CascadeClassifier('haar cascade
      files\haarcascade_lefteye_2splits.xml')
13.    reye = cv2.CascadeClassifier('haar cascade
      files\haarcascade_righteye_2splits.xml')
14.
15.    lbl=['Close','Open']
16.
17.    model = load_model('models/cnncat2.h5')
18.    path = os.getcwd()
19.    cap = cv2.VideoCapture(0)
20.    font = cv2.FONT_HERSHEY_COMPLEX_SMALL
21.    count=0
22.    score=0
23.    thicc=2
24.    rpred=[99]
25.    lpred=[99]
26.
27.    while(True):
28.        ret, frame = cap.read()
```

```
29.        height,width = frame.shape[:2]
30.
31.        gray = cv2.cvtColor(frame, cv2.COLOR_BGR2GRAY)
32.
33.        faces =
      face.detectMultiScale(gray,minNeighbors=5,scaleFactor=1.1,minSize=(25,25))
34.        left_eye = leye.detectMultiScale(gray)
35.        right_eye = reye.detectMultiScale(gray)
36.
37.        cv2.rectangle(frame, (0,height-50) , (200,height) , (0,0,0) ,
      thickness=cv2.FILLED )
38.
39.        for (x,y,w,h) in faces:
40.      cv2.rectangle(frame, (x,y) , (x+w,y+h) , (100,100,100) , 1 )
41.
42.        for (x,y,w,h) in right_eye:
43.            r_eye=frame[y:y+h,x:x+w]
44.            count=count+1
45.            r_eye = cv2.cvtColor(r_eye,cv2.COLOR_BGR2GRAY)
46.            r_eye = cv2.resize(r_eye,(24,24))
47.            r_eye= r_eye/255
48.            r_eye= r_eye.reshape(24,24,-1)
49.            r_eye = np.expand_dims(r_eye,axis=0)
50.            rpred = model.predict_classes(r_eye)
51.            if(rpred[0]==1):
52.                lbl='Open'
53.            if(rpred[0]==0):
54.                lbl='Closed'
55.            break
56.
57.        for (x,y,w,h) in left_eye:
58.            l_eye=frame[y:y+h,x:x+w]
59.            count=count+1
60.            l_eye = cv2.cvtColor(l_eye,cv2.COLOR_BGR2GRAY)

61.            l_eye = cv2.resize(l_eye,(24,24))
62.            l_eye= l_eye/255
63.            l_eye=l_eye.reshape(24,24,-1)
64.            l_eye = np.expand_dims(l_eye,axis=0)
65.            lpred = model.predict_classes(l_eye)
66.            if(lpred[0]==1):
67.                lbl='Open'
68.            if(lpred[0]==0):
69.                lbl='Closed'
70.            break
71.
72.        if(rpred[0]==0 and lpred[0]==0):
73.            score=score+1
74.            cv2.putText(frame,"Closed",(10,height-20), font,
      1,(255,255,255),1,cv2.LINE_AA)
75.        # if(rpred[0]==1 or lpred[0]==1):
76.        else:
77.            score=score-1
78.            cv2.putText(frame,"Open",(10,height-20), font,
      1,(255,255,255),1,cv2.LINE_AA)
79.
80.        if(score<0):
```

```
81.          score=0
82.       cv2.putText(frame,'Score:'+str(score),(100,height-20), font,
        1,(255,255,255),1,cv2.LINE_AA)
83.        if(score>15):
84.           #person is feeling sleepy so we beep the alarm
85.           cv2.imwrite(os.path.join(path,'image.jpg'),frame)
86.           try:
87.               sound.play()
88.
89.           except: # isplaying = False
90.               pass
91.           if(thicc<16):
92.               thicc= thicc+2
93.           else:
94.               thicc=thicc-2
95.               if(thicc<2):
96.                   thicc=2
97.           cv2.rectangle(frame,(0,0),(width,height),(0,0,255),thicc)
98.       cv2.imshow('frame',frame)
99.       if cv2.waitKey(1) & 0xFF == ord('q'):
100.          break
101.   cap.release()
102.   cv2.destroyAllWindows()
```

```
1.    python "drowsiness detection.py"
```

Closed Eye Detection

Open Eyes Detection

Bibliography

1. https://data-flair.training/blogs/python-project-driver-drowsiness-detection-system/

Chatbot Using Python

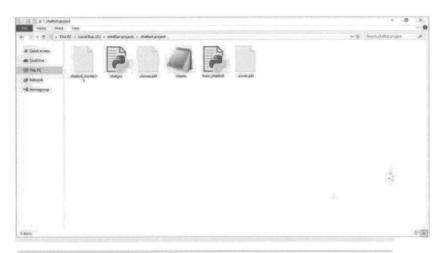

```
1.    import nltk
2.    from nltk.stem import WordNetLemmatizer
3.    lemmatizer = WordNetLemmatizer()
4.    import json
5.    import pickle
6.
7.    import numpy as np
8.    from keras.models import Sequential
9.    from keras.layers import Dense, Activation, Dropout
10.   from keras.optimizers import SGD
11.   import random
12.
13.   words=[]
14.   classes = []
15.   documents = []
16.   ignore_words = ['?', '!']
17.   data_file = open('intents.json').read()
18.   intents = json.loads(data_file)
```

Kolla Bhanu Prakash. Data Science Handbook: A Practical Approach, (357–364) © 2022 Scrivener
Publishing LLC

```
{"intents": [
    {"tag": "greeting",
     "patterns": ["Hi there", "How are you", "Is anyone there?","Hey","Hola", "Hello", "Good day"],
     "responses": ["Hello, thanks for asking", "Good to see you again", "Hi there, how can I help?"
     "context": [""]
    },
    {"tag": "goodbye",
     "patterns": ["Bye", "See you later", "Goodbye", "Nice chatting to you, bye", "Till next time"]
     "responses": ["See you!", "Have a nice day", "Bye! Come back again soon."],
     "context": [""]
    },
    {"tag": "thanks",
     "patterns": ["Thanks", "Thank you", "That's helpful", "Awesome, thanks", "Thanks for helping m
     "responses": ["Happy to help!", "Any time!", "My pleasure"],
     "context": [""]
    },
    {"tag": "noanswer",
     "patterns": [],
     "responses": ["Sorry, can't understand you", "Please give me more info", "Not sure I understan
     "context": [""]
    },
    {"tag": "options",
     "patterns": ["How you could help me?", "What you can do?", "What help you provide?", "How you
     "responses": ["I can guide you through Adverse drug reaction list, Blood pressure tracking, Ho
     "context": [""]
    },
    {"tag": "adverse_drug",
     "patterns": ["How to check Adverse drug reaction?", "Open adverse drugs module", "Give me a li
     "responses": ["Navigating to Adverse drug reaction module"],
```

```
1.   for intent in intents['intents']:
2.       for pattern in intent['patterns']:
3.
4.           #tokenize each word
5.           w = nltk.word_tokenize(pattern)
6.           words.extend(w)
7.           #add documents in the corpus
8.           documents.append((w, intent['tag']))
9.
10.          # add to our classes list
11.          if intent['tag'] not in classes:
12.              classes.append(intent['tag'])
```

```
1.   # lemmatize, lower each word and remove duplicates
2.   words = [lemmatizer.lemmatize(w.lower()) for w in words if w not in
     ignore_words]
3.   words = sorted(list(set(words)))
4.   # sort classes
5.   classes = sorted(list(set(classes)))
6.   # documents = combination between patterns and intents
7.   print (len(documents), "documents")
8.   # classes = intents
9.   print (len(classes), "classes", classes)
10.  # words = all words, vocabulary
11.  print (len(words), "unique lemmatized words", words)
12.
13.  pickle.dump(words,open('words.pkl','wb'))
14.  pickle.dump(classes,open('classes.pkl','wb'))
```

```
1.    # create our training data
2.    training = []
3.    # create an empty array for our output
4.    output_empty = [0] * len(classes)
5.    # training set, bag of words for each sentence
6.    for doc in documents:
7.        # initialize our bag of words
8.        bag = []
9.        # list of tokenized words for the pattern
10.       pattern_words = doc[0]
11.       # lemmatize each word - create base word, in attempt to represent
related words
12.       pattern_words = [lemmatizer.lemmatize(word.lower()) for word in
pattern_words]
13.       # create our bag of words array with 1, if word match found in current
pattern
14.       for w in words:
15.           bag.append(1) if w in pattern_words else bag.append(0)
16.
17.       # output is a '0' for each tag and '1' for current tag (for each
pattern)
18.       output_row = list(output_empty)
19.       output_row[classes.index(doc[1])] = 1
20.
21.       training.append([bag, output_row])
22.   # shuffle our features and turn into np.array
23.   random.shuffle(training)
24.   training = np.array(training)
25.   # create train and test lists. X - patterns, Y - intents
26.   train_x = list(training[:,0])
27.   train_y = list(training[:,1])
28.   print("Training data created")
```

```
1.    # Create model - 3 layers. First layer 128 neurons, second layer 64
      neurons and 3rd output layer contains number of neurons
2.    # equal to number of intents to predict output intent with softmax
3.    model = Sequential()
4.    model.add(Dense(128, input_shape=(len(train_x[0]),), activation='relu'))
5.    model.add(Dropout(0.5))
6.    model.add(Dense(64, activation='relu'))
7.    model.add(Dropout(0.5))
8.    model.add(Dense(len(train_y[0]), activation='softmax'))
9.
10.   # Compile model. Stochastic gradient descent with Nesterov accelerated
      gradient gives good results for this model
11.   sgd = SGD(lr=0.01, decay=1e-6, momentum=0.9, nesterov=True)
12.   model.compile(loss='categorical_crossentropy', optimizer=sgd, metrics=
      ['accuracy'])
13.
14.   #fitting and saving the model
15.   hist = model.fit(np.array(train_x), np.array(train_y), epochs=200,
      batch_size=5, verbose=1)
16.   model.save('chatbot_model.h5', hist)
17.
18.   print("model created")
```

```
1.    import nltk
2.    from nltk.stem import WordNetLemmatizer
3.    lemmatizer = WordNetLemmatizer()
4.    import pickle
5.    import numpy as np
6.
7.    from keras.models import load_model
8.    model = load_model('chatbot_model.h5')
9.    import json
10.   import random
11.   intents = json.loads(open('intents.json').read())
12.   words = pickle.load(open('words.pkl','rb'))
13.   classes = pickle.load(open('classes.pkl','rb'))
```

```
1.    def clean_up_sentence(sentence):
2.        # tokenize the pattern - split words into array
3.        sentence_words = nltk.word_tokenize(sentence)
4.        # stem each word - create short form for word
5.        sentence_words = [lemmatizer.lemmatize(word.lower()) for word in
      sentence_words]
6.        return sentence_words
7.    # return bag of words array: 0 or 1 for each word in the bag that exists
      in the sentence
8.
9.    def bow(sentence, words, show_details=True):
10.       # tokenize the pattern
11.       sentence_words = clean_up_sentence(sentence)
12.       # bag of words - matrix of N words, vocabulary matrix
13.       bag = [0]*len(words)
14.       for s in sentence_words:
15.           for i,w in enumerate(words):
16.               if w == s:
17.                   # assign 1 if current word is in the vocabulary position
18.                   bag[i] = 1
19.                   if show_details:
20.                       print ("found in bag: %s" % w)
```

```
21.         return(np.array(bag))
22.
23.   def predict_class(sentence, model):
24.         # filter out predictions below a threshold
25.         p = bow(sentence, words,show_details=False)
26.         res = model.predict(np.array([p]))[0]
27.         ERROR_THRESHOLD = 0.25
28.         results = [[i,r] for i,r in enumerate(res) if r>ERROR_THRESHOLD]
29.         # sort by strength of probability
30.         results.sort(key=lambda x: x[1], reverse=True)
31.         return_list = []
32.         for r in results:
33.             return_list.append({"intent": classes[r[0]], "probability":
      str(r[1])})
34.         return return_list
```

```
1.    def getResponse(ints, intents_json):
2.         tag = ints[0]['intent']
3.         list_of_intents = intents_json['intents']
4.         for i in list_of_intents:
5.             if(i['tag']== tag):
6.                 result = random.choice(i['responses'])
7.                 break
8.         return result
9.
10.   def chatbot_response(text):
11.         ints = predict_class(text, model)
12.         res = getResponse(ints, intents)
13.         return res
```

```
1.    #Creating GUI with tkinter
2.    import tkinter
3.    from tkinter import *
4.
5.
6.    def send():
7.         msg = EntryBox.get("1.0",'end-1c').strip()
8.         EntryBox.delete("0.0",END)
9.
10.        if msg != '':
11.            ChatLog.config(state=NORMAL)
12.            ChatLog.insert(END, "You: " + msg + '\n\n')
13.            ChatLog.config(foreground="#442265", font=("Verdana", 12 ))
14.
15.            res = chatbot_response(msg)
16.            ChatLog.insert(END, "Bot: " + res + '\n\n')
17.
18.            ChatLog.config(state=DISABLED)
19.            ChatLog.yview(END)
20.
21.    base = Tk()
22.    base.title("Hello")
23.    base.geometry("400x500")
24.    base.resizable(width=FALSE, height=FALSE)
25.
26.    #Create Chat window
27.    ChatLog = Text(base, bd=0, bg="white", height="8", width="50",
      font="Arial",)
28.
29.    ChatLog.config(state=DISABLED)
30.
```

```
31.   #Bind scrollbar to Chat window
32.   scrollbar = Scrollbar(base, command=ChatLog.yview, cursor="heart")
33.   ChatLog['yscrollcommand'] = scrollbar.set
34.
35.   #Create Button to send message
36.   SendButton = Button(base, font=("Verdana",12,'bold'), text="Send",
      width="12", height=5,
37.                         bd=0, bg="#32de97",
      activebackground="#3c9d9b",fg='#ffffff',
38.                         command= send )
39.
40.   #Create the box to enter message
41.   EntryBox = Text(base, bd=0, bg="white",width="29", height="5",
      font="Arial")
42.   #EntryBox.bind("<Return>", send)
43.
44.
45.   #Place all components on the screen
46.   scrollbar.place(x=376,y=6, height=386)
47.   ChatLog.place(x=6,y=6, height=386, width=370)
48.   EntryBox.place(x=128, y=401, height=90, width=265)
49.   SendButton.place(x=6, y=401, height=90)
50.
51.   base.mainloop()
```

| 1. | `python train_chatbot.py` | 1. | `python chatgui.py` |

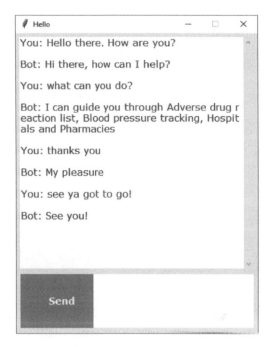

Bibliography

1. https://data-flair.training/blogs/python-chatbot-project/
2. "What is a chatbot?". techtarget.com. Retrieved 30 January 2017.
3. Caldarini, Guendalina; Jaf, Sardar; McGarry, Kenneth (2022). "A Literature Survey of Recent Advances in Chatbots". Information. MDPI. 13 (1): 41. doi:10.3390/info13010041.
4. Luka Bradeško, Dunja Mladenić. "A Survey of Chabot Systems through a Loebner Prize Competition". S2CID 39745939.

Handwritten Digit Recognition Project

```
1.    import keras
2.    from keras.datasets import mnist
3.    from keras.models import Sequential
4.    from keras.layers import Dense, Dropout, Flatten
5.    from keras.layers import Conv2D, MaxPooling2D
6.    from keras import backend as K
7.
8.    # the data, split between train and test sets
9.    (x_train, y_train), (x_test, y_test) = mnist.load_data()
10.
11.   print(x_train.shape, y_train.shape)
```

```
1.    x_train = x_train.reshape(x_train.shape[0], 28, 28, 1)
2.    x_test = x_test.reshape(x_test.shape[0], 28, 28, 1)
3.    input_shape = (28, 28, 1)
4.
5.    # convert class vectors to binary class matrices
6.    y_train = keras.utils.to_categorical(y_train, num_classes)
7.    y_test = keras.utils.to_categorical(y_test, num_classes)
8.
9.    x_train = x_train.astype('float32')
10.   x_test = x_test.astype('float32')
11.   x_train /= 255
12.   x_test /= 255
13.   print('x_train shape:', x_train.shape)
14.   print(x_train.shape[0], 'train samples')
15.   print(x_test.shape[0], 'test samples')
```

```
1.    batch_size = 128
2.    num_classes = 10
3.    epochs = 10
4.
5.    model = Sequential()
6.    model.add(Conv2D(32, kernel_size=(3, 3),activation='relu',input_shape=input
7.    model.add(Conv2D(64, (3, 3), activation='relu'))
8.    model.add(MaxPooling2D(pool_size=(2, 2)))
9.    model.add(Dropout(0.25))
10.   model.add(Flatten())
11.   model.add(Dense(256, activation='relu'))
12.   model.add(Dropout(0.5))
13.   model.add(Dense(num_classes, activation='softmax'))
14.
15.
      model.compile(loss=keras.losses.categorical_crossentropy,optimizer=keras.opt
      ['accuracy'])
```

Kolla Bhanu Prakash. *Data Science Handbook: A Practical Approach*, (365–368) © 2022 Scrivener Publishing LLC

```
1.  hist = model.fit(x_train,
    y_train,batch_size=batch_size,epochs=epochs,verbose=1,validation_data=
    (x_test, y_test))
2.  print("The model has successfully trained")
3.
4.  model.save('mnist.h5')
5.  print("Saving the model as mnist.h5")
```

```
1.  score = model.evaluate(x_test, y_test, verbose=0)
2.  print('Test loss:', score[0])
3.  print('Test accuracy:', score[1])
```

```
1.  from keras.models import load_model
2.  from tkinter import *
3.  import tkinter as tk
4.  import win32gui
5.  from PIL import ImageGrab, Image
6.  import numpy as np
7.
8.  model = load_model('mnist.h5')
9.
10.     def predict_digit(img):
11.         #resize image to 28x28 pixels
12.         img = img.resize((28,28))
13.         #convert rgb to grayscale
14.         img = img.convert('L')
15.         img = np.array(img)
16.         #reshaping to support our model input and normalizing
17.         img = img.reshape(1,28,28,1)
18.         img = img/255.0
19.         #predicting the class
20.         res = model.predict([img])[0]
21.         return np.argmax(res), max(res)
22.
23.     class App(tk.Tk):
24.         def __init__(self):
25.             tk.Tk.__init__(self)
26.
27.             self.x = self.y = 0
28.
29.             # Creating elements
30.             self.canvas = tk.Canvas(self, width=300, height=300, bg = "white",
        cursor="cross")
```

```
31.              self.label = tk.Label(self, text="Thinking..", font=("Helvetica",
      48))
32.              self.classify_btn = tk.Button(self, text = "Recognise", command =
      self.classify_handwriting)
33.              self.button_clear = tk.Button(self, text = "Clear", command =
      self.clear_all)
34.
35.              # Grid structure
36.              self.canvas.grid(row=0, column=0, pady=2, sticky=W, )
37.              self.label.grid(row=0, column=1,pady=2, padx=2)
38.              self.classify_btn.grid(row=1, column=1, pady=2, padx=2)
39.              self.button_clear.grid(row=1, column=0, pady=2)
40.
41.              #self.canvas.bind("<Motion>", self.start_pos)
42.              self.canvas.bind("<B1-Motion>", self.draw_lines)
43.
44.        def clear_all(self):
45.              self.canvas.delete("all")
46.
47.        def classify_handwriting(self):
48.              HWND = self.canvas.winfo_id() # get the handle of the canvas
49.              rect = win32gui.GetWindowRect(HWND) # get the coordinate of the
      canvas
50.              im = ImageGrab.grab(rect)
51.
52.              digit, acc = predict_digit(im)
53.              self.label.configure(text= str(digit)+', '+ str(int(acc*100))+'%')
54.
55.        def draw_lines(self, event):

56.              self.x = event.x
57.              self.y = event.y
58.              r=8
59.              self.canvas.create_oval(self.x-r, self.y-r, self.x + r, self.y +
      r, fill='black')
60.
61.    app = App()
62.    mainloop()
```

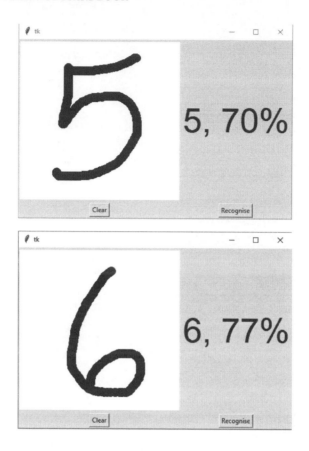

Bibliography

1. https://data-flair.training/blogs/python-deep-learning-project-handwritten-digit-recognition/
2. https://machinelearningmastery.com/handwritten-digit-recognition-using-convolutional-neural-networks-python-keras/
3. https://machinelearningmastery.com/how-to-develop-a-convolutional-neural-network-from-scratch-for-mnist-handwritten-digit-classification/
4. https://www.geeksforgeeks.org/handwritten-digit-recognition-using-neural-network/

Image Caption Generator Project in Python

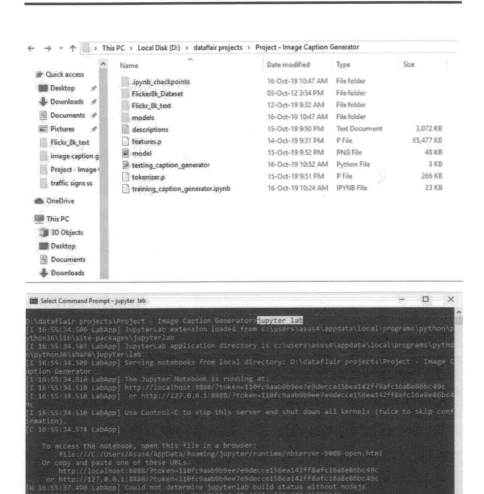

```
1.  import string
2.  import numpy as np
3.  from PIL import Image
4.  import os
5.  from pickle import dump, load
6.  import numpy as np
7.
8.  from keras.applications.xception import Xception, preprocess_input
9.  from keras.preprocessing.image import load_img, img_to_array
10. from keras.preprocessing.text import Tokenizer
11. from keras.preprocessing.sequence import pad_sequences
12. from keras.utils import to_categorical
13. from keras.layers.merge import add
14. from keras.models import Model, load_model
15. from keras.layers import Input, Dense, LSTM, Embedding, Dropout
16.
17. # small library for seeing the progress of loops.
18. from tqdm import tqdm_notebook as tqdm
19. tqdm().pandas()
```

File   Edit   Format   Run   Options   Window   Help

```
1000268201_693b08cb0e.jpg#0    A child in a pink dress is climbing up a set of stairs in an entry way .
1000268201_693b08cb0e.jpg#1    A girl going into a wooden building .
1000268201_693b08cb0e.jpg#2    A little girl climbing into a wooden playhouse .
1000268201_693b08cb0e.jpg#3    A little girl climbing the stairs to her playhouse .
1000268201_693b08cb0e.jpg#4    A little girl in a pink dress going into a wooden cabin .
1001773457_577c3a7d70.jpg#0    A black dog and a spotted dog are fighting
1001773457_577c3a7d70.jpg#1    A black dog and a tri-colored dog playing with each other on the road .
1001773457_577c3a7d70.jpg#2    A black dog and a white dog with brown spots are staring at each other in the
1001773457_577c3a7d70.jpg#3    Two dogs of different breeds looking at each other on the road .
1001773457_577c3a7d70.jpg#4    Two dogs on pavement moving toward each other .
1002674143_1b742ab4b8.jpg#0    A little girl covered in paint sits in front of a painted rainbow with her han
1002674143_1b742ab4b8.jpg#1    A little girl is sitting in front of a large painted rainbow .
1002674143_1b742ab4b8.jpg#2    A small girl in the grass plays with fingerpaints in front of a white canvas w
1002674143_1b742ab4b8.jpg#3    There is a girl with pigtails sitting in front of a rainbow painting .
1002674143_1b742ab4b8.jpg#4    Young girl with pigtails painting outside in the grass .
1003163366_44323f5815.jpg#0    A man lays on a bench while his dog sits by him .
1003163366_44323f5815.jpg#1    A man lays on the bench to which a white dog is also tied .
1003163366_44323f5815.jpg#2    a man sleeping on a bench outside with a white and black dog sitting next to h
1003163366_44323f5815.jpg#3    A shirtless man lies on a park bench with his dog .
1003163366_44323f5815.jpg#4    man laying on bench holding leash of dog sitting on ground
1007129816_e794419615.jpg#0    A man in an orange hat starring at something .
1007129816_e794419615.jpg#1    A man wears an orange hat and glasses .
1007129816_e794419615.jpg#2    A man with gauges and glasses is wearing a Blitz hat .
1007129816_e794419615.jpg#3    A man with glasses is wearing a beer can crocheted hat .
1007129816_e794419615.jpg#4    The man with pierced ears is wearing glasses and an orange hat .
1007320043_627395c3d8.jpg#0    A child playing on a rope net .
```

dataflair.py - C:/Users/Asus4/AppData/Local/Programs/Python/Python37-32/dataflair.py (3.7.4)   —   □   ×

File   Edit   Format   Run   Options   Window   Help

```
{
'3461437556_cc5e97f3ac.jpg': ['dogs on grass',
                              'three dogs are running on the grass',
                              'three dogs one white and two brown are running together
                              'three dogs run along grassy yard',
                              'three dogs run together in the grass'
                              ],

'3461583471_2b8b6b4d73.jpg': ['buy is grinding rail on snowboard',
                              'person is jumping ramp on snowboard',
                              'snowboarder goes down ramp',
                              'snowboarder going over ramp',
                              'snowboarder performs jump on the clean white snow'
                              ],
'997722733_0cb5439472.jpg' : ['man in pink shirt climbs rock face',
                              'man is rock climbing high in the air',
                              'person in red shirt climbing up rock face covered in as
                              'rock climber in red shirt',
                              'rock climber practices on rock climbing wall'
                              ]

}
```

File   Edit   Format   Run   Options   Window   Help

```
1000268201_693b08cb0e.jpg          child in pink dress is climbing up set of stairs in
1000268201_693b08cb0e.jpg          girl going into wooden building
1000268201_693b08cb0e.jpg          little girl climbing into wooden playhouse
1000268201_693b08cb0e.jpg          little girl climbing the stairs to her playhouse
1000268201_693b08cb0e.jpg          little girl in pink dress going into wooden cabin
1001773457_577c3a7d70.jpg          black dog and spotted dog are fighting
1001773457_577c3a7d70.jpg          black dog and tricolored dog playing with each othe
1001773457_577c3a7d70.jpg          black dog and white dog with brown spots are starin
1001773457_577c3a7d70.jpg          two dogs of different breeds looking at each other
1001773457_577c3a7d70.jpg          two dogs on pavement moving toward each other
1002674143_1b742ab4b8.jpg          little girl covered in paint sits in front of paint
1002674143_1b742ab4b8.jpg          little girl is sitting in front of large painted ra
1002674143_1b742ab4b8.jpg          small girl in the grass plays with fingerpaints in
1002674143_1b742ab4b8.jpg          there is girl with pigtails sitting in front of rai
1002674143_1b742ab4b8.jpg          young girl with pigtails painting outside in the gr
1003163366_44323f5815.jpg          man lays on bench while his dog sits by him
```

```python
1.   # Loading a text file into memory
2.   def load_doc(filename):
3.       # Opening the file as read only
4.       file = open(filename, 'r')
5.       text = file.read()
6.       file.close()
7.       return text
8.
9.   # get all imgs with their captions
10.  def all_img_captions(filename):
11.      file = load_doc(filename)
12.      captions = file.split('\n')
13.      descriptions ={}
14.      for caption in captions[:-1]:
15.          img, caption = caption.split('\t')
16.          if img[:-2] not in descriptions:
17.              descriptions[img[:-2]] = [ caption ]
18.          else:
19.              descriptions[img[:-2]].append(caption)
20.      return descriptions
21.
22.  #Data cleaning- lower casing, removing puntuations and words containing
     numbers
23.  def cleaning_text(captions):
24.      table = str.maketrans('','',string.punctuation)
25.      for img,caps in captions.items():
26.          for i,img_caption in enumerate(caps):
27.
28.              img_caption.replace("-"," ")
29.              desc = img_caption.split()
30.
31.              #converts to lowercase
32.              desc = [word.lower() for word in desc]
33.              #remove punctuation from each token
34.              desc = [word.translate(table) for word in desc]
35.              #remove hanging 's and a
36.              desc = [word for word in desc if(len(word)>1)]
37.              #remove tokens with numbers in them
38.              desc = [word for word in desc if(word.isalpha())]
39.              #convert back to string
40.
```

```
41.                    img_caption = ' '.join(desc)
42.                    captions[img][i]= img_caption
43.        return captions
44.
45.    def text_vocabulary(descriptions):
46.        # build vocabulary of all unique words
47.        vocab = set()
48.
49.        for key in descriptions.keys():
50.            [vocab.update(d.split()) for d in descriptions[key]]
51.
52.        return vocab
53.
54.    #All descriptions in one file
55.    def save_descriptions(descriptions, filename):
56.        lines = list()
57.        for key, desc_list in descriptions.items():
58.            for desc in desc_list:
59.                lines.append(key + '\t' + desc )
60.        data = "\n".join(lines)
61.         file = open(filename,"w")
62.         file.write(data)
63.         file.close()
64.
65.
66.     # Set these path according to project folder in you system
67.     dataset_text = "D:\dataflair projects\Project - Image Caption
       Generator\Flickr_8k_text"
68.     dataset_images = "D:\dataflair projects\Project - Image Caption
       Generator\Flicker8k_Dataset"
69.
70.     #we prepare our text data
71.     filename = dataset_text + "/" + "Flickr8k.token.txt"
72.     #loading the file that contains all data
73.     #mapping them into descriptions dictionary img to 5 captions
74.     descriptions = all_img_captions(filename)
75.     print("Length of descriptions =" ,len(descriptions))
76.
77.     #cleaning the descriptions
78.     clean_descriptions = cleaning_text(descriptions)
79.
80.     #building vocabulary
81.     vocabulary = text_vocabulary(clean_descriptions)
82.     print("Length of vocabulary = ", len(vocabulary))
83.
84.     #saving each description to file
85.     save_descriptions(clean_descriptions, "descriptions.txt")
```

```
1.   def extract_features(directory):
2.           model = Xception( include_top=False, pooling='avg' )
3.           features = {}
4.           for img in tqdm(os.listdir(directory)):
5.               filename = directory + "/" + img
6.               image = Image.open(filename)
7.               image = image.resize((299,299))
8.               image = np.expand_dims(image, axis=0)
9.               #image = preprocess_input(image)
10.              image = image/127.5
11.              image = image - 1.0
12.
13.              feature = model.predict(image)
14.              features[img] = feature
15.          return features
16.
17.  #2048 feature vector
18.  features = extract_features(dataset_images)
19.  dump(features, open("features.p","wb"))
```

In [44]:
```
# Now let's extract the features from our xception model
def extract_features(directory):
        model = Xception( include_top=False, pooling='avg' )
        features = {}
        for img in tqdm(os.listdir(directory)):
            filename = directory + "/" + img
            image = Image.open(filename)
            image = image.resize((299,299))
            image = np.expand_dims(image, axis=0)
            #image = preprocess_input(image)
            image = image/127.5
            image = image - 1.0

            feature = model.predict(image)
            features[img] = feature
        return features
```

In [45]:
```
#2048 feature vector
features = extract_features(dataset_images)
dump(features, open("features.p","wb"))
```

100% ████████████████████████ 8091/8091 [06:29<00:00, 20.78it/s]

In [21]:
```
features = load(open("features.p","rb"))
```

```
1.   features = load(open("features.p","rb"))
```

```
1.   #load the data
2.   def load_photos(filename):
3.       file = load_doc(filename)
4.       photos = file.split("\n")[:-1]
5.       return photos
6.
7.
8.   def load_clean_descriptions(filename, photos):
9.       #loading clean_descriptions
10.      file = load_doc(filename)
11.      descriptions = {}
12.      for line in file.split("\n"):
13.
14.          words = line.split()
15.          if len(words)<1 :
16.              continue
17.
18.          image, image_caption = words[0], words[1:]
19.
20.          if image in photos:
21.              if image not in descriptions:
22.                  descriptions[image] = []
23.              desc = '<start> ' + " ".join(image_caption) + ' <end>'
24.              descriptions[image].append(desc)
25.
26.      return descriptions
27.
28.
29.  def load_features(photos):
30.      #loading all features
31.      all_features = load(open("features.p","rb"))
32.      #selecting only needed features
33.      features = {k:all_features[k] for k in photos}
34.      return features
35.
36.
37.  filename = dataset_text + "/" + "Flickr_8k.trainImages.txt"
38.
39.  #train = loading_data(filename)
40.  train_imgs = load_photos(filename)
41.  train_descriptions = load_clean_descriptions("descriptions.txt",
     train_imgs)
42.  train_features = load_features(train_imgs)
```

```
1.   #converting dictionary to clean list of descriptions
2.   def dict_to_list(descriptions):
3.       all_desc = []
4.       for key in descriptions.keys():
5.           [all_desc.append(d) for d in descriptions[key]]
6.       return all_desc
7.
8.   #creating tokenizer class
9.   #this will vectorise text corpus
10.  #each integer will represent token in dictionary
```

```
11.
12.    from keras.preprocessing.text import Tokenizer
13.
14.    def create_tokenizer(descriptions):
15.        desc_list = dict_to_list(descriptions)
16.        tokenizer = Tokenizer()
17.        tokenizer.fit_on_texts(desc_list)
18.        return tokenizer
19.
20.    # give each word an index, and store that into tokenizer.p pickle file
21.    tokenizer = create_tokenizer(train_descriptions)
22.    dump(tokenizer, open('tokenizer.p', 'wb'))
23.    vocab_size = len(tokenizer.word_index) + 1
24.    vocab_size
```

```
1.    #calculate maximum length of descriptions
2.    def max_length(descriptions):
3.        desc_list = dict_to_list(descriptions)
4.        return max(len(d.split()) for d in desc_list)
5.
6.    max_length = max_length(descriptions)
7.    max_length
```

x1(feature vector)	x2(Text sequence)	y(word to predict)
feature	start,	two
feature	start, two	dogs
feature	start, two, dogs	drink
feature	start, two, dogs, drink	water
feature	start, two, dogs, drink, water	end

```
1.    #create input-output sequence pairs from the image description.
2.
3.    #data generator, used by model.fit_generator()
4.    def data_generator(descriptions, features, tokenizer, max_length):
5.        while 1:
6.            for key, description_list in descriptions.items():
7.                #retrieve photo features
8.                feature = features[key][0]
9.                input_image, input_sequence, output_word =
     create_sequences(tokenizer, max_length, description_list, feature)
10.                yield [[input_image, input_sequence], output_word]
11.
12.    def create_sequences(tokenizer, max_length, desc_list, feature):
13.        X1, X2, y = list(), list(), list()
14.        # walk through each description for the image
15.        for desc in desc_list:
16.            # encode the sequence
17.            seq = tokenizer.texts_to_sequences([desc])[0]
18.            # split one sequence into multiple X,y pairs
19.            for i in range(1, len(seq)):
20.                # split into input and output pair
```

```
21.              in_seq, out_seq = seq[:i], seq[i]
22.              # pad input sequence
23.              in_seq = pad_sequences([in_seq], maxlen=max_length)[0]
24.              # encode output sequence
25.              out_seq = to_categorical([out_seq], num_classes=vocab_size)[0]
26.              # store
27.              X1.append(feature)
28.              X2.append(in_seq)
29.              y.append(out_seq)
30.      return np.array(X1), np.array(X2), np.array(y)
31.
32.  #You can check the shape of the input and output for your model
33.  [a,b],c = next(data_generator(train_descriptions, features, tokenizer,
     max_length))
34.  a.shape, b.shape, c.shape
35.  #((47, 2048), (47, 32), (47, 7577))
```

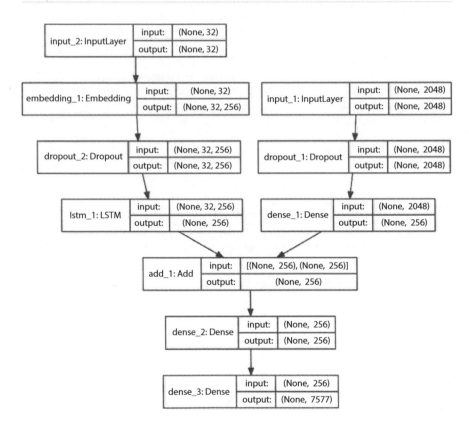

```
1.   from keras.utils import plot_model
2.
3.   # define the captioning model
4.   def define_model(vocab_size, max_length):
5.
6.       # features from the CNN model squeezed from 2048 to 256 nodes
7.       inputs1 = Input(shape=(2048,))
8.       fe1 = Dropout(0.5)(inputs1)
9.       fe2 = Dense(256, activation='relu')(fe1)
10.
11.      # LSTM sequence model
12.      inputs2 = Input(shape=(max_length,))
13.      se1 = Embedding(vocab_size, 256, mask_zero=True)(inputs2)
14.      se2 = Dropout(0.5)(se1)
15.      se3 = LSTM(256)(se2)
16.
17.      # Merging both models
18.      decoder1 = add([fe2, se3])
19.      decoder2 = Dense(256, activation='relu')(decoder1)
20.      outputs = Dense(vocab_size, activation='softmax')(decoder2)
21.
22.      # tie it together [image, seq] [word]
23.      model = Model(inputs=[inputs1, inputs2], outputs=outputs)
24.      model.compile(loss='categorical_crossentropy', optimizer='adam')
25.
26.      # summarize model
27.      print(model.summary())
28.      plot_model(model, to_file='model.png', show_shapes=True)
29.
30.      return model
```

```
1.   # train our model
2.   print('Dataset: ', len(train_imgs))
3.   print('Descriptions: train=', len(train_descriptions))
4.   print('Photos: train=', len(train_features))
5.   print('Vocabulary Size:', vocab_size)
6.   print('Description Length: ', max_length)
7.
8.   model = define_model(vocab_size, max_length)
9.   epochs = 10
10.  steps = len(train_descriptions)
11.  # making a directory models to save our models
12.  os.mkdir("models")
13.  for i in range(epochs):
14.      generator = data_generator(train_descriptions, train_features,
     tokenizer, max_length)
15.      model.fit_generator(generator, epochs=1, steps_per_epoch= steps,
     verbose=1)
16.      model.save("models/model_" + str(i) + ".h5")
```

```
1.   import numpy as np
2.   from PIL import Image
3.   import matplotlib.pyplot as plt
4.   import argparse
5.
6.
7.   ap = argparse.ArgumentParser()
8.   ap.add_argument('-i', '--image', required=True, help="Image Path")
9.   args = vars(ap.parse_args())
10.  img_path = args['image']
11.
12.  def extract_features(filename, model):
13.          try:
14.              image = Image.open(filename)
15.
16.          except:
17.              print("ERROR: Couldn't open image! Make sure the image path
     and extension is correct")
18.          image = image.resize((299,299))
19.          image = np.array(image)
20.          # for images that has 4 channels, we convert them into 3 channels
21.          if image.shape[2] == 4:
22.              image = image[..., :3]
23.          image = np.expand_dims(image, axis=0)
24.          image = image/127.5
25.          image = image - 1.0
26.          feature = model.predict(image)
27.          return feature
28.
29.  def word_for_id(integer, tokenizer):
30.  for word, index in tokenizer.word_index.items():

31.      if index == integer:
32.          return word
33.  return None
34.
35.
36.  def generate_desc(model, tokenizer, photo, max_length):
37.      in_text = 'start'
38.      for i in range(max_length):
39.          sequence = tokenizer.texts_to_sequences([in_text])[0]
40.          sequence = pad_sequences([sequence], maxlen=max_length)
41.          pred = model.predict([photo,sequence], verbose=0)
42.          pred = np.argmax(pred)
43.          word = word_for_id(pred, tokenizer)
44.          if word is None:
45.              break
46.          in_text += ' ' + word
47.          if word == 'end':
48.              break
49.      return in_text
50.
51.
52.  #path = 'Flicker8k_Dataset/111537222_07e56d5a30.jpg'
53.  max_length = 32
54.  tokenizer = load(open("tokenizer.p","rb"))
55.  model = load_model('models/model_9.h5')
56.  xception_model = Xception(include_top=False, pooling="avg")
57.
```

```
58.   photo = extract_features(img_path, xception_model)
59.   img = Image.open(img_path)
60.
61.   description = generate_desc(model, tokenizer, photo, max_length)
62.   print("\n\n")
63.   print(description)
64.   plt.imshow(img)
```

Bibliography

1. https://data-flair.training/blogs/python-based-project-image-caption-generator-cnn/

Credit Card Fraud Detection Project

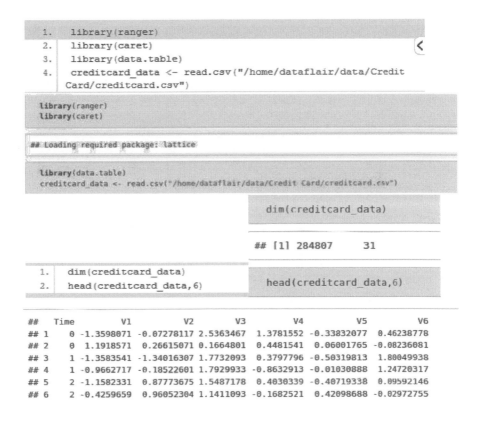

```
1.    library(ranger)
2.    library(caret)
3.    library(data.table)
4.    creditcard_data <- read.csv("/home/dataflair/data/Credit
      Card/creditcard.csv")
```

```
library(ranger)
library(caret)
```

```
## Loading required package: lattice
```

```
library(data.table)
creditcard_data <- read.csv("/home/dataflair/data/Credit Card/creditcard.csv")
```

```
dim(creditcard_data)
```

```
## [1] 284807        31
```

```
1.    dim(creditcard_data)
2.    head(creditcard_data,6)
```

```
head(creditcard_data,6)
```

```
##   Time         V1          V2        V3         V4          V5          V6
## 1    0 -1.3598071 -0.07278117 2.5363467  1.3781552 -0.33832077  0.46238778
## 2    0  1.1918571  0.26615071 0.1664801  0.4481541  0.06001765 -0.08236081
## 3    1 -1.3583541 -1.34016307 1.7732093  0.3797796 -0.50319813  1.80049938
## 4    1 -0.9662717 -0.18522601 1.7929933 -0.8632913 -0.01030888  1.24720317
## 5    2 -1.1582331  0.87773675 1.5487178  0.4030339 -0.40719338  0.09592146
## 6    2 -0.4259659  0.96052304 1.1411093 -0.1682521  0.42098688 -0.02972755
```

Kolla Bhanu Prakash. Data Science Handbook: A Practical Approach, (381–392) © 2022 Scrivener Publishing LLC

```
##              V7          V8          V9         V10         V11         V12
## 1   0.23959855  0.09869790   0.3637870  0.09079417 -0.5515995 -0.61780086
## 2  -0.07880298  0.08510165  -0.2554251 -0.16697441  1.6127267  1.06523531
## 3   0.79146096  0.24767579  -1.5146543  0.20764287  0.6245015  0.06608369
## 4   0.23760894  0.37743587  -1.3870241 -0.05495192 -0.2264873  0.17822823
## 5   0.59294075 -0.27053268   0.8177393  0.75307443 -0.8228429  0.53819555
## 6   0.47620095  0.26031433  -0.5686714 -0.37140720  1.3412620  0.35989384
##             V13         V14         V15         V16         V17         V18
## 1  -0.9913898 -0.3111694   1.4681770 -0.4704005  0.20797124  0.02579058
## 2   0.4890950 -0.1437723   0.6355581  0.4639170 -0.11480466 -0.18336127
## 3   0.7172927 -0.1659459   2.3458649 -2.8900832  1.10996938 -0.12135931
## 4   0.5077569 -0.2879237  -0.6314181 -1.0596472 -0.68409279  1.96577500
## 5   1.3458516 -1.1196698   0.1751211 -0.4514492 -0.23703324 -0.03819479
## 6  -0.3580907 -0.1371337   0.5176168  0.4017259 -0.05813282  0.06865315
```

```
1.   tail(creditcard_data,6)
```

```
tail(creditcard_data,6)
```

```
##             Time          V1          V2          V3          V4          V5
## 284802 172785    0.1203164   0.93100513  -0.5460121  -0.7450968   1.13031398
## 284803 172786  -11.8811179  10.07178497  -9.8347835  -2.0666557  -5.36447278
## 284804 172787   -0.7327887  -0.05508049   2.0350297  -0.7385886   0.86822940
## 284805 172788    1.9195650  -0.30125385  -3.2496398  -0.5578281   2.63051512
## 284806 172788   -0.2404400   0.53048251   0.7025102   0.6897992  -0.37796113
## 284807 172792   -0.5334125  -0.18973334   0.7033374  -0.5062712  -0.01254568
##                 V6          V7          V8          V9         V10         V11
## 284802  -0.2359732   0.8127221   0.1150929  -0.2040635  -0.6574221   0.6448373
## 284803  -2.6068373  -4.9182154   7.3053340   1.9144283   4.3561704  -1.5931053
## 284804   1.0584153   0.0243297   0.2948687   0.5848000  -0.9759261  -0.1501888
## 284805   3.0312601  -0.2968265   0.7084172   0.4324540  -0.4847818   0.4116137
## 284806   0.6237077  -0.6861800   0.6791455   0.3920867  -0.3991257  -1.9338488
## 284807  -0.6496167   1.5770063  -0.4146504   0.4861795  -0.9154266  -1.0404583
##                V12         V13         V14         V15         V16
## 284802  0.19091623  -0.5463289  -0.73170658  -0.80803553   0.5996281
## 284803  2.71194079  -0.6892556   4.62694203  -0.92445871   1.1076406
## 284804  0.91580191   1.2147558  -0.67514296   1.16493091  -0.7117573
## 284805  0.06311886  -0.1836987  -0.51060184   1.32928351   0.1407160
## 284806 -0.96288614  -1.0420817   0.44962444   1.96256312  -0.6085771
## 284807 -0.03151305  -0.1880929  -0.08431647   0.04133346  -0.3026201
```

```
1.   table(creditcard_data$Class)
2.   summary(creditcard_data$Amount)
3.   names(creditcard_data)
4.   var(creditcard_data$Amount)
```

```
table(creditcard_data$Class)
```

```
##
##      0      1
## 284315    492
```

```
summary(creditcard_data$Amount)
```

```
##      Min.  1st Qu.  Median    Mean  3rd Qu.     Max.
##      0.00     5.60   22.00   88.35    77.17 25691.16
```

```
names(creditcard_data)
```

```
## [1] "Time"   "V1"     "V2"     "V3"     "V4"     "V5"     "V6"
## [8] "V7"     "V8"     "V9"     "V10"    "V11"    "V12"    "V13"
## [15] "V14"    "V15"    "V16"    "V17"    "V18"    "V19"    "V20"
## [22] "V21"    "V22"    "V23"    "V24"    "V25"    "V26"    "V27"
## [29] "V28"    "Amount" "Class"
```

```
var(creditcard_data$Amount)
```

```
## [1] 62560.07
```

```
1.  sd(creditcard_data$Amount)
```

```
sd(creditcard_data$Amount)
```

```
## [1] 250.1201
```

```
1.  head(creditcard_data)
```

```
head(creditcard_data)
```

```
##   Time         V1          V2         V3          V4          V5          V6
## 1    0 -1.3598071 -0.07278117  2.5363467  1.3781552 -0.33832077  0.46238778
## 2    0  1.1918571  0.26615071  0.1664801  0.4481541  0.06001765 -0.08236081
## 3    1 -1.3583541  1.34016307  1.7732093  0.3797796 -0.50319813  1.80049938
## 4    1 -0.9662717 -0.18522601  1.7929933 -0.8632913 -0.01030888  1.24720317
## 5    2 -1.1582331  0.87773675  1.5487178  0.4030339 -0.40719338  0.09592146
## 6    2 -0.4259659  0.96052304  1.1411093 -0.1682521  0.42098688 -0.02972755
##           V7          V8         V9         V10         V11         V12
## 1  0.23959855  0.09869790  0.3637870  0.09079417 -0.5515995 -0.61780086
## 2 -0.07880298  0.08510165 -0.2554251 -0.16697441  1.6127267  1.06523531
## 3  0.79146096  0.24767579 -1.5146543  0.20764287  0.6245015  0.06608369
## 4  0.23760894  0.37743587 -1.3870241 -0.05495192 -0.2264873  0.17822823
## 5  0.59294075 -0.27053268  0.8177393  0.75307443 -0.8228429  0.53819555
## 6  0.47620095  0.26031433 -0.5686714 -0.37140720  1.3412620  0.35989384
```

```
##           V13         V14          V15         V16          V17          V18
## 1 -0.9913898  -0.3111694   1.4681770 -0.4704005  0.20797124   0.02579058
## 2  0.4890950  -0.1437723   0.6355581  0.4639170 -0.11480466  -0.18336127
## 3  0.7172927  -0.1659459   2.3458649 -2.8900832  1.10996938  -0.12135931
## 4  0.5077569  -0.2879237  -0.6314181 -1.0596472 -0.68409279   1.96577500
## 5  1.3458516  -1.1196698   0.1751211 -0.4514492 -0.23703324  -0.03819479
## 6 -0.3580907  -0.1371337   0.5176168  0.4017259 -0.05813282   0.06865315
##           V19         V20          V21          V22         V23
## 1  0.40399296  0.25141210 -0.018306778  0.277837576 -0.11047391
## 2 -0.14578304 -0.06908314 -0.225775248 -0.638671953  0.10128802
## 3 -2.26185710  0.52497973  0.247998153  0.771679402  0.90941226
## 4 -1.23262197 -0.20803778 -0.108300452  0.005273597 -0.19032052
## 5  0.80348692  0.40854236 -0.009430697  0.798278495 -0.13745808
## 6 -0.03319379  0.08496767 -0.208253515 -0.559824796 -0.02639767
```

```
1.   creditcard_data$Amount=scale(creditcard_data$Amount)
2.   NewData=creditcard_data[,-c(1)]
3.   head(NewData)
```

```
creditcard_data$Amount=scale(creditcard_data$Amount)
NewData=creditcard_data[,-c(1)]
head(NewData)
```

```
##            V1          V2         V3         V4          V5          V6
## 1 -1.3598071 -0.07278117  2.5363467  1.3781552 -0.33832077  0.46238778
## 2  1.1918571  0.26015071  0.1664801  0.4481541  0.06001765 -0.08236081
## 3 -1.3583541 -1.34016307  1.7732093  0.3797796 -0.50319813  1.80049938
## 4 -0.9662717 -0.18522601  1.7929933 -0.8632913 -0.01030888  1.24720317
## 5 -1.1582331  0.87773675  1.5487178  0.4030339 -0.40719338  0.09592146
## 6 -0.4259659  0.96052304  1.1411093 -0.1682521  0.42098688 -0.02972755

##           V7          V8         V9         V10        V11         V12
## 1  0.23959855  0.09869790  0.3637870  0.09079417 -0.5515995 -0.61780086
## 2 -0.07880298  0.08510165 -0.2554251 -0.16697441  1.6127267  1.06523531
## 3  0.79146096  0.24767579 -1.5146543  0.20764287  0.6245015  0.06608369
## 4  0.23760894  0.37743587 -1.3870241 -0.05495192 -0.2264873  0.17822823
## 5  0.59294075 -0.27053268  0.8177393  0.75307443 -0.8228429  0.53819555
## 6  0.47620095  0.26031433 -0.5686714 -0.37140720  1.3412620  0.35989384
##           V13         V14          V15         V16          V17          V18
## 1 -0.9913898  -0.3111694   1.4681770 -0.4704005  0.20797124   0.02579058
## 2  0.4890950  -0.1437723   0.6355581  0.4639170 -0.11480466  -0.18336127
## 3  0.7172927  -0.1659459   2.3458649 -2.8900832  1.10996938  -0.12135931
## 4  0.5077569  -0.2879237  -0.6314181 -1.0596472 -0.68409279   1.96577500
## 5  1.3458516  -1.1196698   0.1751211 -0.4514492 -0.23703324  -0.03819479
## 6 -0.3580907  -0.1371337   0.5176168  0.4017259 -0.05813282   0.06865315
```

```
##            V19          V20          V21          V22          V23
## 1  0.40399296   0.25141210  -0.018306778   0.277837576  -0.11047391
## 2 -0.14578304  -0.06908314  -0.225775248  -0.638671953   0.10128802
## 3 -2.26185710   0.52497973   0.247998153   0.771679402   0.90941226
## 4 -1.23262197  -0.20803778  -0.108300452   0.005273597  -0.19032052
## 5  0.80348692   0.40854236  -0.009430697   0.798278495  -0.13745808
## 6 -0.03319379   0.08496767  -0.208253515  -0.559824796  -0.02639767
```

```
1.   library(caTools)
2.   set.seed(123)
3.   data_sample = sample.split(NewData$Class,SplitRatio=0.80)
4.   train_data = subset(NewData,data_sample==TRUE)
5.   test_data = subset(NewData,data_sample==FALSE)
6.   dim(train_data)
7.   dim(test_data)
```

```
library(caTools)
set.seed(123)
data_sample = sample.split(NewData$Class,SplitRatio=0.80)
train_data = subset(NewData,data_sample==TRUE)
test_data = subset(NewData,data_sample==FALSE)
dim(train_data)
```

```
## [1] 227846     30
```

```
dim(test_data)
```

```
## [1] 56961     30
```

```
Logistic_Model=glm(Class~.,test_data,family=binomial())
```

```
## Warning: glm.fit: fitted probabilities numerically 0 or 1 occurred
```

```
summary(Logistic_Model)
```

```
##
## Call:
## glm(formula = Class ~ ., family = binomial(), data = test_data)
##
## Deviance Residuals:
##     Min        1Q     Median        3Q       Max
## -4.9019   -0.0254   -0.0156   -0.0078    4.0877
```

```
1.    Logistic_Model=glm(Class~.,test_data,family=binomial())
2.    summary(Logistic_Model)
```

```
Logistic_Model=glm(Class~.,test_data,family=binomial())
```

```
## Warning: glm.fit: fitted probabilities numerically 0 or 1 occurred
```

```
summary(Logistic_Model)
```

```
##
## Call:
## glm(formula = Class ~ ., family = binomial(), data = test_data)
##
## Deviance Residuals:
##     Min       1Q    Median       3Q       Max
## -4.9019   -0.0254   -0.0156   -0.0078    4.0877
```

```
1.    plot(Logistic_Model)
```

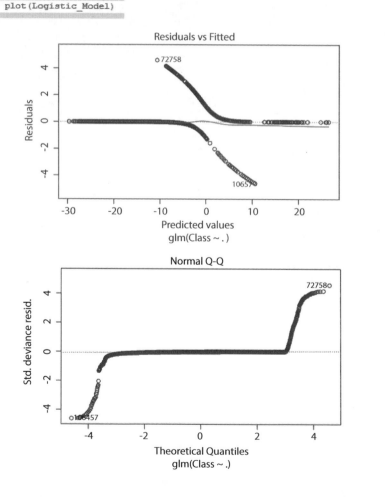

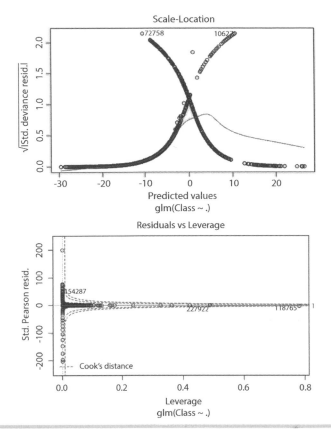

```
1.  library(pROC)
2.  lr.predict <- predict(Logistic_Model,train_data, probability = TRUE)
3.  auc.gbm = roc(test_data$Class, lr.predict, plot = TRUE, col = "blue")
```

```
Logistic_Model=glm(Class~.,train_data,family=binomial())
summary(Logistic_Model)
```

```
##
## Call:
## glm(formula = Class ~ ., family = binomial(), data = train_data)
##
## Deviance Residuals:
##     Min       1Q   Median       3Q      Max
## -4.6108  -0.0292  -0.0194  -0.0125   4.6021
##
## Coefficients:
##              Estimate Std. Error z value Pr(>|z|)
## (Intercept) -8.651305   0.160212 -53.999  < 2e-16 ***
## V1           0.072540   0.044144   1.643 0.100332
## V2           0.014818   0.059777   0.248 0.804220
```

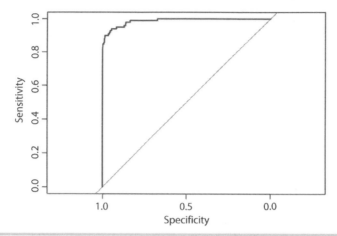

```
1.    library(rpart)
2.    library(rpart.plot)
3.    decisionTree_model <- rpart(Class ~ . , creditcard_data, method = 'class')
4.    predicted_val <- predict(decisionTree_model, creditcard_data, type =
      'class')
5.    probability <- predict(decisionTree_model, creditcard_data, type = 'prob')
6.    rpart.plot(decisionTree_model)
```

```
library(rpart)
library(rpart.plot)
decisionTree_model <- rpart(Class ~ . , creditcard_data, method = 'class')
predicted_val <- predict(decisionTree_model, creditcard_data, type = 'class')
probability <- predict(decisionTree_model, creditcard_data, type = 'prob')

rpart.plot(decisionTree_model)
```

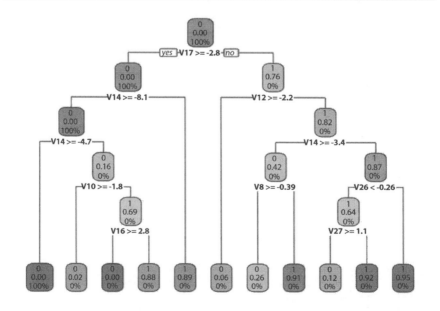

```
1.    library(neuralnet)
2.    ANN_model =neuralnet (Class~.,train_data,linear.output=FALSE)
3.    plot(ANN_model)
4.
5.    predANN=compute(ANN_model,test_data)
6.    resultANN=predANN$net.result
7.    resultANN=ifelse(resultANN>0.5,1,0)
```

```
library(neuralnet)
ANN_model =neuralnet (Class~.,train_data,linear.output=FALSE)
plot(ANN_model)
```

```
predANN=compute(ANN_model,test_data)
resultANN=predANN$net.result
resultANN=ifelse(resultANN>0.5,1,0)
```

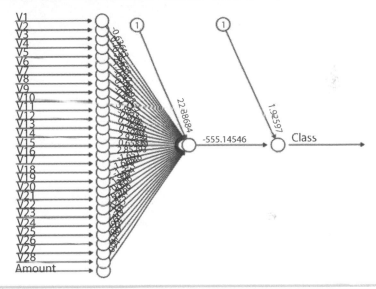

```
1.    library(gbm, quietly=TRUE)
2.
3.    # Get the time to train the GBM model
4.    system.time(
5.            model_gbm <- gbm(Class ~ .
6.                    , distribution = "bernoulli"
7.                    , data = rbind(train_data, test_data)
8.                    , n.trees = 500
9.                    , interaction.depth = 3
10.                   , n.minobsinnode = 100
11.                   , shrinkage = 0.01
12.                   , bag.fraction = 0.5
13.                   , train.fraction = nrow(train_data) / (nrow(train_data) +
      nrow(test_data))
14.           )
15.   )
16.   # Determine best iteration based on test data
17.   gbm.iter = gbm.perf(model_gbm, method = "test")
```

```
library(gbm, quietly=TRUE)
```

```
## Loaded gbm 2.1.5
```

```
# Get the time to train the GBM model
system.time(
    model_gbm <- gbm(Class ~ .
        , distribution = "bernoulli"
        , data = rbind(train_data, test_data)
        , n.trees = 500
        , interaction.depth = 3
        , n.minobsinnode = 100
        , shrinkage = 0.01
        , bag.fraction = 0.5
        , train.fraction = nrow(train_data) / (nrow(train_data) + nrow(test_data))
        )
)
```

```
##    user  system elapsed
## 345.781   0.144 345.971
```

```
# Determine best iteration based on test data
gbm.iter = gbm.perf(model_gbm, method = "test")
```

1. model.influence = relative.influence(model_gbm, n.trees = gbm.iter, sort.
   = TRUE)
2. #Plot the gbm model
3.
4. plot(model_gbm)

```
model.influence = relative.influence(model_gbm, n.trees = gbm.iter, sort. = TRUE)
#Plot the gbm model

plot(model_gbm)
```

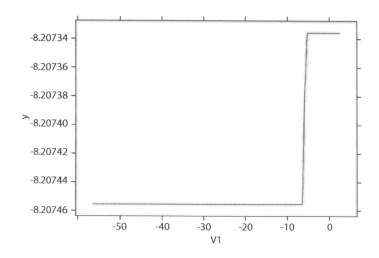

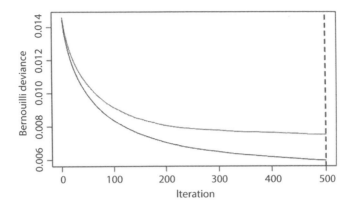

```
1.  # Plot and calculate AUC on test data
2.  gbm_test = predict(model_gbm, newdata = test_data, n.trees = gbm.iter)
3.  gbm_auc = roc(test_data$Class, gbm_test, plot = TRUE, col = "red")
```

```
# Plot and calculate AUC on test data
gbm_test = predict(model_gbm, newdata = test_data, n.trees = gbm.iter)
gbm_auc = roc(test_data$Class, gbm_test, plot = TRUE, col = "red")
```

```
## Setting levels: control = 0, case = 1
```

```
## Setting direction: controls < cases
```

```
1.  print(gbm_auc)
```

```
print(gbm_auc)
```

```
##
## Call:
## roc.default(response = test_data$Class, predictor = gbm_test,    plot = TRUE, col = "red")
##
## Data: gbm_test in 56863 controls (test_data$Class 0) < 98 cases (test_data$Class 1).
## Area under the curve: 0.9555
```

Bibliography

1. https://data-flair.training/blogs/data-science-machine-learning-project-credit-card-fraud-detection/

27

Movie Recommendation System

```
1.    library(recommenderlab)
```

```
library(recommenderlab)
```

```
## Loading required package: Matrix
```

```
## Loading required package: arules
```

```
##
## Attaching package: 'arules'
```

```
## The following objects are masked from 'package:base':
##
##      abbreviate, write
```

```
## Loading required package: proxy
```

```
##
## Attaching package: 'proxy'
```

```
## The following object is masked from 'package:Matrix':
##
##      as.matrix
```

```
1.    library(ggplot2)                          #Author DataFlair
2.    library(data.table)
3.    library(reshape2)
```

Kolla Bhanu Prakash. Data Science Handbook: A Practical Approach, (393–412) © 2022 Scrivener Publishing LLC

```
library(ggplot2)                                          #Author DataFlair
```

```
## Registered S3 methods overwritten by 'ggplot2':
##   method          from
##   [.quosures      rlang
##   c.quosures      rlang
##   print.quosures  rlang
```

```
library(data.table)
library(reshape2)
```

```
##
## Attaching package: 'reshape2'
```

```
## The following objects are masked from 'package:data.table':
##
##      dcast, melt
```

```
1.  setwd("/home/dataflair/data/movie_data")              #Author
    DataFlair
2.  movie_data <- read.csv("movies.csv",stringsAsFactors=FALSE)
3.  rating_data <- read.csv("ratings.csv")
4.  str(movie_data)
```

```
setwd("/home/dataflair/data/movie_data")                 #Author DataFlair
movie_data <- read.csv("movies.csv",stringsAsFactors=FALSE)
rating_data <- read.csv("ratings.csv")
str(movie_data)
```

```
## 'data.frame':    10329 obs. of  3 variables:
## $ movieId: int  1 2 3 4 5 6 7 8 9 10 ...
## $ title  : chr  "Toy Story (1995)" "Jumanji (1995)" "Grumpier Old Men (1995)" "
Waiting to Exhale (1995)" ...
## $ genres : chr  "Adventure|Animation|Children|Comedy|Fantasy" "Adventure|Childr
en|Fantasy" "Comedy|Romance" "Comedy|Drama|Romance" ...
```

```
1.  summary(movie_data)     #Author DataFlair
```

```
summary(movie_data)     #Author DataFlair
```

```
##     movieId              title              genres
## Min.   :     1    Length:10329      Length:10329
## 1st Qu.:  3240    Class :character  Class :character
## Median :  7088    Mode  :character  Mode  :character
## Mean   : 31924
## 3rd Qu.: 59900
## Max.   :149532
```

1. head(movie_data)

```
head(movie_data)
```

```
##    movieId                                   title
## 1        1                        Toy Story (1995)
## 2        2                          Jumanji (1995)
## 3        3                 Grumpier Old Men (1995)
## 4        4                Waiting to Exhale (1995)
## 5        5      Father of the Bride Part II (1995)
## 6        6                             Heat (1995)
##                                                genres
## 1 Adventure|Animation|Children|Comedy|Fantasy
## 2                  Adventure|Children|Fantasy
## 3                              Comedy|Romance
## 4                        Comedy|Drama|Romance
## 5                                      Comedy
## 6                       Action|Crime|Thriller
```

1. summary(rating_data)   #Author DataFlair

```
summary(rating_data)    #Author DataFlair
```

```
##     userId           movieId          rating         timestamp
## Min.   : 1.0     Min.   :      1     Min.   :0.500    Min.   :8.286e+08
## 1st Qu.:192.0    1st Qu.:  1073     1st Qu.:3.000    1st Qu.:9.711e+08
## Median :383.0    Median :  2497     Median :3.500    Median :1.115e+09
## Mean   :364.9    Mean   : 13381     Mean   :3.517    Mean   :1.130e+09
## 3rd Qu.:557.0    3rd Qu.:  5991     3rd Qu.:4.000    3rd Qu.:1.275e+09
## Max.   :668.0    Max.   :149532     Max.   :5.000    Max.   :1.452e+09
```

```
1.    head(rating_data)
```

```
head(rating_data)
```

```
##   userId movieId rating timestamp
## 1      1      16    4.0 1217897793
## 2      1      24    1.5 1217895807
## 3      1      32    4.0 1217896246
## 4      1      47    4.0 1217896556
## 5      1      50    4.0 1217896523
## 6      1     110    4.0 1217896150
```

```
1.   movie_genre <- as.data.frame(movie_data$genres, stringsAsFactors=FALSE)
2.   library(data.table)
3.   movie_genre2 <- as.data.frame(tstrsplit(movie_genre[,1], '[|]',
4.                               type.convert=TRUE),
5.                               stringsAsFactors=FALSE) #DataFlair
6.   colnames(movie_genre2) <- c(1:10)
7.
8.   list_genre <- c("Action", "Adventure", "Animation", "Children",
9.                  "Comedy", "Crime","Documentary", "Drama", "Fantasy",
10.                 "Film-Noir", "Horror", "Musical", "Mystery","Romance",
11.                 "Sci-Fi", "Thriller", "War", "Western")
12.  genre_mat1 <- matrix(0,10330,18)
13.  genre_mat1[1,] <- list_genre
14.  colnames(genre_mat1) <- list_genre
15.
16.  for (index in 1:nrow(movie_genre2)) {
17.    for (col in 1:ncol(movie_genre2)) {
18.      gen_col = which(genre_mat1[1,] == movie_genre2[index,col]) #Author
     DataFlair
19.      genre_mat1[index+1,gen_col] <- 1
20.    }
21.  }
```

```
22.    genre_mat2 <- as.data.frame(genre_mat1[-1,], stringsAsFactors=FALSE)
       #remove first row, which was the genre list
23.    for (col in 1:ncol(genre_mat2)) {
24.      genre_mat2[,col] <- as.integer(genre_mat2[,col]) #convert from
       characters to integers
25.    }
26.    str(genre_mat2)
```

```
movie_genre <- as.data.frame(movie_data$genres, stringsAsFactors=FALSE)
library(data.table)
movie_genre2 <- as.data.frame(tstrsplit(movie_genre[,1], '[|]',
                              type.convert=TRUE),
                    stringsAsFactors=FALSE)        #DataFlair
colnames(movie_genre2) <- c(1:10)

list_genre <- c("Action", "Adventure", "Animation", "Children",
              "Comedy", "Crime","Documentary", "Drama", "Fantasy",
              "Film-Noir", "Horror", "Musical", "Mystery","Romance",
              "Sci-Fi", "Thriller", "War", "Western")
genre_mat1 <- matrix(0,10330,18)
genre_mat1[1,] <- list_genre
colnames(genre_mat1) <- list_genre

for (index in 1:nrow(movie_genre2)) {
  for (col in 1:ncol(movie_genre2)) {
    gen_col = which(genre_mat1[1,] == movie_genre2[index,col])  #Author DataFlair
    genre_mat1[index+1,gen_col] <- 1
  }
}
genre_mat2 <- as.data.frame(genre_mat1[-1,], stringsAsFactors=FALSE) #remove first row, which was the genre list
for (col in 1:ncol(genre_mat2)) {
  genre_mat2[,col] <- as.integer(genre_mat2[,col]) #convert from characters to integers
}
str(genre_mat2)
```

```
## 'data.frame':    10329 obs. of  18 variables:
##  $ Action     : int  0 0 0 0 0 1 0 0 1 1 ...
##  $ Adventure  : int  1 1 0 0 0 0 0 1 0 1 ...
##  $ Animation  : int  1 0 0 0 0 0 0 0 0 0 ...
##  $ Children   : int  1 1 0 0 0 0 0 1 0 0 ...
##  $ Comedy     : int  1 0 1 1 1 0 1 0 0 0 ...
##  $ Crime      : int  0 0 0 0 0 1 0 0 0 0 ...
##  $ Documentary: int  0 0 0 0 0 0 0 0 0 0 ...
##  $ Drama      : int  0 0 0 1 0 0 0 0 0 0 ...
##  $ Fantasy    : int  1 1 0 0 0 0 0 0 0 0 ...
##  $ Film-Noir  : int  0 0 0 0 0 0 0 0 0 0 ...
##  $ Horror     : int  0 0 0 0 0 0 0 0 0 0 ...
##  $ Musical    : int  0 0 0 0 0 0 0 0 0 0 ...
##  $ Mystery    : int  0 0 0 0 0 0 0 0 0 0 ...
##  $ Romance    : int  0 0 1 1 0 0 1 0 0 0 ...
##  $ Sci-Fi     : int  0 0 0 0 0 0 0 0 0 0 ...
##  $ Thriller   : int  0 0 0 0 0 1 0 0 0 1 ...
##  $ War        : int  0 0 0 0 0 0 0 0 0 0 ...
##  $ Western    : int  0 0 0 0 0 0 0 0 0 0 ...
```

```
1.  SearchMatrix <- cbind(movie_data[,1:2], genre_mat2[])
2.  head(SearchMatrix)    #DataFlair
```

```
SearchMatrix <- cbind(movie_data[,1:2], genre_mat2[])
head(SearchMatrix)    #DataFlair
```

```
##   movieId                              title Action Adventure Animation
## 1       1                   Toy Story (1995)      0         1         1
## 2       2                     Jumanji (1995)      0         1         0
## 3       3            Grumpier Old Men (1995)      0         0         0
## 4       4           Waiting to Exhale (1995)      0         0         0
## 5       5 Father of the Bride Part II (1995)      0         0         0
## 6       6                        Heat (1995)      1         0         0
##   Children Comedy Crime Documentary Drama Fantasy Film-Noir Horror Musical
## 1        1      1     0           0     0       1         0      0       0
## 2        1      0     0           0     0       1         0      0       0
## 3        0      1     0           0     0       0         0      0       0
## 4        0      1     0           0     1       0         0      0       0
## 5        0      1     0           0     0       0         0      0       0
## 6        0      0     1           0     0       0         0      0       0
##   Mystery Romance Sci-Fi Thriller War Western
```

```
1.  ratingMatrix <- dcast(rating_data, userId~movieId, value.var = "rating",
    na.rm=FALSE)
2.  ratingMatrix <- as.matrix(ratingMatrix[,-1]) #remove userIds
3.  #Convert rating matrix into a recommenderlab sparse matrix
4.  ratingMatrix <- as(ratingMatrix, "realRatingMatrix")
5.  ratingMatrix
```

```
ratingMatrix <- dcast(rating_data, userId~movieId, value.var = "rating", na.rm=F
ALSE)
ratingMatrix <- as.matrix(ratingMatrix[,-1]) #remove userIds
#Convert rating matrix into a recommenderlab sparse matrix
ratingMatrix <- as(ratingMatrix, "realRatingMatrix")
ratingMatrix
```

```
## 668 x 10325 rating matrix of class 'realRatingMatrix' with 105339 ratings.
```

```
1.  recommendation_model <- recommenderRegistry$get_entries(dataType =
    "realRatingMatrix")
2.  names(recommendation_model)
```

```
recommendation_model <- recommenderRegistry$get_entries(dataType = "realRatingMatrix")
names(recommendation_model)
```

```
## [1] "ALS_realRatingMatrix"      "ALS_implicit_realRatingMatrix"
## [3] "IBCF_realRatingMatrix"     "POPULAR_realRatingMatrix"
## [5] "RANDOM_realRatingMatrix"   "RERECOMMEND_realRatingMatrix"
## [7] "SVD_realRatingMatrix"      "SVDF_realRatingMatrix"
## [9] "UBCF_realRatingMatrix"
```

```
1.  lapply(recommendation_model, "[[", "description")
```

```
lapply(recommendation_model, "[[", "description")
```

```
## $ALS_realRatingMatrix
## [1] "Recommender for explicit ratings based on latent factors, calculated by
alternating least squares algorithm."
##
## $ALS_implicit_realRatingMatrix
## [1] "Recommender for implicit data based on latent factors, calculated by alt
ernating least squares algorithm."
##
## $IBCF_realRatingMatrix
## [1] "Recommender based on item-based collaborative filtering."
##
## $POPULAR_realRatingMatrix
## [1] "Recommender based on item popularity."
##
```

```
1.    recommendation_model$IBCF_realRatingMatrix$parameters
```

```
recommendation_model$IBCF_realRatingMatrix$parameters
```

```
## $k
## [1] 30
##
## $method
## [1] "Cosine"
##
## $normalize
## [1] "center"
##
## $normalize_sim_matrix
## [1] FALSE
##
## $alpha
## [1] 0.5
```

```
1.    similarity_mat <- similarity(ratingMatrix[1:4, ],
2.                                 method = "cosine",
3.                                 which = "users")
4.    as.matrix(similarity_mat)
5.
6.    image(as.matrix(similarity_mat), main = "User's Similarities")
```

```
similarity_mat <- similarity(ratingMatrix[1:4, ],
                             method = "cosine",
                             which = "users")
as.matrix(similarity_mat)
```

```
##             1         2         3         4
## 1 0.0000000 0.9760860 0.9641723 0.9914398
## 2 0.9760860 0.0000000 0.9925732 0.9374253
## 3 0.9641723 0.9925732 0.0000000 0.9888968
## 4 0.9914398 0.9374253 0.9888968 0.0000000
```

```
image(as.matrix(similarity_mat), main = "User's Similarities")
```

```
1.  movie_similarity <- similarity(ratingMatrix[, 1:4], method =
2.                           "cosine", which = "items")
3.  as.matrix(movie_similarity)
4.
5.  image(as.matrix(movie_similarity), main = "Movies similarity")
```

```
movie_similarity <- similarity(ratingMatrix[, 1:4], method =
                         "cosine", which = "items")
as.matrix(movie_similarity)
```

```
##             1         2         3         4
## 1 0.0000000 0.9669732 0.9559341 0.9101276
## 2 0.9669732 0.0000000 0.9658757 0.9412416
## 3 0.9559341 0.9658757 0.0000000 0.9864877
## 4 0.9101276 0.9412416 0.9864877 0.0000000
```

```
image(as.matrix(movie_similarity), main = "Movies similarity")
```

```
1.  rating_values <- as.vector(ratingMatrix@data)
2.  unique(rating_values) # extracting unique ratings
```

```
1.  Table_of_Ratings <- table(rating_values) # creating a count of movie
    ratings
2.  Table_of_Ratings
```

```
rating_values <- as.vector(ratingMatrix@data)
unique(rating_values) # extracting unique ratings
```

```
## [1] 0.0 5.0 4.0 3.0 4.5 1.5 2.0 3.5 1.0 2.5 0.5
```

```
Table_of_Ratings <- table(rating_values) # creating a count of movie ratings
Table_of_Ratings
```

```
## rating_values
##       0     0.5       1     1.5       2     2.5       3     3.5       4
## 6791761    1198    3258    1567    7943    5484   21729   12237   28880
##     4.5       5
##    8187   14856
```

```
1.    library(ggplot2)
2.    movie_views <- colCounts(ratingMatrix) # count views for each movie
3.    table_views <- data.frame(movie = names(movie_views),
4.                                views = movie_views) # create dataframe of views
5.    table_views <- table_views[order(table_views$views,
6.                                decreasing = TRUE), ] # sort by number of
      views
7.    table_views$title <- NA
8.    for (index in 1:10325){
9.      table_views[index,3] <- as.character(subset(movie_data,
10.                                   movie_data$movieId ==
      table_views[index,1])$title)
11.    }
12.    table_views[1:6,]
```

```
library(ggplot2)
movie_views <- colCounts(ratingMatrix) # count views for each movie
table_views <- data.frame(movie = names(movie_views),
                            views = movie_views) # create dataframe of views
table_views <- table_views[order(table_views$views,
                            decreasing = TRUE), ] # sort by number of views
table_views$title <- NA
for (index in 1:10325){
  table_views[index,3] <- as.character(subset(movie_data,
                                 movie_data$movieId == table_views[inde
x,1])$title)
}
table_views[1:6,]
```

```
##     movie views                                     title
## 296   296   325                       Pulp Fiction (1994)
## 356   356   311                       Forrest Gump (1994)
## 318   318   308            Shawshank Redemption, The (1994)
## 480   480   294                       Jurassic Park (1993)
## 593   593   290             Silence of the Lambs, The (1991)
## 260   260   273  Star Wars: Episode IV - A New Hope (1977)
```

```
1.    ggplot(table_views[1:6, ], aes(x = title, y = views)) +
2.      geom_bar(stat="identity", fill = 'steelblue') +
3.      geom_text(aes(label=views), vjust=-0.3, size=3.5) +
4.      theme(axis.text.x = element_text(angle = 45, hjust = 1)) +
5.
6.      ggtitle("Total Views of the Top Films")
```

```
ggplot(table_views[1:6, ], aes(x = title, y = views)) +
  geom_bar(stat="identity", fill = 'steelblue') +
  geom_text(aes(label=views), vjust=-0.3, size=3.5) +
  theme(axis.text.x = element_text(angle = 45, hjust = 1)) +

  ggtitle("Total Views of the Top Films")
```

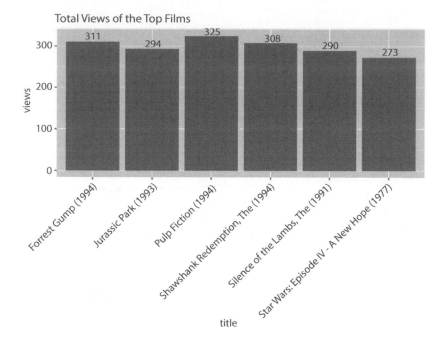

Total Views of the Top Films

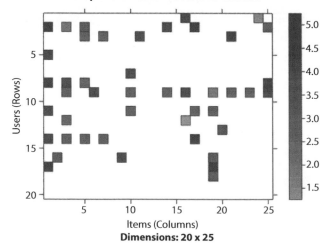

```
1.  image(ratingMatrix[1:20, 1:25], axes = FALSE, main = "Heatmap of the first
    25 rows and 25 columns")
```

```
image(ratingMatrix[1:20, 1:25], axes = FALSE, main = "Heatmap of the first 25 ro
ws and 25 columns")
```

Heatmap of the first 25 rows and 25 columns

```
1.   movie_ratings <- ratingMatrix[rowCounts(ratingMatrix) > 50,
2.                             colCounts(ratingMatrix) > 50]
3.   Movie_ratings
```

```
movie_ratings <- ratingMatrix[rowCounts(ratingMatrix) > 50,
                          colCounts(ratingMatrix) > 50]
movie_ratings
```

```
## 420 x 447 rating matrix of class 'realRatingMatrix' with 38341 ratings.
```

```
1.   minimum_movies<- quantile(rowCounts(movie_ratings), 0.98)
2.   minimum_users <- quantile(colCounts(movie_ratings), 0.98)
3.   image(movie_ratings[rowCounts(movie_ratings) > minimum_movies,
4.                       colCounts(movie_ratings) > minimum_users],
5.   main = "Heatmap of the top users and movies")
```

```
minimum_movies<- quantile(rowCounts(movie_ratings), 0.98)
minimum_users <- quantile(colCounts(movie_ratings), 0.98)
image(movie_ratings[rowCounts(movie_ratings) > minimum_movies,
                  colCounts(movie_ratings) > minimum_users],
main = "Heatmap of the top users and movies")
```

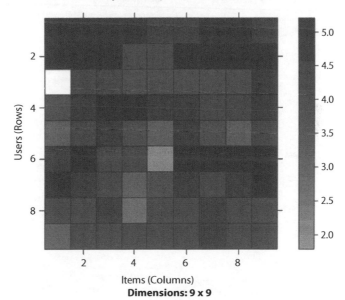

Heatmap of the top users and movies

Items (Columns)
Dimensions: 9 x 9

```
1.   average_ratings <- rowMeans(movie_ratings)
2.   qplot(average_ratings, fill=I("steelblue"), col=I("red")) +
3.     ggtitle("Distribution of the average rating per user")
```

```
average_ratings <- rowMeans(movie_ratings)
qplot(average_ratings, fill=I("steelblue"), col=I("red")) +
  ggtitle("Distribution of the average rating per user")
```

```
## `stat_bin()` using `bins = 30`. Pick better value with `binwidth`.
```

Distribution of the average rating per user

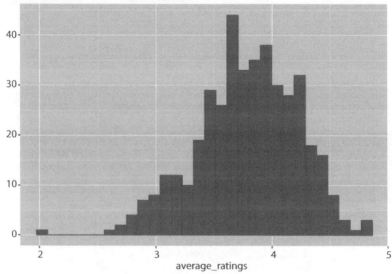

```
1.   normalized_ratings <- normalize(movie_ratings)
2.   sum(rowMeans(normalized_ratings) > 0.00001)
3.
4.   image(normalized_ratings[rowCounts(normalized_ratings) > minimum_movies,
5.                            colCounts(normalized_ratings) > minimum_users],
6.   main = "Normalized Ratings of the Top Users")
```

```
normalized_ratings <- normalize(movie_ratings)
sum(rowMeans(normalized_ratings) > 0.00001)
```

```
## [1] 0
```

```
image(normalized_ratings[rowCounts(normalized_ratings) > minimum_movies,
                         colCounts(normalized_ratings) > minimum_users],
main = "Normalized Ratings of the Top Users")
```

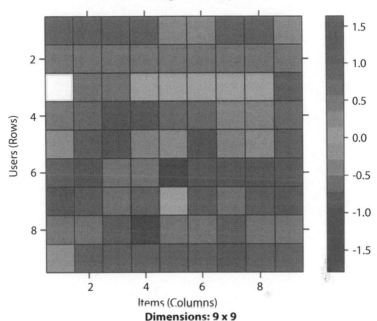

Dimensions: 9 x 9

```
1.    binary_minimum_movies <- quantile(rowCounts(movie_ratings), 0.95)
2.    binary_minimum_users <- quantile(colCounts(movie_ratings), 0.95)
3.    #movies_watched <- binarize(movie_ratings, minRating = 1)
4.
5.    good_rated_films <- binarize(movie_ratings, minRating = 3)
6.    image(good_rated_films[rowCounts(movie_ratings) > binary_minimum_movies,
7.    colCounts(movie_ratings) > binary_minimum_users],
8.    main = "Heatmap of the top users and movies")
```

```r
binary_minimum_movies <- quantile(rowCounts(movie_ratings), 0.95)
binary_minimum_users <- quantile(colCounts(movie_ratings), 0.95)
#movies_watched <- binarize(movie_ratings, minRating = 1)

good_rated_films <- binarize(movie_ratings, minRating = 3)
image(good_rated_films[rowCounts(movie_ratings) > binary_minimum_movies,
colCounts(movie_ratings) > binary_minimum_users],
main = "Heatmap of the top users and movies")
```

Heatmap of the top users and movies

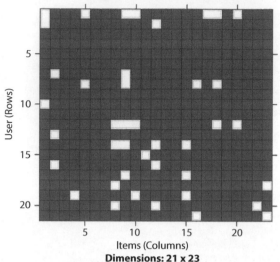

Dimensions: 21 x 23

```
1.    sampled_data<- sample(x = c(TRUE, FALSE),
2.                          size = nrow(movie_ratings),
3.                          replace = TRUE,
4.                          prob = c(0.8, 0.2))
5.    training_data <- movie_ratings[sampled_data, ]
6.    testing_data <- movie_ratings[!sampled_data, ]
```

```
sampled_data<- sample(x = c(TRUE, FALSE),
                      size = nrow(movie_ratings),
                      replace = TRUE,
                      prob = c(0.8, 0.2))
training_data <- movie_ratings[sampled_data, ]
testing_data <- movie_ratings[!sampled_data, ]
```

```
1.    recommendation_system <- recommenderRegistry$get_entries(dataType
      ="realRatingMatrix")
2.    recommendation_system$IBCF_realRatingMatrix$parameters
```

```
recommendation_system <- recommenderRegistry$get_entries(dataType ="realRatingMatrix")
recommendation_system$IBCF_realRatingMatrix$parameters
```

```
## $k
## [1] 30
##
## $method
## [1] "Cosine"
##
## $normalize
## [1] "center"
##
## $normalize_sim_matrix
## [1] FALSE
##
## $alpha
## [1] 0.5
##
## $na_as_zero
## [1] FALSE
```

```
1.    recommen_model <- Recommender(data = training_data,
2.                                  method = "IBCF",
3.                                  parameter = list(k = 30))
4.    recommen_model
5.    class(recommen_model)
```

```
recommen_model <- Recommender(data = training_data,
                              method = "IBCF",
                              parameter = list(k = 30))
recommen_model
```

```
## Recommender of type 'IBCF' for 'realRatingMatrix'
## learned using 337 users.
```

```
class(recommen_model)
```

```
## [1] "Recommender"
## attr(,"package")
## [1] "recommenderlab"
```

```
1.    model_info <- getModel(recommen_model)
2.    class(model_info$sim)
3.    dim(model_info$sim)
4.    top_items <- 20
5.    image(model_info$sim[1:top_items, 1:top_items],
6.        main = "Heatmap of the first rows and columns")
```

```
model_info <- getModel(recommen_model)

class(model_info$sim) # this contains a similarity matrix
```

```
## [1] "dgCMatrix"
## attr(,"package")
## [1] "Matrix"
```

```
dim(model_info$sim)
```

```
## [1] 447 447
```

```
top_items <- 20
image(model_info$sim[1:top_items, 1:top_items],
      main = "Heatmap of the first rows and columns")
```

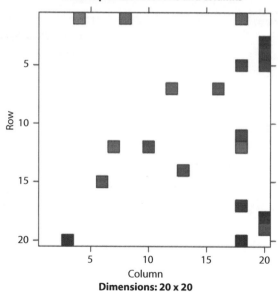

Heatmap of the first rows and columns

Dimensions: 20 x 20

```
1.   sum_rows <- rowSums(model_info$sim > 0)
2.   table(sum_rows)
3.
4.   sum_cols <- colSums(model_info$sim > 0)
5.   qplot(sum_cols, fill=I("steelblue"), col=I("red"))+ ggtitle("Distribution
     of the column count")
```

```
sum_rows <- rowSums(model_info$sim > 0)
table(sum_rows)
```

```
## sum_rows
##  30
## 447
```

```
sum_cols <- colSums(model_info$sim > 0)
qplot(sum_cols, fill=I("steelblue"), col=I("red"))+ ggtitle("Distribution of the
column count")
```

```
## `stat_bin()` using `bins = 30`. Pick better value with `binwidth`.
```

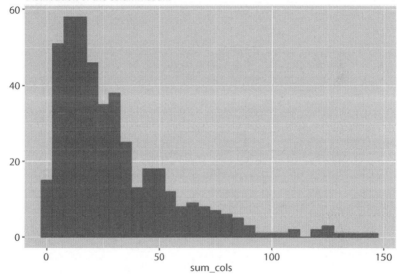

Distribution of the column count

```
1.    top_recommendations <- 10 # the number of items to recommend to each user
2.    predicted_recommendations <- predict(object = recommen_mod
3.                          newdata = testing_data,
4.                          n = top_recommendations)
5.    predicted_recommendations
```

```
top_recommendations <- 10       # the number of items to recommend to each user
predicted_recommendations <- predict(object = recommen_model,
                          newdata = testing_data,
                          n = top_recommendations)
predicted_recommendations
```

```
## Recommendations as 'topNList' with n = 10 for 83 users.
```

```
1.   user1 <- predicted_recommendations@items[[1]] # recommendation for the
     first user
2.   movies_user1 <- predicted_recommendations@itemLabels[user1]
3.   movies_user2 <- movies_user1
4.   for (index in 1:10){
5.     movies_user2[index] <- as.character(subset(movie_data,
6.                                    movie_data$movieId ==
     movies_user1[index])$title)
7.   }
8.   movies_user2
```

```
user1 <- predicted_recommendations@items[[1]] # recommendation for the first use
r
movies_user1 <- predicted_recommendations@itemLabels[user1]
movies_user2 <- movies_user1
for (index in 1:10){
  movies_user2[index] <- as.character(subset(movie_data,
                                  movie_data$movieId == movies_user1[inde
x])$title)
}
movies_user2
```

```
## [1] "Broken Arrow (1996)"
## [2] "Species (1995)"
## [3] "Mask, The (1994)"
## [4] "Executive Decision (1996)"
## [5] "Annie Hall (1977)"
## [6] "Little Miss Sunshine (2006)"
## [7] "Pan's Labyrinth (Laberinto del fauno, El) (2006)"
## [8] "Hangover, The (2009)"
## [9] "Mrs. Doubtfire (1993)"
## [10] "Leaving Las Vegas (1995)"
```

```
1.   recommendation_matrix <- sapply(predicted_recommendations@items,
2.                           function(x){ as.integer(colnames(movie_ratings)[x])
     }) # matrix with the recommendations for each user
3.   #dim(recc_matrix)
4.   recommendation_matrix[,1:4]
```

```
recommendation_matrix <- sapply(predicted_recommendations@items,
                    function(x){ as.integer(colnames(movie_ratings)[x]) }) # m
atrix with the recommendations for each user
#dim(recc_matrix)
recommendation_matrix[,1:4]
```

```
##        [,1] [,2] [,3] [,4]
## [1,]    95    7 1748  145
## [2,]   196  145 2321 1517
## [3,]   367  163  145  163
## [4,]   494  265  141 2005
## [5,]  1230  339  435 4896
## [6,] 46578  350 4022  160
## [7,] 48394  355 5218  420
## [8,] 69122  370  474 2671
```

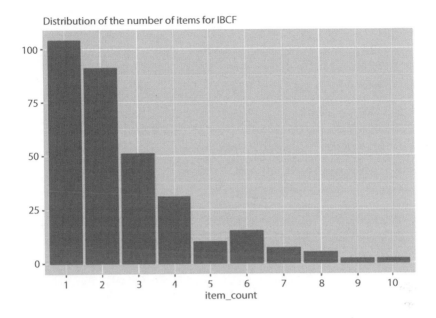

Distribution of the number of items for IBCF

```
##                                       Movie title No of items
## 21                               Get Shorty (1995)          10
## 145                                Bad Boys (1995)          10
## 19   Ace Ventura: When Nature Calls (1995)                   9
## 34                                     Babe (1995)           9
```

Bibliography

1. https://data-flair.training/blogs/data-science r-movie-recommendation/

Customer Segmentation

```
1.   customer_data=read.csv("/home/dataflair/Mall_Customers.csv")
2.   str(customer_data)
3.
4.   names(customer_data)
```

```
customer_data=read.csv("/home/dataflair/Mall_Customers.csv")
str(customer_data)
```

```
## 'data.frame':    200 obs. of  5 variables:
##  $ CustomerID              : int  1 2 3 4 5 6 7 8 9 10 ...
##  $ Gender                  : Factor w/ 2 levels "Female","Male": 2 2 1 1 1 1 1 1 2 1 ...
## ...
##  $ Age                     : int  19 21 20 23 31 22 35 23 64 30 ...
##  $ Annual.Income..k..      : int  15 15 16 16 17 17 18 18 19 19 ...
##  $ Spending.Score..1.100. : int  39 81 6 77 40 76 6 94 3 72 ...
```

```
names(customer_data)
```

```
## [1] "CustomerID"              "Gender"
## [3] "Age"                     "Annual.Income..k.."
## [5] "Spending.Score..1.100."
```

```
1.   head(customer_data)
2.   summary(customer_data$Age)
```

```
head(customer_data)
```

```
##   CustomerID Gender Age Annual.Income..k., Spending.Score..1.100.
## 1          1   Male  19                 15                      39
## 2          2   Male  21                 15                      81
## 3          3 Female  20                 16                       6
## 4          4 Female  23                 16                      77
## 5          5 Female  31                 17                      40
## 6          6 Female  22                 17                      76
```

```
summary(customer_data$Age)
```

```
##    Min. 1st Qu.  Median    Mean 3rd Qu.    Max.
##   18.00   28.75   36.00   38.85   49.00   70.00
```

Kolla Bhanu Prakash. Data Science Handbook: A Practical Approach, (413–432) © 2022 Scrivener Publishing LLC

```
1.    sd(customer_data$Age)
2.    summary(customer_data$Annual.Income..k..)
3.    sd(customer_data$Annual.Income..k..)
4.    summary(customer_data$Age)
```

```
sd(customer_data$Age)
```

```
## [1] 13.96901
```

```
summary(customer_data$Annual.Income..k..)
```

```
##    Min. 1st Qu.  Median   Mean 3rd Qu.    Max.
##   15.00   41.50   61.50   60.56   78.00  137.00
```

```
sd(customer_data$Annual.Income..k..)
```

```
## [1] 26.26472
```

```
summary(customer_data$Age)
```

```
##    Min. 1st Qu.  Median   Mean 3rd Qu.    Max.
##   18.00   28.75   36.00   38.85   49.00   70.00
```

```
1.    sd(customer_data$Spending.Score..1.100.)
```

```
sd(customer_data$Spending.Score..1.100.)
```

```
## [1] 25.82352
```

```
1.    a=table(customer_data$Gender)
2.    barplot(a,main="Using BarPlot to display Gender Comparision",
3.           ylab="Count",
4.           xlab="Gender",
5.           col=rainbow(2),
6.           legend=rownames(a))
```

```
a=table(customer_data$Gender)
barplot(a,main="Using BarPlot to display Gender Comparision",
        ylab="Count",
        xlab="Gender",
        col=rainbow(2),
        legend=rownames(a))
```

Using BarPlot to display Gender Comparision

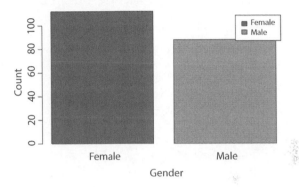

```
1.  pct=round(a/sum(a)*100)
2.  lbs=paste(c("Female","Male")," ",pct,"%",sep=" ")
3.  library(plotrix)
4.  pie3D(a,labels=lbs,
5.     main="Pie Chart Depicting Ratio of Female and Male")
```

```
pct=round(a/sum(a)*100)
lbs=paste(c("Female","Male")," ",pct,"%",sep=" ")
library(plotrix)
pie3D(a,labels=lbs,
     main="Pie Chart Depicting Ratio of Female and Male")
```

Pie Chart Depicting Ratio of Female and Male

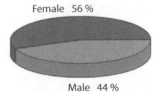

```
1.   summary(customer_data$Age)
```

```
summary(customer_data$Age)
```

```
##     Min. 1st Qu. Median   Mean 3rd Qu.   Max.
##    18.00   28.75  36.00  38.85   49.00  70.00
```

```
1.   hist(customer_data$Age,
2.       col="blue",
3.       main="Histogram to Show Count of Age Class",
4.       xlab="Age Class",
5.       ylab="Frequency",
6.       labels=TRUE)
```

```
hist(customer_data$Age,
    col="blue",
    main="Histogram to Show Count of Age Class",
    xlab="Age Class",
    ylab="Frequency",
    labels=TRUE)
```

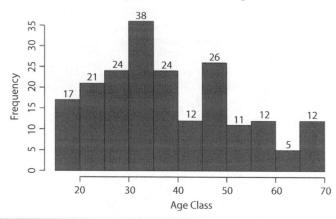

Histogram to Show Count of Age Class

```
1.   boxplot(customer_data$Age,
2.       col="ff0066",
3.       main="Boxplot for Descriptive Analysis of Age")
```

```
boxplot(customer_data$Age,
     col="#ff0066",
     main="Boxplot for Descriptive Analysis of Age")
```

Boxplot for Descriptive Analysis of Age

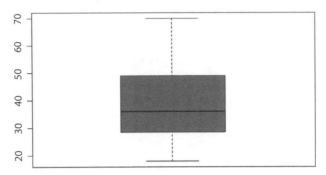

```
1.    summary(customer_data$Annual.Income..k..)
2.    hist(customer_data$Annual.Income..k..,
3.      col="#660033",
4.      main="Histogram for Annual Income",
5.      xlab="Annual Income Class",
6.      ylab="Frequency",
7.      labels=TRUE)
```

```
summary(customer_data$Annual.Income..k..)
```

```
##    Min. 1st Qu. Median   Mean 3rd Qu.    Max.
##   15.00   41.50  61.50  60.56   78.00  137.00
```

```
hist(customer_data$Annual.Income..k..,
    col="#660033",
    main="Histogram for Annual Income",
    xlab="Annual Income Class",
    ylab="Frequency",
    labels=TRUE)
```

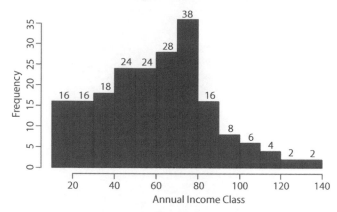

```
1.   plot(density(customer_data$Annual.Income..k..),
2.      col="yellow",
3.      main="Density Plot for Annual Income",
4.      xlab="Annual Income Class",
5.      ylab="Density")
6.   polygon(density(customer_data$Annual.Income..k..),
7.           col="#ccff66")
```

```
plot(density(customer_data$Annual.Income..k..),
    col="yellow",
    main="Density Plot for Annual Income",
    xlab="Annual Income Class",
    ylab="Density")
polygon(density(customer_data$Annual.Income..k..),
        col="#ccff66")
```

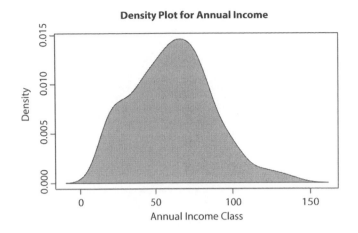

Density Plot for Annual Income

```
1.   summary(customer_data$Spending.Score..1.100.)
2.
3.   Min. 1st Qu. Median Mean 3rd Qu. Max.
4.   ## 1.00 34.75 50.00 50.20 73.00 99.00
5.
6.   boxplot(customer_data$Spending.Score..1.100.,
7.       horizontal=TRUE,
8.       col="#990000",
9.       main="BoxPlot for Descriptive Analysis of Spending Score")
```

```
summary(customer_data$Spending.Score..1.100.)
```

```
##     Min. 1st Qu. Median   Mean 3rd Qu.   Max.
##     1.00   34.75  50.00  50.20   73.00  99.00
```

```
boxplot(customer_data$Spending.Score..1.100.,
        horizontal=TRUE,
        col="#990000",
        main="BoxPlot for Descriptive Analysis of Spending Score")
```

BoxPlot for Descriptive Analysis of Spending Score

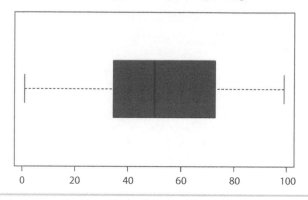

```
1.   hist(customer_data$Spending.Score..1.100.,
2.      main="HistoGram for Spending Score",
3.      xlab="Spending Score Class",
4.      ylab="Frequency",
5.      col="#6600cc",
6.      labels=TRUE)
```

```
hist(customer_data$Spending.Score..1.100.,
   main="HistoGram for Spending Score",
   xlab="Spending Score Class",
   ylab="Frequency",
   col="#6600cc",
   labels=TRUE)
```

HistoGram for Spending Score

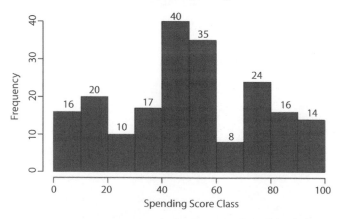

```
1.   library(purrr)
2.   set.seed(123)
3.   # function to calculate total intra-cluster sum of square
4.   iss <- function(k) {
5.     kmeans(customer_data[,3:5],k,iter.max=100,nstart=100,algorithm="Lloyd"
     )$tot.withinss
6.   }
7.
8.   k.values <- 1:10
9.
10.
11.   iss_values <- map_dbl(k.values, iss)
12.
13.   plot(k.values, iss_values,
14.       type="b", pch = 19, frame = FALSE,
15.       xlab="Number of clusters K",
16.       ylab="Total intra-clusters sum of squares")
```

```
library(purrr)
set.seed(123)
# function to calculate total intra-cluster sum of square
iss <- function(k) {
  kmeans(customer_data[,3:5],k,iter.max=100,nstart=100,algorithm="Lloyd" )$tot.withins
s
}

k.values <- 1:10


iss_values <- map_dbl(k.values, iss)          .

plot(k.values, iss_values,
    type="b", pch = 19, frame = FALSE,
    xlab="Number of clusters K",
    ylab="Total intra-clusters sum of squares")
```

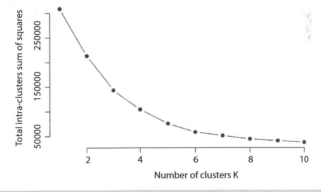

```
1.   library(cluster)
2.   library(gridExtra)
3.   library(grid)
4.
5.
6.   k2<-kmeans(customer_data[,3:5],2,iter.max=100,nstart=50,algorithm="Lloyd")
7.   s2<-plot(silhouette(k2$cluster,dist(customer_data[,3:5],"euclidean")))
```

```
library(cluster)
library(gridExtra)
library(grid)


k2<-kmeans(customer_data[,3:5],2,iter.max=100,nstart=50,algorithm="Lloyd")
s2<-plot(silhouette(k2$cluster,dist(customer_data[,3:5],"euclidean")))
```

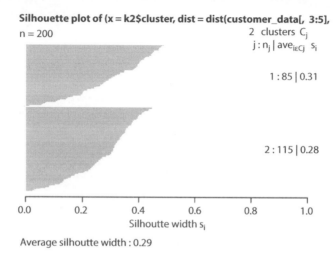

Silhouette plot of (x = k2$cluster, dist = dist(customer_data[, 3:5],

n = 200

2 clusters C_j
$j : n_j \mid ave_{i \in C_j}\ s_i$

1 : 85 | 0.31

2 : 115 | 0.28

Silhoutte width s_i

Average silhoutte width : 0.29

```
1.   k3<-kmeans(customer_data[,3:5],3,iter.max=100,nstart=50,algorithm="Lloyd")
2.   s3<-plot(silhouette(k3$cluster,dist(customer_data[,3:5],"euclidean")))
```

```
k3<-kmeans(customer_data[,3:5],3,iter.max=100,nstart=50,algorithm="Lloyd")
s3<-plot(silhouette(k3$cluster,dist(customer_data[,3:5],"euclidean")))
```

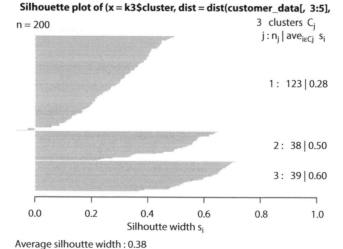

Silhouette plot of (x = k3$cluster, dist = dist(customer_data[, 3:5],

n = 200

3 clusters C_j
$j : n_j \mid ave_{i \in C_j}\ s_i$

1 : 123 | 0.28

2 : 38 | 0.50

3 : 39 | 0.60

Silhoutte width s_i

Average silhoutte width : 0.38

```
1.   k4<-kmeans(customer_data[,3:5],4,iter.max=100,nstart=50,algorithm="Lloyd")
2.   s4<-plot(silhouette(k4$cluster,dist(customer_data[,3:5],"euclidean")))
```

```
k4<-kmeans(customer_data[,3:5],4,iter.max=100,nstart=50,algorithm="Lloyd")
s4<-plot(silhouette(k4$cluster,dist(customer_data[,3:5],"euclidean")))
```

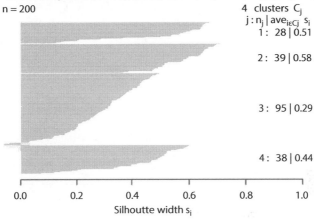

Silhouette plot of (x = k4$cluster, dist = dist(customer_data[, 3:5],

n = 200

4 clusters C_j

$j : n_j \mid ave_{i \in Cj} \; s_i$

1 : 28 | 0.51

2 : 39 | 0.58

3 : 95 | 0.29

4 : 38 | 0.44

Silhoutte width s_i

Average silhoutte width : 0.41

```
1.   k5<-kmeans(customer_data[,3:5],5,iter.max=100,nstart=50,algorithm="Lloyd")
2.   s5<-plot(silhouette(k5$cluster,dist(customer_data[,3:5],"
```

```
k5<-kmeans(customer_data[,3:5],5,iter.max=100,nstart=50,algorithm="Lloyd")
s5<-plot(silhouette(k5$cluster,dist(customer_data[,3:5],"euclidean")))
```

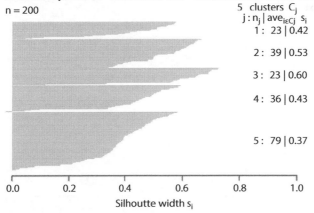

Silhouette plot of (x = k5$cluster, dist = dist(customer_data[, 3:5],

n = 200

5 clusters C_j

$j : n_j \mid ave_{i \in Cj} \; s_i$

1 : 23 | 0.42

2 : 39 | 0.53

3 : 23 | 0.60

4 : 36 | 0.43

5 : 79 | 0.37

Silhoutte width s_i

Average silhoutte width : 0.44

```
1.  k6<-kmeans(customer_data[,3:5],6,iter.max=100,nstart=50,algorithm="Lloyd")
2.  s6<-plot(silhouette(k6$cluster,dist(customer_data[,3:5],"euclidean")))
```

```
k6<-kmeans(customer_data[,3:5],6,iter.max=100,nstart=50,algorithm="Lloyd")
s6<-plot(silhouette(k6$cluster,dist(customer_data[,3:5],"euclidean")))
```

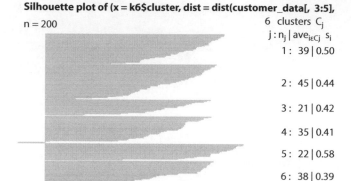

Silhouette plot of (x = k6$cluster, dist = dist(customer_data[, 3:5],

n = 200

6 clusters C_j

$j : n_j \mid ave_{i \in Cj} \; s_i$

1 : 39 | 0.50

2 : 45 | 0.44

3 : 21 | 0.42

4 : 35 | 0.41

5 : 22 | 0.58

6 : 38 | 0.39

Silhoutte width s_i

Average silhoutte width : 0.45

```
1.  k7<-kmeans(customer_data[,3:5],7,iter.max=100,nstart=50,algorithm="Lloyd")
2.  s7<-plot(silhouette(k7$cluster,dist(customer_data[,3:5],"euclidean")))
```

```
k7<-kmeans(customer_data[,3:5],7,iter.max=100,nstart=50,algorithm="Lloyd")
s7<-plot(silhouette(k7$cluster,dist(customer_data[,3:5],"euclidean")))
```

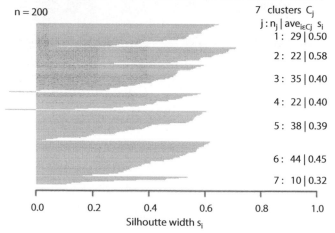

Silhouette plot of (x = k7$cluster, dist = dist(customer_data[, 3:5],

n = 200

7 clusters C_j

$j : n_j \mid ave_{i \in Cj} \; s_i$

1 : 29 | 0.50

2 : 22 | 0.58

3 : 35 | 0.40

4 : 22 | 0.40

5 : 38 | 0.39

6 : 44 | 0.45

7 : 10 | 0.32

Silhoutte width s_i

Average silhoutte width : 0.44

```
1.   k8<-kmeans(customer_data[,3:5],8,iter.max=100,nstart=50,algorithm="Lloyd")
2.   s8<-plot(silhouette{k8$cluster,dist(customer_data[,3:5],"euclidean")})
```

```
k8<-kmeans(customer_data[,3:5],8,iter.max=100,nstart=50,algorithm="Lloyd")
s8<-plot(silhouette(k8$cluster,dist(customer_data[,3:5],"euclidean")))
```

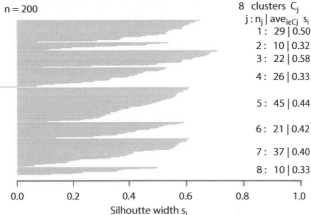

Silhouette plot of (x = k8$cluster, dist = dist(customer_data[, 3:5],

n = 200

8 clusters C_j
$j : n_j \mid ave_{i \in C_j} \, s_i$
1 : 29 | 0.50
2 : 10 | 0.32
3 : 22 | 0.58

4 : 26 | 0.33

5 : 45 | 0.44

6 : 21 | 0.42

7 : 37 | 0.40

8 : 10 | 0.33

0.0   0.2   0.4   0.6   0.8   1.0

Silhoutte width s_i

Average silhoutte width : 0.43

```
1.   k9<-kmeans(customer_data[,3:5],9,iter.max=100,nstart=50,algorithm="Lloyd")
2.   s9<-plot(silhouette{k9$cluster,dist(customer_data[,3:5],"euclidean")})
```

```
k9<-kmeans(customer_data[,3:5],9,iter.max=100,nstart=50,algorithm="Lloyd")
s9<-plot(silhouette(k9$cluster,dist(customer_data[,3:5],"euclidean")))
```

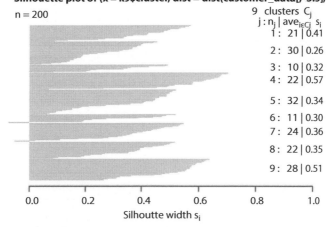

Silhouette plot of (x = k9$cluster, dist = dist(customer_data[, 3:5],

n = 200

9 clusters C_j
$j : n_j \mid ave_{i \in C_j} \, s_i$
1 : 21 | 0.41

2 : 30 | 0.26

3 : 10 | 0.32
4 : 22 | 0.57

5 : 32 | 0.34

6 : 11 | 0.30
7 : 24 | 0.36

8 : 22 | 0.35

9 : 28 | 0.51

0.0   0.2   0.4   0.6   0.8   1.0

Silhoutte width s_i

Average silhoutte width : 0.39

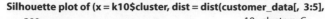

```
k10<-kmeans(customer_data[,3:5],10,iter.max=100,nstart=50,algorithm="Lloyd")
s10<-plot(silhouette(k10$cluster,dist(customer_data[,3:5],"euclidean")))
```

Silhouette plot of (x = k10$cluster, dist = dist(customer_data[, 3:5],

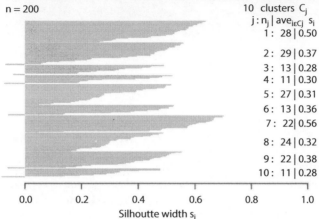

n = 200

10 clusters C_j

$j : n_j \mid ave_{i \in C_j} \, s_i$

1 : 28 | 0.50

2 : 29 | 0.37
3 : 13 | 0.28
4 : 11 | 0.30
5 : 27 | 0.31
6 : 13 | 0.36
7 : 22| 0.56

8 : 24 | 0.32

9 : 22 | 0.38
10 : 11 | 0.28

0.0   0.2   0.4   0.6   0.8   1.0

Silhoutte width s_i

Average silhoutte width : 0.38

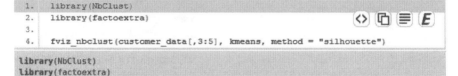

```
library(NbClust)
library(factoextra)

fviz_nbclust(customer_data[,3:5], kmeans, method = "silhouette")
```

```
library(NbClust)
library(factoextra)
```

```
## Loading required package: ggplot2
```

```
## Welcome! Related Books: `Practical Guide To Cluster Analysis in R` at https://goo.g
l/13EFCZ
```

```
fviz_nbclust(customer_data[,3:5], kmeans, method = "silhouette")
```

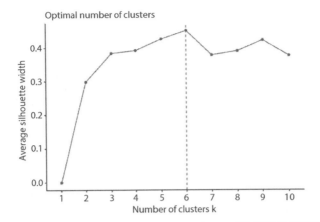

```
1.    set.seed(125)
2.    stat_gap <- clusGap(customer_data[,3:5], FUN = kmeans, nst
3.              K.max = 10, B = 50)
4.    fviz_gap_stat(stat_gap)
```

```
# compute gap statistic
set.seed(123)
gap_stat <- clusGap(customer_data[,3:5], FUN = kmeans, nstart = 25,
              K.max = 10, B = 50)
fviz_gap_stat(gap_stat)
```

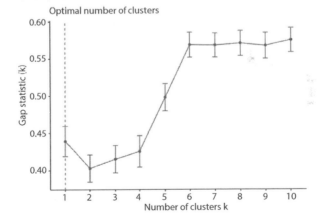

```
1.  k6<-kmeans(customer_data[,3:5],6,iter.max=100,nstart=50,algorithm="Lloyd")
2.  k6
```

```
# compute gap statistic
k6<-kmeans(customer_data[,3:5],6,iter.max=100,nstart=50,algorithm="Lloyd")
k6
```

```
## K-means clustering with 6 clusters of sizes 45, 22, 21, 38, 35, 39
##
## Cluster means:
##      Age Annual.Income..k.. Spending.Score..1.100.
## 1 56.15556           53.37778               49.08889
## 2 25.27273           25.72727               79.36364
## 3 44.14286           25.14286               19.52381
## 4 27.00000           56.65789               49.13158
## 5 41.68571           88.22857               17.28571
## 6 32.69231           86.53846               82.12821
##
## Clustering vector:
##   [1] 3 2 3 2 3 2 3 2 3 2 3 2 3 2 3 2 3 2 3 2 3 2 3 2 3 2 3 2 3 2 3 2 3 2 3
##  [36] 2 3 2 3 2 1 2 1 4 3 2 1 4 4 4 1 4 4 1 1 1 1 1 4 1 1 4 1 1 4 1 1 1 4 1 1 4 4
##  [71] 1 1 1 1 1 4 1 4 4 1 1 4 1 1 1 4 1 1 4 4 1 1 1 4 1 4 1 4 4 1 4 1 4 4 1 1 4 1
```

```
1.  pcclust=prcomp(customer_data[,3:5],scale=FALSE) #principal component
    analysis
2.  summary(pcclust)
3.
4.  pcclust$rotation[,1:2]
```

```
pcclust=prcomp(customer_data[,3:5],scale=FALSE)  #principal component analysis
summary(pcclust)
```

```
## Importance of components:
##                              PC1     PC2     PC3
## Standard deviation       26.4625 26.1597 12.9317
## Proportion of Variance    0.4512  0.4410  0.1078
## Cumulative Proportion     0.4512  0.8922  1.0000
```

```
pcclust$rotation[,1:2]
```

```
##                              PC1         PC2
## Age                    0.1889742 -0.1309652
## Annual.Income..k..    -0.5886410 -0.8083757
## Spending.Score..1.100. -0.7859965  0.5739136
```

```
1.   set.seed(1)
2.   ggplot(customer_data, aes(x =Annual.Income..k.., y =
     Spending.Score..1.100.)) +
3.     geom_point(stat = "identity", aes(color = as.factor(k6$cluster))) +
4.     scale_color_discrete(name=" ",
5.               breaks=c("1", "2", "3", "4", "5","6"),
6.               labels=c("Cluster 1", "Cluster 2", "Cluster 3", "Cluster 4",
     "Cluster 5","Cluster 6")) +
7.     ggtitle("Segments of Mall Customers", subtitle = "Using K-means
     Clustering")
```

```
## VISULIASE THE CLUSTERS
set.seed(1)
ggplot(customer_data, aes(x =Annual.Income..k.., y = Spending.Score..1.100.)) +
   geom_point(stat = "identity", aes(color = as.factor(k6$cluster))) +
   scale_color_discrete(name=" ",
               breaks=c("1", "2", "3", "4", "5","6"),
               labels=c("Cluster 1", "Cluster 2", "Cluster 3", "Cluster 4",
"Cluster 5","Cluster 6")) +
   ggtitle("Segments of Mall Customers", subtitle = "Using K-means Clustering")
```

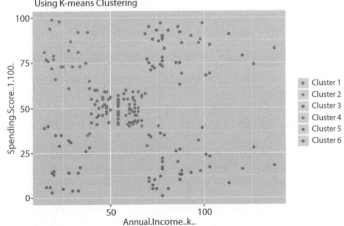

```
1.  ggplot(customer_data, aes(x =Spending.Score..1.100., y =Age)) +
2.    geom_point(stat = "identity", aes(color = as.factor(k6$cluster))) +
3.    scale_color_discrete(name=" ",
4.                    breaks=c("1", "2", "3", "4", "5","6"),
5.                    labels=c("Cluster 1", "Cluster 2", "Cluster 3",
    "Cluster 4", "Cluster 5","Cluster 6")) +
6.      ggtitle("Segments of Mall Customers", subtitle = "Using K-means
    Clustering")
```

```
ggplot(customer_data, aes(x =Spending.Score..1.100., y =Age)) +
  geom_point(stat = "identity", aes(color = as.factor(k6$cluster))) +
  scale_color_discrete(name=" ",
                  breaks=c("1", "2", "3", "4", "5","6"),
                  labels=c("Cluster 1", "Cluster 2", "Cluster 3", "Cluster 4",
"Cluster 5","Cluster 6")) +
    ggtitle("Segments of Mall Customers", subtitle = "Using K-means Clustering")
```

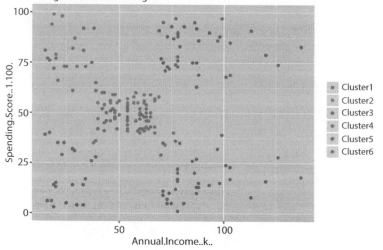

```
1.  kCols=function(vec){cols=rainbow (length (unique (vec)))
2.  return (cols[as.numeric(as.factor(vec))])}
3.
4.  digCluster<-k6$cluster; dignm<-as.character(digCluster); # K-means
    clusters
5.
6.  plot(pcclust$x[,1:2], col =kCols(digCluster),pch =19,xlab ="K-
    means",ylab="classes")
7.  legend("bottomleft",unique(dignm),fill=unique(kCols(digCluster)))
```

```
kCols=function(vec){cols=rainbow (length (unique (vec)))
return (cols[as.numeric(as.factor(vec))])}

digCluster<-k6$cluster; dignm<-as.character(digCluster);    # K-means clusters

plot(pcclust$x[,1:2], col =kCols(digCluster),pch =19,xlab ="K-means",ylab="classes")
legend("bottomleft",unique(dignm),fill=unique(kCols(digCluster)))
```

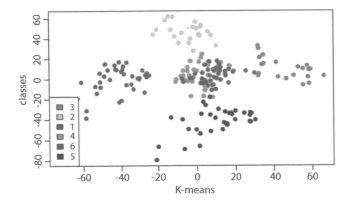

Bibliography

1. https://data-flair.training/blogs/r-data-science-project-customer-segmentation/

Breast Cancer Classification

1.	`pip install numpy opencv-python pillow tensorflow keras imutils scikit-learn matplotlib`

1.	`mkdir datasets`
2.	`mkdir datasets\original`

1.	`cd breast-cancer-classification\breast-cancer-classification\datasets\original`
2.	`tree`

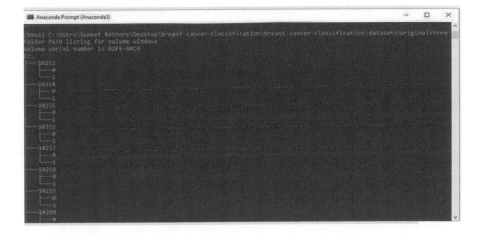

Kolla Bhanu Prakash. Data Science Handbook: A Practical Approach, (433–444) © 2022 Scrivener Publishing LLC

```
1.   import os
2.
3.   INPUT_DATASET = "datasets/original"
4.
5.   BASE_PATH = "datasets/idc"
6.   TRAIN_PATH = os.path.sep.join([BASE_PATH, "training"])
7.   VAL_PATH = os.path.sep.join([BASE_PATH, "validation"])
8.   TEST_PATH = os.path.sep.join([BASE_PATH, "testing"])
9.
10.  TRAIN_SPLIT = 0.8
11.  VAL_SPLIT = 0.1
```

config.py - C:\Users\Sumeet Rathore\Desktop\breast-cancer-classification\breast-cancer-cla...   —   □   ×

File Edit Format Run Options Window Help

```
import os

INPUT_DATASET = "datasets/original"

BASE_PATH = "datasets/idc"
TRAIN_PATH = os.path.sep.join([BASE_PATH, "training"])
VAL_PATH = os.path.sep.join([BASE_PATH, "validation"])
TEST_PATH = os.path.sep.join([BASE_PATH, "testing"])

TRAIN_SPLIT = 0.8
VAL_SPLIT = 0.1
```

Ln: 12 Col: 0

```
1.    from cancernet import config
2.    from imutils import paths
3.    import random, shutil, os
4.
5.    originalPaths=list(paths.list_images(config.INPUT_DATASET))
6.    random.seed(7)
7.    random.shuffle(originalPaths)
8.
9.    index=int(len(originalPaths)*config.TRAIN_SPLIT)
10.   trainPaths=originalPaths[:index]
11.   testPaths=originalPaths[index:]
12.
13.   index=int(len(trainPaths)*config.VAL_SPLIT)
14.   valPaths=trainPaths[:index]
15.   trainPaths=trainPaths[index:]
16.
17.   datasets=[("training", trainPaths, config.TRAIN_PATH),
18.             ("validation", valPaths, config.VAL_PATH),
19.             ("testing", testPaths, config.TEST_PATH)
20.   ]
21.
22.   for (setType, originalPaths, basePath) in datasets:
23.           print(f'Building {setType} set')
24.
25.           if not os.path.exists(basePath):
26.                   print(f'Building directory {base_path}')
27.                   os.makedirs(basePath)
28.
29.           for path in originalPaths:
30.                   file=path.split(os.path.sep)[-1]
31.                   label=file[-5:-4]
32.
33.                   labelPath=os.path.sep.join([basePath,label])
34.                   if not os.path.exists(labelPath):
35.                           print(f'Building directory {labelPath}')
36.                           os.makedirs(labelPath)
37.
38.                   newPath=os.path.sep.join([labelPath, file])
39.                   shutil.copy2(inputPath, newPath)
```

```
build_dataset.py - C:\Users\Sumeet Rathore\Desktop\breast-cancer-classification\breast-can...    —    □    ✕

File   Edit   Format   Run   Options   Window   Help

from cancernet import config
from imutils import paths
import random, shutil, os

originalPaths=list(paths.list_images(config.INPUT_DATASET))
random.seed(7)
random.shuffle(originalPaths)

index=int(len(originalPaths)*config.TRAIN_SPLIT)
trainPaths=originalPaths[:index]
testPaths=originalPaths[index:]

index=int(len(trainPaths)*config.VAL_SPLIT)
valPaths=trainPaths[:index]
trainPaths=trainPaths[index:]

datasets=[("training", trainPaths, config.TRAIN_PATH),
          ("validation", valPaths, config.VAL_PATH),
          ("testing", testPaths, config.TEST_PATH)
]

for (setType, originalPaths, basePath) in datasets:
        print(f'Building {setType} set')

        if not os.path.exists(basePath):
                print(f'Building directory {basePath}')
                os.makedirs(basePath)

        for path in originalPaths:
                file=path.split(os.path.sep)[-1]
                label=file[-5:-4]

                labelPath=os.path.sep.join([basePath,label])
                if not os.path.exists(labelPath):
                        print(f'Building directory {labelPath}')
                        os.makedirs(labelPath)

                newPath=os.path.sep.join([labelPath, file])
                shutil.copy2(path, newPath)
```

```
Command Prompt                                                                        —    □    ✕

C:\Users\ADMIN\Desktop\breast-cancer-classification\breast-cancer-classification>py build_dataset.py
Building training set
Building directory datasets/idc\training
Building directory datasets/idc\training\0
Building directory datasets/idc\training\1
Building validation set
Building directory datasets/idc\validation
Building directory datasets/idc\validation\1
Building directory datasets/idc\validation\0
Building testing set
Building directory datasets/idc\testing
Building directory datasets/idc\testing\1
Building directory datasets/idc\testing\0
```

```
1.    from keras.models import Sequential
2.    from keras.layers.normalization import BatchNormalization
3.    from keras.layers.convolutional import SeparableConv2D
4.    from keras.layers.convolutional import MaxPooling2D
5.    from keras.layers.core import Activation
6.    from keras.layers.core import Flatten
7.    from keras.layers.core import Dropout
8.    from keras.layers.core import Dense
9.    from keras import backend as K
10.
11.   class CancerNet:
12.     @staticmethod
13.     def build(width,height,depth,classes):
14.       model=Sequential()
15.       shape=(height,width,depth)
16.       channelDim=-1
17.
18.       if K.image_data_format()=="channels_first":
19.         shape=(depth,height,width)
20.         channelDim=1
21.
22.       model.add(SeparableConv2D(32, (3,3),
      padding="same",input_shape=shape))
23.         model.add(Activation("relu"))
24.         model.add(BatchNormalization(axis=channelDim))
25.         model.add(MaxPooling2D(pool_size=(2,2)))
26.         model.add(Dropout(0.25))
27.
28.         model.add(SeparableConv2D(64, (3,3), padding="same"))
29.         model.add(Activation("relu"))
30.         model.add(BatchNormalization(axis=channelDim))
31.         model.add(SeparableConv2D(64, (3,3), padding="same"))
32.         model.add(Activation("relu"))
33.         model.add(BatchNormalization(axis=channelDim))
34.         model.add(MaxPooling2D(pool_size=(2,2)))
35.         model.add(Dropout(0.25))
36.
37.         model.add(SeparableConv2D(128, (3,3), padding="same"))
38.         model.add(Activation("relu"))
39.         model.add(BatchNormalization(axis=channelDim))
40.         model.add(SeparableConv2D(128, (3,3), padding="same"))
41.         model.add(Activation("relu"))
42.         model.add(BatchNormalization(axis=channelDim))
43.         model.add(SeparableConv2D(128, (3,3), padding="same"))
44.         model.add(Activation("relu"))
45.         model.add(BatchNormalization(axis=channelDim))
46.         model.add(MaxPooling2D(pool_size=(2,2)))
47.         model.add(Dropout(0.25))
48.
49.         model.add(Flatten())
50.         model.add(Dense(256))
51.         model.add(Activation("relu"))
52.         model.add(BatchNormalization())
53.         model.add(Dropout(0.5))
54.
55.         model.add(Dense(classes))
56.         model.add(Activation("softmax"))
57.
58.         return model
```

```
cancernet.py - C:\Users\Sumeet Rathore\Desktop\breast-cancer-classification\breast-cancer-classification\cancernet\canc...   —   □   X
File  Edit  Format  Run  Options  Window  Help
from keras.models import Sequential
from keras.layers.normalization import BatchNormalization
from keras.layers.convolutional import SeparableConv2D
from keras.layers.convolutional import MaxPooling2D
from keras.layers.core import Activation
from keras.layers.core import Flatten
from keras.layers.core import Dropout
from keras.layers.core import Dense
from keras import backend as K

class CancerNet:
        @staticmethod
        def build(width,height,depth,classes):
                model=Sequential()
                shape=(height,width,depth)
                channelDim=-1

                if K.image_data_format()=="channels_first":
                        shape=(depth,height,width)
                        channelDim=1

                model.add(SeparableConv2D(32, (3,3), padding="same",input_shape=shape))
                model.add(Activation("relu"))
                model.add(BatchNormalization(axis=channelDim))
                model.add(MaxPooling2D(pool_size=(2,2)))
                model.add(Dropout(0.25))

                model.add(SeparableConv2D(64, (3,3), padding="same"))
                model.add(Activation("relu"))
                model.add(BatchNormalization(axis=channelDim))
                model.add(SeparableConv2D(64, (3,3), padding="same"))
                model.add(Activation("relu"))
                model.add(BatchNormalization(axis=channelDim))
                model.add(MaxPooling2D(pool_size=(2,2)))
                model.add(Dropout(0.25))

                model.add(SeparableConv2D(128, (3,3), padding="same"))
                model.add(Activation("relu"))
                model.add(BatchNormalization(axis=channelDim))
                model.add(SeparableConv2D(128, (3,3), padding="same"))
                model.add(Activation("relu"))
                model.add(BatchNormalization(axis=channelDim))
                model.add(SeparableConv2D(128, (3,3), padding="same"))
                model.add(Activation("relu"))
                model.add(BatchNormalization(axis=channelDim))
                model.add(MaxPooling2D(pool_size=(2,2)))
                model.add(Dropout(0.25))

                model.add(Flatten())
                model.add(Dense(256))
                model.add(Activation("relu"))
                model.add(BatchNormalization())
                model.add(Dropout(0.5))

                model.add(Dense(classes))
                model.add(Activation("softmax"))

                return model
                                                                        Ln: 40  Col: 36
```

```
1.    import matplotlib
2.    matplotlib.use("Agg")
3.
4.    from keras.preprocessing.image import ImageDataGenerator
5.    from keras.callbacks import LearningRateScheduler
6.    from keras.optimizers import Adagrad
7.    from keras.utils import np_utils
8.    from sklearn.metrics import classification_report
9.    from sklearn.metrics import confusion_matrix
10.   from cancernet.cancernet import CancerNet
```

```
11.   from cancernet import config
12.   from imutils import paths
13.   import matplotlib.pyplot as plt
14.   import numpy as np
15.   import os
16.
17.   NUM_EPOCHS=40; INIT_LR=1e-2; BS=32
18.
19.   trainPaths=list(paths.list_images(config.TRAIN_PATH))
20.   lenTrain=len(trainPaths)
21.   lenVal=len(list(paths.list_images(config.VAL_PATH)))
22.   lenTest=len(list(paths.list_images(config.TEST_PATH)))
23.
24.   trainLabels=[int(p.split(os.path.sep)[-2]) for p in trainPaths]
25.   trainLabels=np_utils.to_categorical(trainLabels)
26.   classTotals=trainLabels.sum(axis=0)
27.   classWeight=classTotals.max()/classTotals
28.
29.   trainAug = ImageDataGenerator(
30.     rescale=1/255.0,

31.       rotation_range=20,
32.       zoom_range=0.05,
33.       width_shift_range=0.1,
34.       height_shift_range=0.1,
35.       shear_range=0.05,
36.       horizontal_flip=True,
37.       vertical_flip=True,
38.       fill_mode="nearest")
39.
40.     valAug=ImageDataGenerator(rescale=1 / 255.0)
41.
42.     trainGen = trainAug.flow_from_directory(
43.       config.TRAIN_PATH,
44.       class_mode="categorical",
45.       target_size=(48,48),
46.       color_mode="rgb",
47.       shuffle=True,
48.       batch_size=BS)
49.     valGen = valAug.flow_from_directory(
50.       config.VAL_PATH,
51.       class_mode="categorical",
52.       target_size=(48,48),
53.       color_mode="rgb",
54.       shuffle=False,
55.       batch_size=BS)
56.     testGen = valAug.flow_from_directory(
57.       config.TEST_PATH,
58.       class_mode="categorical",
59.       target_size=(48,48),
60.       color_mode="rgb",
```

```
61.      shuffle=False,
62.      batch_size=BS)
63.
64.    model=CancerNet.build(width=48,height=48,depth=3,classes=2)
65.    opt=Adagrad(lr=INIT_LR,decay=INIT_LR/NUM_EPOCHS)
66.    model.compile(loss="binary_crossentropy",optimizer=opt,metrics=
       ["accuracy"])
67.
68.
69.    M=model.fit_generator(
70.       trainGen,
71.       steps_per_epoch=lenTrain//BS,
72.       validation_data=valGen,
73.       validation_steps=lenVal//BS,
74.       class_weight=classWeight,
75.       epochs=NUM_EPOCHS)
76.
77.    print("Now evaluating the model")
78.    testGen.reset()
79.    pred_indices=model.predict_generator(testGen,steps=(lenTest//BS)+1)
80.
81.    pred_indices=np.argmax(pred_indices,axis=1)
82.
83.    print(classification_report(testGen.classes, pred_indices,
       target_names=testGen.class_indices.keys()))
84.
85.    cm=confusion_matrix(testGen.classes,pred_indices)
86.    total=sum(sum(cm))
87.    accuracy=(cm[0,0]+cm[1,1])/total
88.    specificity=cm[1,1]/(cm[1,0]+cm[1,1])
89.    sensitivity=cm[0,0]/(cm[0,0]+cm[0,1])
90.    print(cm)


91.    print(f'Accuracy: {accuracy}')
92.    print(f'Specificity: {specificity}')
93.    print(f'Sensitivity: {sensitivity}')
94.
95.    N = NUM_EPOCHS
96.    plt.style.use("ggplot")
97.    plt.figure()
98.    plt.plot(np.arange(0,N), M.history["loss"], label="train_loss")
99.    plt.plot(np.arange(0,N), M.history["val_loss"], label="val_loss")
100.   plt.plot(np.arange(0,N), M.history["acc"], label="train_acc")
101.   plt.plot(np.arange(0,N), M.history["val_acc"], label="val_acc")
102.   plt.title("Training Loss and Accuracy on the IDC Dataset")
103.   plt.xlabel("Epoch No.")
104.   plt.ylabel("Loss/Accuracy")
105.   plt.legend(loc="lower left")
106.   plt.savefig('plot.png')
```

```
train_model.py - C:\Users\Sumeet Rathore\Desktop\breast-cancer-classification\breast-cancer-classification\train_model.py (3.7.3)
File  Edit  Format  Run  Options  Window  Help

import matplotlib
matplotlib.use("Agg")

from keras.preprocessing.image import ImageDataGenerator
from keras.callbacks import LearningRateScheduler
from keras.optimizers import Adagrad
from keras.utils import np_utils
from sklearn.metrics import classification_report
from sklearn.metrics import confusion_matrix
from cancernet.cancernet import CancerNet
from cancernet import config
from imutils import paths
import matplotlib.pyplot as plt
import numpy as np
import os

NUM_EPOCHS=40; INIT_LR=1e-2; BS=32

trainPaths=list(paths.list_images(config.TRAIN_PATH))
lenTrain=len(trainPaths)
lenVal=len(list(paths.list_images(config.VAL_PATH)))
lenTest=len(list(paths.list_images(config.TEST_PATH)))

trainLabels=[int(p.split(os.path.sep)[-2]) for p in trainPaths]
trainLabels=np_utils.to_categorical(trainLabels)
classTotals=trainLabels.sum(axis=0)
classWeight=classTotals.max()/classTotals

trainAug = ImageDataGenerator(
        rescale=1/255.0,
        rotation_range=20,
        zoom_range=0.05,
        width_shift_range=0.1,
        height_shift_range=0.1,
        shear_range=0.05,
        horizontal_flip=True,
        vertical_flip=True,
        fill_mode="nearest")

valAug=ImageDataGenerator(rescale=1 / 255.0)


trainGen = trainAug.flow_from_directory(
        config.TRAIN_PATH,
        class_mode="categorical",
        target_size=(48,48),
        color_mode="rgb",
        shuffle=True,
        batch_size=BS)
valGen = valAug.flow_from_directory(
        config.VAL_PATH,
        class_mode="categorical",
        target_size=(48,48),
        color_mode="rgb",
        shuffle=False,
        batch_size=BS)
testGen = valAug.flow_from_directory(
        config.TEST_PATH,
        class_mode="categorical",
        target_size=(48,48),
        color_mode="rgb",
        shuffle=False,
        batch_size=BS)

model=CancerNet.build(width=48,height=48,depth=3,classes=2)
opt=Adagrad(lr=INIT_LR,decay=INIT_LR/NUM_EPOCHS)
model.compile(loss="binary_crossentropy",optimizer=opt,metrics=["accuracy"])


M=model.fit_generator(
        trainGen,
        steps_per_epoch=lenTrain//BS,
        validation_data=valGen,
        validation_steps=lenVal//BS,
        class_weight=classWeight,
        epochs=NUM_EPOCHS)
```

```
print("Now evaluating the model")
testGen.reset()
pred_indices=model.predict_generator(testGen,steps=(lenTest//BS)+1)

pred_indices=np.argmax(pred_indices,axis=1)
```

```
H=model.fit_generator(
        trainGen,
        steps_per_epoch=lenTrain//BS,
        validation_data=valGen,
        validation_steps=lenVal//BS,
        class_weight=classWeight,
        epochs=NUM_EPOCHS)

print("Now evaluating the model")
testGen.reset()
pred_indices=model.predict_generator(testGen,steps=(lenTest//BS)+1)

pred_indices=np.argmax(pred_indices,axis=1)

print(classification_report(testGen.classes, pred_indices, target_names=testGen.class_indices.keys()))

cm=confusion_matrix(testGen.classes,pred_indices)
total=sum(sum(cm))
accuracy=(cm[0,0]+cm[1,1])/total
specificity=cm[1,1]/(cm[1,0]+cm[1,1])
sensitivity=cm[0,0]/(cm[0,0]+cm[0,1])
print(cm)
print(f'Accuracy: {accuracy}')
print(f'Specificity: {specificity}')
print(f'Sensitivity: {sensitivity}')

N = NUM_EPOCHS
plt.style.use("ggplot")
plt.figure()
plt.plot(np.arange(0,N), H.history["loss"], label="train_loss")
plt.plot(np.arange(0,N), H.history["val_loss"], label="val_loss")
plt.plot(np.arange(0,N), H.history["acc"], label="train_acc")
plt.plot(np.arange(0,N), H.history["val_acc"], label="val_acc")
plt.title("Training Loss and Accuracy on the IDC Dataset")
plt.xlabel("Epoch No.")
plt.ylabel("Loss/Accuracy")
plt.legend(loc="lower left")
plt.savefig('plot.png')
```

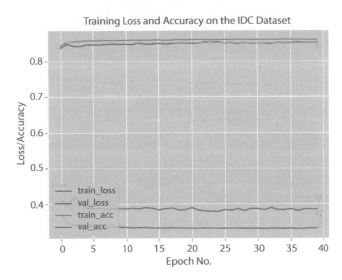

Training Loss and Accuracy on the IDC Dataset

Bibliography

1. https://data-flair.training/blogs/project-in-python-breast-cancer-classification/ "Breast Cancer Treatment (PDQ®)". NCI. 23 May 2014.
2. World Cancer Report 2014. World Health Organization. 2014. pp. Chapter 5.2. ISBN 978-92-832-0429-9.
3. "Klinefelter Syndrome". Eunice Kennedy Shriver National Institute of Child Health and Human Development. 24 May 2007. Archived from the original on 27 November 2012.

4. "SEER Stat Fact Sheets: Breast Cancer". NCI.
5. "Cancer Survival in England: Patients Diagnosed 2007–2011 and Followed up to 2012" (PDF). Office for National Statistics.

Traffic Signs Recognition

```
1.   pip install tensorflow keras sklearn matplotlib pandas pil
```

Name	Date modified	Type	Size
meta	04-Oct-19 12:52 PM	File folder	
test	04-Oct-19 12:52 PM	File folder	
train	04-Oct-19 12:55 PM	File folder	
Meta	25-Nov-18 6:13 PM	Microsoft Excel C...	2 KB
Test	25-Nov-18 6:13 PM	Microsoft Excel C...	418 KB
Train	25-Nov-18 6:13 PM	Microsoft Excel C...	1,896 KB

is PC › Local Disk (D:) › dataflair projects › Project - Traffic sign classification ›

```python
[9]: import numpy as np
import pandas as pd
import matplotlib.pyplot as plt
import tensorflow as tf
from PIL import Image
import os
from sklearn.model_selection import train_test_split
from keras.utils import to_categorical
from keras.models import Sequential
from keras.layers import Conv2D, MaxPool2D, Dense, Flatten, Dropout

data = []
labels = []
classes = 43
cur_path = os.getcwd()

for i in range(classes):
    path = os.path.join(cur_path,'train',str(i))
    images = os.listdir(path)

    for a in images:
        try:
            image = Image.open(path + '\\'+ a)
            image = image.resize((30,30))
            image = np.array(image)
            #sim = Image.fromarray(image)
            data.append(image)
            labels.append(i)
        except:
            print("Error loading image")
data = np.array(data)
labels = np.array(labels)
```

Kolla Bhanu Prakash. Data Science Handbook: A Practical Approach, (445–454) © 2022 Scrivener Publishing LLC

```
[10]: print(data.shape, labels.shape)
      X_train, X_test, y_train, y_test = train_test_split(data, labels, test_size=0.2, random_state=42)


      print(X_train.shape, X_test.shape, y_train.shape, y_test.shape)

      y_train = to_categorical(y_train, 43)
      y_test = to_categorical(y_test, 43)
```

```
(39209, 30, 30, 3) (39209,)
(31367, 30, 30, 3) (7842, 30, 30, 3) (31367,) (7842,)
```

```
[11]: model = Sequential()
      model.add(Conv2D(filters=32, kernel_size=(5,5), activation='relu', input_shape=X_train.shape[1:]))
      model.add(Conv2D(filters=32, kernel_size=(5,5), activation='relu'))
      model.add(MaxPool2D(pool_size=(2, 2)))
      model.add(Dropout(rate=0.25))
      model.add(Conv2D(filters=64, kernel_size=(3, 3), activation='relu'))
      model.add(Conv2D(filters=64, kernel_size=(3, 3), activation='relu'))
      model.add(MaxPool2D(pool_size=(2, 2)))
      model.add(Dropout(rate=0.25))
      model.add(Flatten())
      model.add(Dense(256, activation='relu'))
      model.add(Dropout(rate=0.5))
      model.add(Dense(43, activation='softmax'))

      #Compilation of the model
      model.compile(loss='categorical_crossentropy', optimizer='adam', metrics=['accuracy'])
```

```
[12]: epochs = 15
      history = model.fit(X_train, y_train, batch_size=64, epochs=epochs,validation_data=(X_test, y_test))

      Train on 31367 samples, validate on 7842 samples
      Epoch 1/15
      31367/31367 [==============================] - 82s 3ms/step - loss: 2.3108 - accuracy: 0.4369 - val_lo
      ss: 0.6590 - val_accuracy: 0.8234
      Epoch 2/15
      31367/31367 [==============================] - 82s 3ms/step - loss: 0.8266 - accuracy: 0.7606 - val_lo
      ss: 0.3468 - val_accuracy: 0.9100
      Epoch 3/15
      31367/31367 [==============================] - 83s 3ms/step - loss: 0.5738 - accuracy: 0.8283 - val_lo
      ss: 0.1882 - val_accuracy: 0.9504
      Epoch 4/15
      31367/31367 [==============================] - 85s 3ms/step - loss: 0.4282 - accuracy: 0.8720 - val_lo
      ss: 0.1373 - val_accuracy: 0.9661
      Epoch 5/15
      31367/31367 [==============================] - 84s 3ms/step - loss: 0.3565 - accuracy: 0.8950 - val_lo
      ss: 0.1068 - val_accuracy: 0.9702
      Epoch 6/15
      31367/31367 [==============================] - 81s 3ms/step - loss: 0.3081 - accuracy: 0.9074 - val_lo
      ss: 0.1527 - val_accuracy: 0.9575
      Epoch 7/15
      31367/31367 [==============================] - 81s 3ms/step - loss: 0.2730 - accuracy: 0.9192 - val_lo
      ss: 0.0888 - val_accuracy: 0.9753
      Epoch 8/15
      31367/31367 [==============================] - 81s 3ms/step - loss: 0.2429 - accuracy: 0.9271 - val_lo
      ss: 0.0934 - val_accuracy: 0.9737
      Epoch 9/15
      31367/31367 [==============================] - 84s 3ms/step - loss: 0.2429 - accuracy: 0.9299 - val_lo
      ss: 0.0772 - val_accuracy: 0.9763
      Epoch 10/15
      31367/31367 [==============================] - 81s 3ms/step - loss: 0.2176 - accuracy: 0.9364 - val_lo
      ss: 0.1133 - val_accuracy: 0.9663
      Epoch 11/15
      31367/31367 [==============================] - 82s 3ms/step - loss: 0.2200 - accuracy: 0.9360 - val_lo
      ss: 0.0823 - val_accuracy: 0.9786
      Epoch 12/15
      31367/31367 [==============================] - 80s 3ms/step - loss: 0.2046 - accuracy: 0.9406 - val_lo
      ss: 0.0806 - val_accuracy: 0.9787
      Epoch 13/15
      31367/31367 [==============================] - 80s 3ms/step - loss: 0.1876 - accuracy: 0.9452 - val_lo
      ss: 0.0569 - val_accuracy: 0.9852
      Epoch 14/15
      31367/31367 [==============================] - 81s 3ms/step - loss: 0.2007 - accuracy: 0.9430 - val_lo
      ss: 0.0629 - val_accuracy: 0.9811
      Epoch 15/15
      31367/31367 [==============================] - 81s 3ms/step - loss: 0.1914 - accuracy: 0.9463 - val_lo
      ss: 0.0676 - val_accuracy: 0.9813
```

```
[13]: plt.figure(0)
      plt.plot(history.history['accuracy'], label='training accuracy')
      plt.plot(history.history['val_accuracy'], label='val accuracy')
      plt.title('Accuracy')
      plt.xlabel('epochs')
      plt.ylabel('accuracy')
      plt.legend()

      plt.figure(1)
      plt.plot(history.history['loss'], label='training loss')
      plt.plot(history.history['val_loss'], label='val loss')
      plt.title('Loss')
      plt.xlabel('epochs')
      plt.ylabel('loss')
      plt.legend()
```

```
[13]: <matplotlib.legend.Legend at 0x24eece89e48>
```

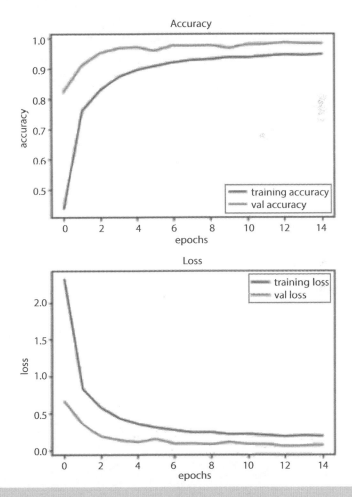

Accuracy and Loss Graphs

```
[14]  from sklearn.metrics import accuracy_score
      import pandas as pd
      y_test = pd.read_csv('Test.csv')

      labels = y_test["ClassId"].values
      imgs = y_test["Path"].values

      data=[]

      for img in imgs:
          image = Image.open(img)
          image = image.resize((30,30))
          data.append(np.array(image))

      X_test=np.array(data)

      pred = model.predict_classes(X_test)

      #Accuracy with the test data
      from sklearn.metrics import accuracy_score
      accuracy_score(labels, pred)
```

```
[14]  0.9532066508313539
```

```
1.    model.save('traffic_classifier.h5')
```

```
1.    import numpy as np
2.    import pandas as pd
3.    import matplotlib.pyplot as plt
4.    import cv2
5.    import tensorflow as tf
6.    from PIL import Image
7.    import os
8.    from sklearn.model_selection import train_test_split
9.    from keras.utils import to_categorical
10.   from keras.models import Sequential, load_model
11.   from keras.layers import Conv2D, MaxPool2D, Dense, Flatten, Dropout
12.
13.   data = []
14.   labels = []
15.   classes = 43
16.   cur_path = os.getcwd()
17.
18.   #Retrieving the images and their labels
19.   for i in range(classes):
20.       path = os.path.join(cur_path,'train',str(i))
21.       images = os.listdir(path)
22.
23.       for a in images:
24.           try:
25.               image = Image.open(path + '\\'+ a)
26.               image = image.resize((30,30))
27.               image = np.array(image)
28.               #sim = Image.fromarray(image)
29.               data.append(image)
30.               labels.append(i)
```

```
31.            except:
32.                print("Error loading image")
33.
34.    #Converting lists into numpy arrays
35.    data = np.array(data)
36.    labels = np.array(labels)
37.
38.    print(data.shape, labels.shape)
39.    #Splitting training and testing dataset
40.    X_train, X_test, y_train, y_test = train_test_split(data, labels,
       test_size=0.2, random_state=42)
41.
42.    print(X_train.shape, X_test.shape, y_train.shape, y_test.shape)
43.
44.    #Converting the labels into one hot encoding
45.    y_train = to_categorical(y_train, 43)
46.    y_test = to_categorical(y_test, 43)
47.
48.    #Building the model
49.    model = Sequential()
50.    model.add(Conv2D(filters=32, kernel_size=(5,5), activation='relu',
       input_shape=X_train.shape[1:]))
51.    model.add(Conv2D(filters=32, kernel_size=(5,5), activation='relu'))
52.    model.add(MaxPool2D(pool_size=(2, 2)))
53.    model.add(Dropout(rate=0.25))
54.    model.add(Conv2D(filters=64, kernel_size=(3, 3), activation='relu'))
55.    model.add(Conv2D(filters=64, kernel_size=(3, 3), activation='relu'))
56.    model.add(MaxPool2D(pool_size=(2, 2)))
57.    model.add(Dropout(rate=0.25))
58.    model.add(Flatten())
59.    model.add(Dense(256, activation='relu'))
60.    model.add(Dropout(rate=0.5))
61.    model.add(Dense(43, activation='softmax'))
62.
63.    #Compilation of the model
64.    model.compile(loss='categorical_crossentropy', optimizer='adam', metrics=
       ['accuracy'])
65.
66.    epochs = 15
67.    history = model.fit(X_train, y_train, batch_size=32, epochs=epochs,
       validation_data=(X_test, y_test))
68.    model.save("my_model.h5")
69.
70.    #plotting graphs for accuracy
71.    plt.figure(0)
72.    plt.plot(history.history['accuracy'], label='training accuracy')
73.    plt.plot(history.history['val_accuracy'], label='val accuracy')
74.    plt.title('Accuracy')
75.    plt.xlabel('epochs')
76.    plt.ylabel('accuracy')
77.    plt.legend()
78.    plt.show()
79.
80.    plt.figure(1)
81.    plt.plot(history.history['loss'], label='training loss')
82.    plt.plot(history.history['val_loss'], label='val loss')
83.    plt.title('Loss')
84.    plt.xlabel('epochs')
```

```
85.    plt.ylabel('loss')
86.    plt.legend()
87.    plt.show()
88.
89.    #testing accuracy on test dataset
90.    from sklearn.metrics import accuracy_score

91.
92.    y_test = pd.read_csv('Test.csv')
93.
94.    labels = y_test["ClassId"].values
95.    imgs = y_test["Path"].values
96.
97.    data=[]
98.
99.    for img in imgs:
100.        image = Image.open(img)
101.        image = image.resize((30,30))
102.        data.append(np.array(image))
103.
104.    X_test=np.array(data)
105.
106.    pred = model.predict_classes(X_test)
107.
108.    #Accuracy with the test data
109.    from sklearn.metrics import accuracy_score
110.    print(accuracy_score(labels, pred))
111.
112.    model.save('traffic_classifier.h5')

1.    import tkinter as tk
2.    from tkinter import filedialog
3.    from tkinter import *
4.    from PIL import ImageTk, Image
5.
6.    import numpy
7.    #load the trained model to classify sign
8.    from keras.models import load_model
9.    model = load_model('traffic_classifier.h5')
10.
11.    #dictionary to label all traffic signs class.
12.    classes = { 1:'Speed limit (20km/h)',
13.                2:'Speed limit (30km/h)',
14.                3:'Speed limit (50km/h)',
15.                4:'Speed limit (60km/h)',
```

```
16.                    5:'Speed limit (70km/h)',
17.                    6:'Speed limit (80km/h)',
18.                    7:'End of speed limit (80km/h)',
19.                    8:'Speed limit (100km/h)',
20.                    9:'Speed limit (120km/h)',
21.                    10:'No passing',
22.                    11:'No passing veh over 3.5 tons',
23.                    12:'Right-of-way at intersection',
24.                    13:'Priority road',
25.                    14:'Yield',
26.                    15:'Stop',
27.                    16:'No vehicles',
28.                    17:'Veh > 3.5 tons prohibited',
29.                    18:'No entry',
30.                    19:'General caution',

31.                    20:'Dangerous curve left',
32.                    21:'Dangerous curve right',
33.                    22:'Double curve',
34.                    23:'Bumpy road',
35.                    24:'Slippery road',
36.                    25:'Road narrows on the right',
37.                    26:'Road work',
38.                    27:'Traffic signals',
39.                    28:'Pedestrians',
40.                    29:'Children crossing',
41.                    30:'Bicycles crossing',
42.                    31:'Beware of ice/snow',
43.                    32:'Wild animals crossing',
44.                    33:'End speed + passing limits',
45.                    34:'Turn right ahead',
46.                    35:'Turn left ahead',
47.                    36:'Ahead only',
48.                    37:'Go straight or right',
49.                    38:'Go straight or left',
50.                    39:'Keep right',
51.                    40:'Keep left',
52.                    41:'Roundabout mandatory',
53.                    42:'End of no passing',
54.                    43:'End no passing veh > 3.5 tons' }
55.
56.    #initialise GUI
57.    top=tk.Tk()
58.    top.geometry('800x600')
59.    top.title('Traffic sign classification')
60.    top.configure(background='#CDCDCD')
61.
62.    label=Label(top,background='#CDCDCD', font=('arial',15,'bold'))
63.    sign_image = Label(top)
64.
65.    def classify(file_path):
```

```
66.        global label_packed
67.        image = Image.open(file_path)
68.        image = image.resize((30,30))
69.        image = numpy.expand_dims(image, axis=0)
70.        image = numpy.array(image)
71.        pred = model.predict_classes([image])[0]
72.        sign = classes[pred+1]
73.        print(sign)
74.        label.configure(foreground='#011638', text=sign)
75.
76.    def show_classify_button(file_path):
77.        classify_b=Button(top,text="Classify Image",command=lambda:
       classify(file_path),padx=10,pady=5)
78.        classify_b.configure(background='#364156', foreground='white',font=
       ('arial',10,'bold'))
79.        classify_b.place(relx=0.79,rely=0.46)
80.
81.    def upload_image():
82.        try:
83.            file_path=filedialog.askopenfilename()
84.            uploaded=Image.open(file_path)
85.            uploaded.thumbnail(((top.winfo_width()/2.25),(top.winfo_height()
       /2.25)))
86.            im=ImageTk.PhotoImage(uploaded)
87.
88.            sign_image.configure(image=im)
89.            sign_image.image=im
90.            label.configure(text='')
91.            show_classify_button(file_path)
92.        except:
93.            pass
94.
95.    upload=Button(top,text="Upload an
       image",command=upload_image,padx=10,pady=5)
96.    upload.configure(background='#364156', foreground='white',font=
       ('arial',10,'bold'))
97.
98.    upload.pack(side=BOTTOM,pady=50)
99.    sign_image.pack(side=BOTTOM,expand=True)
100.   label.pack(side=BOTTOM,expand=True)
101.   heading = Label(top, text="Know Your Traffic Sign",pady=20,
       font=('arial',20,'bold'))
102.   heading.configure(background='#CDCDCD',foreground='#364156')
103.   heading.pack()
104.   top.mainloop()
```

Bibliography

1. https://data-flair.training/blogs/python-project-traffic-signs-recognition/
2. https://www.analyticsvidhya.com/blog/2021/12/traffic-signs-recognition-using-cnn-and-keras-in-python/
3. https://en.wikipedia.org/wiki/Traffic-sign_recognition
4. https://towardsdatascience.com/recognizing-traffic-signs-with-over-98-accuracy-using-deep-learning-86737aedc2ab
5. https://medium.com/dataflair/class-data-science-project-for-2020-traffic-signs-recognition-12b09c131742

Printed and bound by CPI Group (UK) Ltd, Croydon, CR0 4YY

19/04/2024

14485864-0001